P9-CFG-102

The Communicator's Commentary

1, 2 Kings

THE COMMUNICATOR'S COMMENTARY SERIES
OLD TESTAMENT

- I *Genesis* by D. Stuart Briscoe
- II *Exodus* by Maxie D. Dunnam
- III *Leviticus* by Gary W. Demarest
- IV *Numbers* by James Philip
- V *Deuteronomy* by John C. Maxwell
- VI *Joshua* by John A. Huffman, Jr.
- VII *Judges, Ruth* by David Jackman
- VIII *1, 2 Samuel* by Kenneth L. Chafin
- IX *1, 2 Kings* by Russell H. Dilday
- X *1, 2 Chronicles* by Leslie C. Allen
- XI *Ezra, Nehemiah, Esther* by Robert M. Norris
- XII *Job* by David L. McKenna
- XIII *Psalms 1–72* by Donald M. Williams
- XIV *Psalms 73–150* by Donald M. Williams
- XV *Proverbs, Ecclesiastes, Song of Solomon* by David A. Hubbard
- XVI *Isaiah* by David L. McKenna
- XVII *Jeremiah, Lamentations* by John Guest
- XVIII *Ezekiel* by Douglas Stuart
- XIX *Daniel* by Sinclair B. Ferguson
- XX *Hosea, Joel, Amos, Obadiah, Jonah, Micah* by Lloyd J. Ogilvie
- XXI *Nahum, Habakkuk, Zephaniah, Haggai, Zechariah, Malachi* by Lloyd J. Ogilvie

Lloyd J. Ogilvie

General Editor

The Communicator's Commentary

1, 2 Kings

Russell H. Dilday

WORD BOOKS, PUBLISHER • WACO, TEXAS

Library of Congress Cataloging in Publication Data
Main entry under title:

The Communicator's commentary.
Bibliography: p.
Contents: OT9. 1, 2 Kings/by Russell H. Dilday
1. Bible. O.T.—Commentaries. I. Ogilvie, Lloyd John. II. Dilday, Russell H., 1930–
BS1151.2.C66 1986 221.7'7 86–11138
ISBN 0–8499–0414–5 (v. OT9)

Printed in the United States of America

5 6 7 8 9 9 AGF 9 8 7

To Robert, Nancy, and Ellen
whose commitment to our Lord
and service in His kingdom
has been their parents'
greatest reward

Contents

Editor's Preface

God has called all of His people to be communicators. Everyone who is in Christ is called into ministry. As ministers of "the manifold grace of God," all of us—clergy and laity—are commissioned with the challenge to communicate our faith to individuals and groups, classes and congregations.

The Bible, God's Word, is the objective basis of the truth of His love and power that we seek to communicate. In response to the urgent, expressed needs of pastors, teachers, Bible study leaders, church school teachers, small group enablers, and individual Christians, the Communicator's Commentary is offered as a penetrating search of the Scriptures of the Old and New Testament to enable vital personal and practical communication of the abundant life.

Many current commentaries and Bible study guides provide only some aspects of a communicator's needs. Some offer in-depth scholarship but no application to daily life. Others are so popular in approach that biblical roots are left unexplained. Few offer impelling illustrations that open windows for the reader to see the exciting application for today's struggles. And most of all, seldom have the expositors given the valuable outlines of passages so needed to help the preacher or teacher in his or her busy life to prepare for communicating the Word to congregations or classes.

This Communicator's Commentary series brings all of these elements together. The authors are scholar-preachers and teachers outstanding in their ability to make the Scriptures come alive for individuals and groups. They are noted for bringing together excellence in biblical scholarship, knowledge of the original Hebrew and Greek, sensitivity to people's needs, vivid illustrative material from biblical, classical, and contemporary sources, and lucid communication by the use of clear outlines of thought. Each has been selected to contribute to this series because of his Spirit-empowered ability to help people live in the skins of biblical characters and provide a "you-are-there" intensity to the drama of events of the Bible which have so much to say about our relationships and responsibilities today.

The design for the Communicator's Commentary gives the reader an overall outline of each book of the Bible. Following the introduction, which reveals the author's approach and salient background on the book, each chapter of the commentary provides the Scripture to be exposited. The New King James Bible has been chosen for the Communicator's Commentary because it combines with integrity the beauty of language, underlying Hebrew and Greek textual basis, and thought-flow of the 1611 King James Version, while replacing obsolete verb forms and other archaisms with their everyday contemporary counterparts for greater readability. Reverence for God is preserved in the capitalization of all pronouns referring to the Father, Son, or Holy Spirit. Readers who are more comfortable with another translation can readily find the parallel passage by means of the chapter and verse reference at the end of each passage being exposited. The paragraphs of exposition combine fresh insights to the Scripture, application, rich illustrative material, and innovative ways of utilizing the vibrant truth for his or her own life and for the challenge of communicating it with vigor and vitality.

It has been gratifying to me as Editor of this series to receive enthusiastic progress reports from each contributor. As they worked, all were gripped with new truths from the Scripture—God-given insights into passages, previously not written in the literature of biblical explanation. A prime objective of this series is for each user to find the same awareness: that God speaks with newness through the Scriptures when we approach them with a ready mind and a willingness to communicate what He has given; that God delights to give communicators of His Word "I-never-saw-that-in-that-verse-before" intellectual insights so that our listeners and readers can have "I-never-realized-all-that-was-in-that-verse" spiritual experiences.

The thrust of the commentary series unequivocally affirms that God speaks through the Scriptures today to engender faith, enable adventuresome living of the abundant life, and establish the basis of obedient discipleship. The Bible, the unique Word of God, is unlimited as a resource for Christians in communicating our hope to others. It is our weapon in the battle for truth, the guide for ministry, and the irresistible force for introducing others to God.

A biblically rooted communication of the Gospel holds in unity and oneness what divergent movements have wrought asunder. This commentary series courageously presents personal faith, caring for individuals, and social responsibility as essential, inseparable dimensions of biblical Christianity. It seeks to present the quadrilateral Gospel in its fullness which calls us to unreserved commitment to Christ, unrestricted self-esteem in His grace, unqualified love for others in personal evangelism, and undying efforts to work for justice and righteousness in a sick and suffering world.

A growing renaissance in the church today is being led by clergy and laity who are biblically rooted, Christ-centered, and Holy Spirit-empowered. They have dared to listen to people's most urgent questions and deepest needs and then to God as He speaks through the Bible. Biblical preaching is the secret of growing churches. Bible study classes and small groups are equipping the laity for ministry in the world. Dynamic Christians are finding that daily study of God's Word allows the Spirit to do in them what He wishes to communicate through them to others. These days are the most exciting time since Pentecost. The Communicator's Commentary is offered to be a primary resource of new life for this renaissance.

It has been very encouraging to receive the enthusiastic responses of pastors and teachers to the twelve New Testament volumes of the Communicator's Commentary series. The letters from communicators on the firing line in pulpits, classes, study groups, and Bible fellowship clusters across the nation, as well as the reviews of scholars and publication analysts, have indicated that we have been on target in meeting a need for a distinctly different kind of commentary on the Scriptures, a commentary that is primarily aimed at helping interpreters of the Bible to equip the laity for ministry.

This positive response has led the publisher to press on with an additional twenty-one volumes covering the books of the Old Testament. These new volumes rest upon the same goals and guidelines that undergird the New Testament volumes. Scholar-preachers with facility in Hebrew as well as vivid contemporary exposition have been selected as authors. The purpose throughout is to aid the preacher and teacher in the challenge and adventure of Old Testament exposition in communication. In each volume you will meet Yahweh, the "I AM" Lord who is Creator, Sustainer, and Redeemer in the unfolding drama of His call and care of Israel. He is the Lord who acts, intervenes, judges, and presses His people into the immense challenges and privileges of being a chosen people, a holy nation. And in the descriptive exposition of each passage, the implications of the ultimate revelation of Yahweh in Jesus Christ, His Son, our Lord, are carefully spelled out to maintain unity and oneness in the preaching and teaching of the Gospel.

I am pleased to introduce to you the author of this fine commentary on 1 and 2 Kings. Dr. Russell H. Dilday is President of Southwestern Baptist Theological Seminary, where he has taught Philosophy of Religion for the last ten years. He came to Southwestern after twenty-five years of pastoral ministry.

This commentary reflects Dr. Dilday's diverse experience in Christian leadership. In his careful scholarship you will see a man of academia. In his attention to broader theological issues you will interact with a philosopher of religion. As an educator, Dr. Dilday teaches the meaning of the biblical text with clarity. As a pastor, he allows the text to speak to our generation with insight and power. This volume fulfills perfectly the purpose of the Communicator's Commentary series: to combine scholarly excellence with pastoral relevance in order to assist the contemporary communicator of God's Word.

As the English titles indicate, 1 and 2 Kings recount the history of the kings of Israel and Judah. In what way, we might wonder, do these records matter to us today? Dr. Dilday explains: "Even if you have no overbearing curiosity about the lives of the rich and famous, the accounts of the kings of Israel and Judah are still a valuable and intriguing subject for study. These reigns provided a ready framework on which the author built his inspired story of God's dealings with His people, and if we are to learn God's truth from this period for our own age, we can find it clearly in these two books." The books of Kings illustrate in vivid detail how the Almighty God deals with His people—yesterday and today!

Perhaps more than anything else, we see in Kings that our God is the God of history. Dr. Dilday notes that the writer of these books understood that history was "His-story," and that God was the Sovereign Lord of history, using men and nations to work out His redemptive purposes. Such a perspective is sadly lacking in much of contemporary Christianity. We pride ourselves on being modern and technologically advanced. But in so doing we may lose touch with our own history—and even with our God who reveals Himself in history. We may compromise the breadth of God's vision for the world and the majesty of His sovereignty. 1 and 2 Kings restore our perspective. We are reminded that the God who numbers every hair on our heads is also the King of kings who oversees the affairs of all nations.

In showing us again the God of history, the books of Kings call us to global perspective, to personal obedience, and to profound worship. Russell Dilday enables the voice of Kings to speak again. I am excited to commend to you this volume!

LLOYD OGILVIE

Introduction

When I was invited to write a commentary for the Word Communicator's Commentary series, my great appreciation for those volumes in the series already in print led me to accept the invitation eagerly, with a sense of excitement and humility. Technical biblical commentaries are important to the scholarly study of Scripture, a fact which I have come to appreciate more during these past ten years at Southwestern Seminary. But from the perspective of a pastor, a position I held for over twenty-five years, there is also a great need for commentaries designed to help with the weekly task of sermon preparation, with communicating the word of God to congregations who gather Sunday by Sunday. Most analytical commentaries do not go beyond exegesis and hermeneutics to the next step of applying the inspired revelation to present-day situations. Wisely, in addition to its widely acclaimed technical commentaries, Word has launched an ambitious effort to produce another set designed for this very purpose: to help the preacher/teacher not only to interpret the Word of God but to proclaim its inspired message to contemporary listeners. I was honored to be asked to contribute. It should be stated here, therefore, that this volume does not claim to be a technical, critical analysis of 1 and 2 Kings, nor does the author claim to be a specialist in Old Testament studies. Since my academic discipline is philosophy of religion, and my vocational calling, until these last ten years in academia, has been the pastoral ministry, my qualifications for making this study are those of a generalist.

Had the invitation to write for this series included the freedom to choose the biblical books I preferred, I probably would not have chosen the Books of Kings. These were more or less assigned to me, and now that the project has been completed, I am grateful for the appointment. It has been a fascinating and inspiring experience, one I might otherwise have missed.

The whole world, it seems, has an incurable fascination with royalty. That enchantment may have existed for centuries, but it seems recent developments within the British royal family, especially the escapades of HRH Prince Charles and Lady "Di" and HRH Prince Andrew and the Duchess of York, affectionately known as "Fergie," have captivated the public more than ever. We are enchanted by the lives of kings and queens.

There must have been a similar fascination with monarchs in the ancient world as well. The author of the Books of Kings acknowledged his dependence on several written sources that had been collected and preserved by generations of persons in the ancient world who were obviously impressed with royalty.

Even if you have no overbearing curiosity about the lives of the rich and famous, the accounts of the kings of Israel and Judah are still a valuable and intriguing subject for study. These reigns provided a ready framework on which the author built his inspired story of God's dealings with His people, and if we are to learn God's truth from this period for our own age, we can find it clearly in these two books.

Authorship and Date

1 and 2 Kings cover about four centuries of history from the close of David's reign to the release of Jehoiachin from Babylon during the reign of Evil-Merodach (approximately 1000 B.C. to 500 B.C.). If Kings was written by one author, then he must have lived until this last event, and completed his work while he was with the children of Israel in exile.

While the text itself does not identify the author, Jewish tradition (Mishna *Baba Bathra* 15a) attributes Kings to Jeremiah, the prophet. To be sure, the tone and perspective of the books are prophetic, and since Jeremiah was contemporary with Josiah and the remaining kings of Judah down to the fall of Jerusalem, this theory has an attractive appeal. Furthermore, it would help explain why Jeremiah, in spite of his importance, is noticeably absent from Kings. However, Jeremiah's authorship seems unlikely, since he was taken to Egypt where he died (Jer. 43:6, 7), and the ending of 2 Kings comes from someone who was obviously in Babylon, sometime before the return under Cyrus, which is not mentioned. A good guess, then, is that

Kings was written by an unidentified prophet in Babylon about 550 B.C.

Other Old Testament scholars attribute Kings to a prophet who lived and wrote during the reign of Josiah, which was approximately 640–604 B.C. Some credit a second inspired author who lived in Babylonian captivity with the conclusion of the Book of 2 Kings, which would be from the death of Josiah to the release of Jehoiachin about 550 B.C.

Purpose

Clearly, the author of Kings was trying to do more than merely write a history of Israel in the technical sense. Instead his purpose was didactic, to teach important lessons, to convey a spiritual message. That message and those lessons were "Deuteronomic" (cf. Deuteronomy 7, 9, 11, especially 11:26–28). The nation is supposed to keep the Law of Yahweh. If they do, they will be blessed. If they do not, they will be cursed.

The writer understood that history was "His-story," and that God was the Sovereign Lord of History using men and nations to work out His redemptive purposes. So he was not just interested in facts, but the meaning, the divine revelation behind the facts. Since the king stood in the place of the nation, the author chose to proclaim his message by telling the story of the kings, judging each king not on political grounds but on religious and spiritual grounds. He also wanted to magnify the roles of certain great prophets, to show how the kingdom was divided and taken away in fulfillment of prophecy, and to demonstrate God's faithfulness in fulfilling His promise to David to establish his house and throne forever.

Sources

Some commentators have divided the books radically into fragments: L, J, E, Davidic court narrative, Elijah cycle, Elisha cycle, Ahab source, Isaiah source, other prophetic sources, pre-Deuteronomic editor, and finally, the Deuteronomic author. It is better to recognize that, as the text itself indicates, the author, under the inspiration of the Holy Spirit, used various sources including some stilted court records and some powerful prophetic messages. Some of the sources are named in the Books of Kings: The Book of the Acts of Solomon (1 Kings 11:41), The Book of the Chronicles of Kings of Judah (1 Kings 14:29), The Book of the Chronicles of Kings of Israel (1 Kings 14:19), eyewitness accounts of prophets: Nathan, Abijah, Iddo, Shemaiah, Jehu, and Isaiah, and certain Court Histories.

Method

The author uses a chronological method to tell his story, interweaving the accounts of the kings of both Judah and Israel. He tells the complete story of one king's reign then goes back to pick up the story of his contemporary or contemporaries in the other kingdom. He uses a routine formula to discuss and judge each king. Of course, interspersed at appropriate points are the activities of the prophets.

Place in the Canon

Kings is obviously a sequel to 1 and 2 Samuel. In fact in the LXX (Septuagint, Greek translation of the Old Testament in the third century B.C.), where the division of Kings into two books is first found, 1 Kings is called "Of the Kingdoms 3" and 2 Kings is called "Of the Kingdoms 4." 1 and 2 Samuel are designated "Of the Kingdoms 1 and 2."

In our English Bible, the Books of Kings are grouped under "history," but in the Hebrew scriptures they are considered together as the fourth of the Former Prophets (Joshua, Judges, Samuel, and Kings). The division of Kings into two books, which probably occurred to help the scribes find references more readily in their debates with Christians, was picked up by Jerome in the Vulgate (Latin translation in the fourth century A.D.).

An Outline of 1 and 2 Kings

I. From the Last Days of David to the Divided Kingdom 970–932 B.C.: 1 Kings 1:1–11:43
   A. The Death of David and the Accession of Solomon: 1:1–2:12
      1. David's Old Age: 1:1–4
      2. Adonijah's Quest for Power: 1:5–10
      3. Nathan's and Bathsheba's Counterplot: 1:11–27
      4. Solomon's Selection as King: 1:28–37
      5. Solomon's Anointing by Zadok: 1:38–53
      6. David's Last Words and Death: 2:1–12
   B. The Wisdom and Wealth of Solomon: 2:13–4:34
      1. Solomon's Position Secured: 2:13–46
      2. Solomon's Marriage and God's Gift of Wisdom: 3:1–15
      3. Solomon's Wise Judgment: 3:16–28
      4. Solomon's Rich Resources: 4:1–34
   C. The Building and Dedication of the Temple: 5:1–8:66
      1. Solomon Recruits Hiram and Plans the Temple: 5:1–18
      2. Solomon Builds the Temple: 6:1–38
      3. Solomon Furnishes the Temple and Completes Other Buildings: 7:1–51
      4. Solomon Dedicates the Temple: 8:1–66
   D. The Golden Age of Solomon: 9:1–10:29
      1. God Appears to Solomon a Second Time: 9:1–9
      2. Solomon Establishes Financial, Labor, and Trade Policies: 9:10–28
      3. The Queen of Sheba Visits King Solomon: 10:1–13
      4. The Great Wealth and Power of King Solomon: 10:14–29

- E. The Decline and Death of Solomon: 11:1–43
  1. Solomon's Foreign Wives Lead Him Astray: 11:1–13
  2. God Raises up Enemies against Solomon: 11:14–25
  3. Jeroboam Rebels and Solomon Dies: 11:26–43

II. From the Divided Kingdom to the Fall of Israel 932–722 B.C.: 1 Kings 12:1–2 Kings 17:41

- A. The Reigns of Jeroboam of Israel and Rehoboam of Judah: 12:1–14:31
  1. The Division of the Kingdom: 12:1–16
  2. The Reign of Jeroboam in Israel: 12:17–33
  3. The Message of the Man of God: 13:1–34
  4. The Conclusion of Jeroboam's Reign: 14:1–20
  5. The Reign of Rehoboam in Judah: 14:21–31
- B. The Reigns of Two Kings in Judah and Five Kings in Israel: 15:1–16:28
  1. Abijam Reigns in Judah: 15:1–8
  2. Asa Reigns in Judah: 15:9–24
  3. Nadab Reigns in Israel: 15:25–32
  4. Baasha Reigns in Israel: 15:33–16:7
  5. Elah Reigns in Israel: 16:8–14
  6. Zimri Reigns in Israel: 16:15–20
  7. Omri (and Tibni) Reigns in Israel: 16:21–28
- C. The Early Reign of Ahab of Israel and the Early Ministry of Elijah: 16:29–18:46
  1. Ahab and His Evil Reign in Israel: 16:29–34
  2. Elijah and the Widow of Zarephath: 17:1–24
  3. Elijah and Obadiah: 18:1–16
  4. Elijah and the Prophets of Baal: 18:17–46
- D. The Account of Elijah's Confrontation with Ahab: 19:1–22:40
  1. Elijah Escapes from Jezebel: 19:1–14
  2. Elijah Receives a New Task: 19:15–21
  3. Ahab Defeats the Syrians: 20:1–43
  4. Ahab Takes Naboth's Vineyard: 21:1–16
  5. Elijah Condemns Ahab: 21:17–29
  6. Ahab Is Warned by Micaiah: 22:1–28
  7. Ahab Is Slain in Battle: 22:29–40
- E. The Reigns of Jehoshaphat of Judah and Ahaziah of Israel and the Conclusion of Elijah's Ministry: 22:41–2 Kings 2:14

1. Jehoshaphat's Reign Summarized: 22:41–50
2. Ahaziah's Reign Summarized: 22:51–53
3. Ahaziah's Reign Judged by Elijah: 2 Kings 1:1–18
4. Elijah's Ministry Ended: 2:1–14

F. The Beginning of Elisha's Ministry and the Reign of Jehoram of Israel: 2:15–3:27
   1. Elisha Begins His Miraculous Ministry: 2:15–25
   2. Jehoram Makes an Alliance and Seeks Elisha's Prophecy: 3:1–20
   3. Jehoram Quells the Moabite Rebellion: 3:21–27

G. The Account of Elisha's Miracles: 4:1–6:7
   1. Elisha and the Widow's Oil: 4:1–7
   2. Elisha and the Shunammite's Son: 4:8–37
   3. Elisha and the Miraculous Food: 4:38–44
   4. Elisha and the Leper Naaman: 5:1–27
   5. Elisha and the Floating Ax Head: 6:1–7

H. The Account of Elisha's Role in the Syrian Wars: 6:8–8:15
   1. The Blinded Syrians Are Captured: 6:8–23
   2. The City of Samaria Is Besieged: 6:24–33
   3. The City of Samaria Is Delivered: 7:1–20
   4. The Shunammite's Land Is Restored: 8:1–6
   5. The King of Syria Is Replaced: 8:7–15

I. The Reigns of Jehoram and Ahaziah of Judah and Jehu of Israel: 8:16–10:36
   1. Jehoram Reigns in Judah: 8:16–24
   2. Ahaziah Reigns in Judah: 8:25–29
   3. Elisha Anoints Jehu of Israel: 9:1–13
   4. Jehu Slays Jehoram of Israel and Claims the Throne: 9:14–26
   5. Jehu Slays Ahaziah of Judah and Jezebel: 9:27–37
   6. Jehu Slays the Families of Ahab and Ahaziah: 10:1–17
   7. Jehu Slays the Worshipers of Baal and Dies: 10:18–36

J. The Reigns of Athaliah the Queen and Jehoash of Judah: 11:1–12:21
   1. Athaliah Assumes the Throne, but Jehoash Is Spared and Crowned: 11:1–12
   2. Athaliah Is Killed and Jehoash Is Enthroned: 11:13–21

3. Jehoash Restores the Temple: 12:1–16
4. Jehoash Pays Tribute to Syria and Dies: 12:17–21

K. The Reigns of Jehoahaz, Jehoash, and Jeroboam II of Israel; Amaziah and Azariah of Judah; the Last Days of Elisha: 13:1–15:7
1. Jehoahaz Reigns in Israel: 13:1–9
2. Jehoash Reigns in Israel: 13:10–13
3. Elisha Prophesies and Dies: 13:14–21
4. Israel Recaptures Cities from Syria: 13:22–25
5. Amaziah Reigns in Judah: 14:1–22
6. Jeroboam II Reigns in Israel: 14:23–29
7. Azariah Reigns in Judah: 15:1–7

L. The Last Six Kings of Israel, Jotham and Ahaz of Judah, and the Captivity of Israel: 15:8–17:41
1. Zechariah, Shallum, and Menahem Reign in Israel: 15:8–22
2. Pekahiah and Pekah Reign in Israel: 15:23–31
3. Jotham and Ahaz Reign in Judah: 15:32–16:20
4. Hoshea Reigns in Israel: 17:1–4
5. Assyria Carries Israel into Captivity: 17:5–23
6. Assyria Resettles Samaria: 17:24–41

III. The Kingdom of Judah from the Fall of Samaria to the Fall of Jerusalem 722–587 B.C.: 2 Kings 18:1–25:30

A. The Reign of Hezekiah in Judah: 18:1–20:21
1. Hezekiah's Initial Reforms: 18:1–16
2. Sennacherib's Boast against the Lord: 18:17–37
3. Isaiah's Prophecy of Deliverance: 19:1–7
4. Hezekiah's Prayer for Help: 19:8–19
5. Isaiah's Word Concerning Sennacherib: 19:20–37
6. Hezekiah's Illness and God's Cure: 20:1–11
7. Babylon's Envoys and Hezekiah's Death: 20:12–21

B. The Reigns of Manasseh and Amon: 21:1–26
1. Manasseh Reigns in Judah: 21:1–9
2. The Prophets Judge Manasseh and He Dies: 21:10–18
3. Amon Reigns in Judah: 21:19–26

C. The Reign and Reforms of Josiah: 22:1–23:30
1. The Discovery of the Book of the Law: 22:1–13
2. The Prophecy of Huldah: 22:14–20
3. The Reforms of Josiah: 23:1–30

D. The Last Days of Judah and the Fall of Jerusalem: 23:31–25:30
   1. Jehoahaz's Reign and Captivity: 23:31–34
   2. Jehoiakim's Reign: 23:35–24:7
   3. Jehoiachin's Reign and the First Deportation: 24:8–16
   4. Zedekiah's Reign as a Vassal: 24:17–20
   5. The Siege and Fall of Jerusalem: 25:1–21
   6. The Appointment of Gedaliah and the Release of Jehoiachin: 25:22–30

SECTION ONE

From the Last Days of David to the Divided Kingdom 970–932 B.C.

1 Kings 1:1–11:43

CHAPTER ONE

The Death of David and the Accession of Solomon

1 Kings 1:1–2:12

Introduction

This first chapter along with the first twelve verses of the second chapter originally may have been a part of the conclusion of 2 Samuel. In early Hebrew scriptures, the Books of Kings were undivided and were considered the fourth book of the "Former Prophets" (Joshua, Judges, Samuel, Kings). The division of Kings into separate books, which comes, it seems, at an awkward place in the story, may have been made arbitrarily by the Greek translators, perhaps to conform with the size of the scrolls available to them.[1] Or, according to Francisco, the divisions may have been made to help the Jews find references more readily in their controversies with Christians.[2]

Additional evidence that the early Hebrews considered Samuel and Kings as a unit is seen in the names given to the books by the Greek translators after they created the divisions. The two books of Samuel were called "Of the Kingdoms 1" and "Of the Kingdoms 2," and the books of the Kings were called "Of the Kingdoms 3" and "Of the Kingdoms 4."

Whatever the reasons for the divisions, adding the last days of David's reign here at the beginning allows the story to flow naturally from the last chapter of 2 Samuel into 1 Kings, coming to a logical transition where David's reign ends and Solomon's begins at verse 12 of chapter 2.

David ruled Israel from about 1010 to 970 B.C., a period of forty years and six months (2:11). So the events in this section of 1 Kings can be dated and located with some accuracy. They took place during the last few years of the Davidic monarchy in the city of Jerusalem.

When Joshua led the Children of Israel into the promised land, Jerusalem was an ancient fortress-city belonging to a Canaanite tribe called the Jebusites. Following the conquest, the city was assigned to the tribe of Benjamin who allowed the Jebusites to live there unmolested until their king rebelled and was slain by Joshua. Even then, the city continued as a Jebusite fortress until approximately 1000 B.C. when David sent Joab, his trusted military strategist, to scale the walls and capture the city for his new capital (2 Sam. 5:6–9). Jerusalem was very small then, only 1,250 feet long and 400 feet wide, shaped like a giant human footprint. Enlarging the Jebusite fortress, building a palace, and erecting a sacred tent for the Ark of the Covenant, David then gave Jerusalem the name "The City of David."

Later, Solomon enlarged the city northward to include Mount Moriah, where Abraham offered up Isaac, where David purchased the threshing floor of Araunah the Jebusite (2 Sam. 24:18), and where he eventually built his great temple. After the destruction of Jerusalem in A.D. 70, the ancient City of David was abandoned and its present location lies outside the walls of modern Jerusalem.

It was here in Jerusalem, a city no larger than twelve acres with a population of about twelve hundred, that the events of this first section of Kings take place.

DAVID'S OLD AGE

1:1 Now King David was old, advanced in years; and they put covers on him, but he could not get warm.

2 Therefore his servants said to him, "Let a young woman, a virgin, be sought for our lord the king, and let her stand before the king, and let her care for him; and let her lie in your bosom, that our lord the king may be warm."

3 So they sought for a lovely young woman throughout all the territory of Israel, and found Abishag the Shunammite, and brought her to the king.

> 4 The young woman *was* very lovely; and she cared for the king, and served him; but the king did not know her.
>
> *1 Kings 1:1–4*

Any historical account that begins with the word "now" and tells about an old man who couldn't get warm even though his servants piled covers on him is obviously not a formal, technical chronicle. Instead, the style of the author of Kings is personal, colorful, dramatic, even folksy. A lively, well-written narrative, it was obviously composed by someone who had access to firsthand information about the inner life of the court with its plots and counterplots. The word "now" in verse 1, which is literally "and" in Hebrew, adds credence to the theory that this verse is not necessarily the beginning of a new book but the continuation of 2 Samuel.

David was about seventy years old. Even though his weakened physical condition was not out of the ordinary for a man of his age in ancient times, some commentators have felt compelled to offer explanations for what they consider to be David's "abnormal" poor health. Keil believes the king's enfeebled condition was not the result of senility, but of a sickly constitution brought on by the hardships of his agitated and restless life.[3] The rabbinical tradition claimed David's shivering coldness was inflicted upon him by God as a punishment for cutting off a piece of Saul's robe (1 Sam. 24:5).[4] Whatever its cause, David's physical condition, while not unusual for his age, was a critical factor in the consideration of his continued effectiveness as king. The imperfect tense used in verse 1 expresses the continuous, habitual character of the king's condition, literally, "he used not to be warm."

It was this concern that led to the suggested cure in verse 2. The enlisting of a lovely young virgin to nurse the king and *"lie in [his] bosom, that our lord the king may be warm"* was a traditional cure prescribed by ancient medicine. For example, Galen, the Greek physician, recommended that the health and heat of a young body could be transferred to that of an aging patient as a medical treatment.[5] Josephus also describes the procedure as a medical one, and calls the servants in verse 2 "physicians" (*Antiquities,* 7.19.3).

After a thorough search throughout the kingdom, Abishag the Shunammite was the young woman selected (v. 3). The author's use of "the" Shunammite instead of "a" Shunammite indicates she was well known. Her hometown, Shunem, on the western slope of Moreh northwest of Jezreel, was the place where Elisha raised the widow's son (2 Kings 4:8). There has been a great deal of speculation about the identity of this intriguing character in David's life. The similarity of the names "Shunammite" and "Shulammite" in the Song of Songs has led to an undocumented theory that Abishag is the one Solomon wrote about in that book. According to the theory, as she ministered to David, she became romantically involved with his son Solomon and was later the subject of his love poem.[6] In a classic allegorical interpretation, Jerome makes Abishag "the ever-virgin wisdom of God so extolled by Solomon."[7]

Obviously, Abishag was to be more than a nurse for the king. The Septuagint translation makes it specific: "let her excite him and lie with him."[8] On the basis of the incident in 1 Kings 2:13, some have suggested David took her as his wife, but more than likely she became one of his several concubines. Although monogamy was the ideal marriage principle given by God in Genesis, polygamy was a widespread practice in Israel at this time. Even David, who was a man after God's own heart, had numerous wives and concubines.

"But the king did not know her" (v. 4). While this passage may imply that David made a moral choice not to be sexually involved with Abishag, it may also indicate that he did not have the physical capacity to do so. Anthropologists have shown how ancient cultures sometimes required a test of virility to see if their aging king had the strength to continue ruling.[9] David would not have been expected to abdicate the throne just because he could not keep warm with covers piled on his bed, but if he failed the test of vigor, then according to the custom of that period, some would assume a new king needed to be named.

There is pathos in this graphic description of the aging king. Here is David the athletic giant-killer, David the valiant warrior-hero, David the noble ruler, David the talented musician, now weak, trembling, unable to leave his bed. This pathetic picture of the man whose name was synonymous with valor and strength reveals the honest realism of the Old Testament record. Even if it was unflattering, the inspired writers of the Word of God did not glamorize their heroes at the expense of truth. David was a "legend in his own time," but the Bible reminds us he was also an imperfect sinner who, in spite of his admirable traits, had to face the common enemies of all humanity, old age and eventually death.

However, it is clear that while the king was limited physically, his personality remained vibrant and his spirit resolute. Later in verses 28–35, the flash of his former fire blazes up again. The old lion could yet be roused and could strike when roused. His decisive declaration of Solomon as his successor shows his inner spiritual strength still remained vital. This is encouraging to men and women of faith who want to retain youthful vigor in old age in spite of physical limitations.

George Burns, the comedian, on the eve of his ninetieth birthday, donated a million dollars to build an intensive care unit for a film industry retirement home in Los Angeles. He was interviewed by reporters who asked him about his long life. "I've lived a very exciting life so far," he said. He then paused and added, "I expect the second half to be just as good!" When asked why he chose to give his money to the retirement home, he responded drily, "I may finish up there when I get old." "I'm never going to retire," he said with his eyes sparkling behind his owl-eyed spectacles. "I'm going to stay in show business until I'm the only one left."[10]

Such an optimistic, forward-looking attitude in senior years is appealing because the desire to face aging gracefully and positively is universal. That's why we consider heroic the statement of South Carolina Senator Strom Thurmond when he was asked about getting married at age seventy, "In my old age I'd rather smell perfume than liniment." That's what appeals to us when we read the scriptural description of Moses at the age of 120, "his eyes were not dim nor his natural vigor abated" (Deut. 34:7). We want very much to overcome time and remain useful, vigorous, and wise in old age. And that's why we should be grateful that the Bible gives us valuable insights about coping with aging.

For instance, the Bible teaches that we retain spiritual youthfulness by adopting a positive personal outlook. "For as he thinks in his heart, so is he" (Prov. 23:7). "Keep your heart with all diligence, for out of it spring the issues of life" (Prov. 4:23). Old age is something other than chronological years; one's attitude and outlook are what determine one's age. Maybe the truths Solomon wrote in Ecclesiastes 12 were learned from watching his aging father David. Solomon declares that we are old when:

1. We stagger at trifles or let little things throw us. "The grasshopper is a burden" (v. 5).

2. We tremble at challenges or let the spirit of adventure die. "They are afraid of height" (v. 5). Caleb was eighty-five when he said, "Lord, give me this mountain." Compare him with the teenager who says, "I don't want to be heroic, just comfortable." Which one is really old?

3. We glorify the past and resign from the present. "I have no pleasure in the years" (v. 1).

Robert Browning captured this biblical truth in his poem *Rabbi ben Ezra:*

> Grow old along with me!
> The best is yet to be,
> The last of life, for which the first was made!

Second, according to the word of God, we retain spiritual youthfulness by maintaining a positive personal faith in God. The good news of the Bible is that personal faith in Jesus Christ generates indescribable new life and then floods that life with fulfillment, joy, meaning, peace, purpose, and power. A personal relationship with God through Christ transforms a life of deterioration and boredom into a life of constant renewal. "Those who wait upon the Lord shall renew their strength; they shall mount up with wings like eagles, they shall run and not be weary, they shall walk and not faint" (Isa. 40:31). "The fear of the Lord prolongs days" (Prov. 10:27). "Therefore we do not lose heart. Even though our outward man is perishing, yet the inward man is being renewed day by day" (2 Cor. 4:16).

Browning continued his poem with the words:

> Our times are in His hand
> Who saith, "A whole I planned,
> Youth shows but half; trust God; see all, nor
> be afraid!"

Adonijah's Quest for Power

1:5 Then Adonijah the son of Haggith exalted himself, saying, "I will be king"; and he prepared for

himself chariots and horsemen, and fifty men to run
before him.
6 (And his father had not rebuked him at any
time by saying, "Why have you done so?" He *was* also
very good-looking. *His mother* had borne him after
Absalom.)
7 Then he conferred with Joab the son of Zeruiah
and with Abiathar the priest, and they followed and
helped Adonijah.
8 But Zadok the priest, Benaiah the son of
Jehoiada, Nathan the prophet, Shimei, Rei, and the
mighty men who *belonged* to David were not with
Adonijah.
9 And Adonijah sacrificed sheep and oxen and
fattened cattle by the stone of Zoheleth, which *is* by
En Rogel; he also invited all his brothers, the king's
sons, and all the men of Judah, the king's servants.
10 But he did not invite Nathan the prophet, Benaiah, the mighty men, or Solomon his brother.

1 Kings 1:5–10

Adonijah, now about thirty-five years old, was David's fourth son. We know nothing of his mother, Haggith, one of David's wives. Adonijah was by now the king's oldest son since Amnon, David's firstborn, was slain by the order of Absalom. Absalom, after his unsuccessful coup d'état, was in turn killed by Joab's men; another son, Chileab, is not mentioned in Scripture, probably indicating he died young. This left Adonijah as the oldest, and even though primogeniture had not yet been established as the rule of monarchical succession in Israel, he assumed, as the oldest, he had a right to the throne. Actually, the early Hebrew kings could name whomever they wished as their successors without regard to the age or rank of the heirs.

Saying, *"I will be king,"* Adonijah *"exalted himself"* (v. 5) and launched his campaign for the crown. This statement uses a participle and should be translated, "was exalting himself," emphasizing the continuous process of a developing scheme. Adonijah's actions, therefore, were not spontaneous but premeditated, planned over a period of time, as he watched the encroaching weakness of his father.

It is interesting to note that much of his plan for rebellion was identical to the plan his brother Absalom used in his abortive attempt at overthrowing his father David's regime. For example, the numbers of chariots, horsemen, and runners are exactly the same as those Absalom recruited in 2 Sam. 15:1. Adonijah obviously took a lesson from his rebellious older brother.

"Horsemen" in verse 5 is actually the word *horses.* Mounted cavalry were not employed by Israel until Solomon's day, although they were used by Egypt and other cultures earlier.[11] *"Men to run before him"* is the usual Hebrew terminology for royal bodyguards, similar no doubt to today's secret service men who run beside the presidential limousine in national parades.

Adonijah is described as handsome, a desirable leadership quality in ancient cultures, but he was spoiled by a doting father. *"His father had not rebuked him at any time"* (v. 6). David may have been a heroic king, but he had a history of paternal weakness toward his sons. The Scriptures tell us he was unable to rebuke Amnon (2 Sam. 13:21) or to discipline Absalom (2 Sam. 18:5), and here he is described as unsuccessful in restraining Adonijah.

David may have been so engrossed in his kingly responsibilities that he neglected his sons. Whatever the reason for the failure, it is clear that a child who does not learn early to subordinate his selfish interests to a greater loyalty is left like Adonijah, ill-prepared for life. Think what David could have done for Adonijah if he had taken time to share some of his own rich experiences as a youth. If he had demanded responsibility and accountability, or as verse 6 expresses it, if he had confronted Absalom with the words, *"Why have you done so?"* Since, as a father, David had failed to teach his son to obey him or the Lord and thereby encouraged him to pursue whatever he wanted regardless of what was right, it is no surprise that Adonijah rebelled. Although he knew Solomon was God's as well as his father's choice for a successor, Adonijah was not willing to accept it.

The Bible uniformly points out the importance of strong parental discipline in the development of mature, responsible children. It teaches us that the family is the first training ground for trusteeship at every level in life. Sometimes these lessons are presented in the form of negative examples such as Eli's failure with his children (1 Sam. 3:13) or Samuel's failure with his (1 Sam. 8:3). At other times the teaching is by direct admonition:

> He who spares his rod hates his son, but he who loves him disciplines him promptly (Prov. 13:24).
>
> Do not withhold correction from a child (Prov. 23:13).
>
> Train up a child in the way he should go, and when he is old he will not depart from it (Prov. 22:6).
>
> And you fathers, do not provoke your children to wrath, but bring them up in the training and admonition of the Lord (Eph. 6:4).
>
> One who rules his own house well, having his children in submission with all reverence (1 Tim. 3:4).
>
> That they admonish the young women . . . to love their children (Titus 2:4).

While unstructured, relaxed theories of parenting have been popular in the past, a new consensus is emerging even among secular psychologists that a firm, loving parental style is best. Public school systems are discovering the same principles and are replacing social promotions and other unstructured policies. Calling for stricter discipline in the classrooms and a return to "old-fashioned" priorities in learning, some school systems have implemented "no pass–no play" rules that require greater accountability from students before they can participate in extracurricular activities. How often so-called new educational developments and parenting styles are in reality rediscoveries of ancient biblical principles.

Coconspirators in Adonijah's attempted coup are named in verse 7. First is Joab, the son of Zeruiah, David's sister and therefore Adonijah's cousin. He was a long-time military leader in David's regime, but he had earned the king's disfavor by having Absalom, David's rebellious son, killed and by slaying two trusted leaders, Abner and Amasa (2 Sam. 18:9–17; 3:22–39; 20:8–10). No doubt, David had made Joab feel rejected, especially when he appointed Benaiah to the military post Joab once held. Joab's professional jealousy degenerated into hate. He wanted to be indispensable. As a fighter, he knew that would never be the case in a peaceful regime, so he rallied behind Adonijah, risking everything on the hope that the pretender to the throne would emerge the winner.

Another in Adonijah's political party was Abiathar the priest. He was the sole survivor of Saul's massacre of the house of Eli, the hereditary priests of the ark of Shiloh (1 Sam. 22). Abiathar and Zadok had apparently shared the high priesthood between them when David ordered the ark to be brought to Jerusalem (1 Chron. 15:11). For some unknown reason, David preferred Zadok, and Abiathar assumed that his own future under the present monarchy was bleak. He would have a better chance for power under Adonijah as king, so he joined the rebellion. The statement, *"They followed and helped Adonijah"* in verse 7 is a pregnant construction in Hebrew, meaning literally, "they supported after Adonijah."[12]

Here is a tragic illustration of how a selfish grasping after power can destroy relationships as well as individual personalities. Over the years Joab and Abiathar had developed intimate friendships with their colleagues Benaiah and Zadok. Their fellowship, which had been made closer because of shared dangers and suffering, now crumbled under the sad pressure of petty personal jealousies. As leaders, these two should have been more concerned for the welfare of the king and the nation than for the protection of their own futures.

Once a self-centered quest for personal position or power gets into a relationship, it is like a trickle of water in the crack of a huge rock. Even though it appears harmless, when the water freezes in winter it can split even the hardest of stones. To be heroic and effective in a great cause, leaders must suppress side glances toward personal advantage and, like Paul, decide, "This one thing I do." Joab and Abiathar tarnished their sacred commitments, discarded precious friendships, and self-destructed because they thought more of themselves than of God's will.

In verse 8, the list of those not invited to Adonijah's feast indicates he knew his claim to the throne would be contested. In fact the persons named here and in verse 10 became the nucleus of an opposition party favoring David's appointment of Solomon as the next ruler. Zadok, Benaiah, Jehoiada, and Nathan are identified later as members of this group. Nothing is known about Shimei and Rei. *"The mighty men"* were a select group of seasoned soldiers who had fought with the king through the years since his wilderness exploits (2 Sam. 23:8).[13] The Hebrew word *gibbōrîm* is kin to an Arabic word meaning "giant" or "bully." Here its meaning is primarily "a person of substance."[14]

Combining a religious ceremony with a celebrative announcement party, Adonijah hosted a feast. *"Sheep and oxen and fattened cattle"* were slaughtered and prepared for his guests gathered by *"the stone of Zoheleth, which is by En Rogel"* (v. 9). The location of the stone (which is also called "the rolling stone" or "the serpent's stone") is most likely the water supply southwest of the Davidic-Jebusite city of Jerusalem in the Kidron Valley slightly lower down than the junction with the Hinnom Valley.[15]

Adonijah's premature celebration is a classic example of counting chickens before they hatch. Such a feast should have climaxed, not initiated his dash for the throne. His quick defeat teaches us to weigh the outcome of our deeds before we commit ourselves to a course of action. It warns us to see a challenge through to completion before we start planning a victory dinner. As Maclaren put it, "They who feast when they should fight are likely to end their mirth with sorrow."[16]

Adonijah was guilty of another offense that is frequently repeated today. He tried to disguise his self-promotion as God's will. He *"exalted himself, saying, 'I will be king'"* (v. 5), then planned a religious feast to mask his selfish manipulations hoping they would pass as God's will.

Adonijah is not the first nor the last personality in history to enlist both the military and the church to gain power. More often than not, the plan fails as it did here. It seems clear from his proud claim, "I would be king," that Adonijah wanted to rule, not serve. How strikingly different was the pattern of Jesus who came "not to be ministered unto, but to minister."

Nathan's and Bathsheba's Counterplot

1:11 So Nathan spoke to Bathsheba the mother of Solomon, saying, "Have you not heard that Adonijah the son of Haggith has become king, and David our lord does not know *it?*

12 "Come, please, let me now give you advice, that you may save your own life and the life of your son Solomon.

13 "Go immediately to King David and say to him, 'Did you not, my lord, O king, swear to your

maidservant, saying, "Assuredly your son Solomon shall reign after me, and he shall sit on my throne"? Why then has Adonijah become king?'

14 "Then, while you are still talking there with the king, I also will come in after you and confirm your words."

15 So Bathsheba went into the chamber to the king. (Now the king was very old, and Abishag the Shunammite was serving the king.)

16 And Bathsheba bowed and did homage to the king. Then the king said, "What is your wish?"

17 Then she said to him, "My lord, you swore by the LORD your God to your maidservant, *saying,* 'Assuredly Solomon your son shall reign after me, and he shall sit on my throne.'

18 "So now, look! Adonijah has become king; and now, my lord the king, you do not know about *it.*

19 "He has sacrificed oxen and fattened cattle and sheep in abundance, and has invited all the sons of the king, Abiathar the priest, and Joab the commander of the army; but Solomon your servant he has not invited.

20 "And as for you, my lord, O king, the eyes of all Israel *are* on you, that you should tell them who will sit on the throne of my lord the king after him.

21 "Otherwise it will happen, when my lord the king rests with his fathers, that I and my son Solomon will be counted as offenders."

22 And just then, while she was still talking with the king, Nathan the prophet also came in.

23 So they told the king, saying, "Here is Nathan the prophet." And when he came in before the king, he bowed down before the king with his face to the ground.

24 And Nathan said, "My lord, O king, have you said, 'Adonijah shall reign after me, and he shall sit on my throne'?

25 "For he has gone down today, and has sacrificed oxen and fattened cattle and sheep in abundance, and has invited all the king's sons, and the commanders of the army, and Abiathar the priest; and look! They are

eating and drinking before him; and they say, *'Long live King Adonijah!'*
26 "But he has not invited me—me your servant—
nor Zadok the priest, nor Benaiah the son of Jehoiada,
nor your servant Solomon.
27 "Has this thing been done by my lord the king,
and you have not told your servant who should sit on
the throne of my lord the king after him?"

1 Kings 1:11-27

Nathan the prophet, first mentioned in verse 8 as one of those Adonijah did not invite to his banquet, played a large role in the establishment of the kingdom under David and Solomon. His enormous influence is reflected in a long list of events. He was the one who persuaded David to delegate to his son Solomon the responsibility for building the temple. He also courageously reproved the king for his adultery and his treatment of Uriah. His strong interest in Solomon began at the moment of his birth and led to Solomon's being given another name, Jedidiah, "beloved of Yahweh." Now in this passage he bravely took the initiative in opposing Adonijah's coup and ensuring the anointing of Solomon as king. Later Nathan is identified as the one who wrote the chronicles of the reign of David and the history of the reign of Solomon (1 Chron. 29:29; 2 Chron. 9:29). Maybe Nathan's bold example of faithfulness undergirded the future role of the prophets recorded in the remainder of 1 and 2 Kings.

Obviously, Nathan, Bathsheba, and even David were unaware of Adonijah's plan until it was already under way. The secretive hatching of the conspiracy shows Adonijah knew he was not David's choice and that his initial steps would arouse significant opposition. Cleverly, Nathan stirred the maternal instincts of Bathsheba in identifying Adonijah the contender as *"the son of Haggith,"* a rival wife in David's harem (v. 11).

The word *"save"* in verse 12 is from the same root as the word "Malta," the port of refuge in Phoenician navigation. The word *"life"* translates the Hebrew word *nepeš,* which means "life-breath" or "vitality."[17] In her plea before David, Bathsheba reminded him of an oath he made to name Solomon king. While the oath is not mentioned elsewhere in Scripture, it was probably made after God told David in

2 Sam. 7:12 that a son not yet born would rule after him. This ruled out Adonijah, as well as Absalom, and obviously pointed to Solomon. Just because there is no other record of the oath is not sufficient reason to assume, as some commentators do, that Bathsheba and Nathan fabricated the story to trick the feeble king.

The *"he"* in verse 17 (also in verses 13, 14, 30, and 35) is given emphasis by its position in the sentence. It suggests, "he and no other." The word *"assuredly"* in these same verses is the Hebrew particle *kî* and probably should not be translated at all. It is usually intended for nothing more than a quotation mark.

Bathsheba reminded David in verse 20 that as king he had the right to name his successor. While no official plan for succession had yet been established, it was assumed that an Israelite king could choose anyone to succeed him. Only if a dead king's wishes were unknown could the eldest son claim the right of succession.[18] She and Nathan were not suggesting the immediate abdication of David, only the appointment of Solomon as the one who would be a co-regent or king-designate until David's death. Only then would he become the sole ruler of Israel and Judah. *"Rests with his fathers"* was a frequently used euphemism for death in Old Testament times. This limited view of life after death was later replaced by the glorious concept of the resurrection.

Nathan entered the king's chamber with proper respect. Verse 23 literally says, "He bowed to the king upon his nose, earthward."[19] With deference to the king's authority, he assumed David not only knew about Adonijah's plans, but had instituted them without informing anyone. Then he asked the king a question, *"Have you said, 'Adonijah shall reign after me . . . ?'"* To be sure, the question carried with it a sting of rebuke, but it shows Nathan's sensitive and tactful spirit. The same spirit was reflected in his indirectly confronting David with his adultery by telling the story of the poor man with one lamb. While maintaining tactful respect, Nathan still got his message across: David should have been more aware; he should have acted sooner to stop Adonijah and not put his friends in danger. He showed full confidence in David that he would act to correct the situation.

In this passage, as throughout his life, Nathan performed the work of God's prophet admirably, setting a noble example not only for those prophets who followed him in Judah and Israel, but for present-day prophetic ministers as well. Some commentaries take a different view. They believe Nathan was a conniver with Bathsheba in a manipulative plot using lies and subterfuge to take advantage of David's pitiful senility and ensure their own futures in the kingdom.[20] It seems better to see Nathan as an astute planner who, at great personal risk, carried out his responsibility to see that God's declared will in the succession of the monarchy was carried out. His design was not only clever but also courageous and was carried out with due respect for David's honored position. In this way Nathan showed what a real prophet is to be and do. He acted not so much out of concern for his own safety but for the will of God. It was risky going to the king during his weakness. It could have cost him his life had Adonijah won. But he was brave. Had he not acted responsibly, there might not have been a "Solomonic era" in Israel.

Clearly, Nathan understood that a call to prophetic ministry was a call to interfere, to counsel, to warn, and to punish whenever self-will threatened to divert the will of God and injure God's people. What a noble example for preachers today. Isn't it tragic that some contemporary ministers seem more interested in promoting their individual careers, more concerned about popular acceptance, about being on the winning side of a denominational power struggle, more interested in surviving or "succeeding" than they are in risking everything for the sake of integrity and faithfulness? Nathan's example is needed today.

Solomon's Selection as King

1:28 Then King David answered and said, "Call Bathsheba to me." So she came into the king's presence and stood before the king.

29 And the king took an oath and said, "*As* the Lord lives, who has redeemed my life from every distress,

30 "just as I swore to you by the Lord God of Israel, saying, 'Assuredly Solomon your son shall be king after me, and he shall sit on my throne in my place,' so I certainly will do this day."

31 Then Bathsheba bowed with *her* face to the earth, and paid homage to the king, and said, "Let my lord King David live forever!"

32 And King David said, "Call to me Zadok the
priest, Nathan the prophet, and Benaiah the son of
Jehoiada." So they came before the king.
33 The king also said to them, "Take with you the
servants of your lord, and have Solomon my son ride
on my own mule, and take him down to Gihon.
34 "There let Zadok the priest and Nathan the
prophet anoint him king over Israel; and blow
the horn, and say, '*Long* live King Solomon!'
35 Then you shall come up after him, and he shall
come and sit on my throne, and he shall be king in
my place. For I have appointed him to be ruler over
Israel and Judah."
36 Benaiah the son of Jehoiada answered the king
and said, "Amen! May the LORD God of my lord the
king say so *too.*
37 "As the LORD has been with my lord the king,
even so may He be with Solomon, and make his
throne greater than the throne of my lord King
David."

1 Kings 1:28–37

Notice the quick and decisive response of the aging David to Bathsheba and Nathan's announcement. The old leader could yet be roused. It took a lot to awaken him, but now his former fervor flashed to life in the dying embers of David's life. Knowing that the king's word was still respected by the people and would be absolutely obeyed, all Nathan and Bathsheba wanted was for David to name Solomon as his royal choice. David, however, did more than that. With one stroke of decisive action he set in motion events that would completely frustrate Adonijah's plot and immediately install Solomon in office. Swearing an oath to Bathsheba he called in his "faithful three"—Zadok the priest, Nathan the prophet, and Benaiah the warrior—and commanded them to take immediate steps to anoint Solomon king.

"And the king took an oath . . ." (v. 29). The oath was a favorite statement for David. Repeatedly, throughout the biblical accounts of his life, he is seen taking an oath. He considered such oaths important. In the Psalms, he said, "I will pay my vows to the Lord . . ." (Ps. 116:14). He understood that a vow, or an oath, buttressed one's will and resolve.

As a pastor I have counseled with husbands who described how they resisted temptations to unfaithfulness by remembering they had made a promise at the wedding altar to "keep myself only for her so long as we both shall live." When you go back on a vow, you go back on yourself, on God, on those who trust and love you. Breaking an oath is like dropping a spool of thread that has been wound up with great effort. It unravels. Something irrecoverable is lost.

That's why the making of a public decision in an evangelistic service is important, why signing a pledge card in a stewardship campaign is crucial, why marriage vows are vital. A couple may share their commitments to each other privately, but when they stand before a crowd and say, "I do," they are strongly reinforcing those promises by a formal oath. A believer may secretly tell the Lord, "I will follow you," but when that believer walks down an aisle in church and stands before others with a public confession, that vow cannot be easily ignored. A vow or an oath "nails it down," puts you on record before witnesses, encourages you to follow through on your commitment. No wonder Jesus said, "Therefore whoever confesses Me before men, him I will also confess before My Father who is in heaven" (Matt. 10:33).

The instructions David gave his staff are specific and clear. *"Have Solomon my son ride on my own mule"* (v. 33). Mules were traditionally reserved for the royal family (2 Sam. 13:29; 18:9). Horses were not introduced into Jewish military life until Solomon's reign and then only for pulling chariots, not for riding. Mounted warriors were used in other cultures during this period of history, but not in Israel until much later. Since Hebraic law forbade crossbreeding (Lev. 19:19), mules had to be imported and were therefore very expensive.[21] So while the common people rode donkeys, the mule was reserved for royalty. It is interesting to note that the Hebrew word for mule, *pirdâ*, is feminine. The female mule is still preferred to the male for riding.[22]

SOLOMON'S ANOINTING BY ZADOK

1:38 So Zadok the priest, Nathan the prophet, Benaiah the son of Jehoiada, the Cherethites, and the

Pelethites went down and had Solomon ride on King
David's mule, and took him to Gihon.
39 Then Zadok the priest took a horn of oil from
the tabernacle and anointed Solomon. And they blew
the horn, and all the people said, "Long live King
Solomon!"
40 And all the people went up after him; and the
people played the flutes and rejoiced with great joy,
so that the earth *seemed to* split with their sound.
41 Now Adonijah and all the guests who *were* with
him heard *it* as they finished eating. And when Joab
heard the sound of the horn, he said, "Why *is* the city
in such a noisy uproar?"
42 While he was still speaking, there came Jonathan, the son of Abiathar the priest. And Adonijah
said to him, "Come in, for you *are* a prominent man,
and bring good news."
43 Then Jonathan answered and said to Adonijah,
"No! Our lord King David has made Solomon king.
44 "The king has sent with him Zadok the priest,
Nathan the prophet, Benaiah the son of Jehoiada, the
Cherethites, and the Pelethites; and they have made
him ride on the king's mule.
45 "So Zadok the priest and Nathan the prophet
have anointed him king at Gihon; and they have
gone up from there rejoicing, so that the city is in an
uproar. This *is* the noise that you have heard.
46 "Also Solomon sits on the throne of the kingdom.
47 "And moreover the king's servants have gone
to bless our lord King David, saying, 'May God make
the name of Solomon better than your name, and
may He make his throne greater than your throne.'
Then the king bowed himself on the bed.
48 "Also the king said thus, 'Blessed *be* the LORD
God of Israel, who has given *one* to sit on my throne
this day, while my eyes see *it!*'"
49 So all the guests who were with Adonijah were
afraid, and arose, and each one went his way.
50 Now Adonijah was afraid of Solomon; so
he arose, and went and took hold of the horns of
the altar.

> 51 And it was told Solomon, saying, "Indeed Adonijah is afraid of King Solomon; for look, he has taken hold of the horns of the altar, saying, 'Let King Solomon swear to me today that he will not put his servant to death with the sword.'"
>
> 52 Then Solomon said, "If he proves himself a worthy man, not one hair of him shall fall to the earth; but if wickedness is found in him, he shall die."
>
> 53 So King Solomon sent them to bring him down from the altar. And he came and fell down before King Solomon; and Solomon said to him, "Go to your house."
>
> *1 Kings 1:38–53*

David's three faithful servants carried out his instructions precisely. The *"Cherethites, and the Pelethites"* in verse 38 were foreign mercenaries commanded by Benaiah who served as the king's personal bodyguards. They were Cretans and Philistines recruited from outside Israel and Judah when David was in exile.[23] David probably selected foreigners to ensure that his closest guards would be independent of any internal party bickering in his court (2 Sam. 8:18). While they still carried the same title, they may not all have been foreigners during these last years of David's reign.[24]

It is interesting to note that both Solomon and Adonijah were anointed in places where there was running water: Adonijah beside the water supply at En Rogel, and Solomon beside the famous stream Gihon. Could this suggest that a process of purification was part of the ceremony?

The horn of oil mentioned in verse 39 was the sacred olive oil compounded by Moses (Exod. 30:23) and preserved in a ram's horn in the sanctuary tent on the Ophel, the hill in the city where David's citadel was built and where the ark was kept. (The translation should be "the" horn of oil rather than "a" horn of oil.) The Ophel was the highest point on the southeastern hill of Jerusalem, so verse 38 is accurate when it says they *"went down,"* since they traveled from the Ophel to the deep cleft of the Kidron Valley. Anointing with this special oil was an act whereby the king was brought into intimate relationship with God and became God's intermediary with the community. In this act special power and vitality through the spirit of God was conveyed to the king so he became something more than ordinary men.[25]

The other "horn" in verse 39 was the Shophar, a musical instrument like a trumpet made by heating and straightening a ram's horn. It was the sound of this horn that alerted Adonijah and his rebels at their premature feast a few miles away, out of sight but not out of hearing. Notice it was Joab, the old warrior whose ear was trained to such sounds on the battlefield, who heard the trumpet first. In questioning the *"uproar,"* Joab used a word for the sound of a beehive. He employed the imperfect tense suggesting the continuous sound and commotion of a swarm of bees.[26]

Jonathan, the son of the rebel priest Abiathar, ran to the hapless celebrants with the news that Solomon had been anointed king. (It is interesting that Ahimaaz, the son of the other priest, Zadok, was also a long-distance runner [cf. 2 Sam. 15:27; 17:17; 18:27]. Does this indicate that preachers' sons make good athletes?) They hoped for *"good tidings"* (the word in v. 42 is "gospel" or "evangelize"), but the news was bad for Adonijah and his party. Upon hearing it, Adonijah's erstwhile supporters scattered in panic.

How fickle the crowd can be. They followed Adonijah with fawning loyalty when they thought he was going to win, but when it appeared the tide was shifting, they quickly changed their minds. It is tragic to see instances of this same fickle loyalty today. During a recent denominational debate, I watched preachers who decided being on the "winning" side was more important than standing alone by convictions no matter what the cost.

On one occasion, I attended a rally sponsored by a group that was critical of the seminaries. After the meeting, a pastor who had obviously played to the gallery during his message before the group, and who later realized I had been present, rushed to the back of the auditorium to explain to me, "I'm not really with this crowd. I love the Seminary. I'm on your side." How tragic when the people of God are unwilling to stand by what they believe for fear of losing popularity. Fearful that they may not be recommended to another position, they follow the majority where they perceive the power to be. However, when the power begins to shift to other leaders, they quickly reverse directions and proclaim their loyalty to the new party. The Bible says we should not practice "eye-service as men-pleasers," but should serve "in sincerity of heart, fearing God" (Col. 3:22). It also says,

"The fear of man brings a snare, but whoever trusts in the Lord shall be safe" (Prov. 29:25).

Adonijah was afraid of Solomon (v. 50). He was afraid because he knew what he was planning to do to Solomon if *his* coup had succeeded. No doubt Solomon had the same fate in mind for him. So he took the easy way out and rushed to the sacred tent on Mount Zion where he sought asylum by symbolically grasping the horns of the altar for sanctuary. Abiathar, his priestly colleague, was in charge here, and he may have taken this step on the advice of Abiathar. The horns were wooden projections overlaid with brass protruding from the four corners of the altar (Exod. 27:2). The practice of finding safety in the sanctuary was common enough among the various cultures in the ancient Near East. It was so abused among the Romans that sacred asylum was abolished by the Emperor Tiberius as the temples became overcrowded with the worst criminals in the empire.[27] Although it was provided for in Exod. 21:12–14, the only record of such sanctuary in the Old Testament is here and in 1 Kings 2:28. It should be noted that this asylum was intended to protect innocent persons. Hence, Adonijah's and Joab's use was really an abuse and explains why Solomon later had no compunction to punish them both.

The cowardly flight of Adonijah is hardly the action of a man with character enough to be a strong king. By fleeing, he not only took the easy way out, but he admitted the immoral nature of his plot. Adonijah is a pathetic example of a man who as a child was spoiled and indulged by his parents and who made the mistake of listening to the empty compliments and promptings of his vacillating supporters. It's dangerous to take compliments and adulation too seriously.

Adonijah's quest for power is also a classic example of the manipulative style of leadership that centers its attention on self-promotion. Positions of high responsibility and power in the kingdom of God must be earned rather than sought. Adonijah's philosophy is reflected in his statement, "I will be king" (v. 5). The Bible says of high positions, "And no man takes this honor to himself, but he who is called by God" (Heb. 5:4). In sharp contrast, Solomon's magnanimous, unthreatened decision to offer clemency to his enemy shows the bigness of character befitting a king. It gained him the love and respect of his people. Bigness is seen not only in how one handles defeat but more so in how one handles victory.

DAVID'S LAST WORDS AND DEATH

2:1 Now the days of David drew near that he
should die, and he charged Solomon his son, saying:
2 "I go the way of all the earth; be strong, therefore, and prove yourself a man.
3 "And keep the charge of the LORD your God: to
walk in His ways, to keep His statutes, His commandments, His judgments, and His testimonies, as
it is written in the Law of Moses, that you may prosper in all that you do and wherever you turn;
4 "that the LORD may fulfill His word which He
spoke concerning me, saying, 'If your sons take heed
to their way, to walk before Me in truth with all their
heart and with all their soul,' He said, 'you shall not
lack a man on the throne of Israel.'
5 "Moreover you know also what Joab the son of
Zeruiah did to me, *and* what he did to the two commanders of the armies of Israel, to Abner the son of
Ner and Amasa the son of Jether, whom he killed.
And he shed the blood of war in peacetime, and put
the blood of war on his belt that *was* around his
waist, and on his sandals that *were* on his feet.
6 "Therefore do according to your wisdom, and do
not let his gray hair go down to the grave in peace.
7 "But show kindness to the sons of Barzillai the
Gileadite, and let them be among those who eat at
your table, for so they came to me when I fled from
Absalom your brother.
8 "And see, *you have* with you Shimei the son of
Gera, a Benjamite from Bahurim, who cursed me
with a malicious curse in the day when I went to
Mahanaim. But he came down to meet me at the Jordan, and I swore to him by the LORD saying, 'I will
not put you to death with the sword.'
9 "Now therefore, do not hold him guiltless, for
you *are* a wise man and know what you ought to do
to him; but bring his gray hair down to the grave
with blood."
10 So David rested with his fathers, and was buried
in the City of David.

11 The period that David reigned over Israel *was*
forty years; seven years he reigned in Hebron, and in
Jerusalem he reigned thirty-three years.
12 Then Solomon sat on the throne of his father
David; and his kingdom was firmly established.

1 Kings 2:1–12

In the Old Testament, a person's dying words were especially significant. So the setting here calls readers to give particular attention to this portion of the book. Adding to this urgency is the word *"charged."* The Hebrew word *ṣiwwâ* carries a special force when it is used of a dying man's last instructions. It comes from the same root as the word for last will or testament.[28]

We do not know how much time elapsed between the anointing of Solomon and the death of David, a period called a coregency. According to Josephus, all the events recorded in 1 Chronicles 28 and 29 took place during this interval. Apparently David recovered somewhat from the illness described in chapter 1, and enjoyed a few additional years of joint rule with his son. Eventually, however, the old king ended his illustrious reign, and before "going the way of all the earth" he left Solomon with some urgent instructions.

In light of the statement in verse 2, *"prove yourself a man,"* one wonders how old Solomon was when he assumed the throne. He was considerably younger than his older brother Adonijah. In his prayer in 3:7 he admitted, "I am a little child; I do not know how to go out or come in," but this could be a humble confession of his insufficiency rather than a reference to his age. Some Greek manuscripts add the information that Solomon was twelve years old at his accession; however, this is legend.[29]

In his last words, David asked Solomon to do four things:

1. Keep God's law. *"Statutes, commandments, and judgments"* are terms referring to the three portions of the divine law—the ceremonial, moral, and judicial. *"Testimonies"* may be those shared evidences of God's will made clear by his dealings with bygone generations.

2. Execute Joab, the murderer of Abner, Amasa, and Absalom (cf. notes on 1:7). David somehow believed their blood was on his hands, and he could not be free from that curse until Joab died.

3. Reward the loyalty of Barzillai. *"Show kindness"* in verse 7 is

literally *ḥesed,* meaning "keep agreement with."[30] Barzillai was a Transjordan chieftain who brought food to David's people in the wilderness (2 Sam. 17:27–29; 19:31–39). He later declined David's offer to come to Jerusalem with him. Instead, since he was old, he decided to stay in the city of his fathers. Now his descendants were to receive the reward he had earned.

4. Execute Shemei, whose curse on David was considered a capital offense (Exod. 22:28). Some commentaries believe David blackened his record by ordering revenge on his enemies because he feared the result of a superstitious curse. This view, however, does not take into account the scriptural admonition against offenses like murder and the cursing of an anointed one. David was simply following the legal code of his day relating to capital offenses.

David made it clear that if Solomon obeyed God's law, he would *"prosper in all that you do and wherever you turn."* This promise, similar to the one God gave Joshua in the first chapter of the book of Joshua, is not a textual basis for the theology of prosperity so popular today. Instead, it is a declaration consistent with many other Scriptures that no life can fulfill its highest potential unless that life is lived with a healthy reliance on the word of God.

After forty years and six months, David *"rested with his fathers."* When speaking of death, the Old Testament reserved this term for kings or persons of equal importance.[31] He was buried in the City of David in tombs he himself had prepared for the kings of Israel and Judah. The burial place was held in such high esteem that the location was still known in Christ's day (Acts 2:29). According to 2 Kings 11:10, David's weapons were preserved as relics in the sanctuary, while, according to Josephus, other representative treasures of his reign were buried with him in his tomb. The great Jewish historian details the wealth Solomon deposited in his father's grave and states that the tomb was looted by Hyrcanus, the high priest during the siege of Antiochus, and on another occasion by Herod the Great. Apparently the treasure chamber could be reached without disturbing the royal crypt.[32] Some archaeologists believe recent excavations have located the royal tombs in modern Jerusalem.[33]

Some manuscripts make verse 12 the beginning verse of 1 Kings, assigning chapter 1 and the first eleven verses of chapter 2 to the ending of 2 Samuel. Others begin 1 Kings with verse 13.

NOTES

1. Gwilym H. Jones, *1 and 2 Kings,* New Century Bible Commentary, ed. Ronald E. Clements (Grand Rapids: Eerdmans, 1984), 2.

2. Clyde T. Francisco, "First and Second Kings," in *Introducing the Old Testament* (Nashville: Broadman, 1953), 67.

3. C. F. Keil, *The Books of the Kings,* Biblical Commentary on the Old Testament, ed. C. F. Keil and F. Delitzsch, vol. 4 (Grand Rapids: Eerdmans, 1950), 17.

4. I. W. Slotki, *Kings* (London: Soncino Press, 1950), 1.

5. James A. Montgomery, *A Critical and Exegetical Commentary on the Books of Kings,* International Critical Commentary, ed. Henry Snyder Gehman, vol. 10 (New York: Scribner, 1951), 72.

6. Jones, 89.

7. Karl Chr. W. F. Bähr, *The Books of the Kings,* Commentary on the Holy Scriptures, ed. John Peter Lange (Grand Rapids: Zondervan, 1960), 22.

8. Norman H. Snaith, Ralph W. Sockman, and Raymond Calkins, "The First and Second Books of Kings," in *The Interpreter's Bible,* vol. 3 (Nashville: Abingdon, 1954), 20.

9. John Gray, *I and II Kings,* Old Testament Library (Philadelphia: Westminster, 1963), 76.

10. *Dallas Morning News,* 8 November 1985.

11. Jones, 90; Gray, 77.

12. Gray, 80.

13. M. Pierce Matheney and Roy Honeycutt, "1–2 Kings," in *The Broadman Bible Commentary,* ed. Clifton J. Allen, vol. 3 (Nashville: Broadman, 1970), 151.

14. Gray, 81.

15. Jones, 92.

16. Alexander Maclaren, *Second Samuel and the Books of Kings,* Expositions of Holy Scripture, vol. 2 (Grand Rapids: Eerdmans, 1952), 153.

17. Gray, 86.

18. Slotki, 4.

19. Simon J. DeVries, *1 Kings,* Word Biblical Commentary, ed. John D. W. Watts, vol. 12 (Waco, TX: Word Books, 1985), 15.

20. Jones, 93–94.

21. DeVries, 16.

22. Keil, 22.

23. Matheney and Honeycutt, 166.

24. Robert C. Dentan, *Kings and Chronicles,* Layman's Bible Commentary, vol. 7 (Richmond: John Knox Press, 1964), 17.

25. Gray, 90.
26. Ibid., 91.
27. Ibid., 94.
28. Slotki, 12.
29. Jones, 110.
30. Snaith, Sockman, and Calkins, 33.
31. Matheney and Honeycutt, 163.
32. J. Rawson Lumby, *I and II Kings,* The Cambridge Bible, ed. J. J. S. Perowne (Cambridge: Cambridge University Press, 1889), 20.
33. Matheney and Honeycutt, 163.

CHAPTER TWO

The Wisdom and Wealth of Solomon

1 Kings 2:13–4:34

Introduction

Because verse 13, like verse 1 in chapter 1, begins with the introductory word "now," and because it identifies Adonijah and Bathsheba as though the reader were meeting them for the first time, some say it appears the author is starting a new section and that the original book of 1 Kings probably began at this point.

Having traced the rise of Solomon to the throne in the place of his father David, the historian sets out to illustrate why God chose the younger son to rule instead of Adonijah, the oldest. He does so by describing the remarkable wisdom and ability of Solomon as demonstrated in four diverse categories of his royal responsibilities: Solomon as Administrative Organizer (4:1–28), as Patron of Culture (4:29–34), as Creative Builder (5:1–9:25), and as Shrewd Merchant-prince (9:26–20:29).[1]

Some commentators, incorrectly I believe, suggest that the author of 1 Kings knew that Solomon had taken advantage of his aging father, and, with the help of Nathan and Bathsheba, had assumed the throne by means of a manipulative plot. The author felt obligated, therefore, to add this section on Solomon's God-given wisdom and ability in order to justify his self-appointment as king. Such an explanation is unnecessary, and the account flows naturally and logically from Solomon's accession to the throne to this discussion of his wisdom and wealth.

SOLOMON'S POSITION SECURED

2:13 Now Adonijah the son of Haggith came to
Bathsheba the mother of Solomon. So she said, "Do
you come peaceably?" And he said, "Peaceably."
14 Moreover he said, "I have something *to say* to
you." And she said, "Say it."
15 Then he said, "You know that the kingdom was
mine, and all Israel had set their expectations on me,
that I should reign. However, the kingdom has been
turned over, and has become my brother's; for it was
his from the LORD.
16 "Now I ask one petition of you; do not deny
me." And she said to him, "Say it."
17 Then he said, "Please speak to King Solomon,
for he will not refuse you, that he may give me
Abishag the Shunammite as wife."
18 So Bathsheba said, "Very well, I will speak for
you to the king."
19 Bathsheba therefore went to King Solomon, to
speak to him for Adonijah. And the king rose up
to meet her and bowed down to her, and sat down
on his throne and had a throne set for the king's
mother; so she sat at his right hand.
20 Then she said, "I desire one small petition of
you; do not refuse me." And the king said to her,
"Ask it, my mother, for I will not refuse you."
21 So she said, "Let Abishag the Shunammite be
given to Adonijah your brother as wife."
22 And King Solomon answered and said to his
mother, "Now why do you ask Abishag the Shunammite for Adonijah? Ask for him the kingdom also—
for he *is* my older brother—for him, and for Abiathar
the priest, and for Joab the son of Zeruiah."
23 Then King Solomon swore by the LORD, saying,
"May God do so to me, and more also, if Adonijah
has not spoken this word against his own life!
24 "Now therefore, *as* the LORD lives, who has confirmed me and set me on the throne of David my
father, and who has established a house for me, as
He promised, Adonijah shall be put to death today!"
25 So King Solomon sent by the hand of Benaiah

the son of Jehoiada; and he struck him down, and he died.

26 And to Abiathar the priest the king said, "Go to Anathoth, to your own fields, for you *are* deserving of death; but I will not put you to death at this time, because you carried the ark of the Lord GOD before my father David, and because you were afflicted every time my father was afflicted."

27 So Solomon removed Abiathar from being priest to the LORD, that he might fulfill the word of the LORD which He spoke concerning the house of Eli at Shiloh.

28 Then news came to Joab, for Joab had defected to Adonijah, though he had not defected to Absalom. So Joab fled to the tabernacle of the LORD, and took hold of the horns of the altar.

29 And King Solomon was told, "Joab has fled to the tabernacle of the LORD; there *he is,* by the altar." Then Solomon sent Benaiah the son of Jehoiada, saying, "Go, strike him down."

30 So Benaiah went to the tabernacle of the LORD, and said to him, "Thus says the king, 'Come out!'" And he said, "No, but I will die here." And Benaiah brought back word to the king, saying, "Thus said Joab, and thus he answered me."

31 Then the king said to him, "Do as he has said, and strike him down and bury him, that you may take away from me and from the house of my father the innocent blood which Joab shed.

32 "So the LORD will return his blood on his head, because he struck down two men more righteous and better than he, and killed them with the sword—Abner the son of Ner, the commander of the army of Israel, and Amasa the son of Jether, the commander of the army of Judah—though my father David did not know *it.*

33 "Their blood shall therefore return upon the head of Joab and upon the head of his descendants forever. But upon David and his descendants, upon his house and his throne, there shall be peace forever from the LORD."

34 So Benaiah the son of Jehoiada went up and

struck and killed him; and he was buried in his own house in the wilderness.

35 The king put Benaiah the son of Jehoiada in his place over the army, and the king put Zadok the priest in the place of Abiathar.

36 Then the king sent and called for Shimei, and said to him, "Build yourself a house in Jerusalem and dwell there, and do not go out from there anywhere.

37 "For it shall be, on the day you go out and cross the Brook Kidron, know for certain you shall surely die; your blood shall be on your own head."

38 And Shimei said to the king, "The saying *is* good. As my lord the king has said, so your servant will do." So Shimei dwelt in Jerusalem many days.

39 Now it happened at the end of three years, that two slaves of Shimei ran away to Achish the son of Maachah, king of Gath. And they told Shimei, saying, "Look, your slaves *are* in Gath!"

40 So Shimei arose, saddled his donkey, and went to Achish at Gath to seek his slaves. And Shimei went and brought his slaves from Gath.

41 And Solomon was told that Shimei had gone from Jerusalem to Gath and had come back.

42 Then the king sent and called for Shimei, and said to him, "Did I not make you swear by the LORD, and warn you, saying, 'Know for certain that on the day you go out and travel anywhere, you shall surely die'? And you said to me, 'The word I have heard *is* good.'

43 "Why then have you not kept the oath of the LORD and the commandment that I gave you?"

44 The king said moreover to Shimei, "You know, as your heart acknowledges, all the wickedness that you did to my father David; therefore the LORD will return your wickedness on your own head.

45 "But King Solomon *shall be* blessed, and the throne of David shall be established before the LORD forever."

46 So the king commanded Benaiah the son of Jehoiada; and he went out and struck him down, and

> he died. Thus the kingdom was established in the hand of Solomon.
>
> *1 Kings 2:13–46*

When David died, he left Solomon some loose ends to tie up before the kingdom could be secured. It was these matters of unfinished business David addressed in his last instructions to Solomon. Verse 46 says, *"Thus the kingdom was established in the hand of Solomon."* But before that assessment could be made, the young king was forced to deal with some lingering opposition that might well have destroyed his reign before it started. And deal with them he did, forthrightly and wisely.

First, there was his brother Adonijah who had just failed in his attempt to assume the throne. With the condition that he prove himself worthy and engage in no *"wickedness,"* Solomon pardoned the insurrectionist and sent him to his house. Adonijah, however, would not give up. This time, his futile attempt at power cost him his life.

His request to have the beautiful Abishag, David's nurse and concubine, as his wife appeared on the surface to be an innocent if presumptuous one. She would be a kind of consolation prize for the man who came in second in the race for kingship. Abishag is described as young and lovely (1:4) and Adonijah as very good-looking (1:6). They would have made a handsome couple, and perhaps Bathsheba's "match-making" instinct led her to assume his request was nothing more than a harmless, romantic affair of the heart, certainly not another conniving plot to take over the throne.

By ancient custom, however, claiming the widow or the harem of a deceased king was an indirect way of claiming the right to the vacated throne (2 Sam. 16:20–22; 12:8; 3:6–7). So Adonijah's request may have been tantamount to another coup d'état and was, therefore, treason. Some believe Adonijah was simply driven by lust for the beautiful woman, reflecting the same weakness that infected Ammon and even his father David, but it seems clear from the suspicious manner in which he approached Bathsheba that Adonijah knew very well what he was doing. Verse 15 implies he still believed that since he was the oldest son, he had the right to the throne. *"Mine"* is given emphasis by being placed before the word *"kingdom."*[2] He admitted God gave the kingdom to Solomon, but he hinted that the common people supported his own claim. His appeal was coated with false piosity, contrived humility, and a pretense of "peace." With a martyr-spirit he played on Bathsheba's sympathy.

Here is a powerful reminder that those are least to be trusted who have once proved themselves to be enemies, especially when they suddenly appear with tokens of peace. While we must never become cynical and suspicious of every act of untrustworthy people, we must be aware that the most presumptuous motive is often hidden under the mask of unassuming deportment. Ambitious and power-hungry people do not hesitate to use any means to obtain the ends they cannot acquire by force. When they can no longer demand, they beg. This pitiful scene of a contender for the throne of Israel begging help from the queen mother is further evidence of the flawed character that made Adonijah unfit for kingly responsibility.

Did Bathsheba fall for his insidious plot? It appeared so. She personally petitioned Solomon on behalf of Adonijah saying his request was a *"small petition"* (v. 20). I'm not so sure Bathsheba was that naïve; Adonijah obviously believed she was. Why else would he have asked for help from the one who had so recently helped wrench the kingdom from his hands? But Bathsheba was clever. It may be she went along with Adonijah knowing full well that when she mentioned the request for Abishag to Solomon, her wise son would see through the disguised plot and get rid of the contender once and for all. Maybe her lingering jealousy and mistrust of the young and beautiful Abishag (who had been introduced into her husband David's harem) motivated her to go along with Adonijah's plan in order to get Abishag into trouble. Whatever her intentions, she brought the request before the king, who saw through the plot and put his brother to death for the crime of treasonous insurrection.

Notice the respect Solomon paid his mother when she sought an audience in his throne room (vv. 19–20). In ancient oriental courts, the queen mother was the first lady of the realm, taking precedence over any other woman in the royal harem.[3] Solomon's respect toward his mother, however, goes beyond the traditional throne room protocol. He stood, bowed down, ordered a throne for her, and seated her on his right, the place of honor. Even though he was caught up in the heady atmosphere of national leadership, Solomon did not forget what he owed his mother. Just as he had shown due honor for his noble father, so the young king boldly demonstrates to the gathered royal court his love and respect for Bathsheba.

How often children forget their parents and nearest relatives and may at times even become ashamed of them when they attain great riches and honor. I remember a brilliant young businessman in a large city where I was pastor who rocketed to success in the field of commercial real estate development. He not only became wealthy, but he also attained celebrity status because of frequent appearances on television. He was front-page copy in the local papers and was even featured in a national news magazine. Considering himself too busy for church responsibilities he once held, he eventually joined a "less demanding" congregation where social status was the primary motivation for membership. That was bad enough. Even worse was his neglect of his parents. At first it was incidental. His aging father and mother told me they understood why his demanding schedule kept him away. They were a little embarrassed to call on others for the help their son should have rendered, but, after all, he was occupied with the demands of the booming business everyone in town was reading about. Slowly, as the young man climbed the social ladder into the rarified strata of the elite, his neglect became more than incidental. There developed a studied rejection. He employed strangers to become "companions" for his parents. They were more than just hired helpers to run errands, they were surrogates to whom he tried to delegate the attention only a child can give. That attention had become odious to the young business star on his way up.

On one occasion, when a civic organization was honoring the young man, they surprised him by having his parents present at the dinner. Until he caught himself and put on a respectable mask of parental appreciation, it was sadly obvious to all who were there that his first reaction was to be ashamed of the plain and simple couple who seemed so out of place at the elaborate affair. Ashamed of a father and mother? No personal achievements or status should cause us to forget the fourth commandment. Solomon remembered. His example of respect and love for his mother is a lesson not only in filial relationship, but also in divine obedience as well.

The respectful king, however, can also be the angry king. His quick answer to Bathsheba's request was filled with insight and irony (v. 22). Insight because he immediately saw through what appeared on the surface to be a harmless request. Irony in his statement "you might as well ask the kingdom for him and for his cohorts, Abiathar and Joab." It was obvious Solomon did not underestimate the seriousness of a plot led by Adonijah, who apparently had strong popular support (cf. v. 15) and who was assisted by the top leaders in the religious and military establishments. His action was decisive. Adonijah, who had failed to appreciate his brother's mercy, now received the king's swift judgment.

The oath in verse 23, *"May God do so to me, and more also . . ."* is literally, "Thus shall God do unto me and thus shall He add that."[4] A familiar idiomatic expression in the Old Testament (cf. Ruth 1:17), it is an oath of assertion meaning, "May God kill me, if I do not kill Adonijah." Another oath was introduced in verse 24 with the words, *"as the Lord lives."* So with resolute decisiveness the first of a bloody trilogy of executions was carried out as the new king consolidated his power.

The next threat to be dealt with was Abiathar the high priest who helped Adonijah with his unsuccessful coup (cf. 1:7, 25). Even though he deserved death (v. 26 literally, "you are a man of death"), the king could not execute Abiathar. He was a priest and therefore beyond the royal jurisdiction as far as matters of life and death were concerned.[5] So he did what he could do. He exiled him to his hometown, Anathoth, about three miles northeast of Jerusalem. Anathoth was the hometown of the prophet Jeremiah. Solomon's command in verse 26 was literally, "To Anathoth." The abruptness of the command was indicative of his rage.

Verse 35 adds that Solomon appointed Zadok the priest in the place of Abiathar. That is, the king gave to Zadok the responsibilities of the high priest. He could not take away the status of priest from Abiathar, for that was his by birth. Neither could he name Zadok as a priest by political appointment. He was already a priest by inheritance. The king, however, could assign national responsibilities, and so Zadok was given the national religious leadership role while the exiled Abiathar, still a priest, was retired.

Some churches have a policy of deacon service that illustrates this situation. Following their ordination, the deacons are deacons for life. Yet the church has a rotating plan for active service, with only a certain number of the deacons assigned that status for a limited period of time. So while some deacons may be inactive, not attending meetings or taking official assignments, they are still nevertheless deacons. This explanation helps us understand why Abiathar, even though exiled, is still listed with Zadok as a priest in 1 Kings 4:4.

The prophecy referred to in verse 27 is found in 1 Sam. 2:30–33 where God promised to end the priestly line of Eli because of the wickedness of his sons and Eli's unwillingness to control them. Now, as a result of Solomon's decisions, the priestly office was transferred from the lineage of Eli through Zadok into the sole possession of the line of Eleazar the son of Aaron.[6] The priestly supremacy remained in Zadok's family until Menelaus of the tribe of Benjamin outbid Jason for the high priesthood in 171 B.C. (2 Macc. 4:24). Scholars believe that the Qumran sect may have rejected traditional Judaism because they believed the priestly office had been contaminated by events such as this occasion in 171 B.C. or when the office as a political bribe was accepted by Jonathan the brother of Judas Maccabeaeus, who was not of the priestly family.[7]

Nothing is related concerning the subsequent fate of Abiathar, probably because the death of a high priest who had been deprived of office was a matter of little consequence in the history of the kingdom. Since he was about eighty years old at the time of his exile, he apparently did not long survive his punishment.

The third opponent to be eliminated was Joab, David's nephew and former military commander in chief. He had been demoted by David for killing Absalom, and believing he therefore had a better future with Adonijah, he had joined the rebellion (1:7, 41). When he heard what had happened to Abiathar and Adonijah, and presuming he would be next on Solomon's list, he took refuge in the sanctuary, grasping the horns of the altar for asylum. This would have pardoned him had he been guilty only of aiding Adonijah, but Joab forgot about two other crimes of which he was guilty—the murders of Abner and Amasa, commanders of the army. The law provided sanctuary at the altar for all crimes except murder (Exod. 21:13–14).[8] So Solomon was justified in having him executed, thus ridding the kingdom of another adversary and fulfilling his father's last wish concerning Joab (2:5–6).

Joab was buried *"in his own house in the wilderness"* (v. 34). This "wilderness" was not a barren desert but the fertile plains outside the city. (Compare the statements in Matthew 14 that Jesus fed the multitudes in a "desert place" where there was "much grass.") Joab was possibly buried literally "in" his house, that is, under the floor of the house; although the land adjacent to the dwelling was also considered "the house."[9] To be buried in one's own property was a mark of distinction, so at the end, Solomon allowed the old general this final honor.[10]

The fourth target of Solomon's campaign to put down his opposition was Shimei, a Benjamite of the house of Saul and son of Gera. There are twenty different persons in the Old Testament who bear that name, including the one in 1:8 who remained loyal to David during Adonijah's rebellion. The Shimei in this passage is the same one David referred to in his final instructions to Solomon in 2:8. Cursing David, he had thrown stones at him when David was fleeing from Absalom his son. In spite of the grievous consequences of cursing God's anointed, David refused to let his cousin Abishai slay Shimei, and when David returned in victory, Shimei repented and David forgave him (2 Sam. 16:5–14; 19:16–23). Yet David believed the curse somehow remained in effect and could be canceled only by Shimei's death. He asked Solomon to carry out his execution.

By putting him under a limited house arrest with the condition that he remain in Jerusalem, Solomon wisely allowed Shimei a reprieve from execution. This would win popular favor for the new king as a just and merciful ruler. The reprieve, however, did not work. Shimei broke the agreement, and Solomon had him killed. In so doing, Solomon not only obeyed his dying father's last wish, but he diminished the likelihood of another Benjamite uprising like the one that threatened his father's rule (2 Samuel 20). The brook Kidron, which Solomon named as the limit beyond which Shimei could not cross, was the boundary between the tribe of Judah and the tribe of Benjamin. Solomon was therefore restricting Shimei's access to his tribal kinsmen and thereby reducing the possibility of future trouble.

One lesson in the passage is the caution against presuming on our opportunities. Shimei had chance after chance. David had spared him in spite of his insulting and treacherous hostility. Now Solomon let him live in Jerusalem in spite of his father's clear request to execute him. The conditions imposed upon him were not that unreasonable, but Shimei kept pressing. Like a little child testing his parents to see how far they will let him go, Shimei seemed to be reaching for the limits of mercy and long-suffering. He found them, and he died.

Neither should we presume on God. When a child of God piously prays for divine protection and safety, and then speeds down the interstate at eighty miles per hour with the safety belt dangling unfastened on the seat, he is dangerously presuming on God. There are other more subtle ways to repeat the mistake of Shimei, but the tragic outcome of his presumption should be a warning. So is the experience of our Lord during His temptation. In resisting Satan in the wilderness, Jesus refused to jump from the temple, even though God's word promised that the angels would "bear him up." He answered, "It has been said, 'You shall not tempt the Lord your God'" (Luke 4:12).

With the death of Shimei, Solomon had now eliminated every known opposition to his rule and at the same time completed the full charge made to him by his father David. If only he had been as zealous to obey the will of his Heavenly Father. While he started out with a commendable desire to follow God's law, Solomon, in spite of being the wisest man of his day, soon drifted into compromise, and eventually his glorious rule collapsed.

Solomon's Marriage and God's Gift of Wisdom

> 3:1 Now Solomon made a treaty with Pharaoh king of Egypt, and married Pharaoh's daughter; then he brought her to the City of David until he had finished building his own house, and the house of the LORD, and the wall all around Jerusalem.
>
> 2 Meanwhile the people sacrificed at the high places, because there was no house built for the name of the LORD until those days.
>
> 3 And Solomon loved the LORD, walking in the statutes of his father David, except that he sacrificed and burned incense at the high places.
>
> 4 Now the king went to Gibeon to sacrifice there, for that *was* the great high place: Solomon offered a thousand burnt offerings on that altar.
>
> 5 At Gibeon the LORD appeared to Solomon in a dream by night; and God said, "Ask! What shall I give you?"
>
> 6 And Solomon said: "You have shown great mercy to Your servant David my father, because he walked before You in truth, in righteousness, and in

uprightness of heart with You; You have continued
this great kindness for him, and You have given him
a son to sit on his throne, as *it is* this day.
7 "Now, O LORD my God, You have made Your
servant king instead of my father David, but I *am* a
little child; I do not know *how* to go out or come in.
8 "And Your servant *is* in the midst of Your people whom You have chosen, a great people, too numerous to be numbered or counted.
9 "Therefore give to Your servant an understanding heart to judge Your people, that I may discern
between good and evil. For who is able to judge this
great people of Yours?"
10 The speech pleased the LORD, that Solomon had
asked this thing.
11 Then God said to him: "Because you have asked
this thing, and have not asked long life for yourself,
nor have asked riches for yourself, nor have asked
the life of your enemies, but have asked for yourself
understanding to discern justice,
12 "behold, I have done according to your words;
see, I have given you a wise and understanding heart,
so that there has not been anyone like you before you,
nor shall any like you arise after you.
13 "And I have also given you what you have not
asked: both riches and honor, so that there shall not
be anyone like you among the kings all your days.
14 "So if you walk in My ways, to keep My statutes
and My commandments, as your father David walked,
then I will lengthen your days."
15 Then Solomon awoke; and indeed it had been a
dream. And he came to Jerusalem and stood before
the ark of the covenant of the LORD, offered up burnt
offerings, offered peace offerings, and made a feast
for all his servants.

1 Kings 3:1–15

Under the inspiration of the Holy Spirit, the author of 1 Kings was compelled to insert at this point in his story the account of Solomon's worship experience at Gibeon. The great king of Israel was known for his wisdom and wealth, so chapter 3 tells how he got these gifts. Furthermore, since Solomon came to power, wresting the kingdom from his brother in a deadly campaign against popular military leaders and a high priest, the writer felt it was important to show the other, more benevolent, side of the famous leader. He was not only a shrewd politician but also a mild and pious ruler whom God blessed with great abilities. Some commentators have labeled this section, "The Divine Legitimation at Gibeon."[11]

In 3:1 the writer used the term, *"Pharaoh king of Egypt,"* as though it were the proper name for the ruler. But "Pharaoh" is actually a transliteration of an Egyptian word meaning "king" or "ruler."[12] It is not known for sure which pharaoh became Solomon's father-in-law, although some interesting speculations have been offered. Some identify him as Siamun, the next to the last pharaoh of the twenty-first or Tanite dynasty because it is known that he made excursions into Palestine.[13] Others believe he was Pasebkhanuk II (also called Psusennes), who reigned 987–952 B.C. and was the last king of the twenty-first dynasty.[14] Some identify the pharaoh with Sheshonk (or Shishak as the Bible calls him), the first king of the twenty-second dynasty who is mentioned in 14:25. Whoever the princess was, the marriage was politically motivated and may well have been arranged for Solomon by David, who enjoyed friendly relations with Egypt before his death. We are told in 9:16 that the wedding dowry was the city of Gezer. It may be that the marriage song of Psalm 45 was composed in commemoration of this royal wedding.[15]

Before his coronation, Solomon had married Naamah the Ammonitess, by whom he had a son named Rehoboam (14:21). So this was at least his second marriage. Apparently the Egyptian princess forsook her own religion and worshiped Yahweh, for at this time Solomon was not likely to have allowed idolatry in Jerusalem. He brought his new bride to the City of David, the eastern portion of the hill of Zion on which the temple was later built. Solomon considered it too sacred a place for his own house because the ark was there. In 7:8 we learn that the queen's house was close to Solomon's and equally as grand. It took thirteen years to build his house, during which time the queen lived in the City of David.

"The high places" mentioned in the next verses were ancient sites where pagan Canaanite worship was carried out. God had forbidden Israel to adopt the religious customs of the foreigners among whom they lived (Deut. 12:1–14), but since *"there was no house built for the name of the Lord"* (v. 2), the people felt it was permissible to rebuild

and consecrate for the worship of Yahweh these ancient centers of pagan sacrifice. Evidence of this has been found through archaeological excavations of Kadesh Naphtali. A third-century B.C. Jewish altar was discovered there with traces underneath of an ancient pagan temple of a much earlier date.[16] Later the prophets denounced this practice as abominable, and even here in this passage there seems to be the insinuation that it was wrong. *"Solomon loved the Lord . . . except that he sacrificed . . . at the high places"* (v. 3). Even though it was not the ideal He wanted His people to follow, God still met them wherever they turned their hearts to Him.

It seems ironic that just before the author describes the glory of Solomon's reign, he first pointed to certain seeds of disobedience that would eventually take root and bring down the great ruler's kingdom. Solomon loved the Lord, but his marriage to Ammonitish and Egyptian wives and his worship in forbidden places were already beginning to taint his devotion. Soon that disobedience would lead to apostasy causing the kingdom to be divided. His sins cast a spell of doom over all his wisdom, wealth, and achievements.

Robert Louis Stevenson's *Strange Case of Dr. Jekyll and Mr. Hyde* illustrates the insidious encroachment of sin in a person's life. The magic potion that turned the respected Dr. Jekyll into the wicked Mr. Hyde provided the noble physician a convenient way to enjoy sinful pleasure without losing his reputation. When he had his fill of wickedness, he needed only one sip of the antidote to become Dr. Jekyll again, all without a hint of scandal. One day, however, Dr. Jekyll awakened to discover that in his sleep, without the help of the potion, he had become Mr. Hyde. It frightened him. He went into his laboratory to take the antidote, but nothing happened. He drank it all. Nothing happened. Try as he would, no formula he concocted would restore his identity as the genial, gracious gentleman he had been. The evil he had voluntarily unleashed in his life had become dominant, supreme, uncontrollable.

This was Stevenson's literary technique to illustrate the superhuman power of evil. If you give sin an inch in your life, it will take a mile. Give it a tiny foothold, and it runs rampant, getting the upper hand and destroying the quality of your life. As Tennyson said of evil influences, "You have made us lords and now you cannot put us down."

David was teaching this same serious truth when in the first

Psalm he described the man who "walks" in the counsel of the ungodly, "stands" in the path of sinners, and "sits" in the seat of the scornful. There is a subtle pattern of progression in those verbs "walk," "stand," "sit," suggesting that sin creeps up on its unsuspecting victims with tiny steps of encroachment that may at first seem harmless. Solomon started out with a love for God, a commendable faithfulness in prayer and worship, and a humble and teachable spirit. But he let Satan in the door by what must have seemed to him at the time trivial compromises. They would bear their poisonous fruit later.

Meanwhile, there follows in verse 4 the beautiful account of Solomon's prayer and God's gift of wisdom. *"He went to Gibeon to sacrifice."* Why there? Gibeon was about six miles northwest of Jerusalem at the location of modern El-Jîb. Excavations there have uncovered a number of jar handles with the name *gb'n* inscribed on them, leading archaeologists to confirm El-Jîb as the site of ancient Gibeon.[17] The city is identified as another of the "high places." Yet because Gibeon was also the last resting place for the tabernacle and had been the popular center of worship before the temple was built, Solomon chose Gibeon as the location for what 2 Chron. 1:1–13 calls his inaugural ceremony.

Much earlier, Joshua, obeying the command of God, had set up the tabernacle of Moses with its Ark of the Covenant at Shiloh, where it remained until the war with the Philistines during the last days of Eli. Then the ark was captured and later returned to Kiriath-jearim, where it stayed until David brought it up to his newly captured capital, Jerusalem, making a special tent for it until the temple could be erected. Meanwhile, the tabernacle at Shiloh was moved by Saul to Nob, closer to his home, where it was cared for by Ahimelech the priest. Later Saul had it moved to Gibeon, and there it stood up to Solomon's day.

In the tabernacle at Gibeon was the great bronze altar of Bezaleel, described in 2 Chron. 1:5. It was here, according to 3:4, Solomon "used to offer" a thousand burnt offerings. The imperfect tense of the verb indicates a regular, continuous act.[18] Even though the tent in Jerusalem where the ark was kept would have been a more appropriate place for Solomon to worship, God graciously met him at Gibeon. The account of Solomon's petition and God's answer provides a classic lesson in prayer.

In a dream, which was a frequent channel of revelation in Old Testament days, God appeared with a forthright invitation, *"Ask! What shall I give you?"* (3:5). Here the God of heaven bends down to grant the supplication of a man and graciously puts the key to all His treasures in the young king's hand. Within the bounds of reason, Solomon could have obtained anything he wished.

How often in God's word are we reminded that every faithful believer has that same privilege? "And I say unto you, ask, and it will be given to you" (Luke 11:9). "If you abide in Me, and My words abide in you, you will ask what you desire, and it shall be done for you" (John 15:7). Even though we are not kings on royal thrones, every time we come before the gracious Heavenly Father through Jesus Christ our Mediator, it is as though God were saying to us, "Ask! What shall I give you?" The doors to His unlimited blessings are opened to us. If young men and women at the beginning of their careers could see the possibilities of their futures and the issues that hang on early choices as clearly as they will see them someday, there would be fewer wasted mornings of life and fewer gloomy sunsets.

Of course God knew Solomon well enough to know he could be trusted with this wide open offer to grant anything he wished. No parent offers to give a child anything he wishes without knowing what the child is likely to ask. Similarly, God gives us a carte blanche choice only if our wills run parallel with His. The promise has a condition: "If you abide in Me. . . ." David wrote, "He shall give you the desires of your heart," but he preceded that promise with the condition: "Delight yourself also in the Lord" (Ps. 37:4).

Another prayer truth in this passage is found in that even though God knew what Solomon needed, He wanted the king to ask. Sometimes as a pastor I've been asked, "If God knows my thoughts, isn't it redundant to come before Him to express those thoughts in prayer? "If God knows all things, even the number of hairs on my head, then He certainly knows what is best for me. Why doesn't He provide those things without my asking?" Sometimes He does, but as a Heavenly Father, He wants His children to communicate with Him.

My wife Betty was taking care of our two-year-old granddaughter the other day and overheard her talking to herself and her dolls as she played in her room. "If I pick up my toys, Nana will see it and say, 'Oh, Elizabeth, you've picked up your toys. You're such a big girl!'" Having overheard that, Betty (or "Nana" as Elizabeth calls her) walked into the room and fulfilled Elizabeth's wish. She said to our beaming granddaughter, "Oh, Elizabeth, you've picked up your toys You're such a big girl!" And Elizabeth was pleased.

The Heavenly Father, reading our minds, overhearing our cries, knowing our needs better than we know them ourselves, often grants them without our asking. But He still wants us to ask, and some of His gifts come only when we ask. Wise parents know what their children need, but they also know how important it is that their children be encouraged to talk to them. Keeping the lines of unthreatened communication open in the home is essential to healthy childhood development. So even parents who know their children's needs want to have fellowship with their children. They want to be approachable, to encourage their children to talk to them. They want to be asked.

There is another lesson in this passage related to the proper attitude of those who approach God in prayer. Solomon begins his prayer in the spirit of gratitude, acknowledging the bountiful blessings of God in the life of his father David as well as in his own experience (v. 6). He prays humbly. *"I am a little child,"* Solomon admits (v. 7). Although he was young, probably in his early twenties, this does not indicate as some have taught that Solomon became king as a child. Rabbinic tradition says he was twelve. Josephus, in *Antiquities* 7.7.8, says he was fourteen. But the statement is actually Solomon's poetic way of expressing his inadequacies as he faced the awesome tasks of leadership. Jeremiah used the same plea when God called him.

Imagine the pressures facing Solomon as he looked to the future. He was young and inexperienced. He stood in the shadow of his father David's glorious reign, which could be intimidating to a young man. His brother, with pretensions for the throne, had rallied an unknown quantity of popular support among the people. There were still the smoldering hostilities of Saul's old partisans. His was a difficult position in an unsteady situation. In verse 9 he calls the Israelites a *"great people."* Literally it reads, "heavy people." They were great in the sense of a great burden, great in number, and difficult to lead. He was not a typical overconfident youth who believed he could do better than his old-fashioned father. Solomon recognized the heaviness of his burden, and he had the wisdom to admit his insufficiency before God. The Bible repeatedly teaches us that God hears the plea of a humble petitioner who admits his need. "All the fitness he requireth is to feel your need of Him." And so Solomon asked God for *"an understanding heart to judge Your people, that I may discern between good and evil"* (v. 9).

The heart in Hebrew philosophy represented both emotion and intellect, but it is closer to our idea of mind. *"Understanding"* is literally, "hearing." Solomon asked God for "a hearing mind" inclined to hear and do God's will.[19] In asking for discernment, a hearing heart, or wisdom, Solomon had asked for the highest gift. Wisdom, being more than apprehension, comprehension, or knowledge, was considered in the Old Testament to be the greatest gift. Since it includes sensitivity and imagination, it can put itself in the place of others. Therefore, great leaders must know more than facts about others, they must also be able to feel for them, to get inside their situation. Worthy leaders must be able to love people who are unlovable, see them as God sees them. A hearing heart is an indispensable quality of leadership. He who seeks this kind of wisdom first is already wise.

That's why this request has been considered a model for political leaders since Solomon's day. His prayer has often been repeated by great rulers as they assumed office. For example, when Harry Truman was inaugurated as president of the United States, he offered this same petition as his own prayer for guidance.

"The speech pleased the Lord" (v. 10). Because the prayer was pleasing to God, He promised to answer it. In fact verse 12 indicates God was already answering before the prayer was finished. *"Behold I have done according to your words. . . ."* The perfect tense indicates completed action. He also gave Solomon more than he asked. In addition to wisdom, Solomon was to receive riches and honor in unprecedented portions (v. 13). Ironically, his not wishing for material things was the reason he got them. Isn't it true that the people who do not make wealth their priority are the people who can be most safely trusted with it and who, when they receive it, usually enjoy it the most? "Seek ye first the Kingdom of God and His righteousness, and all these things shall be added to you" (Matt. 6:33).

We learn here also that God gives sufficiency to the one upon whom He confers responsibility, to the one who doesn't rush into an office or responsibility but rather is called to the task by God. In Solomon's case the need God met with His sufficiency was the need for divine wisdom, a wisdom that made its recipient legendary.

SOLOMON'S WISE JUDGMENT

3:16 Now two women *who were* harlots came to the king, and stood before him.

17 And one woman said, "O my lord, this woman and I dwell in the same house; and I gave birth while she *was* in the house.

18 "Then it happened, the third day after I had given birth, that this woman also gave birth. And we *were* together; no one *was* with us in the house, except the two of us in the house.

19 "And this woman's son died in the night, because she lay on him.

20 "So she arose in the middle of the night and took my son from my side, while your maidservant slept, and laid him in her bosom, and laid her dead child in my bosom.

21 "And when I rose in the morning to nurse my son, there he was, dead. But when I had examined him in the morning, indeed, he was not my son whom I had borne."

22 Then the other woman said, "No! But the living one *is* my son, and the dead one *is* your son." And the first woman said, "No! But the dead one *is* your son, and the living one *is* my son." Thus they spoke before the king.

23 And the king said, "The one says, 'This *is* my son, who lives, and your son *is* the dead one'; and the other says, 'No! But your son *is* the dead one, and my son *is* the living one.'"

24 Then the king said, "Bring me a sword." So they brought a sword before the king.

25 And the king said, "Divide the living child in two, and give half to one, and half to the other."

26 Then the woman whose son *was* living spoke to the king, for she yearned with compassion for her

son; and she said, "O my lord, give her the living child, and by no means kill him!" But the other said, "Let him be neither mine nor yours, *but* divide *him.*"

27 So the king answered and said, "Give the first woman the living child, and by no means kill him; she *is* his mother."

28 And all Israel heard of the judgment which the king had rendered; and they feared the king, for they saw that the wisdom of God *was* in him to administer justice.

1 Kings 3:16–28

There follows in this section a convincing illustration of the supernatural wisdom with which Israel's legendary young king was blessed. Two prostitutes who were roommates approached King Solomon with a delicate and complicated legal problem: namely, the true identity of a newborn baby. Both distraught women claimed the baby as theirs: the plaintiff accusing the defendant of intentionally switching her dead baby for the plaintiff's live one; the defendant countering that the plaintiff was lying and that the living baby belonged to the defendant. Notice that the common people, even prostitutes, had right of access to the king for judgment.

No doubt embarrassed with the term "harlots" in verse 16, the Targum substitutes the word "innkeepers." Even though prostitution and fornication are uniformly condemned throughout the Bible, in this case as in others in Scripture, the prostitute was seen as a helpless victim before the law, with no one to plead her case.

Exercising a discernment and practical judgment beyond his years, Solomon proposed a drastic and shocking solution that would kill the remaining child. He knew he could count on the tender love of the real mother. Her concern for the safety of her child would surface and identify her. He was right. Verse 26 literally says, "her compassion grew warm." The real mother was willing to lose her child in order to let it live.

There is a lesson here for all close relationships. We must not let our love for someone else stifle that person's life and spiritual growth by holding that person too close to ourselves. Genuine love is willing to give up the beloved.

SOLOMON'S RICH RESOURCES

4:1 So King Solomon was king over all Israel.
2 And these *were* his officials: Azariah the son of
Zadok, the priest;
3 Elihoreph and Ahijah, the sons of Shisha,
scribes; Jehoshaphat the son of Ahilud, the recorder;
4 Benaiah the son of Jehoiada, over the army;
Zadok and Abiathar, the priests;
5 Azariah the son of Nathan, over the officers;
Zabud the son of Nathan, a priest *and* the king's
friend;
6 Ahishar, over the household; and Adoniram the
son of Abda, over the labor force.
7 And Solomon had twelve governors over all Israel, who provided food for the king and his household; each one made provision for one month of the
year.
8 These *are* their names: Ben-Hur, in the mountains of Ephraim;
9 Ben-Deker, in Makaz, Shaalbim, Beth Shemesh,
and Elon Beth Hanan;
10 Ben-Hesed, in Arubboth; to him *belonged* So-
choh and all the land of Hepher;
11 Ben-Abinadab, *in* all the regions of Dor; he had
Taphath the daughter of Solomon as wife;
12 Baana the son of Ahilud, *in* Taanach, Megiddo,
and all Beth Shean, which *is* beside Zaretan below
Jezreel, from Beth Shean to Abel Meholah, as far as
the other side of Jokneam;
13 Ben-Geber, in Ramoth Gilead; to him *belonged*
the towns of Jair the son of Manasseh, in Gilead; to
him *also belonged* the region of Argob in Bashan—
sixty large cities with walls and bronze gate-bars;
14 Ahinadab the son of Iddo, *in* Mahanaim;
15 Ahimaaz, in Naphtali; he also took Basemath
the daughter of Solomon as wife;
16 Baanah the son of Hushai, in Asher and Aloth;
17 Jehoshaphat the son of Paruah, in Issachar;
18 Shimei the son of Elah, in Benjamin;
19 Geber the son of Uri, in the land of Gilead, *in*
the country of Sihon king of the Amorites, and of Og

king of Bashan. *He was* the only governor who *was* in
the land.
20 Judah and Israel *were* as numerous as the sand
by the sea in multitude, eating and drinking and rejoicing.
21 So Solomon reigned over all kingdoms from the
River *to* the land of the Philistines, as far as the border
of Egypt. *They* brought tribute and served Solomon all
the days of his life.
22 Now Solomon's provision for one day was
thirty kors of fine flour, sixty kors of meal,
23 ten fatted oxen, twenty oxen from the pastures,
and one hundred sheep, besides deer, gazelles, roe-
bucks, and fatted fowl.
24 For he had dominion over all *the region* on this
side of the River from Tiphsah even to Gaza, namely
over all the kings on this side of the River; and he
had peace on every side all around him.
25 And Judah and Israel dwelt safely, each man
under his vine and his fig tree, from Dan as far as
Beersheba, all the days of Solomon.
26 Solomon had forty thousand stalls of horses for
his chariots, and twelve thousand horsemen.
27 And these governors, each man in his month,
provided food for King Solomon and for all who came
to King Solomon's table. There was no lack in their
supply.
28 They also brought barley and straw to the
proper place, for the horses and steeds, each man according to his charge.
29 And God gave Solomon wisdom and exceedingly great understanding, and largeness of heart like
the sand on the seashore.
30 Thus Solomon's wisdom excelled the wisdom of
all the men of the East and all the wisdom of Egypt.
31 For he was wiser than all men—than Ethan the
Ezrahite, and Heman, Chalcol, and Darda, the sons
of Mahol; and his fame was in all the surrounding
nations.
32 He spoke three thousand proverbs, and his
songs were one thousand and five.
33 Also he spoke of trees, from the cedar tree of

> Lebanon even to the hyssop that springs out of the wall; he spoke also of animals, of birds, of creeping things, and of fish.
>
> 34 And men of all nations, from all the kings of the earth who had heard of his wisdom, came to hear the wisdom of Solomon.
>
> *1 Kings 4:1–34*

The prevailing philosophical view during this period of Israel's history suggested that a righteous, godly person would automatically prosper, while an evil person would suffer and be deprived. Since he was a godly man, Solomon, according to this view, would naturally be prosperous and strong. While we must not build a theology of prosperity on this chapter, it does teach that, in Solomon's case, his faithful, obedient, and prayerful manner of life resulted in great success as a leader and great material possessions as well.

Verses 1–19 describe how the king's administrative gifts allowed him to put together a strong government organization. The passage apparently reflects conditions at a later time in Solomon's reign, since two of the officers mentioned married Solomon's daughters, who were not even born at this point in the king's life (vv. 11, 15).

Some say the *"officials"* in verse 2 were princes, probably cabinet level officers. The *"scribes"* in verse 3 were secretaries, who took minutes of important state events. The *"recorder"* is literally the "remembrancer" whose duty was to bring to the king's attention matters of importance affecting the state.

Since Abiathar (v. 4) had been exiled by Solomon (1 Kings 2:26ff.), his inclusion here as a priest seems to be a problem. It must be remembered, however, that while Solomon could only reassign Abiathar's responsibility, he could not take away his title nor his dignity as a priest. Those were his by inheritance. The Nathan in verse 5 is not the prophet, but the son of David (2 Sam. 5:14). *"The king's friend"* is a phrase used for a petty official (cf. 2 Sam. 15:37).

The five with no proper names (Ben-Hur, Ben-Deker, Ben-Hesed, Ben-Abinadab, and Ben-Geber) may have taken the designation *Ben,* which means "son of," as their proper names. In this case the names should be spelled together like *Benjamin.* Montgomery offers another explanation. Since this list was taken from a tabular form in the royal archives, he believes the edge of the manuscript was damaged so that their first names could not be read.[20] Slotki notes that five of the twelve leaders are known by their fathers' names, six have their own names added to their fathers' names, while only one is mentioned by his name alone. He believes the first five may have owed their appointment to their fathers' influence alone, the six to their own as well as their fathers', while Ahimaaz owed it to his personal merit without any support from his father.[21] Maybe that was one reason he married the king's daughter!

The concluding verses tell of Solomon's remarkable power and prosperity. In verse 21 the river is the Euphrates, and the territory designated is precisely what God promised to Abraham. *"From the River"* is literally "this side of the River" (cf. also v. 24), but it does not necessarily mean that the author was from that area. This was a common term for this territory.

Some estimate the household of Solomon, for which the enormous provisions in verses 22–23 had to be gathered, consisted of fifteen thousand persons. Others suggest as many as thirty-six thousand. The *"fatted oxen"* were pen-fed cattle in contrast to the more common variety that grazed in the pastures.

The beautiful phrase for an idyllic time of secure enjoyment of modest, material good in a simple state of agricultural society occurs frequently in the Old Testament: *"dwelt safely, each man under his vine and his fig tree"* (v. 25). It breathes the very essence of calm peace and contentment. Isn't this the ultimate goal of governments and rulers, not to gain prominence and power but to provide the common people with individual peace and prosperity?

Since at this period in history the use of horses and chariots was a new military strategy, Solomon's possession of so many was a sign of growing luxury, which may have carried the seeds of future evil. 2 Chron. 9:25, the parallel passage, has four thousand in the place of forty thousand in verse 26.

What an impressive inventory of wealth, even for a king; but the crown of Solomon's gifts, in the mind of the author, was still his wisdom. His *"largeness of heart"* referred to in verse 29 points to his broad interests in poetry, botany, biology, ornithology, ichthyology, astronomy, arithmetic, and medicine. The wisdom of Egypt in verse 30 refers to geometry, astronomy, and the preparation of ointments and medicines.

Jewish tradition (as well as the Koran) credits Solomon with the ability to converse in the language of every beast, fowl, fish, plant, and demon. Ancient rankings put the cedar tree at the top of the list of plants and hyssop at the lowest level; thus Solomon's botanical interests were all-inclusive.

Even though they are mentioned again in 1 Chron. 6:18, 29 and in Psalms 87 and 89, the names in verse 31 are unknown to us. Jewish tradition associates Ethan with Abraham, Heman with Moses, Chalcol with Joseph, and Darda with the generation of the wilderness. They were no doubt household names in the ancient world, but today they are forgotten. Human wisdom is fleeting and transient, but the wisdom that comes from above is eternal. Solomon's wisdom was of the latter variety, and his wisdom has been preserved by inspiration as a part of the eternal word of God.

NOTES

1. Robert C. Dentan, *Kings and Chronicles,* Layman's Bible Commentary, vol. 7 (Richmond: John Knox Press, 1964), 22.
2. I. W. Slotki, *Kings* (London: Soncino Press, 1950), 15.
3. John Gray, *I and II Kings,* Old Testament Library (Philadelphia: Westminster, 1963), 17.
4. Slotki, 17.
5. Norman H. Snaith, Ralph W. Sockman, and Raymond Calkins, "The First and Second Books of Kings," in *The Interpreter's Bible,* vol. 3 (Nashville: Abingdon, 1954), 34.
6. C. F. Keil, *The Books of the Kings,* Biblical Commentary on the Old Testament, ed. C. F. Keil and F. Delitzsch, vol. 4 (Grand Rapids: Eerdmans, 1950), 34.
7. Gray, 104.
8. Gwilym H. Jones, *1 and 2 Kings,* New Century Bible Commentary, ed. Ronald E. Clements (Grand Rapids: Eerdmans, 1984), 115.
9. William Sanford La Sor, "1 and 2 Kings," in *The New Bible Commentary: Revised,* ed. D. Guthrie and J. A. Motyer (Grand Rapids: Eerdmans, 1970), 326.
10. John T. Gates, "First Kings," *Wycliffe Bible Commentary,* ed. Charles F. Pfeiffer and Everett F. Harrison (Chicago: Moody Press, 1963), 312.
11. Jones, 120.

12. Simon J. DeVries, *1 Kings,* Word Biblical Commentary, ed. John D. W. Watts, vol. 12 (Waco, TX: Word Books, 1985), 50.

13. Ibid., 37.

14. Slotki, 15; Keil, 38.

15. Slotki, 15.

16. Stanley A. Cook, *The Religion of Ancient Palestine in Light of Archaeology* (London: Oxford University Press, 1930), 196–97.

17. Jones, 124.

18. La Sor, 326.

19. Gates, 312.

20. James A. Montgomery, *A Critical and Exegetical Commentary on the Books of Kings,* International Critical Commentary, ed. Henry Snyder Gehman, vol. 10 (New York: Scribner, 1951), 327.

21. Slotki, 15.

CHAPTER THREE

The Building and Dedication of the Temple

1 Kings 5:1–8:66

INTRODUCTION

The building of the temple in Jerusalem marks a high point in the development of Israel's faith. Their long history as a nomadic people, living in tents and following their flocks and herds, had made them content with a portable worship center. The tabernacle was perfectly adapted to a tent-dwelling society, and besides that, Yahweh, who gave them the instructions for the tabernacle in the first place, had suggested to David that there was no need to build Him a "house of cedar" (2 Sam. 7:7). But now Israel was a settled community with cities and fortresses and even a capital with plans for a palace. In God's providence, it was now time to give more permanence to their worship center as David had dreamed of doing.

Understanding it to be God's will, Solomon willingly accepted the task of building the house of God in the place of his father David. As soon as he had consolidated his kingdom, he began to make preparation to begin construction. How extensively and in what detail King David had already planned, we don't know. But apparently Solomon inherited substantial architectural studies, specifications of materials, and probably the establishment of negotiations with King Hiram, David's good friend. Further evidence of this is found in verse 3 where Solomon said to King Hiram, *"You know. . . ."* This may indicate earlier conferences between the two rulers.[1]

We are told in 6:1 that the work on the temple began in the fourth year of Solomon's reign, so even with a substantial head start, it still took the young king several years just to get ready for such a complex project.

In 2 Chronicles 2, the parallel passage is very similar, leaving out some items mentioned here and adding a few others. One addition to the record tells how Solomon enlisted Tyrian craftsmen who could work with gold, silver, bronze, and iron and who knew how to engrave and use purple, crimson, and blue. This is the only source of knowledge we have about the colors of the temple. The Chronicles passage also adds a third type of lumber to Solomon's requisition list. He ordered almug logs along with cedar and cypress.

These two separate accounts of one of the most important events in Israel's history may both be condensations of a common, more elaborate record. Based on the same record, each author prepared his account under the guidance of inspiration to fit his particular situation and purpose.[2]

SOLOMON RECRUITS HIRAM AND PLANS THE TEMPLE

5:1 Now Hiram king of Tyre sent his servants to
Solomon, because he heard that they had anointed
him king in place of his father, for Hiram had always
loved David.

2 Then Solomon sent to Hiram, saying:

3 You know how my father David could not build a house for the name of the LORD his God because of the wars which were fought against him on every side, until the LORD put *his foes* under the soles of his feet.

4 But now the LORD my God has given me rest on every side; *there is* neither adversary nor evil occurrence.

5 And behold, I propose to build a house for the name of the LORD my God, as the LORD spoke to my father David, saying, "Your son, whom I will set on your throne in your place, he shall build the house for My name."

6 Now therefore, command that they cut down cedars for me from Lebanon; and my servants will be with your servants, and I will pay you wages for your servants according to whatever

you say. For you know *there is* none among us
who has skill to cut timber like the Sidonians.

7 So it was, when Hiram heard the words of
Solomon, that he rejoiced greatly and said,

Blessed *be* the LORD this day, for He has given
David a wise son over this great people!

8 Then Hiram sent to Solomon, saying:

I have considered *the message* which you sent
me, *and* I will do all you desire concerning the
cedar and cypress logs.

9 My servants shall bring *them* down from
Lebanon to the sea; I will float them in rafts by
sea to the place you indicate to me, and will
have them broken apart there; then you can
take *them* away. And you shall fulfill my desire
by giving food for my household.

10 Then Hiram gave Solomon cedar and cypress
logs *according to* all his desire.

11 And Solomon gave Hiram twenty thousand
kors of wheat *as* food for his household, and twenty
kors of pressed oil. Thus Solomon gave to Hiram year
by year.

12 So the LORD gave Solomon wisdom, as He had
promised him; and there was peace between Hiram
and Solomon, and the two of them made a treaty together.

13 Then King Solomon raised up a labor force out
of all Israel; and the labor force was thirty thousand
men.

14 And he sent them to Lebanon, ten thousand a
month in shifts: they were one month in Lebanon *and*
two months at home; Adoniram *was* in charge of the
labor force.

15 Solomon had seventy thousand who carried
burdens, and eighty thousand who quarried *stone* in
the mountains,

16 besides three thousand three hundred from the
chiefs of Solomon's deputies, who supervised the people who labored in the work.

17 And the king commanded them to quarry large
stones, costly stones, *and* hewn stones, to lay the foundation of the temple.

> 18 So Solomon's builders, Hiram's builders, and the Gebalites quarried *them;* and they prepared timber and stones to build the temple.
>
> *1 Kings 5:1–18*

Hiram is an abbreviation of Ahiram which means "Brother of Ram," or "My brother is exalted," or "Brother of the lofty one."[3] Archaeologists have discovered a royal sarcophagus in Byblos of Tyre dated about 1200 B.C. inscribed with the king's name, "Ahiram." Apparently it belonged to the man in this passage.

His servants (v. 1) were actually official envoys or ambassadors sent to congratulate Solomon on his inauguration, and possibly to offer condolences for the recent death of his father. The friendship between David and Hiram is recorded in 2 Sam. 5:11–12, a friendship Hiram described as "love" in this verse. Building on that friendship to strengthen their own diplomatic relations was mutually beneficial to Solomon and Hiram. Tyre would gain the advantage of using the Israel-controlled "King's Highway" through Transjordan and of relying on Israel's military protection of their hinterland to the east.[4] Also, Israel would continue to supply grain for the Phoenicians.[5] No wonder verse 7 indicates Hiram "rejoiced greatly" at the prospects of a treaty with Israel. Solomon, on the other hand, would not only gain a military ally with naval capabilities but also an invaluable helper in the massive temple project.[6]

Solomon's official reply to Hiram quoted in the next verses was delivered by Israel's own embassy, probably in the form of a letter. The word *"sent"* implies correspondence. According to Josephus, copies of such a letter along with Hiram's reply were preserved in both Hebrew and Tyrian archives and were extant in his day (*Antiquities,* 8.2.8).

Why was David not permitted to build the house for Yahweh? In 2 Chron. 22:8 David gave two reasons which came from the Lord: (1) "You have shed much blood." (2) "You have made great wars." Perhaps out of a feeling of filial respect, Solomon mentioned only the latter, which he interpreted in the best possible light. According to Solomon, the warfare his father waged was defensive and not so much displeasing to God as it was a demand on his time, leaving the king no opportunity to build. The implication is that if the Lord had "put his foes under the soles of his feet" sooner, David would have had time to build the temple, and God would have permitted it. Whatever the intended restriction on David, it seems that warfare was more to blame than bloodshed. After all, Solomon, who was allowed to construct the sacred house, had just completed a bloody purge to secure his power. Even though he had been involved in a number of killings, he was free from involvement in war.

The unusual construction of the sentence in verse 5 points to an interesting feature in Hebrew thought. *"I propose to build a house for the name of the Lord. . . ."* Not for the Lord, but for the name of the Lord. The Hebrews reverenced the name of the Lord so deeply, they would not even speak it, substituting instead the word *Adonai* meaning "Lord." God's name was the manifestation of the divine nature in a visible sign as a pledge of His presence. They considered the name almost as sacred as God Himself, and to build a house for His name was tantamount to building it for God. Ancient cultures, including the Hebrews, believed that to know the name of a deity allowed the worshiper to claim the power of that deity.

To know another person's name is to have, in some sense, power over that person. I was walking through the Atlanta airport one day transferring from one gate to another. As usual, the wide corridor of the "B" concourse was packed with passengers from around the world hustling in both directions to catch their planes. Like an all-pro running back, I zigzagged through the slower people ahead of me. Having tuned out the babble of all those voices, I was engulfed in my own private, anonymous world, when suddenly one word stopped me in my tracks. "Russell!" It was my name, and it pierced through all that unintelligible noise around me like a trumpet blast. It stopped me so suddenly in my tracks that I created a chain of pile-ups behind me all the way back to gate 22! It was a friend of mine, an airline pilot from Atlanta on his way to another gate, who had spotted me and called my name. We apologized to a few people we had stacked up and stepped out of the stream of traffic for a quick visit. Afterwards, I thought of how those who know your name can, just by calling it, control you.

God had revealed Himself to the Hebrews as one God, the only God, holy, omnipotent, the creator of heaven and earth. Then, wonder of wonders, this mighty God willingly told them His name! He was approachable. He wanted fellowship with His people. He invited them to speak to Him and listen to Him. Now, no matter how busy He is with His world, when we call on Him, He will answer. He promised, "Whosoever shall call upon the name of the Lord shall be saved." Little wonder the name of the Lord was held in such high esteem by His people.

"Rest" in verse 4 is used in the sense of "peace." *"Evil occurrence"* may refer to internal rebellions such as those of Absalom and Sheba during David's reign or coup d'état like that of Adonijah in Solomon's. *"Adversary"* is the Hebrew word *śāṭān,* which we have brought over into English as a transliteration. It originally referred to a human enemy or opponent, but later became a proper name for the Devil. He is called at times in Scripture, "The Adversary." In this verse, of course, the general meaning "enemy" is intended.[7]

Peace and prosperity affect different people in different ways. Solomon said, "Since God has given me rest on every side, since there is neither adversary nor evil occurrence, since He has bestowed upon me unprecedented wealth and wisdom, therefore I will build Him a house." The wise king did not take his happy situation as an opportunity for selfish, luxurious repose, but heard in it God's call to a great task.

In His parable, Jesus identified a successful man who reacted in the opposite way from Solomon. "I have many goods laid up for many years." What then? "I propose to build a house for the name of the Lord my God?" Not this man. "I will build myself bigger barns to keep busy, then I will take my ease, eat, drink, and be merry." Jesus called this successful man a fool. If more contemporary Christians in prosperous America, surrounded by unparalleled freedom and leisure, would follow the example of Solomon rather than the example of the rich fool, there would be plenty of workers and ample resources for the urgent work of the kingdom.

In Old Testament days, cedar was a very desirable material for fine woodwork, and the best cedar was that found in the legendary forests of Lebanon (v. 6). It was a hardwood that resisted dry rot and insects. Its narrow grain was suitable for carving, and its fragrance was pleasant.[8]

Identifying the Sidonians (Phoenicians) in verse 6 as King Hiram's subjects reflects conditions somewhat later than the time of Solomon, when Sidon was subject to Tyre.[9] However, since Sidon was considered the stronger kingdom, it may have been used as a general term for the entire region.[10]

The Sidonians were noted as timber craftsmen in the ancient world, a fact that is substantiated on the famous Palmero Stone. Its inscription from 2200 B.C. tells about timber-carrying ships that sailed from Byblos to Egypt about four hundred years previously. The skill of the Sidonians was expressed in their ability to pick the most suitable trees, know the right time to cut them, fell them with care, and then properly treat the logs.[11]

In Alaska, I saw loggers floating their newly cut timber down the river to the sawmill. At times the logs were loose and ended up with acres of other logs in a holding reservoir at the mill. Each log had been branded so that, when it was taken out to be cut, its owner could be identified. But other logs in the river were tied together in huge, rough rafts, some with lumberjacks riding on them to assure that they arrived safely at their destination. That seems to be the plan Hiram had for transporting the cedars of Lebanon to Israel. They were probably imported at Joppa, near modern Jaiffa.[12]

Does the pagan Hiram's praise of Yahweh in verse 7 indicate he acknowledged Him as the only true God? Not necessarily. It probably means that the King of Tyre simply regarded the God of Israel to be as real as his own deities. He does, however, in 2 Chron. 2:11 call Yahweh the creator of heaven and earth.

Shrewdly, Hiram refused to let Solomon pay his craftsmen individual wages, suggesting instead a general compensation of wheat and oil over a period of years (v. 11). This prevented Hiram's workers from being directly controlled by Solomon.[13]

The pressed oil (literally "beaten oil") was obtained by crushing olives that were not quite ripe in a mortar. This produced an oil whiter in color and purer in flavor than common oil from ripe olives. A similar procedure was specified for the lamps of the tabernacle.[14]

Some say the high price Solomon had to pay for Hiram's provisions sapped his resources to the point of bankruptcy and that he had to cede part of his territory to Tyre to settle the debt (cf. 9:11ff.).[15]

"There was peace between Hiram and Solomon" (v. 12). "Peace" is the Hebrew word *šālôm,* which means more than just the absence of conflict. Hiram and Solomon had not been at war, so the idea of peace here is that of wholeness, concord, well-being, security.[16] God's peace is also more than just the absence of conflict, although it does include that. Through Christ, we are reconciled to God, who loved us even when we were enemies. But there is more to the

experience of God's peace than that. It creates perfect wholeness, concord, well-being, and security. It is the peace which "passes understanding."

There is an important distinction to be made between the *"labor force"* in verse 13 and the workers in verse 15. The "labor force" was made up of Israelites, drafted into national service on rotating shifts. The workers, on the other hand, were tribute-slaves from among the Canaanites and other conquered nations.[17] The Israelite draftees worked in Lebanon one month, then were furloughed back to their homes and families for two months before returning for another thirty-day shift. This plan was instituted because Solomon knew the prolonged absence of the Hebrew workmen would have weakened both their family ties and their national loyalty. He recognized the importance of a healthy home life and strong families as the tough fiber that held the nation together, an emphasis that has remained a strong feature of Jewish life until the present day.

Certain totalitarian states in modern times have minimized the family unit in unsuccessful attempts to develop national strength. The Nazi experiment, for example, of weakening home ties for the sake of strengthening the state did not prove successful.[18]

"Costly stones" in verse 17 means "quality stones," revealing the emphasis Solomon placed on providing the best in his construction of God's house. These quality stones were to be hidden from sight beneath the ground as a foundation, but even though no one would see them, the wise king wanted the best. The present-day foundation of the temple has impressive squared-off stones, but they are the ones Herod, not Solomon, placed there. Little remains of the temple Solomon built, except what is still out of sight underground. However, we know that Solomon constructed his building with skill and care that rivaled that of Herod even though its date was many centuries earlier.[19]

"Gebalites" (v. 18) may be a Hebrew word meaning "stone-squarers," but more likely it means the people from Gebal, possibly another name for Byblos.[20] It was a Phoenician city known as a timber port to the Egyptians as early as 3000 B.C. A bronze ax head with the name and title of Cheops belonging to an Egyptian lumber-gang was found at the mouth of the river near Byblos or Gebal.[21]

Solomon Builds the Temple

6:1 And it came to pass in the four hundred and eightieth year after the children of Israel had come out of the land of Egypt, in the fourth year of Solomon's reign over Israel, in the month of Ziv, which *is* the second month, that he began to build the house of the LORD.

2 Now the house which King Solomon built for the LORD, its length *was* sixty cubits, its width twenty, and its height thirty cubits.

3 The vestibule in front of the sanctuary of the house *was* twenty cubits long across the width of the house, *and* the width of *the vestibule extended* ten cubits from the front of the house.

4 And he made for the house windows with beveled frames.

5 Against the wall of the temple he built chambers all around, *against* the walls of the temple, all around the sanctuary and the inner sanctuary. Thus he made side chambers all around it.

6 The lowest chamber *was* five cubits wide, the middle *was* six cubits wide, and the third *was* seven cubits wide; for he made narrow ledges around the outside of the temple, so that *the support beams* would not be fastened into the walls of the temple.

7 And the temple, when it was being built, was built with stone finished at the quarry, so that no hammer or chisel *or* any iron tool was heard in the temple while it was being built.

8 The doorway for the middle story *was* on the right side of the temple. They went up by stairs to the middle *story,* and from the middle to the third.

9 So he built the temple and finished it, and he paneled the temple with beams and boards of cedar.

10 And he built side chambers against the entire temple, each five cubits high; they were attached to the temple with cedar beams.

11 Then the word of the LORD came to Solomon, saying:

12 "*Concerning* this temple which you are building,

if you walk in My statutes, execute My judgments,
keep all My commandments, and walk in them, then
I will perform My word with you, which I spoke to
your father David.
13 "And I will dwell among the children of Israel,
and will not forsake My people Israel."
14 So Solomon built the temple and finished it.
15 And he built the inside walls of the temple with
cedar boards; from the floor of the temple to the ceiling he paneled the inside with wood; and he covered
the floor of the temple with planks of cypress.
16 Then he built the twenty-cubit room at
the rear of the temple, from floor to ceiling, with
cedar boards; he built *it* inside as the inner sanctuary, as the Most Holy *Place.*
17 And in front of it the temple sanctuary was
forty cubits *long.*
18 The inside of the temple was cedar, carved with
ornamental buds and open flowers. All *was* cedar;
there was no stone *to be* seen.
19 And he prepared the inner sanctuary inside the
temple, to set the ark of the covenant of the LORD
there.
20 The inner sanctuary *was* twenty cubits long,
twenty cubits wide, and twenty cubits high. He overlaid it with pure gold, and overlaid the altar of cedar.
21 So Solomon overlaid the inside of the temple
with pure gold. He stretched gold chains across the
front of the inner sanctuary, and overlaid it with
gold.
22 The whole temple he overlaid with gold, until
he had finished all the temple; also he overlaid with
gold the entire altar that *was* by the inner sanctuary.
23 Inside the inner sanctuary he made two cherubim *of* olive wood, *each* ten cubits high.
24 One wing of the cherub *was* five cubits, and the
other wing of the cherub five cubits: ten cubits from
the tip of one wing to the tip of the other.
25 And the other cherub *was* ten cubits; both
cherubim *were* of the same size and shape.
26 The height of one cherub *was* ten cubits, and so
was the other cherub.

27 Then he set the cherubim inside the inner room; and they stretched out the wings of the cherubim so that the wing of the one touched *one* wall, and the wing of the other cherub touched the other wall. And their wings touched each other in the middle of the room.
28 Also he overlaid the cherubim with gold.
29 Then he carved all the walls of the temple all around, both the inner and outer *sanctuaries,* with carved figures of cherubim, palm trees, and open flowers.
30 And the floor of the temple he overlaid with gold, both the inner and outer *sanctuaries.*
31 For the entrance of the inner sanctuary he made doors *of* olive wood; the lintel *and* doorposts *were* one-fifth *of the wall.*
32 The two doors *were of* olive wood; and he carved on them figures of cherubim, palm trees, and open flowers, and overlaid *them* with gold; and he spread gold on the cherubim and on the palm trees.
33 So for the door of the sanctuary he also made doorposts *of* olive wood, one-fourth *of the wall.*
34 And the two doors *were of* cypress wood; two panels *comprised* one folding door, and two panels *comprised* the other folding door.
35 Then he carved cherubim, palm trees, and open flowers *on them,* and overlaid *them* with gold applied evenly on the carved work.
36 And he built the inner court with three rows of hewn stone and a row of cedar beams.
37 In the fourth year the foundation of the house of the LORD was laid, in the month of Ziv.
38 And in the eleventh year, in the month of Bul, which is the eighth month, the house was finished in all its details and according to all its plans. So he was seven years in building it.

1 Kings 6:1–38

The structure of Solomon's temple consisted of four areas: (1) The main chamber of the house, a rectangle ninety feet long by thirty feet wide by forty-five feet high. Like the tabernacle, it faced east with the holy place comprising the eastern sixty feet and the holy of holies comprising the western thirty feet. (2) The vestibule or entrance hall attached to the eastern front of the chamber. It measured thirty feet wide by fifteen feet deep. (3) The three-storied side chambers which were part of the walls on the north, west, and south sides. These chambers, serving as sleeping quarters, rose twenty-two feet high with the wall above them extending another twenty-two feet. Windows in the wall gave light to the holy place. (4) A large courtyard surrounding the entire structure. The temple itself was exactly twice the size of the tabernacle.[22]

There was no room inside the temple for worshipers because it was the house of God, not the house of His people. A royal palace has no room for large groups of ordinary citizens. Only the king's servants and officials are admitted to his palace. If the people want to show devotion to their king, they gather outside the palace and shout acclamations.[23] So the temple itself was entered only by the official worship leaders. The people stood in the courtyard and worshiped God from outside. Later, of course, through the redemptive work of Christ, believers were given direct access to the throne of God without the intercession or interference of human priests.

On the site now called "The Dome of the Rock" outside the walls of the ancient "City of David," Jerusalem proper, Solomon began his monumental project. This location outside the city departed from the ancient tradition of placing sacred temples in the center of town. DeVries explains that isolating the temple in this way showed the uniqueness of Yahweh in contrast to other deities. As was sometimes the case with other altars to Yahweh in Israel, this was not the worship site of a previous deity taken over and rededicated for the worship of Israel's God. The revealed faith of the Hebrews was not a revised version of some existing pagan religion; it was radically new.[24]

The running account of the construction is neatly divided into four sections. (1) The construction of the exteriors of the buildings, verses 1–10. (2) A reminder of God's conditional promise through Solomon to dwell among the children of Israel, verses 11–13. (3) The construction of the interior of the temple, verses 14–36. (4) A statement of the time consumed in building, verses 37–38.

There is a curious statement in verse 7. *"No hammer or chisel or any iron tool was heard in the temple while it was being built."* Theodoret believed this meant that the temple was built with stones God had miraculously shaped to the precise dimensions so that no cutting was required.[25] A rabbinic tradition offers another explanation with a legend that tells how Solomon secured the "shamir," a small worm with wonderful powers, by whose mere touch, stones could be split to any desired shape. The magic worm enabled him to build the temple without the use of noisy iron tools.[26] Actually, the verse means that the stones were so carefully tooled and skillfully prepared when first cut from the remote quarries that they needed no major adjustments when they were transported to the construction site.[27]

Maclaren finds a beautiful spiritual lesson in the verse: namely, the importance of silence in the work of the kingdom and in the life of the believer. God's message is not always heard in the earthquake or fire, but in the still, small voice. The incarnation did not occur with sensationalism, but unobtrusively, silently. The early spread of the kingdom was unnoticed by the world's great ones—the caesars, philosophers, and patricians. It grew silently like a seed underground. This illustration should be an encouragement to humble Christians who with servant hearts work inconspicuously, and should remind us not to mistake noise and hype for spiritual progress.

In our media-centered society, where the competition for the attention of jaded audiences forces every new advertiser to increase the sensationalism of his presentation, this lesson on the importance of silence is timely. We tend to measure the importance of things by the excitement they generate. Even in appraising the quality of ministry, we are overly impressed by numbers and measurable statistics.

While the so-called super churches are encouraging reminders of the unlimited possibilities of God's power, they may tend to conceal the truth that there are other criteria for measuring "successful" ministry than the secular criteria of success. Sudden, spectacular progress is often short-lived. As they say, "easy come, easy go." Conversely, much that is done silently, without the world's attention, is often what will last the longest.

When I see the tribute the world pays to the superstars of the ecclesiastical world today, especially those who are media personalities, I think of the work of a capable pastor who serves in the inner city of Detroit. He faithfully ministers year after year in a church located in a racially mixed section in the shadows of Detroit's skyscrapers. This is the neighborhood that was torn by riots and burning a few years ago. No one sees this preacher's face on national television. His story doesn't sparkle with the dazzling glitter of which headlines are made, nor does it attract an admiring mailing list of contributors. But I have a strong feeling that on that day when the Lord recognizes those good and faithful servants with His "well done," my servant friend will be near the front of the line, well ahead of some of our sensational religious stars.

However magnificent a temple may be, the message of verses 12–13 is that it has no spiritual value unless the people who use it devote themselves totally to God's control. The sanctuary is but a symbol. The essentials are obedience to His will and observance of His commandments.

Notice that God did not say He would dwell in the temple, but "among" His people. Furthermore, He does not dwell with them just because they built Him a magnificent house. Not even Solomon's wealth could bribe God to favor him or his subjects. As always, God's presence is conditional, depending upon the moral and spiritual quality of those who call upon Him.

It took Solomon seven years and six months to finish the temple. As it turned out, the glory of the great edifice was short-lived. Because of his disobedience, it was plundered just five short years after his death (14:2–6). Furthermore, the continued disobedience of the people led to its total destruction in 586 B.C.

SOLOMON FURNISHES THE TEMPLE AND COMPLETES OTHER BUILDINGS

7:1 But Solomon took thirteen years to build his own house; so he finished all his house.

2 He also built the House of the Forest of Lebanon; its length *was* one hundred cubits, its width fifty cubits, and its height thirty cubits, with four rows of cedar pillars, and cedar beams on the pillars.

3 And *it was* paneled with cedar above the beams that *were* on forty-five pillars, fifteen *to* a row.

4 *There were* windows *with beveled frames in* three rows, and window *was* opposite window *in* three tiers.

5 And all the doorways and doorposts *had*

rectangular frames; and window *was* opposite window *in* three tiers.

6 He also made the Hall of Pillars: its length *was* fifty cubits, and its width thirty cubits; and in front of them *was* a portico with pillars, and a canopy *was* in front of them.

7 Then he made a hall for the throne, the Hall of Judgment, where he might judge; and *it was* paneled with cedar from floor to ceiling.

8 And the house where he dwelt *had* another court inside the hall, of like workmanship. Solomon also made a house like this hall for Pharaoh's daughter, whom he had taken *as wife.*

9 All these *were of* costly stones cut to size, trimmed with saws, inside and out, from the foundation to the eaves, and also on the outside to the great court.

10 The foundation *was of* costly stones, large stones, some ten cubits and some eight cubits.

11 And above *were* costly stones, hewn to size, and cedar wood.

12 The great court *was* enclosed with three rows of hewn stones and a row of cedar beams. So were the inner court of the house of the LORD and the vestibule of the temple.

13 Now King Solomon sent and brought Huram from Tyre.

14 He *was* the son of a widow from the tribe of Naphtali, and his father *was* a man of Tyre, a bronze worker; he was filled with wisdom and understanding and skill in working with all kinds of bronze work. So he came to King Solomon and did all his work.

15 And he cast two pillars of bronze, each one eighteen cubits high, and a line of twelve cubits measured the circumference of each.

16 Then he made two capitals *of* cast bronze, to set on the tops of the pillars. The height of one capital *was* five cubits, and the height of the other capital *was* five cubits.

17 *He made* a lattice network, with wreaths of chainwork, for the capitals which *were* on top of the

pillars: seven chains for one capital and seven for the other capital.

18 So he made the pillars, and two rows of pomegranates above the network all around to cover the capitals that *were* on top; and thus he did for the other capital.

19 The capitals which *were* on top of the pillars in the hall *were* in the shape of lilies, four cubits.

20 The capitals on the two pillars also *had pomegranates* above, by the convex surface which *was* next to the network; and there *were* two hundred such pomegranates in rows on each of the capitals all around.

21 Then he set up the pillars by the vestibule of the temple; he set up the pillar on the right and called its name Jachin, and he set up the pillar on the left and called its name Boaz.

22 The tops of the pillars were in the shape of lilies. So the work of the pillars was finished.

23 And he made the Sea of cast bronze, ten cubits from one brim to the other; *it was* completely round. Its height *was* five cubits, and a line of thirty cubits measured its circumference.

24 Below its brim *were* ornamental buds encircling it all around, ten to a cubit, all the way around the Sea. The ornamental buds *were* cast in two rows when it was cast.

25 It stood on twelve oxen: three looking toward the north, three looking toward the west, three looking toward the south, and three looking toward the east; the Sea *was set* upon them, and all their back parts *pointed* inward.

26 It *was* a handbreadth thick; and its brim was shaped like the brim of a cup, *like* a lily blossom. It contained two thousand baths.

27 He also made ten carts of bronze; four cubits *was* the length of each cart, four cubits its width, and three cubits its height.

28 And this *was* the design of the carts: They had panels, and the panels *were* between frames;

29 on the panels that *were* between the frames *were* lions, oxen, and cherubim. And on the frames *was* a

pedestal on top. Below the lions and oxen *were* wreaths of plaited work.

30 Every cart had four bronze wheels and axles of bronze, and its four feet had supports. Under the laver *were* supports of cast *bronze* beside each wreath.

31 Its opening inside the crown at the top *was* one cubit in diameter; and the opening *was* round, shaped *like* a pedestal, one and a half cubits in outside diameter; and also on the opening *were* engravings, but the panels were square, not round.

32 Under the panels *were* the four wheels, and the axles of the wheels *were joined* to the cart. The height of a wheel *was* one and a half cubits.

33 The workmanship of the wheels *was* like the workmanship of a chariot wheel; their axle pins, their rims, their spokes, and their hubs *were* all of cast *bronze.*

34 And *there were* four supports at the four corners of each cart; its supports *were* part of the cart itself.

35 On the top of the cart, at the height of half a cubit, *it was* perfectly round. And on the top of the cart, its flanges and its panels *were* of the same casting.

36 On the plates of its flanges and on its panels he engraved cherubim, lions, and palm trees, wherever there was a clear space on each, with wreaths all around.

37 Thus he made the ten carts. All of them were of the same mold, one measure, *and* one shape.

38 Then he made ten lavers of bronze; each laver contained forty baths, *and* each laver *was* four cubits. On each of the ten carts *was* a laver.

39 And he put five carts on the right side of the house, and five on the left side of the house. He set the Sea on the right side of the house, toward the southeast.

40 Huram made the lavers and the shovels and the bowls. So Huram finished doing all the work that he was to do for King Solomon *for* the house of the LORD:

41 the two pillars, the *two* bowl-shaped capitals that *were* on top of the two pillars; the two networks

covering the two bowl-shaped capitals which *were* on top of the pillars;

42 four hundred pomegranates for the two networks (two rows of pomegranates for each network, to cover the two bowl-shaped capitals that *were* on top of the pillars);

43 the ten carts, and ten lavers on the carts;

44 one Sea, and twelve oxen under the Sea;

45 the pots, the shovels, and the bowls. All these articles which Huram made for King Solomon *for* the house of the LORD *were of* burnished bronze.

46 In the plain of Jordan the king had them cast in clay molds, between Succoth and Zaretan.

47 And Solomon did not weigh all the articles, because *there were* so many; the weight of the bronze was not determined.

48 Thus Solomon had all the furnishings made for the house of the LORD: the altar of gold, and the table of gold on which *was* the showbread;

49 the lampstands of pure gold, five on the right *side* and five on the left in front of the inner sanctuary, with the flowers and the lamps and the wick-trimmers of gold;

50 the basins, the trimmers, the bowls, the ladles, and the censers of pure gold; and the hinges of gold, *both* for the doors of the inner room (the Most Holy *Place*) *and* for the doors of the main hall of the temple.

51 So all the work that King Solomon had done for the house of the LORD was finished; and Solomon brought in the things which his father David had dedicated: the silver and the gold and the furnishings. He put them in the treasuries of the house of the LORD.

1 Kings 7:1–51

The conjunction *"but"* in verse 1 is intended to contrast the thirteen years required to build Solomon's own house with the seven years required to build the temple (6:38). However, what this difference implies is not clear. To some commentators it seems to condemn Solomon for spending twice as much time building his own house as he spent building the temple of God. Were worldly power and luxury already going to the young king's head? Were secular ideals beginning to overshadow spiritual ideals in his court? It is true that in later years Solomon began to minimize the high priority he had given to serving the Lord, but that was not the case in these early years.

A better interpretation of verse 1 is that Solomon purposely allowed the construction of his house to drag on for thirteen years, while he had accelerated the temple construction and finished it in seven years.[28] Also, we must remember that many years of preparation, planning, and accumulation of materials had preceded the seven-year temple project, while the work on the palace apparently had no such head start. Furthermore, while the temple was more elaborate and intricate, the palace complex was more widespread, involving a number of separate buildings, and thereby more time-consuming. Considering these factors, Solomon probably gave priority to the temple and put more attention and time on its construction than on his palace.

"His own house" refers to the entire royal complex, including the House of the Forest of Lebanon, the Hall of the Pillars, the Hall of the Throne, the house for Pharaoh's daughter, and his own residence. Detailed descriptions of the first three are given, but the king's house and that of the princess are hardly mentioned. We are told merely that the two palaces were similar in style to the Hall of the Throne. They were *"of like workmanship"* and *"like this hall"* (v. 8).

The House of the Forest of Lebanon was not a summer home in the cool mountains of the north as some have suggested, but a royal armory. Its four rows of cedar columns, standing like trees in a forest, probably gave the building its name. It was on these columns that the royal collection of armor was hung, including the five hundred golden shields referred to in 10:16–17. Isaiah specifically calls the building an armory in Isa. 22:8.[29]

There is no doubt as to the purpose of the Hall of the Throne (v. 7), but what function the Hall of Pillars had is not so clear. Perhaps it was a waiting chamber for those who came seeking an audience with the king or who came to plead a law case in the Hall of the Throne.[30]

The remainder of chapter 7 deals with the furnishings and decorations inside the temple. A noted bronze craftsman from Tyre was commissioned to oversee these artistic final touches. Hiram, the same name as the famous king who supplied Solomon with timber and workmen, was a common Phoenician name, so we are not to confuse him with the Tyrian ruler in chapter 5. It seemed important to the author of 1 Kings to show by Hiram's lineage that he was one-half Israelite, his father a Tyrian bronze worker and his mother an Israelite from the tribe of Dan and a widow of a man from Naphtali (cf. 2 Chron. 2:14, where Hiram's name is Huram-abi).

His first project was to build two huge free-standing pillars topped with intricately decorated, blossom-shaped capitals. The open capitals on top of the thirty-foot-high columns may have been filled with oil and then ignited to serve as huge lampstands in the courtyard in front of the temple proper. The one on the right was given the name *"Jachin,"* meaning "He shall establish," and the one on the left the name *"Boaz,"* meaning "in strength."

Why the columns were named is not revealed, but some interesting guesses have been proposed. One is that when he had completed the pillars, Hiram the metal worker stepped back to admire his work. Looking at the column on the right he exclaimed, "It is so solid!" (the approximate meaning of "Jachin"), and then looking at the one on the left he remarked, "With what strength!" (the approximate meaning of "Boaz"). The names were therefore merely the expressions of a satisfied craftsman at the completion of the task, and they caught on.[31]

Another speculation is that the two Hebrew words, "Jachin" and "Boaz" were the first words of Hebrew inscriptions which may have been carved on the pillars.[32] The one on the right declaring the promise of God to establish David's line, and the one on the left declaring the power of Yahweh. Some credence is given this theory by the fact that the word "Jachin" is the same root used by God in His promise to David.[33]

The simplest explanation is that the columns were named to symbolize the presence of the strong name of Yahweh in the temple, and the permanence of His covenant with Israel. Whatever the meaning of the names, the columns must have been an awesome sight to those who approached the vestibule of the temple.

In addition to some miscellaneous bronze implements mentioned in verse 40, Hiram's next project was to fashion an enormous bronze water basin resting on twelve bronze oxen. With a diameter of seven feet and a depth of three feet, it held water for cleaning the altars and implements used in the bloody sacrifices and for use in ceremonial purifications.[34] Called "the Sea" because of its volume, the heavy basin required a more portable distribution system to carry the water to the various worship stations in the temple. So Hiram fashioned ten smaller lavers on wheeled carts which could be pushed about the temple grounds.

The closing verses of chapter 7 recapitulate the list of gold furnishings already described in chapter 6, adding to them some smaller gold appointments. Then, Solomon, we are told, deposited in the temple the treasures collected over the years by King David. These included the gifts from defeated monarchs such as Toi of Hamath and the spoils of wars with Syria, Moab, Ammon, Philistia, and Edom (2 Sam. 8:9–14). Some of this booty was melted into bullion and molded into other objects of art.[35]

SOLOMON DEDICATES THE TEMPLE

8:1 Now Solomon assembled the elders of Israel and all the heads of the tribes, the chief fathers of the children of Israel, to King Solomon in Jerusalem, that they might bring up the ark of the covenant of the LORD from the City of David, which *is* Zion.

2 Therefore all the men of Israel assembled with King Solomon at the feast in the month of Ethanim, which *is* the seventh month.

3 So all the elders of Israel came, and the priests took up the ark.

4 Then they brought up the ark of the LORD, the tabernacle of meeting, and all the holy furnishings that *were* in the tabernacle. The priests and the Levites brought them up.

5 Also King Solomon, and all the congregation of Israel who were assembled with him, *were* with him before the ark, sacrificing sheep and oxen that could not be counted or numbered for multitude.

6 Then the priests brought in the ark of the covenant of the LORD to its place, into the inner sanctuary of the temple, to the Most Holy *Place,* under the wings of the cherubim.

7 For the cherubim spread *their* two wings over the place of the ark, and the cherubim overshadowed the ark and its poles.

8 The poles extended so that the ends of the poles
could be seen from the holy *place,* in front of the
inner sanctuary; but they could not be seen from
outside. And they are there to this day.
9 Nothing *was* in the ark except the two tablets of
stone which Moses put there at Horeb, when the
LORD made *a covenant* with the children of Israel,
when they came out of the land of Egypt.
10 And it came to pass, when the priests came out
of the holy *place,* that the cloud filled the house of
the LORD,
11 so that the priests could not continue minister-
ing because of the cloud; for the glory of the LORD
filled the house of the LORD.
12 Then Solomon spoke:
"The LORD said
He would dwell in the dark cloud.
13 I have surely built You an exalted house,
And a place for You to dwell in forever."
14 Then the king turned around and blessed the
whole assembly of Israel, while all the assembly of
Israel was standing.
15 And he said: "Blessed *be* the LORD God of Israel,
who spoke with His mouth to my father David, and
with His hand has fulfilled *it,* saying,
16 'Since the day that I brought My people Israel
out of Egypt, I have chosen no city from any tribe of
Israel *in which* to build a house, that My name might
be there; but I chose David to be over My people
Israel.'
17 "Now it was in the heart of my father David to
build a temple for the name of the LORD God of Israel.
18 "But the LORD said to my father David, 'Whereas it was in your heart to temple a house for My
name, you did well that it was in your heart.
19 'Nevertheless you shall not build the temple,
but your son who will come from your body, he shall
build the temple for My name.'
20 "So the LORD has fulfilled His word which He
spoke; and I have filled the position of my father
David, and sit on the throne of Israel, as the LORD

promised; and I have built a temple for the name of
the LORD God of Israel.
21 "And there I have made a place for the ark, in
which *is* the covenant of the LORD which He made
with our fathers, when He brought them out of the
land of Egypt."
22 Then Solomon stood before the altar of the
LORD in the presence of all the assembly of Israel,
and spread out his hands toward heaven;
23 and he said: "LORD God of Israel, *there is* no God
in heaven above or on earth below like You, who keep
Your covenant and mercy with Your servants who
walk before You with all their hearts.
24 "You have kept what You promised Your servant
David my father; You have both spoken with Your
mouth and fulfilled *it* with Your hand, as *it is* this
day.
25 "Therefore, LORD God of Israel, now keep what
You promised Your servant David my father, saying,
'You shall not fail to have a man sit before Me on the
throne of Israel, only if your sons take heed to their
way, that they walk before Me as you have walked
before Me.'
26 "And now I pray, O God of Israel, let Your word
come true, which You have spoken to Your servant
David my father.
27 "But will God indeed dwell on the earth? Behold, heaven and the heaven of heavens cannot contain You. How much less this temple which I have
built!
28 "Yet regard the prayer of Your servant and his
supplication, O LORD my God, and listen to the cry
and the prayer which Your servant is praying before
You today:
29 "that Your eyes may be open toward this temple
night and day, toward the place of which You said,
'My name shall be there,' that You may hear the prayer
which Your servant makes toward this place.
30 "And may You hear the supplication of Your
servant and of Your people Israel, when they pray toward this place. Hear in heaven Your dwelling place;
and when You hear, forgive.

31 "When anyone sins against his neighbor, and is forced to take an oath, and comes *and* takes an oath before Your altar in this temple,

32 "then hear in heaven, and act, and judge Your servants, condemning the wicked, bringing his way on his head, and justifying the righteous by giving him according to his righteousness.

33 "When Your people Israel are defeated before an enemy because they have sinned against You, and when they turn back to You and confess Your name, and pray and make supplication to You in this temple,

34 "then hear in heaven, and forgive the sin of Your people Israel, and bring them back to the land which You gave to their fathers.

35 "When the heavens are shut up and there is no rain because they have sinned against You, when they pray toward this place and confess Your name, and turn from their sin because You afflict them,

36 "then hear in heaven, and forgive the sin of Your servants, Your people Israel, that You may teach them the good way in which they should walk; and send rain on Your land which You have given to Your people as an inheritance.

37 "When there is famine in the land, pestilence *or* blight *or* mildew, locusts *or* grasshoppers; when their enemy besieges them in the land of their cities; whatever plague or whatever sickness *there is;*

38 "whatever prayer, whatever supplication is made by anyone, *or* by all Your people Israel, when each one knows the plague of his own heart, and spreads out his hands toward this temple:

39 "then hear in heaven Your dwelling place, and forgive, and act, and give to everyone according to all his ways, whose heart You know (for You alone, know the hearts of all the sons of men),

40 "that they may fear You all the days that they live in the land which You gave to our fathers.

41 "Moreover, concerning a foreigner, who *is* not of Your people Israel, but has come from a far country for Your name's sake

42 "(for they will hear of Your great name and Your strong hand and Your outstretched arm), when he comes and prays toward this temple,

43 "hear in heaven Your dwelling place, and do according to all for which the foreigner calls to You, that all peoples of the earth may know Your name and fear You, as *do* Your people Israel, and that they may know that this temple which I have built is called by Your name.

44 "When Your people go out to battle against their enemy, wherever You send them, and when they pray to the LORD toward the city which You have chosen and the temple which I have built for Your name,

45 "then hear in heaven their prayer and their supplication, and maintain their cause.

46 "When they sin against You (for *there is* no one who does not sin), and You become angry with them and deliver them to the enemy, and they take them captive to the land of the enemy, far or near;

47 "*yet* when they come to themselves in the land where they were carried captive, and repent, and make supplication to You in the land of those who took them captive, saying, 'We have sinned and done wrong, we have committed wickedness';

48 "and *when* they return to You with all their heart and with all their soul in the land of their enemies who led them away captive, and pray to You toward their land which You gave to their fathers, the city which You have chosen and the temple which I have built for Your name:

49 "then hear in heaven Your dwelling place their prayer and their supplication, and maintain their cause,

50 "and forgive Your people who have sinned against You, and all their transgressions which they have transgressed against You; and grant them compassion before those who took them captive, that they may have compassion on them

51 "(for they *are* Your people and Your inheritance, whom You brought out of Egypt, out of the iron furnace),

52 "that Your eyes may be open to the supplication of Your servant and the supplication of Your
people Israel, to listen to them whenever they call to
You.
53 "For You separated them from among all the
peoples of the earth *to be* Your inheritance, as You
spoke by Your servant Moses, when You brought our
fathers out of Egypt, O Lord GOD."
54 And so it was, when Solomon had finished
praying all this prayer and supplication to the LORD,
that he arose from before the altar of the LORD, from
kneeling on his knees with his hands spread up to
heaven.
55 Then he stood and blessed all the assembly of
Israel with a loud voice, saying:
56 "Blessed *be* the LORD, who has given rest to
His people Israel, according to all that He promised.
There has not failed one word of all His good promise,
which He promised through His servant Moses.
57 "May the LORD our God be with us, as He was
with our fathers. May He not leave us nor forsake
us,
58 "that He may incline our hearts to Himself, to
walk in all His ways, and to keep His commandments
and His statutes and His judgments, which He commanded our fathers.
59 "And may these words of mine, with which I
have made supplication before the LORD, be near the
LORD our God day and night, that He may maintain
the cause of His servant and the cause of His people
Israel, as each day may require,
60 "that all the peoples of the earth may know that
the LORD *is* God; *there is* no other.
61 "Let your heart therefore be loyal to the LORD
our God, to walk in His statutes and keep His commandments, as at this day."
62 Then the king and all Israel with him offered
sacrifices before the LORD.
63 And Solomon offered a sacrifice of peace offerings, which he offered to the LORD, twenty-two thousand bulls and one hundred and twenty thousand

sheep. So the king and all the children of Israel dedicated the house of the LORD.
64 On the same day the king consecrated the middle of the court that *was* in front of the house of the
LORD; for there he offered burnt offerings, grain offerings, and the fat of the peace offerings, because
the bronze altar that *was* before the LORD *was* too
small to receive the burnt offerings, the grain offerings, and the fat of the peace offerings.
65 At that time Solomon held a feast, and all Israel
with him, a great assembly from the entrance of
Hamath to the Brook of Egypt, before the LORD our
God, seven days and seven *more* days—fourteen days.
66 On the eighth day he sent the people away; and
they blessed the king, and went to their tents joyful
and glad of heart for all the good that the LORD had
done for His servant David, and for Israel His people.

1 Kings 8:1–66

Chapter 8 is composed of three distinct sections: (1) the bringing of the ark and the tabernacle together with its vessels into the temple, and the message of Solomon on that occasion; (2) the dedicatory prayer of Solomon; and (3) the blessing of the congregation followed by their sacrifices. Since the temple was completed in the eighth month (6:38) and not officially dedicated until the seventh month (8:2), it must have stood empty and unused for eleven months, probably so that the dedication could coincide with the Feast of the Tabernacles. No doubt during this interim, the finishing touches were put on the new facility and detailed preparations made for the elaborate dedicatory ceremonies.[36] Although some commentators disagree, the tabernacle in verse 4 is apparently the historical one which had been at Gibeon. It had housed the ark for many years before David made a interim home for it in Jerusalem. The old tent was probably deposited somewhere in the temple as a sacred relic.[37]

The two tablets of stone that Moses had deposited in the ark at Horeb were still there as the only objects in the sacred chest. (However, Heb. 9:4 indicates that Aaron's rod and a pot of manna were also kept in the ark.) As the ark was put in place, a cloud, representing the approving presence of Yahweh, filled the house, and inspired

Solomon to quote the short poem that introduced his formal dedicatory address (vv. 12–13). Language experts say the poem is incomplete and fragmented, and that it apparently had another opening line in its original form. While it is not included in most English translations, the Greek text of this passage gives an opening line, "The Lord has set the sun in the heavens."[38]

The most impressive section of the chapter is the prayer of Solomon beginning with verse 22. It is actually a series of short petitions asking God:

1. To keep His promise to David (vv. 23–26).
2. To maintain His constant presence in the temple and accept the prayers of the worshipers (vv. 27–30).
3. To punish those who swear falsely (vv. 31–32).
4. To send rain during droughts (vv. 35–36).
5. To help Israel in other calamities (vv. 37–40).
6. To hear the prayers of strangers (vv. 41–43).
7. To give Israel victory in battle (vv. 44–45).
8. To have mercy and forgiveness during captivity (vv. 46–51).
9. To answer both the king and his people (vv. 52–53).

Apparently Solomon prayed in the open courtyard beside the altar of burnt offerings, standing, as Chronicles adds, on a scaffold or pulpit. The custom of standing with hands upraised to God was a more common stance of prayer in the Old Testament than kneeling, although verse 54 indicates Solomon was kneeling with his hands spread up to heaven. Obviously during the lengthy prayer the king changed his posture from standing to kneeling. It was not unusual for the king to assume the priestly role as Solomon does in leading this worship service. Other kings, including David, Ahaz, Jeroboam, and Hezekiah, did the same thing, indicating that Israel's monarchs must have enjoyed priestly prerogatives.[39]

Solomon's petition has some important features that provide valuable lessons in prayer. Notice that God answered the request for an everlasting kingdom, but in God's own way and in His own time. Eventually David's line showed itself unworthy of God's blessings and it died away. But in the mystery of God's providence, He restored it again through the perfect obedience of David's Son, Jesus of Nazareth, who reigns forever and forever!

Often, just when we think our prayer has not been heard or our request denied, God in His own time answers us in far better ways than we could imagine. A middle manager who had worked for an independent oil company in Houston for thirty years was a faithful member of our suburban church. In prayer meeting one Wednesday night, he shared with the church family his anxiety about a financial squeeze in the company that had spawned rumors about cut-backs and employee layoffs. While he felt relatively safe with thirty years of seniority, he asked the church to join him in the prayer that he would not be fired. Within a few weeks, Tom came to my study devastated. The worst had happened. He had been fired. "What do I do now?" he asked. "I'm fifty-four. I've invested all my working life with this company. There's nothing else I'm trained to do." But the most painful question he raised was not really expressed, just latent in his plaintive statement: "We all prayed so hard this wouldn't happen, and I really believed. . . ." His voice trailed off without saying it, but the unspoken problem was obvious, "Why didn't God answer my prayer?" A difficult eleven months followed with numerous temporary positions and disappointing job searches. But before a year had passed, Tom joined another firm. A few months later, he stood before the same Wednesday night crowd with a beaming face. His salary was 50 percent higher than he had earned in the old job, and the opportunities for advancement much better. "God answered my prayers after all—and He provided more than I asked!" It reminds us of Paul's promise that God "is able to do exceedingly abundantly above all that we ask or think" (Eph. 3:20).

Some of the words in this passage are interesting. For example, there are three different words for prayer in verse 28: *Tĕpillâ,* meaning "intercession" or "supplication"; *Tĕḥinnâ,* "entreaty" or "earnest plea for mercy"; and *Rinnâ,* "a wailing cry of petition."[40]

The word *ʾānap,* translated *"become angry"* in verse 46, literally means "flare the nostrils," a vivid description of the wrath of God. In verse 50 one of the strongest words for sin in the Hebrew language is used. The word *pešaʿ,* "transgression," stands for a deliberate rebellion against the known will of God. This is in contrast to a milder word used elsewhere in this passage, *ḥāṭāʾ,* which refers to an unwitting delinquency or a minor ritual infringement.[41]

Notice the many words for law in verse 58: *"ways,"* referring to God's providential plan, *"commandments,"* pointing to authority that obligates one to absolute obedience, *"statutes,"* describing a code written down like the laws on the tables of stone, and *"judgments,"* meaning those divine decisions that provide clues to the mysteries of life. These are only a few of numerous synonyms for God's law in the Hebrew language. Why did the language of the Israelites have so many? Possibly for the same reason that there are so many synonyms for "money" in English—because those who helped frame the language thought so much about that subject and took great delight in it.

Having completed his prayer, Solomon stood to bless the people. And what a moving scene it must have been: standing there in the newly constructed temple, with a united nation gathered before him, the cloud of God's presence still filling the house, and unprecedented peace on every border. The inspired man of prayer looked back on the long road from Sinai and the wilderness and summed up the entire history of Israel in one sentence: *"There has not failed one word of all His good promise, which He promised through His servant Moses"* (v. 56). There had been many a dark day when their enemies had been victorious, and many a hard-fought battlefield had been stained with martyrs' blood, but it had all pointed to this calm moment when the nation's multitudes were gathered in worship and their land was safe.

Looking back, he saw many heroes in the long line behind them. Like the writer of Hebrews, he had no time to tell of Gideon, Barak, Samson, Jephthah, Samuel, and David, who through faith had "turned to flight the armies of the aliens" (Heb. 11:34). There was time to point to one name only—the name of the true Deliverer of Israel. It was the Lord who had given rest to His people (v. 56). We will learn that same truth today in prosperous America if we look at history from the vantage point of the temple. From that perspective we will see it as His Story, and while being grateful for a noble heritage of patriotic heroes, we must acknowledge that all our national blessings have come ultimately from the Lord.

Verse 60 is one of several texts in the Old Testament that reveal God's missionary purpose for Israel, *"that all the peoples of the earth may know that the Lord is God."* Solomon understood this divine plan and asked for God's blessing upon the nation, not for their own sakes alone but also for the eternal benefit of those nations who would come to God through their witness.

NOTES

1. C. F. Keil, *The Books of the Kings,* Biblical Commentary on the Old Testament, ed. C. F. Keil and F. Delitzsch, vol. 4 (Grand Rapids: Eerdmans, 1950), 51.

2. Ibid., 57ff.

3. Charles F. Burney, *Notes on the Hebrew Text of the Books of Kings* (Oxford: Clarendon Press, 1903), 527ff.

4. Gwilym H. Jones, *1 and 2 Kings,* New Century Bible Commentary, ed. Ronald E. Clements (Grand Rapids: Eerdmans, 1984), 154.

5. Keil, 57.

6. Jones, 154.

7. Keil, 57.

8. Norman H. Snaith, Ralph W. Sockman, and Raymond Calkins, "The First and Second Books of Kings," in *The Interpreter's Bible,* vol. 3 (Nashville: Abingdon, 1954), 52.

9. John Gray, *I and II Kings,* Old Testament Library (Philadelphia: Westminster, 1963), 146.

10. Keil, 57.

11. Ibid.

12. Ibid.

13. Jones, 156.

14. Burney, 53.

15. Robert C. Dentan, *Kings and Chronicles,* Layman's Bible Commentary, vol. 7 (Richmond: John Knox Press, 1964), 30.

16. Gray, 147.

17. Keil, 57.

18. Snaith, Sockman, and Calkins, 51.

19. Simon J. DeVries, *1 Kings,* Word Biblical Commentary, ed. John D. W. Watts, vol. 12 (Waco, TX: Word Books, 1985), 83.

20. Burney, 53.

21. Gray, 148.

22. Dentan, 24.

23. Ibid., 31.

24. DeVries, 97.

25. Keil, 71.

26. I. W. Slotki, *Kings* (London: Soncino Press, 1950), 41.

27. Keil, 71.

28. Slotki, 47.

29. Gray, 167.

30. Slotki, 48.

31. Jones, 183.
32. Dentan, 35.
33. Ibid., 26.
34. Gray, 180.
35. Ibid., 188.
36. DeVries, 124.
37. Keil, 120.
38. Jones, 196.
39. Ibid., 200.
40. Ibid., 201.
41. Gray, 211.

CHAPTER FOUR

The Golden Age of Solomon

1 Kings 9:1–10:29

INTRODUCTION

Twenty-four years had passed since the aging David had named Solomon his son as the successor to the throne and the new king had been hurriedly anointed in an emergency ceremony at Gihon. After putting down all internal political opposition and consolidating his kingdom with Israel's international allies, Solomon had gone to the ancient worship center at Gibeon to offer sacrifices to Yahweh. There God appeared to him in a dream, offering him the gift of wisdom and the promise of riches, honor, and long life. Now, twenty-four years later, God appeared to Solomon a second time, reminding the king that his prayers were still being answered and promising continued blessings on his kingdom if certain conditions were met by Solomon and the people.

With this renewed "covenant" reinforcing his efforts, Solomon moved on to establish a rich and powerful nation that for many years was the center of wealth and wisdom for the entire world. This section describes the glory of the "Golden Age of Israel," and how the nations of the world, acknowledging that glory, paid homage to Solomon.

GOD APPEARS TO SOLOMON A SECOND TIME

9:1 And it came to pass, when Solomon had finished building the house of the LORD and the king's house, and all Solomon's desire which he wanted to do,

2 that the LORD appeared to Solomon the second
time, as He had appeared to him at Gibeon.
3 And the LORD said to him: "I have heard your
prayer and your supplication that you have made before Me; I have consecrated this house which you
have built to put My name there forever, and My
eyes and My heart will be there perpetually.
4 "Now if you walk before Me as your father
David walked, in integrity of heart and in uprightness, to do according to all that I have commanded
you, *and* if you keep My statutes and My judgments,
5 "then I will establish the throne of your kingdom over Israel forever, as I promised David your
father, saying, 'You shall not fail to have a man on
the throne of Israel.'
6 "But if you or your sons at all turn from following Me, and do not keep My commandments *and* My
statutes which I have set before you, but go and
serve other gods and worship them,
7 "then I will cut off Israel from the land which I
have given them; and this house which I have consecrated for My name I will cast out of My sight. Israel
will be a proverb and a byword among all peoples.
8 "And *as for* this house, *which* is exalted, everyone who passes by it will be astonished and will
hiss, and say, 'Why has the LORD done thus to this
land and to this house?'
9 "Then they will answer, 'Because they forsook
the LORD their God, who brought their fathers out
of the land of Egypt, and have embraced other gods,
and worshiped them and served them; therefore the
LORD has brought all this calamity on them.'"

1 Kings 9:1–9

We are not told where or exactly when the appearance took place, but we are given a clue in verse 2 where it says, *"as He had appeared to him at Gibeon."* In the Gibeon experience, God appeared at night in a dream, so we may assume this second appearance was also in a dream, perhaps in the king's private chambers in the palace. Some confirmation of this is found in the parallel passage in Chronicles, which adds that the appearance occurred at night.

God's first appearance to Solomon was no surprise, since Solomon had gone to Gibeon specifically to worship the Lord and seek His face. But this second appearance may have come unexpectedly, not in response to Solomon's worshipful seeking, but by God's own initiative. It may be that the Lord decided to confront Solomon again, because the king was slipping deeper and deeper into apostasy.

Sometimes, when we have completed a demanding and challenging task, we are tempted to relax our commitment, slacken our discipline, and give in to self-indulgence. It is in these moments that we need spiritual encouragement. God, knowing our weaknesses, often schedules His manifestations to bring that motivation to us at just the right moment. So He appeared to Solomon as he finished the great work on the temple and the palace. During the excitement and pressure of building, such a manifestation was not so important, but now with the work completed, there was the danger that the king would grow spiritually insensitive and indifferent. So God appeared to speak words of stimulus, promise, and warning.

The answered prayers to which Yahweh refers in His message to Solomon were not only those delivered at the dedication of the temple thirteen years earlier but also, no doubt, many other unrecorded prayers Solomon had offered since that time. Notice how God gave Solomon more than he requested. In his prayer requests at the dedication of the temple, the king had asked God to let His name and His eyes be in the temple perpetually. In His answer, God sanctified the temple not only with His name and His eyes but with His heart as well. The truth of this passage, echoed in so many others, is that God always gives more than we think or ask. Once we realize that this pattern of abundant giving is typical of God, we should ask with greater faith when we approach the Father for His blessings.

While there is a special sense in which God promised His presence in the temple, He has also promised to be with all His people wherever they may be. God's immanence is never limited to sacred places like the temple. This was the glorious truth Solomon's father, David, sang about in Psalm 139, "Where can I go from Your spirit? Or where can I flee from Your presence? If I ascend into heaven, You are there; If I make my bed in hell, behold, You are there."

Every time I read that verse, I think of my friend Jim Irwin, the astronaut who was one of the first men to walk on the moon. We have shared fellowship on the tennis court, around the dinner table, and at the launch site at Cape Canaveral. He has preached in our church and spoken in the chapel of our seminary, and every time I visit with him I am inspired by his testimony. He tells how he drove the moon buggy to the foot of the majestic mountains on the moon's surface and looked back at the beautiful but fragile globe we call Earth. Then he says, "There on the lunar surface, I felt God's presence very real and close." God's presence on the moon! What a confirmation of this ancient promise from God's word that His presence would be with us wherever we are.

Beginning with verse 3, God sets forth certain conditions under which He will act toward Solomon and the people of Israel in the future. They are expressed in the literary forms of "if . . . then" and "if not . . . then." The list of positive conditions is given first and forms a basic outline of the devout life:

1. *"If you walk before Me as David did."* In other words, we are continually to be conscious of His presence and live and work knowing that the Father's watchful eye oversees everything we do.

2. *If you walk "in integrity of heart."* The heart was considered, as it is symbolically today, the center of the personality and the will of humankind. "As a man thinks in his heart, so is he," was one of Solomon's proverbs. So sincerity of heart in one's relationship with God is of ultimate importance to God.

3. *If you walk "in uprightness."* Integrity of heart comes first, because it does no good to perform righteous deeds if our hearts are not right with God first. Neither is it enough to have our hearts right if we do not walk uprightly. Faith without works is dead. Orthodoxy and emotional experiences are important, but they lack fulfillment if they do not issue in holy and God-pleasing living.

4. *If you "do according to all I have commanded you."* Obedience has always been the test of true faith. So God included in this condition, and in the next two, the necessity to obey all His laws.

5. *"If you keep My statutes."*

6. *If you keep "My judgments."*

The reward for meeting the positive conditions is that God would establish Solomon's throne forever as He had promised David his father. (That Davidic promise is recorded in 2:4 and in 2 Sam. 7:16.) Isn't it encouraging that God continued to honor David in spite of his imperfections? Looking back on David's somewhat blemished career, one wonders how God could use a man who, even though he maintained his devout faith and trust in Yahweh, was morally flawed. It seems to suggest that God can work with us if we continue to trust Him, even though our lives are not perfect. The moon is pitted with the scars of thousands of volcanoes and meteor craters, but when we see it in its fullness on a dark night, it shines like a disc of silver in spite of the scars. If we continue to surrender our imperfect lives to Him, God can make them effective in spite of our failures.

The negative conditions are listed in verse 6. Here the singular "you" is changed to the plural as God included the children of Solomon and the entire nation of Israel. In this case the King James translation is more accurate because it uses the singular word "thou" in verse 4 and the plural word "ye" in verse 6 to show where the Hebrew changes the pronoun. More recent English translations do not make this distinction and the change from singular to plural is hidden. The negative conditions are:

1. *If you "turn from following Me."*
2. *If you "do not keep My commandments."*
3. *If you do not keep "My statutes."*
4. *If you "go and serve other Gods and worship them."*

The punishments for committing these negative shortcomings are related to the land, the temple, and the people. They are listed in verse 7:

1. *"Then I will cut off Israel from the land."* The word is literally "send away" from the land.[1]

2. *Then I will cast the temple out of My sight.* He had promised that His eye would be in the temple perpetually if they obeyed Him. But if they disobeyed, then the opposite would take place: the temple would be out of His sight.

3. *Then "Israel will be a proverb and a byword."* The word *"proverb"* is *māšāl,* meaning "a pithy statement made in mockery." The word *"byword"* is *šĕnînâ,* meaning "a pointed, witty, or spiteful saying."[2] Israel's tragic experience would become an example and an admonition to others. The ruins of their culture would stand as a proverbial symbol of disaster like "Sodom and Gomorrah" or "Waterloo."

4. *Then passersby will hiss and question the destruction in astonishment.* The temple was exalted by virtue of being built on a high

mountain. It was lifted up that all might see the glory of God. Now its ruins, standing high and exalted, would be an example to the world of the punishment of God. Peake believes the translation in verse 8 should be "shall be a heap of ruins" instead of "which is exalted."[3]

5. *Then the answer will be "They forsook the Lord."* Those who see the destruction or read about it in this book would know that Israel's calamity was not because God was powerless to protect His people, but because they forsook Him.

The grim punishments in verses 7–9 are the other side to the bright promises in verse 5. This teaches that God draws us to Himself both by holding out His hand full of good things and also by stretching out His hand of judgment and punishment. The promises come first, the threats second, because it is God's nature to bless rather than to smite. To lavish blessings is His delight, but judgment is a work forced on Him by our sin. Some would call God's threat of judgments harsh, but it is never harsh to warn a potential victim of the dangers that lie ahead. To say that the Bible is harsh when it warns us that "the wages of sin is death," is to miss the point that these warnings are given in love to keep us from danger.

Following the nuclear explosion and fire at the Soviet power plant in Chernobyl near Kiev, the radioactive fuel core had to be buried under a mountain of concrete. There seemed to be no way to repair or remove the dangerous and volatile substance as it smoldered and continued to emit radiation. So the engineers decided to seal it off, to leave it buried beneath the cement and steel for centuries until the core would eventually lose its power to destroy. So the monument of cement and steel stands as a symbol of man's ineffective efforts to control the power of nature and of man's fragility and dependence in spite of his technological advances. All who pass by Chernobyl will look and be reminded.

In like manner, the destruction of the temple and subsequent calamities of Israel would become as God said, a warning to others of the tragic results of disobedience. In a forest, those trees whose leaves are vibrant and green give eloquent testimony of the power of light, but so does the white lifeless trunk of the dead tree that was struck by lightning. It may be that Israel has been as convincing a witness for God in its suffering as it was when the nation was at rest in the promised land.

Solomon Establishes Financial, Labor, and Trade Policies

9:10 Now it happened at the end of twenty years,
when Solomon had built the two houses, the house
of the LORD and the king's house
11 (Hiram the king of Tyre had supplied Solomon
with cedar and cypress and gold, as much as he desired), *that* King Solomon then gave Hiram twenty
cities in the land of Galilee.
12 Then Hiram went from Tyre to see the cities
which Solomon had given him, but they did not
please him.
13 So he said, "What *kind of* cities *are* these which
you have given me, my brother?" And he called them
the land of Cabul, as they are to this day.
14 Then Hiram sent the king one hundred and
twenty talents of gold.
15 And this *is* the reason for the labor force which
King Solomon raised: to build the house of the LORD,
his own house, the Millo, the wall of Jerusalem,
Hazor, Megiddo, and Gezer.
16 (Pharaoh king of Egypt had gone up and taken
Gezer and burned it with fire, had killed the Canaanites who dwelt in the city, and had given it *as* a dowry
to his daughter, Solomon's wife.)
17 And Solomon built Gezer, Lower Beth Horon,
18 Baalath, and Tadmor in the wilderness, in the
land *of Judah,*
19 all the storage cities that Solomon had, cities for
his chariots and cities for his cavalry, and whatever
Solomon desired to build in Jerusalem, in Lebanon,
and in all the land of his dominion.
20 All the people *who were* left of the Amorites,
Hittites, Perizzites, Hivites, and Jebusites, who *were*
not of the children of Israel—
21 that is, their descendants who were left in the
land after them, whom the children of Israel had not
been able to destroy completely—from these Solomon
raised forced labor, as it is to this day.
22 But of the children of Israel Solomon made no
forced laborers, because they *were* men of war and

his servants: his officers, his captains, commanders
of his chariots, and his cavalry.
23 Others *were* chiefs of the officials who *were*
over Solomon's work: five hundred and fifty, who
ruled over the people who did the work.
24 But Pharaoh's daughter came up from the City
of David to her house which *Solomon* had built for
her. Then he built the Millo.
25 Now three times a year Solomon offered burnt
offerings and peace offerings on the altar which he
had built for the LORD, and he burned incense with
them *on the altar* that *was* before the LORD. So he
finished the temple.
26 King Solomon also built a fleet of ships at Ezion
Geber, which *is* near Elath on the shore of the Red
Sea, in the land of Edom.
27 Then Hiram sent his servants with the fleet,
seamen who knew the sea, to work with the servants
of Solomon.
28 And they went to Ophir, and acquired four
hundred and twenty talents of gold from there, and
brought *it* to King Solomon.

1 Kings 9:10–28

This section explains how Solomon was able to build his extensive buildings and bring Jerusalem to its high level as a world-class capital, the undisputed center of wealth and power. His accomplishments were made possible by (1) his financial alliance with King Hiram (vv. 10–14), (2) his forced labor plan (vv. 15–25), and (3) his shipping fleet to Ophir (vv. 26–28).

First, the passage reviews the financial arrangements Solomon made with King Hiram of Tyre. In part, these were outlined in chapter 5, where Hiram supplied certain raw materials and craftsmen in exchange for wheat and oil from Solomon. Now in this passage we learn that additional financial arrangements were necessary. It may be that Solomon ran short of cash because of his ambitious building plans and was unable to pay the agreed price of wheat and oil. The shortage necessitated the payment of twenty cities.[4] Another explanation is that the wheat and oil paid for the timber and craftsmen Hiram supplied, but that the twenty cities were payment for the gold Hiram gave Solomon, some of which is mentioned in verse 14.[5] Still others believe that after Solomon's building campaign was over, the two kings exchanged gifts as a celebration. Solomon gave Hiram twenty cities; Hiram gave Solomon 120 talents of gold.[6] Yet another explanation is that the cities, which were on the border nearest Tyre and were inhabited by non-Israelites, were cities of disputed ownership, and Solomon "gave in" and ceded them to Hiram in order to keep peace between the two friendly nations.[7]

Whatever the explanation for the exchange, it is clear that Hiram considered the cities to be worthless, and taunted Solomon for giving him "good-for-nothing" towns. Hiram nicknamed the cities *kābûl,* which literally means "good-for-nothing." Even though he was displeased with the trade, Hiram went ahead with it in good humor and sent Solomon the 120 talents of gold. A talent is calculated to be about 70.4 pounds. Using that equivalent, and the current price for gold of about $500 a troy ounce, one can calculate Hiram's gift to be about $50,688,000. Not a bad trade for twenty good-for-nothing villages on a distant frontier. Solomon was a clever if not a devious trader, and the author gives this as one explanation of how he was able to accomplish so much.

Second, Solomon's vast accomplishments were due in part to the labor force he enlisted for the work. In addition to the fortification of Jerusalem, including *"the Millo"* which was probably a famous tower on the wall, the king also built fortress cities, chariot cities, and store cities across the land. The strategic locations of these military installations have been approvingly vindicated by military strategists through the centuries.

For example, the chariot city of Megiddo was strategically located at the entrance to the Plain of Jezreel on the trunk highway from the Euphrates to the Nile. I visited the archaeological excavation of this ancient city where sections of the fortifications from Solomon's day can still be seen. Stables, chariot stalls, barracks, and stone walls all give evidence of the wise military planning that elevated Israel to prominence as a world power in this period. Anyone analyzing the British campaign in Palestine during the First World War will observe Solomon's acumen in seizing and fortifying strategic points in the land.

How was Solomon able to accomplish all this? Manpower. He raised a labor force from among the captive people whom Israel conquered as they occupied the land. Usually seven different groups are listed: the Canaanites, the Girgazites, the Amorites, the Hittites, the Perizzites, the Hivites, and the Jebusites. Only five are mentioned here. From among these Solomon conscripted forced labor. It is made very clear that he did not use the Israelites as forced laborers. They were recruited only on a rotating plan of service described in chapter 5. Here, we are told that the Israelites were used, not as common laborers, but as men of war, servants to the king, officers, captains, commanders of chariots, cavalry, and chiefs of officials.

The interesting phrase in verse 21, *"as it is to this day,"* suggests that such labor practices were still in effect when the author of 1 Kings wrote his book. This would seem to argue for an authorship before the destruction of Jerusalem in 586 B.C.

Third, Solomon was able to accomplish so much because of his fleet of merchant ships sailing from Ezion Geber to Ophir (vv. 26–28). With the help of his friend Hiram, Solomon built and launched a fleet of trade vessels on the Red Sea to bring supplies to Israel. The locations of Ezion Geber and Ophir are uncertain. The port, Ezion Geber, must have been on the northern shore of the Gulf of Akabah. Ophir is thought to have been in southern Arabia or possibly in Africa or India.

The Queen of Sheba Visits King Solomon

> 10:1 Now when the queen of Sheba heard of the fame of Solomon concerning the name of the LORD, she came to test him with hard questions.
>
> 2 She came to Jerusalem with a very great retinue, with camels that bore spices, very much gold, and precious stones; and when she came to Solomon, she spoke with him about all that was in her heart.
>
> 3 So Solomon answered all her questions; there was nothing so difficult for the king that he could not explain *it* to her.
>
> 4 And when the queen of Sheba had seen all the wisdom of Solomon, the house that he had built,
>
> 5 the food on his table, the seating of his servants, the service of his waiters and their apparel, his cupbearers, and his entryway by which he went up to the house of the LORD, there was no more spirit in her.

6 Then she said to the king: "It was a true report
which I heard in my own land about your words and
your wisdom.
7 "However I did not believe the words until I
came and saw with my own eyes; and indeed the
half was not told me. Your wisdom and prosperity
exceed the fame of which I heard.
8 "Happy *are* your men and happy *are* these your
servants, who stand continually before you *and* hear
your wisdom!
9 Blessed be the LORD your God, who delighted
in you, setting you on the throne of Israel! Because
the LORD has loved Israel forever, therefore He made
you king, to do justice and righteousness."
10 Then she gave the king one hundred and twenty
talents of gold, spices in great quantity, and precious
stones. There never again came such abundance of
spices as the queen of Sheba gave to King Solomon.
11 Also, the ships of Hiram, which brought gold
from Ophir, brought great *quantities* of almug wood
and precious stones from Ophir.
12 And the king made steps of the almug wood for
the house of the LORD and for the king's house, also
harps and stringed instruments for singers. There
never again came such almug wood, nor has the like
been seen to this day.
13 Now King Solomon gave the queen of Sheba
all she desired, whatever she asked, besides what
Solomon had given her according to the royal generosity. So she turned and went to her own country,
she and her servants.

1 Kings 10:1–13

These verses tell one of the most intriguing and fascinating stories in the Books of Kings. The story must have had that same appeal in the first century, because Jesus referred to it in Matt. 12:42. "The queen of the South will rise up in the judgment with this generation and condemn it, for she came from the ends of the earth to hear the wisdom of Solomon; and indeed a greater than Solomon is here." It was this story in chapter 10 that caught the attention of Jesus and seemed to Him to be a good illustration of His point in Matthew 12.

Scholars generally agree the kingdom of Sheba was in the southern part of ancient Arabia. According to Genesis 25, Sheba was the oldest son of Jokshan, Abraham's son by Keturah. It is probable that this man's descendants became identified with the grandson of Cush and the grandson of Eber, both of whom bore the name Sheba, and that together they established the kingdom of Sheba or Sabea in Arabia.[8]

She was a queen, not the wife of a king, but the ruler of this pre-Islamic kingdom. She traveled fifteen hundred miles with a retinue of camels bearing precious gifts. Having heard of his legendary wisdom, she came to test Solomon with hard questions, or riddles. The word is the same one used for the riddles by which Samson confounded the Philistines in the Book of Judges. Apparently such tests of sagacity, wit, and poetic skill were traditional in the ancient Oriental courts. Josephus describes a similar test of Solomon's wisdom by King Hiram.[9] The Arabians were especially famous for their collections of riddles. One, by a collector named Meidani, contains six thousand riddles.[10] Solomon himself is credited in chapter 4 as having composed three thousand such riddles.

Solomon, of course, passed her test with flying colors, and she exclaimed that *"the half was not told me. Your wisdom and prosperity exceed the fame of which I heard"* (v. 7).

The queen was also impressed with the wealth and splendor of the buildings in Jerusalem, the king's banquets, his servants, and the rich apparel they wore. Especially magnificent was the *"entryway by which he went up to the house of the Lord."* This may have been an elaborately decorated private approach that only the king used.[11] Or she may have been awed by the splendid retinue that accompanied the king when he went to the temple. (See comments below concerning v. 16 and the golden shields used in such processions.)

She was overwhelmed. Verse 5 says when she saw it all *"there was no more spirit in her."* Spirit is also the word for breath, so some translations say, "she was breathless" or "it took her breath away." Her blessing in verses 8–9 probably should begin, "Happy are your wives" instead of *"Happy are your men."* The parallel passage in Chronicles uses this phraseology, and it seems like something a queen would say.

After leaving gifts of gold, precious stones, and spices, the queen began her long journey home. Following a parenthetical insertion about the wealth brought to Solomon by the ships of Hiram, the story of the queen of Sheba concludes with verse 13, where it says Solomon *"gave the queen of Sheba all she desired, whatever she asked, besides what Solomon had given her according to the royal generosity."* Some ancient interpreters have given this passage a sexual meaning, maintaining that the queen desired a son by Solomon. In Jewish tradition, such a union transpired and their son was Nebuchadrezzar, while in Ethiopic tradition, their son was Merelik I, the founder of the Ethiopic dynasty.[12]

The glory of the temple was intended to draw the attention of the world to the majesty of God, and to turn the minds of foreign visitors toward Him in faith. Solomon made that very clear in his dedicatory prayer in 8:41–43. "Moreover, concerning a foreigner, who is not of Your people Israel, but has come from a far country for Your name's sake . . . when he comes and prays toward this temple, hear in heaven . . . that all peoples of the earth may know Your name and fear You . . . and that they may know that this temple which I have built is called by Your name."

But here is the first test of that purpose, and it apparently didn't work. The queen of Sheba was impressed with the majestic architecture of the temple, but she did not turn in faith to Yahweh. Her statement about the blessings of the Lord on Israel and Solomon in verse 9 were no more than a polite reference to Solomon's God. And the Scripture plainly says that having seen the splendor of the temple, *"she turned and went to her own country, she and her servants."* There is no record that she accepted Solomon's God, who was so majestically edified by the temple.

Does that not suggest that there must be more than magnificent buildings and elaborate ceremonies to draw unbelieving men and women to faith in God? To the queen of Sheba, the temple with all its glory was only an emotional spectacle with temporary effects. It was a momentary thrill and aroused her wonder, but it did not make her a convert to Yahweh. By contrast, many others have been drawn to God by plainer and simpler aids to worship. David knew God under the stars in the Judean desert. He was deeply moved by the simple architecture of the ark and the tabernacle tent in the wilderness. The queen, on the other hand, saw the mighty temple, but was not moved toward God. Vast cathedrals, super church mega-sanctuaries, vast throngs of worshipers, and massive organizations may impress unbelievers with the greatness of deity, but without a sense of His personal presence, no converts will be made.

She did not take God home to Sheba with her. That's the real test of the genuineness of a spiritual encounter. Perhaps some church groups in our day are putting too much emphasis on large buildings and spectacular programs, which arouse curiosity and draw the crowds. But if, once their attention is attracted, we do not give them an opportunity for a personal encounter with God through faith in Jesus Christ, they too will "turn, go to their own country" without Him.

Here is another of those biblical references to God's missionary purpose for His chosen people. The story of a foreign queen drawn to the wisdom of Israel from a distant land is a picture of the true relation Israel was to have with other nations in God's plan. They were not to be competing with other nations for wealth and military power. They were not to be at war with other nations, but they were chosen to point other nations to God. They were to be a light to enlighten the Gentiles.

It is obvious that the queen came for some purpose more serious than exchanging riddles with the wise king. A journey of fifteen hundred miles is too long and the rigors of travel in that century across desert lands too demanding for such a trivial purpose. The gifts were too great, the cost too high for her to have come just to satisfy her curiosity about the rumors she had heard. She must have been a serious seeker after deeper truth. She must have had a yearning, a hunger for God that drove her to Jerusalem. She came to Solomon tortured by eternal questions, and apparently the king was so anxious to show her the secular glories of his kingdom that he forgot the noble purpose for which he and the nation had been chosen. It's a tragedy easily repeated by individuals and churches today.

When Jesus used the queen of Sheba as an illustration in Matthew 12, He pointed to the fact that she was a seeker, and that she was to be commended for her quest. At great sacrifice, humility, and effort she made her way to the best source of truth available to her. The passage has a lesson for desperate seekers today. A greater than Solomon has come. His wisdom is infinitely greater. His power is greater. He is the way and the truth. Every question has its ultimate answer in Him. He is the satisfaction of every yearning. And when we meet Him, we too find that the half has not been told. He is greater than our highest expectations.

THE GREAT WEALTH AND POWER OF KING SOLOMON

10:14 The weight of gold that came to Solomon yearly
was six hundred and sixty-six talents of gold,
15 besides *that* from the traveling merchants, from
the income of traders, from all the kings of Arabia,
and from the governors of the country.
16 And King Solomon made two hundred large
shields *of* hammered gold; six hundred *shekels* of gold
went into each shield.
17 He also *made* three hundred shields *of* hammered gold; three minas of gold went into each shield.
The king put them in the House of the Forest of
Lebanon.
18 Moreover the king made a great throne of
ivory, and overlaid it with pure gold.
19 The throne had six steps, and the top of the
throne *was* round at the back; *there were* armrests on
either side of the place of the seat, and two lions
stood beside the armrests.
20 Twelve lions stood there, one on each side of
the six steps; nothing like *this* had been made for any
other kingdom.
21 All King Solomon's drinking vessels *were*
gold, and all the vessels of the House of the Forest
of Lebanon *were* pure gold. Not *one was* silver, for
this was accounted as nothing in the days of
Solomon.
22 For the king had merchant ships at sea with the
fleet of Hiram. Once every three years the merchant
ships came bringing gold, silver, ivory, apes, and
monkeys.
23 So King Solomon surpassed all the kings of the
earth in riches and wisdom.
24 Now all the earth sought the presence of
Solomon to hear his wisdom, which God had put in
his heart.
25 Each man brought his present: articles of silver
and gold, garments, armor, spices, horses, and mules,
at a set rate year by year.
26 And Solomon gathered chariots and horsemen;
he had one thousand four hundred chariots and

twelve thousand horsemen, whom he stationed in the chariot cities and with the king at Jerusalem.

27 The king made silver *as common* in Jerusalem as stones, and he made cedar trees as abundant as the sycamores which *are* in the lowland.

28 Also Solomon had horses imported from Egypt and Keveh; the king's merchants bought them in Keveh at the *current* price.

29 Now a chariot that was imported from Egypt cost six hundred *shekels* of silver, and a horse one hundred and fifty; and thus, through their agents, they exported *them* to all the kings of the Hittites and the kings of Syria.

1 Kings 10:14–29

The last verses of chapter 10 provide a final review of the fabulous wealth and power of Solomon's monarchy before the tragic ending described in chapter 11. First, we read about his gold. An annual income over and above what he received from merchants, traders, and other kings and governors was $281,318,400. He had so much gold, he had to think up creative ways to use it, and when it came to gold, Solomon could be very creative. For example, he fashioned ceremonial shields out of gold to hang on the columns of the House of the Forest of Lebanon when they were not being used in his kingly processions. The large shields, like those the soldiers used to protect the entire body, would be valued today at $120,000 each, and he made two hundred of them. Then he made three hundred small round shields like those the soldiers carried on their left arms, each costing, in current dollars, $30,000. That was $33,000,000 in gold shields alone, just to be used by his guards when the king went up to the temple. No wonder the queen of Sheba was amazed at "his entryway by which he went up to the house of the Lord" (v. 5).

Next we are told Solomon built himself an ivory and gold throne decorated with the figures of lions (probably representing the lion of the tribe of Judah). Verse 19 says it was *"round at the back,"* but other translations say "the back of the throne was a calf's head." Since the calf was the symbol of pagan worship, could this indicate that already the influence of foreign gods was creeping into Solomon's kingdom? The throne had six steps leading to the top level, which would be the seventh, a number with important meaning in ancient Israel.

As further evidence of Solomon's wealth, the passage describes how not only the rare ceremonial vessels but even the common drinking vessels of the king were made of gold. Gold was so common a commodity in Israel that silver was *"accounted as nothing"* (v. 21), and was *"as common in Jerusalem as stones"* (v. 27). Much of his wealth was imported from visiting dignitaries who came to pay respects to the king and by his own fleet of trading ships. His fleet in the Red Sea was described in chapter 9, but here in verse 22 we are told he had another fleet of trading ships in the Mediterranean. The word translated *"merchant ships"* is literally "ships of Tarshish," indicating deep-sea vessels that sailed to iron smelters on the coasts of Spain. The three years required for their journey does not necessarily point to a long journey, since the ships stopped at numerous ports along the way. What Solomon did with the imported apes and baboons (or peacocks as some translations have it) is not known.[13] Finally, the passage indicates that Solomon had so many horses and chariots that he made additional income by exporting them to the king of the Hittites and the king of Syria.

His wealth was seen as the fulfillment of God's promises to Solomon at Gibeon at the beginning of his reign. But the prosperity Solomon enjoyed and the wisdom that God gave him in such abundance did not save his kingdom. While much of Solomon's life reads like a happy fairy tale, it certainly doesn't end like one—with everybody living happily ever after. Chapter 11 introduces the final chapter of Israel's golden age, and it has a sad ending.

NOTES

1. I. W. Slotki, *Kings* (London: Soncino Press, 1950), 70.
2. Charles F. Burney, *Notes on the Hebrew Text of the Books of Kings* (Oxford: Clarendon Press, 1903), 132.
3. John Mauchline, "I and II Kings," in *Peake's Commentary on the Bible,* ed. Matthew Black and H. H. Rowley (London: Thomas Nelson and Sons, 1962), 342.

4. Gwilym H. Jones, *1 and 2 Kings,* New Century Bible Commentary, ed. Ronald E. Clements (Grand Rapids: Eerdmans, 1984), 212.

5. Ibid.

6. Slotki, 72.

7. Simon J. DeVries, *1 Kings,* Word Biblical Commentary, ed. John D. W. Watts, vol. 12 (Waco, TX: Word Books, 1985), 132.

8. Merrill C. Tenney, ed., *The Zondervan Pictorial Bible Dictionary* (Grand Rapids: Zondervan, 1963), 779.

9. Jones, 222.

10. Karl Chr. W. F. Bähr, *The Books of the Kings,* Commentary on the Holy Scriptures, ed. John Peter Lange (Grand Rapids: Zondervan, 1960), 117.

11. Ibid.

12. Jones, 225.

13. W. F. Albright, "Ivory and Apes of Ophir," *The American Journal of Semitic Languages* 37 (1920–21): 144.

CHAPTER FIVE

The Decline and Death of Solomon

1 Kings 11:1–43

INTRODUCTION

It is a striking characteristic of Scripture that its accounts of its heroes never conceal their faults. Most secular histories, speaking of the noblest leader of a nation, would at least tend to "soft pedal" the negative aspects of the leader's life. But the Bible is different, painfully honest. It doesn't paint over the wrinkles in its portraits, but with absolute fidelity gives all the faults along with the virtues.

After the glowing descriptions of Solomon's awesome wealth and power in the preceding section, the writer now begins a stark portrayal of his failures. Some say that this narrative of Israel's great king is "idealized." But it is a strange idealizing that leaves the ideal king entangled in a web of abject sensuality and spiritual apostasy.

It is sad to see the monarchy, which under Saul began as a simple military leadership over a tribal confederacy, now degenerate under Solomon into a typical Oriental despotism. We should not be surprised to see civil rebellion and the breaking up of the great kingdom looming on the horizon. A nation ground down by heavy taxation and forced labor to keep up the luxury of a lavish court with its degrading crowd of foreign wives and concubines is ripe for revolt. The king and his successors are about to reap what they have sown.

SOLOMON'S FOREIGN WIVES LEAD HIM ASTRAY

11:1 But King Solomon loved many foreign women,
as well as the daughter of Pharaoh: women of the

Moabites, Ammonites, Edomites, Sidonians, *and* Hittites—

2 from the nations of whom the LORD had said to the children of Israel, "You shall not intermarry with them, nor they with you. Surely they will turn away your hearts after their gods." Solomon clung to these in love.

3 And he had seven hundred wives, princesses, and three hundred concubines; and his wives turned away his heart.

4 For it was so, when Solomon was old, that his wives turned his heart after other gods; and his heart was not loyal to the LORD his God, as *was* the heart of his father David.

5 For Solomon went after Ashtoreth the goddess of the Sidonians, and after Milcom the abomination of the Ammonites.

6 Solomon did evil in the sight of the LORD, and did not fully follow the LORD, as *did* his father David.

7 Then Solomon built a high place for Chemosh the abomination of Moab, on the hill that *is* east of Jerusalem, and for Molech the abomination of the people of Ammon.

8 And he did likewise for all his foreign wives, who burned incense and sacrificed to their gods.

9 So the LORD became angry with Solomon, because his heart had turned from the LORD God of Israel, who had appeared to him twice,

10 and had commanded him concerning this thing, that he should not go after other gods; but he did not keep what the LORD had commanded.

11 Therefore the LORD said to Solomon, "Because you have done this, and have not kept My covenant and My statutes, which I have commanded you, I will surely tear the kingdom away from you and give it to your servant.

12 "Nevertheless I will not do it in your days, for the sake of your father David; I will tear it out of the hand of your son.

13 "However I will not tear away the whole kingdom; I will give one tribe to your son for the sake of

my servant David, and for the sake of Jerusalem
which I have chosen."

1 Kings 11:1–13

This section begins with the word *"but,"* an important conjunction marking a dramatic transition from the breathtaking appraisal of Solomon's power in chapter 10. The word "but" is a verbal warning of impending disaster.

"But King Solomon loved many foreign women, as well as the daughter of Pharaoh" (v. 1). Polygamy in ancient Israel was apparently permitted, even though it obviously contradicted God's ideal of one man for one woman for life. Most of the biblical patriarchs had numerous wives. David had fifteen. Abijah had fourteen. Rehoboam, Solomon's son, had eighteen wives and sixty concubines. So except for the unprecedented number, Solomon's marital situation was not unusual for that historical period.

While the daughter of Pharaoh held a special position as the number one wife of the king, verse 3 tells us Solomon also had 699 other wives as well as 300 concubines. The fact that this number far exceeds the typical harems of other contemporary monarchs should not cause a problem with credibility, since Solomon diligently competed to exceed the other nations in every way. He had accumulated greater wealth, wisdom, and power than all the others; and, since virility was supposed to be an indicator of royal greatness in that day, he wanted to surpass them in this category too. Some interpreters who doubt the accuracy of the number in verse 3 point out that in the Song of Sol. 6:8 Solomon speaks of only "sixty queens and eighty concubines and virgins without number." But the supposed discrepancy can be explained by the fact that the "virgins without number" could have brought the total to a thousand. It can also be explained by reckoning that the number listed in the Song of Solomon may have come earlier in Solomon's reign before he had accumulated the full number in this chapter.

It is interesting to learn that ancient allegorists interpreted this passage as a typology of Christ's kingdom. They taught that just as these hundreds of foreign women were subject unto King Solomon, so Christ has dominion over all the nations of the world.[1]

Notice that the women came from those countries that were near neighbors to Israel, indicating that Solomon's purpose for these marriages was not altogether sensual nor to surpass the harems of other monarchs but also to seal political alliances that would strengthen his country. The word *"princesses"* does not suggest a third category of women in addition to *"wives"* and *"concubines,"* but is a further description of "wives." The wives were from royal families; they were the daughters of kings and therefore "princesses."

It was bad enough that Solomon went along with customs of his day and practiced polygamy in defiance of the ideal God set forth in Genesis. It was bad enough that he took so many wives and concubines, straining the financial budget of his court. It was bad enough that they were foreigners, inciting great suspicion among the Israelites. But what made the situation intolerable was that he chose the women from among those nations God had specifically warned him to avoid. In several places in the Scriptures, which Solomon knew well, God had forbidden intermarriage with the Moabites, Ammonites, Edomites, Sidonians, and Hittites. In defiance of God's clear command, Solomon chose his harem from these very nations.

God's pointed restrictions against intermarriage were not for racial reasons, but for religious reasons. That fact is spelled out very clearly in verse 2, *"Surely they will turn away your hearts after their gods."* For some reason, Egypt was not on God's list of forbidden nations. And, interestingly, there is no record of even the least influence of Egyptian religion on the Israelites throughout this period of their history. The fact that Egypt was not included among the restricted nations may explain why Pharaoh's daughter is listed separately from the other "foreign" women he loved. There must have been certain features in the particular pagan cults on God's list that He considered especially dangerous to His people.

Out of respect for the wisdom and greatness of Solomon, we are inclined to soften somehow the seriousness of his apostasy. After all, even the Bible seems to suggest an excuse when it says that Solomon was old (v. 4). But this is no excuse. In fact, he should have known better after all those years of experience. Besides that, there are evidences that the negative influence of his foreign wives began much earlier in his reign, even though it bore its destructive fruit much later, toward the end. Actually, his untimely failure is a lesson that even at the end of life a fall is possible. As Alexander Maclaren put it, Solomon's ship went down when the voyage was nearly over.[2] Was this the truth John Bunyan had in mind in his allegory when Pilgrim saw a door opening down to hell close by the very gates to the Celestial City itself? He was implying that this side of heaven we never outlive the dangerous undertow of temptation.

There are few real-life illustrations any sadder than those in which noble pastors in their later years fall away from earlier patterns of exemplary ministry. Some have become naïve pawns, manipulated by younger zealots who use their long-established reputations to support their own causes, causes that those senior preachers would have courageously opposed in their younger years. Others have given in to a pitiful pragmatism, adopting inappropriate popular trends that seem to be succeeding in a frantic attempt to rescue what they fear is a declining ministry. Still others in their senior years become obsessed with establishing some kind of earthly immortality and begin to erect monuments in hopes of perpetuating their names. Friends look on sympathetically, excusing their actions as senility, but in truth, as Maclaren says, it is more likely the assault of Satan toward the end of the journey.

Thank God, even though the passage highlights Solomon's old age as a factor in his failure, it doesn't mean such a decline is inevitable toward the end of life. Thank God, too, there are abundant examples of faithful saints whose spirit and faith are at their strongest in old age. "The longer I serve Him, the sweeter He grows." That's the normative pattern that is God's will for us, and with His help it is attainable.

There are other interpreters who try to soften Solomon's failure by pointing out that he did not engage in idolatry *himself;* he only allowed his wives the freedom to practice *their* idolatrous faith. But verse 5 is clear, *"Solomon went after Ashtoreth."* That's the language the Bible uses to describe the worship of idols. Verse 4 is also clear, *"his wives turned his heart after other gods." He* built altars to these pagan deities on the Mount of Olives, directly opposite the beautiful temple, where crowds of passersby would see them and be tempted to imitate the worship practices of the royal harem. The influence of these pagan "high places" *he* built was long-lasting. They were still standing three hundred years later when Josiah began his reign over Judah and finally destroyed them (2 Kings 23:13)! Solomon's direct, personal involvement in idolatry, even if it was for pragmatic, political reasons, is impossible to disregard.

It would also be difficult to lessen the seriousness of Solomon's decline because of God's strong rebuke in this passage. His actions are called *"evil"* in verse 6. Verse 9 says God was *"angry with Solomon, because his heart had turned from the Lord."* The severity of God's punishment also points to the severity of Solomon's sin. The kingdom would be torn away from Solomon and his heirs (vv. 11–13). Add to that the fact that there is no evidence Solomon repented after the Lord confronted him. Following God's stinging rebuke, we hear only the king's dull silence. Years later, when the prophet Ahijah announced to Jeroboam that he would rule the ten tribes, evidence of Solomon's continued apostasy is still there (vv. 33–40). Furthermore, the seriousness of his disobedience is intensified enormously when we remember that Solomon deliberately violated the command of God in spite of God's gracious personal appearances (v. 9).

Now it is true that the king did not totally abandon his worship of Yahweh; he is actually guilty of a kind of half-heartedness. He *"did not fully follow the Lord"* (v. 6). The rabbis tried to excuse Solomon by explaining that he thought he could consummate these foreign marriages for political reasons without incurring the consequences of disloyalty to God. He believed his faith and wisdom were strong enough to inoculate him against their influences.[3] But therein is another indication of the seriousness of his sin. It was based on a false pride. He had become so proud of his wisdom, that he thought he was smarter than God. Remember Satan's temptation in the Garden? "You shall not surely die. You can be as wise as God." Solomon thought his wisdom was strong enough to see him through, but he was wrong.

It may sound less serious to say Solomon did not give up his worship of Yahweh, but we must remember that in God's eyes half-heartedness is no better than outright apostasy. Stubborn disobedience is obviously a sin, but so is falling short, so is halting between two opinions, so is trying to serve two masters. The Bible consistently condemns divided allegiance as a sin. Solomon mistakenly assumed that allowing idolatry to exist alongside Yahweh worship was a commendable form of neutrality, an admirable example of broad-mindedness. But in actuality, his actions were an abomination to God. In his epistle, James warns that the double-minded man is like the waves of the sea, tossed and unstable, blowing aimlessly before every gust of wind.

James Moffat suggested that a sixth beatitude might be added to the others, "Blessed are they who are not double-minded, for they shall be admitted into the intimate presence of God."[4] It seems apparent that years before, David had learned this lesson that his son Solomon so tragically ignored. In Ps. 86:11 David prayed, "O Lord . . . unite my heart," admitting that his heart was divided and that he needed God to pull the competitive strands of his life together into spiritual unity. If only Solomon had listened more carefully to the poetic wisdom of his father and had prayed that same prayer.

Another lesson comes to light in this passage, namely, the gradual degeneration of Solomon's commitment as a warning that sin's victory in our lives most often occurs not by sudden satanic assaults but by slow moral erosion. Romans 5 tells how tribulation produces patience, and patience produces character, and character, hope. But in this story we are reminded that power produces pride, and pride produces arrogance, and arrogance, forgetfulness of God. Solomon's failure seems to have resulted from a gradual loosening of his firm grip on God's will.

An industrious engineer has invented a device to awaken sleepy drivers before they lose control of the car and have an accident. It attaches to the steering wheel in such a way that the driver must maintain a firm grip on the wheel, or a buzzer will sound to awaken him. If he begins to relax his grip, a trigger is released and the alarm goes off. The only way the driver can keep the buzzer from sounding is to keep a firm grip on the wheel. So we must keep a firm grip on the principles of our faith to avoid the same gradual decline that wrecked the life of Israel's greatest king.

In spite of his abundant blessings, in spite of God's miraculous appearances to him on two different occasions, in spite of his incomparable God-given wisdom, Solomon still failed. And if *he* failed, how can we hope to avoid the fatal consequences of sin without a firm and undiluted faith?

God Raises up Enemies against Solomon

11:14 Now the LORD raised up an adversary against Solomon, Hadad the Edomite; he *was* a descendant of the king in Edom.

15 For it happened, when David was in Edom, and
Joab the commander of the army had gone up to bury
the slain, after he had killed every male in Edom
16 (because for six months Joab remained there
with all Israel, until he had cut down every male in
Edom),
17 that Hadad fled to go to Egypt, he and certain
Edomites of his father's servants with him. Hadad
was still a little child.
18 Then they arose from Midian and came to Paran;
and they took men with them from Paran and came to
Egypt, to Pharaoh king of Egypt, who gave him a
house, apportioned food for him, and gave him land.
19 And Hadad found great favor in the sight of
Pharaoh, so that he gave him as wife the sister of his
own wife, that is, the sister of Queen Tahpenes.
20 Then the sister of Tahpenes bore him Genubath
his son, whom Tahpenes weaned in Pharaoh's house.
And Genubath was in Pharaoh's household among
the sons of Pharaoh.
21 So when Hadad heard in Egypt that David
rested with his fathers, and that Joab the commander
of the army was dead, Hadad said to Pharaoh, "Let
me depart, that I may go to my own country."
22 Then Pharaoh said to him, "But what have you
lacked with me, that suddenly you seek to go to your
own country?" So he answered, "Nothing, but do let
me go anyway."
23 And God raised up *another* adversary against
him, Rezon the son of Eliadah, who had fled from his
lord, Hadadezer king of Zobah.
24 So he gathered men to him and became captain
over a band *of raiders,* when David killed those *of
Zobah.* And they went to Damascus and dwelt there,
and reigned in Damascus.
25 He was an adversary of Israel all the days of
Solomon (besides the trouble that Hadad *caused*);
and he abhorred Israel, and reigned over Syria.

1 Kings 11:14–25

Webster's dictionary has a very interesting definition of the word "tragedy." Its origin is from two Greek words: *tragos,* meaning "a he-goat;" and *oide* meaning "a song." Tragedy then literally means "the song of the goat." That meaning may stem from the practice in Greek drama festivals of giving an unwanted goat as a kind of consolation prize to a loser. So tragedy is defined as "a serious play having an unhappy or disastrous ending brought about by moral weakness."

According to this definition, Solomon's life was a tragedy, having a disastrous ending brought about by moral weakness. Even though through most of its years his life was characterized by wisdom and wealth, in the end he received the goat, the consolation prize. In these verses we can see inevitable trouble looming on the horizon. Israel's golden age and Solomon's splendid reign are about to come to an end.

Verse 14 says, *"The Lord raised up an adversary against Solomon, Hadad the Edomite."* Verse 23 says, *"And God raised up another adversary against him, Rezon the son of Eliadah."* The word "adversary" is the Hebrew word *śāṭān,* which literally means "opponent" or "enemy."[5] It is, of course, the very descriptive name the Bible gives to the Devil, the personal power of evil. Here it is used in its general sense of an enemy. And Solomon, who in 5:4 told King Hiram, "God has given me rest on every side, so that there is no adversary," now has two.

First there was Hadad mentioned in verses 1–22. Hadad, a royal heir to the Edomite throne, was a little child when David's military campaign against Edom wiped out the entire male population. He escaped with friends to Midian and Paran where he stayed until a pharaoh less friendly with Solomon came to the throne in Egypt. Then, as a young prince, he moved there, was befriended by the Egyptian ruler and given land and a bride, who was the sister of Queen Tahpenes. Toward the close of Solomon's reign, Hadad saw a chance to return to Edom and arouse his people to revenge David's massacre. While nothing is said about Hadad's anti-Solomon crusade, we must assume he became a troublesome guerrilla fighter against Israel during the years that followed.[6]

The Edomites were the descendants of Esau, the twin brother of Jacob. Even before their birth, these twin brothers were adversaries. In Genesis 25, Rebekah, their mother, said "the children struggled together within her." At birth, Esau came first, but Jacob had a grip on his little brother's ankle as if to trip him or take his place. Seeing that, they named him Jacob, which means "a tripper" or "a supplanter." And from that moment on, the two brothers were constant competitors, and their descendants carried on the feud.

Israel, the descendants of Jacob, and Edom, the descendants of Esau, were continually at war. Most of Israel's enemies came and went like waves of the sea. There were the Canaanites, followed by the Philistines, followed by the Syrians, the Egyptians, the Babylonians, and the Persians. But Edom was always there. These two nations scorned, hated, and scourged each other with a relentlessness that finds no parallel between kindred and neighboring nations anywhere else in history. Little wonder that "Edom" became the rabbinic code word for "enemy" in the ancient writings. Nor is it surprising to see Solomon's God-appointed adversary coming from this land. While Hadad was raised up as Solomon's adversary to the south, in Edom, Rezon was raised up as his adversary to the north, in Damascus. Like Hadad, Rezon was also uprooted by David's military conquests, and he organized a band of raiders who eventually captured Solomon's fortress at Damascus. Although he was unable to completely block Israel's trade routes to the north, he did manage to become a serious thorn in Solomon's side. During the next two centuries, until it was crushed by the Assyrians, the Aramaen kingdom of Damascus became Israel's most formidable enemy.[7]

In addition to providing information about the decline of Solomon's empire, these verses also offer some important spiritual insights for every age. First, they remind us that incidental, unimportant actions often result in calamitous events many years later. David could not have known that his minor military actions in the third-rate country of Edom would lead to disastrous consequences years after his death. A nameless little boy fleeing David's army would later become Solomon's dreaded adversary. David was unaware that an anonymous bandit driven into the Damascus wilderness by his army would help found a mighty empire that would seriously threaten Israel in years to come. Since we cannot foresee the eventual outcome of even the least important of our actions, we must pray for God's direction and constantly follow what we believe to be His will for us.

The passage also teaches us that the consequences of our lives continue on—long after we die. That's why God delays His final judgment until the end of time, rather than weighing our lives when we meet Him at death. The lingering evil of a life like Adolph Hitler's continues long after death. Forty-five years later, headlines in the papers are still pointing to war trials and uncovering atrocities of

Hitler's Nazi regime. In like manner, the influences for good of a life like the apostle Paul's continue to bless people years after that life ends on earth. That's why judgment has to wait until the final curtain goes down on the cosmic drama, when the unforeseen results of every life can be weighed.

We learn another lesson from this passage: namely, that God can and does use godless, pagan people to accomplish His will. While evil and suffering are not always the result of sin, and while trouble in our lives is not always sent by God, there are times when He uses evil, as He did with Hadad and Rezon, to chastise His children and to direct them to follow His path.

JEROBOAM REBELS AND SOLOMON DIES

11:26 Then Solomon's servant, Jeroboam the son of Nebat, an Ephraimite from Zereda, whose mother's name *was* Zeruah, a widow, also rebelled against the king.

27 And this *is* what caused him to rebel against the king: Solomon had built the Millo *and* repaired the damages to the City of David his father.

28 The man Jeroboam *was* a mighty man of valor; and Solomon, seeing that the young man was industrious, made him the officer over all the labor force of the house of Joseph.

29 Now it happened at that time, when Jeroboam went out of Jerusalem, that the prophet Ahijah the Shilonite met him on the way; and he had clothed himself with a new garment, and the two *were* alone in the field.

30 Then Ahijah took hold of the new garment that *was* on him, and tore it *into* twelve pieces.

31 And he said to Jeroboam, "Take for yourself ten pieces, for thus says the LORD, the God of Israel: 'Behold, I will tear the kingdom out of the hand of Solomon and will give ten tribes to you

32 '(but he shall have one tribe for the sake of My servant David, and for the sake of Jerusalem, the city which I have chosen out of all the tribes of Israel),

33 'because they have forsaken Me, and worshiped

Ashtoreth the goddess of the Sidonians, Chemosh the god of the Moabites, and Milcom the god of the people of Ammon, and have not walked in My ways to do *what is* right in My eyes and *keep* My statutes and My judgments, as *did* his father David.

34 'However I will not take the whole kingdom out of his hand, because I have made him ruler all the days of his life for the sake of My servant David, whom I chose because he kept My commandments and My statutes.

35 'But I will take the kingdom out of his son's hand and give it to you—ten tribes.

36 'And to his son I will give one tribe, that My servant David may always have a lamp before Me in Jerusalem, the city which I have chosen for Myself, to put My name there.

37 'So I will take you, and you shall reign over all your heart desires, and you shall be king over Israel.

38 'Then it shall be, if you heed all that I command you, walk in My ways, and do *what is* right in My sight, to keep My statutes and My commandments, as My servant David did, then I will be with you and build for you an enduring house, as I built for David, and will give Israel to you.

39 'And I will afflict the descendants of David because of this, but not forever.'"

40 Solomon therefore sought to kill Jeroboam. But Jeroboam arose and fled to Egypt, to Shishak king of Egypt, and was in Egypt until the death of Solomon.

41 Now the rest of the acts of Solomon, all that he did, and his wisdom, *are* they not written in the book of the acts of Solomon?

42 And the period that Solomon reigned in Jerusalem over all Israel *was* forty years.

43 Then Solomon rested with his fathers, and was buried in the City of David his father. And Rehoboam his son reigned in his place.

1 Kings 11:26–43

God said in verse 11 that He would tear the kingdom from Solomon and give it to his servant. We are now told in verse 26 who that servant was—Jeroboam, the son of Nebat. As the founder and ruler of the Northern Kingdom of Israel he became known as Jeroboam I. His name means "may the people be great," and it stands in competitive opposition to his opponent in the Southern Kingdom of Judah, Rehoboam, whose name means "may the people be extended."[8] Following in the steps of his father, who was an official under Solomon, the young Jeroboam won recognition as a man of high qualities and was appointed to a place of importance on Solomon's staff. The phrase *"man of valor"* in verse 28 may also be translated "man of material means," and may suggest that he was a wealthy property owner. Since his mother is described as a widow, it may be that Jeroboam had inherited wealth at the death of his father.[9]

Solomon, removed from the man in the street in the splendid isolation of his palace, was insulated from the plight of the masses. But not Jeroboam. Working with the common people on the construction projects in Jerusalem and as an overseer of the labor force from the House of Joseph, he had a chance to learn firsthand about the bitterness of the oppressed citizens. Jeroboam sympathized with the bitterness of those with whom he worked as they chafed under the heavy taxation and forced labor imposed on them to keep up Solomon's inflated lifestyle. And he used his position to stir up disaffection against the government.

With providential timing God sent his prophet Ahijah to meet Jeroboam in the wilderness outside Jerusalem to call him dramatically to his destiny as the leader of the ten tribes. This encounter with the word of the Lord galvanized Jeroboam's revolutionary intent and he *"rebelled against the king"* (v. 26). We are not told the details of the rebellion. It must have been significant, however, since verse 40 indicates that Solomon tried to kill him and that Jeroboam had to flee in exile to Egypt.

We are introduced to an example of prophetic drama in verse 30, when Ahijah removes his new cloak and rips it into twelve pieces in front of the startled Jeroboam. This spectacular visual aid underlined the seriousness of God's promise to "tear the kingdom away" from Solomon (v. 11). There is some confusion in the passage about the twelve tribes being divided—ten for Jeroboam and one for Rehoboam, which add up to only eleven. The answer seems to be found in 12:23 where the tribe of Benjamin is counted with Judah as one tribe, apparently because Benjamin was so insignificant.

The breakup of the kingdom was not a part of God's original plan. In the beginning under David, the noble purposes of the united kingdom were outlined and it appeared they were being marvelously advanced under the wise leadership of Solomon. But as it often does, human sin intervened in God's plan, and He had to make a revision. The Great Potter often has to take a vessel that becomes cracked or flawed and reshape it, not in as beautiful a form as He first intended, but nevertheless still useful. So God arranges for the division of the kingdom as a secondary plan in the light of Solomon's failure.

It seems there are frequent occasions when God does the same for us. He has an ideal plan for us, and we are happiest and most complete when we follow it. But if we fail and repent, He forgives us, takes us where we are, and uses us at a secondary but still effective level for His glory. For instance, divorce is never God's ideal, which the Bible describes as "one man for one woman for life." But when human sin intervenes in a marriage and the union is broken, God can take the divided "kingdom" and use it at a secondary level for His purposes. It may not be at the highest strata, where He intended it to be in His ideal, but nevertheless, He can reshape the flawed vessel and put it to useful purposes in His master plan.

There are older students in the seminary who believe they were called by God into the ministry in early life. They refused to follow that call and pursued secular vocations. Now, in some cases after disappointments, they have come back to that call of earlier years. Their lives may not be as effective as they might have been had they obeyed God's initial instructions, but He graciously accepts them and uses them with effectiveness.

Notice how God kept coming back to the same conditions of His covenant relationship with His people. In verse 38, He repeats it again to Jeroboam. "If . . . then." When will humankind learn that receiving His highest blessings is contingent upon obedience to His ways, His statutes, and His commandments?

Notice also the glimmers of anticipation of the Messiah. The eternal nature of David's reign is symbolized in verse 36 by the burning lamp. This apparently refers to the customary practice in Israel of burning a lamp in the window of a house to indicate the family was at home. When the lamp was extinguished, it indicated the breaking up of the home and the destruction of the family.[10] That lamp of

David's promised reign would be ignited once and for all in the eternal reign of the Messiah, Jesus Christ, whom the Scriptures say was "of the house of David." That future messianic anticipation is seen also in verse 39, where the afflictions on David's descendants were not to continue forever. There would come a day when, through Christ's kingdom, the afflictions would cease and Christ would reign as King of kings and Lord of lords.

Upon fleeing from Solomon's wrath, Jeroboam took refuge in Egypt, which always seemed eager to shelter a future potential leader of Israel as a political hedge. The pharaoh who gave him exile is identified as Shishak in verse 40. He followed Solomon's father-in-law on the throne of Egypt and therefore was not as friendly toward Israel. This is the first time in the Old Testament that an Egyptian pharaoh is named.[11] He was the same Shishak who, as an ally of Jeroboam, invaded Judah and plundered the temple and the palace during the fifth year of Rehoboam's reign (14:25–26). It is noted there that he took away the golden shields of Solomon and that Rehoboam had to replace them with cheaper substitutes of bronze.

In verses 41–43 we find the conclusion to Solomon's life written in the standard form the historian used to conclude the lives of all the kings. The Book of the Acts of Solomon was evidently a unique source separate from the Book of the Chronicles of the Kings referred to in other cases. It was a chronological journal of Solomon's accomplishments similar to other court annals, but with more emphasis on the wisdom of the king.[12]

He reigned about forty years and was about sixty years old when he died in approximately 932 B.C. The plainly worded summary seems an unworthy conclusion to such a wonderful life. But Solomon did not die like his father David had died. David remained faithful to the Lord to the very last, and he died nobly, with words of wisdom for his heir. If Solomon's reign had ended as gloriously as it had begun, the Jewish nation would have held him in higher esteem than David his father. But this was not the case, and the unique and radiant career of Israel's wisest man is summed up with a stereotyped formula similar to that of scores of ordinary kings. Here again is the reminder that even the mightiest vessel may be shipwrecked within sight of home port.

This final chapter in Solomon's life is written with the spotlight centered not on the king but on his enemies: Hadad, Rezon, and

Jeroboam. Solomon slowly fades into the background and his adversaries become more prominent than he. As long as he walked with God, he was important to the inspired historians, but as soon as he forsook Yahweh, he became insignificant, an empty vessel discarded by the wayside. The spotlight of God's plan now shifts from the noble life of Solomon to shine on other summits. And it is a sad eclipse.

It is noteworthy that the only mention of Solomon's activities after his lapse is in verse 40, where it says he sought to kill Jeroboam. What a contrast to the unprecedented accomplishments of earlier years. The activities of the great king are now reduced to the level of vengeance, murder, protecting his turf, shoring up his weaknesses, and frantically trying to postpone the inevitable.

How can we assess his life? He was a man of peace, not warlike as David was. He sought wisdom—not the world's variety, but wisdom from God. It was his desire to administer his government according to the law and will of Yahweh. His enormous talents included knowledge of the world as a naturalist, knowledge of humans as an expert in their behavior, knowledge of literature as a poet and writer. He had splendid tastes, which he bestowed upon his kingdom in vast building projects and cultural enhancements. He not only made Israel a majestic kingdom of this world, but he erected the temple to the glory of the spiritual world, lavishing upon it countless treasures. At its dedication, Solomon stood as one of the most imposing figures in human history.

But gradually, almost imperceptibly, his glory began to fade. Brought on by luxury, pleasure, compromise, and disobedience, he began to exchange his godly wisdom for the wisdom of the world. He lost the strength of his convictions and, of all things, began to justify idolatry! Can you imagine? The same man who built the magnificent temple on Mount Zion also built, in order to please his mistresses from Ammon and Moab, altars to Chemosh and Molech on Mount Zion in the very face of God's house. By degrees the glory passed away, and darkness and hopelessness triumphed in the end. He wore one of the fairest and noblest crowns a mortal could wear, but it was perishable, not enduring like the crown of life promised to the faithful.

Finally, the wisest king in history is the personification of four biblical truths:

(1) "For what profit is it to a man if he gains the whole world, and loses his own soul? Or what will a man give in exchange for his soul?" (Matt. 16:26).

(2) "And the world is passing away, and the lust of it; but he who does the will of God abides forever" (1 John 2:17).

(3) "Then I looked on all the works that my hands had done . . . and indeed all was vanity and grasping for the wind" (Eccl. 2:11).

(4) "Fear God and keep His commandments, for this is man's all" (Eccl. 12:13).

NOTES

1. Karl Chr. W. F. Bähr, *The Books of the Kings,* Commentary on the Holy Scriptures, ed. John Peter Lange (Grand Rapids: Zondervan, 1960), 126.
2. Alexander Maclaren, *Second Samuel and the Books of Kings,* Expositions of Holy Scripture, vol. 2 (Grand Rapids: Eerdmans, 1952), 202.
3. I. W. Slotki, *Kings* (London: Soncino Press, 1950), 82.
4. Norman H. Snaith, Ralph W. Sockman, and Raymond Calkins, "The First and Second Books of Kings," in *The Interpreter's Bible,* vol. 3 (Nashville: Abingdon, 1954), 101.
5. Gwilym H. Jones, *1 and 2 Kings,* New Century Bible Commentary, ed. Ronald E. Clements (Grand Rapids: Eerdmans, 1984), 237.
6. Simon J. DeVries, *1 Kings,* Word Biblical Commentary, ed. John D. W. Watts, vol. 12 (Waco, TX: Word Books, 1985), 150.
7. Slotki, 84.
8. Jones, 241.
9. Charles F. Burney, *Notes on the Hebrew Text of the Books of Kings* (Oxford: Clarendon Press, 1903), 169.
10. Slotki, 89.
11. M. Pierce Matheney and Roy Honeycutt, "1-2 Kings," in *The Broadman Bible Commentary,* ed. Clifton J. Allen, vol. 3 (Nashville: Broadman, 1970), 193.
12. Jones, 241.

SECTION TWO

From the Divided Kingdom to the Fall of Israel 932–722 B.C.

1 Kings 12:1–2 Kings 17:41

CHAPTER SIX

The Reigns of Jeroboam of Israel and Rehoboam of Judah

1 Kings 12:1–14:31

INTRODUCTION

There had always been tension between the tribes of the North and the South, due in part to the jealousy between Ephraim and Judah, the two major tribes. Some scholars believe that the friction may have begun even before they entered Canaan and that only the Ephraim tribes were brought into the promised land by Joshua, while Judah came in separately from the South.[1]

Years later, King David, well aware of the continuing animosity between North and South, had to make allowances for it in organizing his monarchy, and actually reigned over two separate entities from a tribally neutral capital, Jerusalem, which, even though it was in the South, was his own personal property. David managed to hold the two groups together in a loose tribal confederacy by a covenant with the elders of the Northern tribes, who had formerly been loyal to Saul. There were, nevertheless, at least two outbreaks of rebellion, one led by Absalom and the other by Sheba (2 Sam. 20:1).

During the early part of Solomon's reign the North and South moved closer to unity, but even the wisest of kings could not totally wipe out the smoldering division he had inherited. In fact, in his later years he actually inflamed the embers of rebellion by his oppressive policies of taxation and labor, wiping out the freedoms that helped hold the old confederacy together. So to the observer of this period of history, the rebellion of the Northern tribes should not be an unexpected event.

He began the story of the division in 11:26 with Jeroboam as the main actor; now the writer continues the account of Jeroboam's reign in the North. Then, after Jeroboam's death, in the typical alternating pattern of the Book of Kings, he returns to pick up the story of Rehoboam's reign in the Southern kingdom of Judah.

The Division of the Kingdom

12:1 And Rehoboam went to Shechem, for all Israel had gone to Shechem to make him king.

2 So it happened, when Jeroboam the son of Nebat heard *it* (he was still in Egypt, for he had fled from the presence of King Solomon and had been dwelling in Egypt),

3 that they sent and called him. Then Jeroboam and the whole assembly of Israel came and spoke to Rehoboam, saying,

4 "Your father made our yoke heavy; now therefore, lighten the burdensome service of your father, and his heavy yoke which he put on us, and we will serve you."

5 So he said to them, "Depart *for* three days, then come back to me." And the people departed.

6 Then King Rehoboam consulted the elders who stood before his father Solomon while he still lived, and he said, "How do you advise *me* to answer these people?"

7 And they spoke to him, saying, "If you will be a servant to these people today, and serve them, and answer them, and speak good words to them, then they will be your servants forever."

8 But he rejected the advice which the elders had given him, and consulted the young men who had grown up with him, who stood before him.

9 And he said to them, "What advice do you give? How should we answer this people who have spoken to me, saying, 'Lighten the yoke which your father put on us'?"

10 Then the young men who had grown up with him spoke to him, saying, "Thus you should speak to this people who have spoken to you, saying, 'Your

father made our yoke heavy, but you make *it* lighter
on us'—thus you shall say to them: 'My little *finger*
shall be thicker than my father's waist!
11 'And now, whereas my father put a heavy yoke
on you, I will add to your yoke; my father chastised you with whips, but I will chastise you with
scourges!'"
12 So Jeroboam and all the people came to Rehoboam the third day, as the king had directed, saying, "Come back to me the third day."
13 Then the king answered the people roughly,
and rejected the advice which the elders had given
him;
14 and he spoke to them according to the advice of
the young men, saying, "My father made your yoke
heavy, but I will add to your yoke; my father chastised
you with whips, but I will chastise you with scourges!"
15 So the king did not listen to the people; for the
turn *of events* was from the LORD, that He might fulfill His word, which the LORD had spoken by Ahijah
the Shilonite to Jeroboam the son of Nebat.
16 Now when all Israel saw that the king did not
listen to them, the people answered the king, saying:

"What share have we in David?
We have no inheritance in the son of Jesse.
To your tents, O Israel!
Now, see to your own house, O David!"

So Israel departed to their tents.

1 Kings 12:1–16

From the brief reference in 11:43, "And Rehoboam his son reigned in his place," we assume that Solomon's son had already been officially recognized, if not anointed, as king in the city of Jerusalem. That coronation meant little to Rehoboam, however, without a confirmation from the major part of his kingdom, which was in the North. So Rehoboam made his way to Shechem where the Northern tribes were already assembled. It was not a prudent political strategy. He, the king, was "humbly" coming to their turf in Shechem rather than the Northern tribes coming to his throne room in Jerusalem. They already had Rehoboam in a weak, defensive posture before the negotiations even started.

Why did they choose Shechem as the location for their confrontation with Rehoboam? For one thing, it was a city of rich historical significance. It was there Abram had first worshiped the Lord in the promised land (Gen. 12:6). Jacob built an altar there. Shechem was the first parcel of ground owned by Israel in Canaan (Gen. 33:18–20). Joseph was buried here (Josh. 24:32). Surely, its historical significance appealed to the leaders of Israel as an appropriate site for such an urgent gathering.

Second, it was far enough away from Jerusalem, where Rehoboam had strong support, to rob him of any political advantage. Third, Shechem was in the home territory of their rebel hero Jeroboam, who had returned from Egyptian exile to lead them. Fourth, Shechem was in the geographical center of the Northern tribes, at the foot of Mount Gerezim, and therefore easily accessible to their constituency. Later, for these same reasons Shechem became the first capital of the Northern Kingdom under Jeroboam.

What an emotional scene it must have been! The colorful tents of the various clans spread out across the valley. The shouts of the multitudes. The tense atmosphere of anxiety and anticipation. There are always exciting vibrations in such a gathering, but there is also danger. Some call it mob hysteria. The over-confident Rehoboam should have been more cautious that day as he approached Shechem. Dr. Karl Bähr comments on such a scene in Lange's commentary:

> The gathering of great crowds in a small place has long been the device of demagogues. These crowds mutually excite each other, masses of men, like-minded, inspire each other with confidence. Peaceful councils vanish, men become accustomed to the shouts of the insurgents, and imbibe their principles. They venture no contradiction against the outburst of passion, especially when swelled by numbers, and, thus inflamed, are dragged onwards in paths from which later repentance can never bring them back.[2]

The demands of the rebels, recorded in verse 4, were not all that unreasonable. They were not calling for total abolition of Solomon's oppressive yoke, only that the new king make their yoke lighter. They were asking for no more than Rehoboam's timely redress of legitimate tribal grievances, which had been so long neglected by his father Solomon. Even with Jeroboam poised to lead the tribes to break away, there is no reason to doubt that they would have remained loyal to Rehoboam had he agreed with their reasonable demands.

Some commentators have pointed out that the nature of their complaints showed how serious the degeneration of the nation's religious life had become as a result of the shameful idolatry Solomon had brought to Israel. Without a word about declining faith in God, they complained exclusively about physical and material deprivation. Obviously, they had long ago forgotten the spiritual purity that God expected of their nation and were more concerned with the body than the soul.[3]

Having listened patiently to their proposals, Rehoboam's response must be the most foolish political blunder he could have committed. To the young king's credit, he did take three days to think about their requests, but that was the only sensible action he took. His foolish mistakes were compounded one upon another to make his total response all the more ludicrous.

First, he sought council in the wrong places. On the surface, asking advice from the older statesmen who had counseled his father appears to have been a good move. To what better source of wisdom could the young king have turned? But if these old men ever had possessed wisdom, it had long since degenerated into cunning political expediency. In verse 7 these worldly-wise veterans suggested that Rehoboam at first flatter the complainers with gentle words. He should offer them promises he did not mean to keep, and then after a while, when his power was firmly entrenched, when he was seated securely in the saddle, he could let them feel the bit and spur of increased oppression. By first pretending to be *their* servant, he could win their confidence and later make them *his* slaves. If that's all these grey-headed men had learned about wisdom, and if their advice is a sample of what passed for sage counsel in the latter days of Solomon's rule, then no wonder rebellion broke out.

Normally, the advice of seasoned experience should be trusted, but these "elders" would have led Rehoboam into a tangled web of dishonest political intrigue that would have been disastrous. You don't have to dig very deeply into the politics of the state legislature, or the Congress, or shamefully, even of religious denominations today, to realize we have some contemporary political manipulators who obviously have taken lessons from the old men of Shechem.

There are some interpreters, however, who read this passage another way. They believe the advice the old men gave Rehoboam was not all that bad. Urging the king to be a servant leader, if indeed they were sincere, was appropriate (v. 7). Indeed, servant leadership is still appropriate, especially for the church leader. It was the leadership style of Jesus—the style He in turn called His disciples to imitate. If their plea to Rehoboam was authentic, these elders were pointing their young leader in the right direction. There are too many heavy-handed, dictatorial leaders today, even in the church, who have forgotten the importance of that biblical pattern of servant leadership.

I met one of these monarchical church leaders the other day who carried out his leadership role by authoritarian decree. He continually spoke of *my* staff, *my* budget, *my* program. He boasted about being in control, how the buck stopped at his desk, how he refused to waste time taking decisions before committees. It seemed to me he was more interested in protecting his dignity and position than in leading the congregation. I also had the distinct impression that he was basically insecure and threatened.

By contrast, another pastor I know is a secure and unthreatened leader. He is unafraid to delegate responsibility. He shares his leadership, making his work more effective by involving numbers of gifted people in the process. He speaks of *our* staff, *our* budget, *our* goals. He sees his leadership role as an opportunity to serve, thereby helping others find fulfillment in their accomplishments too. This style seems to me to be closer to the biblical pattern.

If, indeed, the counsel of the old men was sincere, if they were simply suggesting prudent caution and diplomacy, if their advice came from insights of experienced statesmanship, then Rehoboam would have done well to listen to them rather than the young upstarts with whom he had grown up. Apparently the Talmud understood the advice of the elders to have been authentic. It used this incident to illustrate one of its proverbs: "If the young tell you to build and the old to destroy, pay heed to the latter; for the building of youth is destruction, while the destruction of the old is building."[4] But the tone of the passage seems to point to the conclusion that the old men's advice was faulty.

Unfortunately, the advice Rehoboam received from the young men was no better. Verse 8 tells us they were contemporaries of his who had shared with him the pleasures of court life under his father.

While they were younger than the elders mentioned earlier, they must not have been all that youthful. 1 Kings 14:21 tells us Rehoboam was forty-one years old when be became king, and we know from 2 Chron. 11:18–23 that he had a large harem with twenty-eight sons and sixty daughters. So these cronies of the royal prince were not exactly inexperienced neophytes. Rehoboam's question to them is similar but not identical to the question he brought to the old men. The subtle change is the use of the word *"we"* in verse 9. To the old men Rehoboam said, *"How do you advise me to answer these people?"* To his young companions he said, *"How should we answer this people?"* revealing the fact that he had already identified with their counsel.

If the advice of the old men failed because it was nothing more than cunning expediency, the advice of the young men failed because it was insolent and undiplomatic. Like Rehoboam, they had grown up in luxury and assumed, as he did, that there was no end to the material prosperity that came to them as a result of their royal privileges. So, out of brash self-interest, they encouraged Rehoboam to increase the burdens on the people, by saying, *"My little finger shall be thicker than my father's waist. . . . I will add to your yoke . . . I will chastise you with scourges"* (vv. 10–11). The scourge probably refers to a leather lash tipped with bags filled with sand and covered with spikes.

Unfortunately, Rehoboam heeded the insensitive advice of the young men with their cute rhymes and clever ditties about "little fingers" and "scourges." It was trivial advice from spoiled counselors to a spoiled ruler. A generation earlier, David had spoiled his sons Amnon, Absalom, and Adonijah. Because David indulged them, they rejected his wise counsel in exchange for foolish vanities. Now it appears Solomon did no better than David in rearing his own son Rehoboam.

So this was Rehoboam's first blunder. He trusted the wrong advice. Instead of listening to worldly politicians and trivial courtiers, he should have used the three days to pray for God's wisdom as his father Solomon had done at Gibeon. Rehoboam needed Isaiah's warning in 30:1, "'Woe to the rebellious children,' says the Lord, 'who take counsel, but not of Me.'" James's advice centuries later is also timely, "If any of you lacks wisdom, let him ask of God, who gives to all liberally . . . " (James 1:5).

But Rehoboam's first blunder was followed by another, more serious. He mistakenly assumed he was smarter than his father, Solomon. But his self-appraisal of his wisdom was vastly exaggerated. His little finger might have been larger than Solomon's waist, but his mind was not half the size of his father's.

The Bible places great importance on learning, understanding, knowledge, and truth. One of the most brilliant men in the history of the Christian faith, the apostle Paul, encouraged followers of Jesus Christ to "study" or "be diligent" to become "a worker who does not need to be ashamed, rightly dividing the word of truth" (2 Tim. 2:15). Paul knew it was not Christ-honoring to be a "know-nothing." But he was also aware of the subtle temptation to let learning and wisdom become the supreme value in life. Perhaps from his own proud past the apostle had learned how easily pedantic, scholastic rationalism could become the central focus of life, crowding faith out of the central spotlight of life. It was that pride of knowledge that led Paul to limit and qualify the place of knowledge in the believer's experience. While giving it its proper place high in the scale, Paul was quick to reserve the central position for faith. He was determined not to be a "know-nothing." But he was just as determined not to be a "know-something." In 1 Cor. 8:1–2 he wrote, "Knowledge puffs up . . . and if anyone thinks that he knows anything, he knows nothing yet as he ought to know." In fact a literal translation of that passage expresses it even more succinctly, "For I did not judge it fit to be a know-something." How valuable that advice would have been to Rehoboam, whose opinion of his own mediocre wisdom was grossly inflated.

Now add to the others listed above one final and far more serious blunder—the king gave the people the worst possible reply to their request. If he had intentionally wished to split the kingdom, he could have found no better wedge than his blustering threat of increased tyranny (v. 14). His announced intention to intensify their suffering was imperious, unbecoming of a wise sovereign. With a dozen rash words, Rehoboam, the bungling dictator, opened the door for four hundred years of strife, weakness, and, eventually, the destruction of the entire nation.

Isn't it ironic that the message of the Preacher in Ecclesiastes, usually attributed to Solomon, points prophetically to just such a tragedy? "Then I hated all my labor in which I had toiled under the sun, because I must leave it to the man who will come after me. And who knows whether he will be wise or a fool?" (Eccl. 2:18–19). The one who followed Solomon was indeed a fool.

The reaction to Rehoboam's cruel pronouncement was quick. *"To your tents, O Israel!"* (v. 16). The national rupture was sudden and irrevocable. The ten tribes of the North with their rebel leader Jeroboam now set a separate course, severing all diplomatic relationships and leaving Rehoboam and his single tribe to exist alone. Their answer was given in a poetic form, like a rhyme, a rhythmic chant. It is as though they were saying to Rehoboam, "You and your young advisers came to us with uncaring rhymes and trivial ditties. Now we have a ditty for you! What portion have we in David? Now, see to your own house." That last phrase rings with sarcasm. "Now look at your pitiful kingdom of only one tribe. Look what has become of your dynasty!"

Theirs was the same battle cry Sheba had used in 2 Sam. 20:1 to incite his rebellion during David's reign. It rang with a familiar appeal like "Remember the Alamo!" As the great crowd turned and resolutely walked away, it was obvious that Solomon had sown the wind, but Rehoboam had reaped the whirlwind.

The only bright spot in this entire bleak account is in verse 15. Here the writer, under divine inspiration, seeks to explain what was happening at Shechem from God's perspective. It is one of many places in Kings where it is clear that the biblical historian was interested in doing more than merely cataloging chronological lists of facts and events as a secular historian might do. His task was broader and more important: namely, to explain and interpret those historical events from a spiritual perspective. To the biblical writer, history was "His Story," and he wanted the historical accounts to preach lessons of eternal significance for every age.

So amid the dark, senseless confusion of sinful man's struggles, verse 15 shines through. Here the writer lets us know that there is more to this passage than the grim and disheartening events he has just chronicled. He draws back the curtain for a moment and shows us the true cause behind the events. God is in control. The enthroned Lord of history is working through the ignoble strife to fulfill His word. James Russell Lowell reflects that belief in his poem, "The Present Crisis."

Truth forever on the scaffold, Wrong forever on the
throne,—
Yet that scaffold sways the future, and, behind the
deep unknown,
Standeth God within the shadow, keeping watch
above his own.

The Reign of Jeroboam in Israel

12:17 But Rehoboam reigned over the children of Israel who dwelt in the cities of Judah.
18 Then King Rehoboam sent Adoram, who *was*
in charge of the revenue; but all Israel stoned him
with stones, and he died. Therefore King Rehoboam
mounted his chariot in haste to flee to Jerusalem.
19 So Israel has been in rebellion against the
house of David to this day.
20 Now it came to pass when all Israel heard that
Jeroboam had come back, they sent for him and called
him to the congregation, and made him king over all
Israel. There was none who followed the house of
David, but the tribe of Judah only.
21 And when Rehoboam came to Jerusalem, he
assembled all the house of Judah with the tribe of
Benjamin, one hundred and eighty thousand chosen
men who were warriors, to fight against the house
of Israel, that he might restore the kingdom to
Rehoboam the son of Solomon.
22 But the word of God came to Shemaiah the man
of God, saying,
23 "Speak to Rehoboam the son of Solomon, king
of Judah, to all the house of Judah and Benjamin, and
to the rest of the people, saying,
24 'Thus says the LORD: "You shall not go up nor
fight against your brethren the children of Israel. Let
every man return to his house, for this thing is from
Me."'" Therefore they obeyed the word of the LORD,
and turned back, according to the word of the LORD.
25 Then Jeroboam built Shechem in the mountains
of Ephraim, and dwelt there. Also he went out from
there and built Penuel.

26 And Jeroboam said in his heart, "Now the kingdom may return to the house of David:
27 "If these people go up to offer sacrifices in the
house of the LORD at Jerusalem, then the heart of this
people will turn back to their lord, Rehoboam king of
Judah, and they will kill me and go back to Rehoboam
king of Judah."
28 Therefore the king asked advice, made two
calves of gold, and said to the people, "It is too much
for you to go up to Jerusalem. Here are your gods, O
Israel, which brought you up from the land of Egypt!"
29 And he set up one in Bethel, and the other he
put in Dan.
30 Now this thing became a sin, for the people
went *to worship* before the one as far as Dan.
31 He made shrines on the high places, and made
priests from every class of people, who were not of
the sons of Levi.
32 Jeroboam ordained a feast on the fifteenth day
of the eighth month, like the feast that *was* in Judah,
and offered sacrifices on the altar. So he did at Bethel,
sacrificing to the calves that he had made. And at
Bethel he installed the priests of the high places
which he had made.
33 So he made offerings on the altar which he had
made at Bethel on the fifteenth day of the eighth
month, in the month which he had devised in his own
heart. And he ordained a feast for the children of Israel, and offered sacrifices on the altar and burned
incense.

1 Kings 12:17–33

From this point in the book to its conclusion, the author employs a standard literary pattern to present his accounts of the various kings of Israel and Judah. Up to this point, he has written at length about the stellar careers of David and Solomon, who played such significant roles in launching the kingdom. But now the speed of the narrative accelerates, as each king is ushered across the stage of history and appraised. While the standard literary pattern is not slavishly followed in every detail, it is clear that the author is using a common outline for each royal biography. He skillfully interweaves the chronological account, telling the complete story of one king's reign then going back to pick up the story of his contemporary in the other kingdom.

His purpose is not merely a retelling of history, but, wanting to convey an important message, his aim is didactic, the teaching of lessons. Writing from what has been called a "Deuteronomistic" perspective, he lets each ruler demonstrate that obeying God brings blessings and that disobedience brings punishment. Each king's reign is appraised not on political grounds, as might be done by a secular historian, but rather on religious grounds. At the conclusion of each standard biographical formula he writes either, "He did what was good in the sight of Yahweh," or "He did what was evil in the sight of Yahweh."

Not one of the kings in the Northern Kingdom of Israel escapes his blacklist, and his judgment falls severely on most of the kings of Judah too. Only two Southern kings (Hezekiah and Josiah) come through with clean records. Six receive only a mediocre grade of "passing," and ten "flunk" the inspired historian's appraisal.[5]

So, having finished with David and Solomon, he begins his new series with Jeroboam, the first king of the newly established kingdom to the north, which came to be known as Israel.

We have already seen how insensitive Rehoboam was in attempting to negotiate with the disgruntled rebels at Shechem. Now this weak, faltering leader clumsily tries again to heal the schism. Of all the people in his court, he sent the one man who would be the most unlikely to bring about reconciliation, Adoram, the leader of his forced labor department (v. 18). It shows how little Rehoboam and his youthful advisers understood the gravity of the political situation. Adoram (sometimes identified as Adoniram) may have been the same man whom David appointed to be minister of labor (2 Sam. 20:24). Later, Solomon named him to the same post (4:6). If so, he had served for fifty years and would be quite aged at this time. On the other hand, it may be that the man mentioned here was the son of Adoram and bore the same name. At any rate, just the presence of the man who symbolized one of their primary complaints aroused the ire of Israel's oppressed citizens, and they rose up and stoned him.

Finally, King Rehoboam got the message. He immediately fled for his life to Jerusalem (v. 18). Here was a man who, when it was relatively safe, could show defiant bravado, but when the critical time for action came, he ran.

This futile attempt to heal the division demonstrates how much easier it is to break up what belongs together than it is to restore what is broken. That goes for a home, a church, a denomination, or a friendship, as well as a kingdom. It also shows why Jesus placed such a high value on peacemakers, promising they would inherit the kingdom.

Verse 19 is one of several throughout Kings that gives us some hint as to the dating of the book. "To this day" suggests that it was written before the captivity of the North in 722 B.C.

One final attempt to restore his divided kingdom was mounted by Rehoboam, this time a last-ditch military attack to force the Northern tribes into line (vv. 21–24). But God directly intervened through the prophet Shemaiah, forbidding Rehoboam to go to war against Israel. (With the exception of the parallel passages in Chronicles, this is the only biblical reference to this prophet.) At least on this occasion, Rehoboam had the sense to obey, and the divided kingdom became a reality. The spotlight is now turned on the newly formed kingdom of Israel and its first king, Jeroboam.

What behavior would you expect from a man who had been miraculously informed by a godly prophet that Yahweh had chosen him to be the king of Israel? God had said to Jeroboam, "If you heed all that I command you, walk in My ways, and do what is right in My sight, to keep My statutes and My commandments, as My servant David did, then I will be with you and build for you an enduring house, as I built for David, and will give Israel to you" (11:38). What would you expect a man so clearly directed by God to do? Certainly something other than what Jeroboam did. Had he really believed God, he would have had something more on his mind than erecting golden bulls, establishing deviant shrines, changing God's feast days, appointing improper priests, and fortifying cities. If not missing altogether, Jeroboam's faith was at best weak. To him, divine promises were all right, but armed fortresses with thick walls were better. It is true that God expects us to match His promises with hard work and common sense, rather than sitting back and expecting Him to do it all for us. But Jeroboam fortified his cities because he did not believe God's word.

He began his reign not with bold confidence based on God's promise, but with fear that the loyalty of the people might return to Rehoboam (vv. 26–27). He might be excused for being afraid. That is a common human failing, and certainly understandable under the circumstances. But what he did in response to this fear was inexcusable. His first mistake is recorded in verse 28, "Therefore the king asked advice. . . ." It literally says, "Therefore the king took counsel of *himself*. . . ."[6] Prayer would have been far better than talking to himself.

How many times, by painful experience, I have learned that when we decide we know better than God and we pursue our own course rather than seeking and fulfilling His will, we get into trouble. Thank God for convincing illustrations like this one from the life of Jeroboam and for clear admonitions like the one in Prov. 14:12, "There is a way that seems right to a man, But its end is the way of death."

Jeroboam feared that the appeal of the beautiful temple in Jerusalem would lure his Israelite worshipers back to Rehoboam. So he decided to invent a better version of Yahweh worship that, because of convenience and innovations, would improve on the real thing.

"Why travel all the way to Jerusalem to worship? I will build you more convenient locations in Dan and Bethel near your homes. You say the golden ark and the golden cherubim in the temple are symbols which help you worship? Forget them. I will build you better golden images, young bulls, to remind you of the strength and virility of Yahweh. These images will help you worship here, closer to home." He had apparently learned about the golden bulls while he was exiled in Egypt, where the people worshiped these animals in impressive ceremonies.

Most commentators believe the golden bulls of Jeroboam were not intended as idols or false gods, but rather as images of Yahweh. The Canaanites had images of their gods. Why could not the Israelites have images of Yahweh's strength? In verse 28 Jeroboam used the identical language of Aaron, who built the golden calf in the wilderness, "Here are your God." No, that is not a grammatical error in the last sentence. The word "gods" in verse 28 is singular in meaning even though the verb is plural. Jeroboam was speaking of the one God. He was not introducing idolatry or polytheism into the life of his new kingdom. Nevertheless, he was introducing something just as dangerous, a religion of convenience and popular appeal.

But the king forgot that in the ten commandments God not only forbade the worship of false gods, but He also said, "You shall not make for yourself a carved image—any likeness of anything . . ." (Exod. 20:4–5). Oh, how the people of God yearned for an image of Yahweh. All the other nations had them. Why could Israel not have an image of their God? Without the least intention of withdrawing their homage from Yahweh, the people wanted a symbol, an image to perpetuate in visible form the impressions He had made upon them. But God forbade it. It was not that God did not want His people to *have* an image of Himself. He did not want them to have a *manmade* one—no graven, carved, molten, chiseled likeness from human hands that would mislead His people. Later, in the fullness of time, God would give His yearning people an image that He Himself had created, a perfect image, His only begotten son. In the New Testament Jesus is described as "the image of the invisible God . . . in Him all the fullness [of God] should dwell" (Col. 1:15, 19).

Jeroboam ignored the law of God, capitalized on the yearning of the people, took matters into his royal hands, and built the images anyway. As the governmental ruler, he felt he had the power to determine the nation's religious beliefs. Here a warning flag ought to be raised for modern believers who sometimes seek to use civil power to promote their religious beliefs. The intrusion of civil authority into religious affairs always brings trouble. It was for that reason our forefathers built into the constitution the principle of religious liberty and the separation of church and state. Even when they are in the majority and can enlist the power of government to fulfill church goals, Christians should remember tragic examples like this one. We are to use persuasion, prayer, witnessing, and preaching, not the power of government. In a pluralistic democracy like ours we are to rely on the power of the Holy Spirit, not the secular power of civil authority to further the kingdom.

Even though he did not intend it that way, it did not take long for Jeroboam's people to associate the images with the Canaanite fertility cult of their pagan neighbors, and the golden bulls themselves became objects of worship. That's the danger of symbols in worship. They may at first be transparent aids through which the devout look to God, but inevitably the images turn opaque, hiding God and becoming the object of worship themselves.

"This thing became a sin . . ." (v. 30). Jeroboam may not have designed his images of Yahweh to lead the people into idolatry, but

they did, and they were condemned as idols by Hosea (Hosea 8:5–6; 10:5–6; 13:2).

Added to that serious sin were others. Jeroboam changed the date of the sacred harvest festival from the seventh month, as God had commanded, to the eighth month. He appointed non-Levitical priests in defiance of God's command. He himself officiated at the altars of worship. He maintained the "high places," allowing the people to worship Yahweh at the locations of pagan shrines.

Verse 33 points to one of many clues to the king's failure. *"He had devised in his own heart."* He was guilty of redesigning the faith for his own personal ends. When today's politicians join the church to get votes, when high achievers unite with a prestigious congregation for "social reasons," when opportunists identify with a certain religious group because it is popular, are their actions any better than Jeroboam's? Not really. A religion of convenience, devised in one's own heart, is an abomination to God and is condemned by history as was the substitute faith of Jeroboam. He was branded forever as, "Jeroboam the son of Nebat, who made Israel sin" (2 Kings 23:15).

The Message of the Man of God

> 13:1 And behold, a man of God went from Judah to Bethel by the word of the LORD, and Jeroboam stood by the altar to burn incense.
>
> 2 Then he cried out against the altar by the word of the LORD, and said, "O altar, altar! Thus says the LORD: 'Behold, a child, Josiah by name, shall be born to the house of David; and on you he shall sacrifice the priests of the high places who burn incense on you, and men's bones shall be burned on you.'"
>
> 3 And he gave a sign the same day, saying, "This *is* the sign which the LORD has spoken: Surely the altar shall split apart, and the ashes on it shall be poured out."
>
> 4 So it came to pass when King Jeroboam heard the saying of the man of God, who cried out against the altar in Bethel, that he stretched out his hand from the altar, saying, "Arrest him!" Then his hand, which he stretched out toward him, withered, so that he could not pull it back to himself.

5 The altar also was split apart, and the ashes
poured out from the altar, according to the sign which
the man of God had given by the word of the LORD.
6 Then the king answered and said to the man of
God, "Please entreat the favor of the LORD your God,
and pray for me, that my hand may be restored to me."
So the man of God entreated the LORD, and the king's
hand was restored to him, and became as before.
7 Then the king said to the man of God, "Come
home with me and refresh yourself, and I will give
you a reward."
8 But the man of God said to the king, "If you were
to give me half your house, I would not go in with you;
nor would I eat bread nor drink water in this place.
9 "For so it was commanded me by the word of
the LORD, saying, 'You shall not eat bread, nor drink
water, nor return by the same way you came.'"
10 So he went another way and did not return by
the way he came to Bethel.
11 Now an old prophet dwelt in Bethel, and his
sons came and told him all the works that the man of
God had done that day in Bethel; they also told their
father the words which he had spoken to the king.
12 And their father said to them, "Which way did
he go?" For his sons had seen which way the man of
God went who came from Judah.
13 Then he said to his sons, "Saddle the donkey for
me." So they saddled the donkey for him; and he
rode on it,
14 and went after the man of God, and found him
sitting under an oak. Then he said to him, "*Are* you
the man of God who came from Judah?" And he
said, "I *am.*"
15 Then he said to him, "Come home with me and
eat bread."
16 And he said, "I cannot return with you nor go
in with you; neither can I eat bread nor drink water
with you in this place.
17 "For I have been told by the word of the LORD,
'You shall not eat bread nor drink water there, nor
return by going the way you came.'"
18 He said to him, "I too *am* a prophet as you *are,*

and an angel spoke to me by the word of the LORD,
saying, 'Bring him back with you to your house, that
he may eat bread and drink water.'" (He was lying to
him.)
19 So he went back with him, and ate bread in his
house, and drank water.
20 Now it happened, as they sat at the table, that
the word of the LORD came to the prophet who had
brought him back;
21 and he cried out to the man of God who came
from Judah, saying, "Thus says the LORD: 'Because
you have disobeyed the word of the LORD, and have
not kept the commandment which the LORD your
God commanded you,
22 'but you came back, ate bread, and drank water
in the place of which *the LORD* said to you, "Eat no
bread and drink no water," your corpse shall not
come to the tomb of your fathers.'"
23 So it was, after he had eaten bread and after he
had drunk, that he saddled the donkey for him, the
prophet whom he had brought back.
24 When he was gone, a lion met him on the road
and killed him. And his corpse was thrown on the
road, and the donkey stood by it. The lion also stood
by the corpse.
25 And there, men passed by and saw the corpse
thrown on the road, and the lion standing by the
corpse. Then they went and told *it* in the city where
the old prophet dwelt.
26 Now when the prophet who had brought him
back from the way heard *it,* he said, "It *is* the man of
God who was disobedient to the word of the LORD.
Therefore the LORD has delivered him to the lion,
which has torn him and killed him, according to the
word of the LORD which He spoke to him."
27 And he spoke to his sons, saying, "Saddle the
donkey for me." So they saddled *it.*
28 Then he went and found his corpse thrown on
the road, and the donkey and the lion standing by the
corpse. The lion had not eaten the corpse nor torn
the donkey.
29 And the prophet took up the corpse of the man

> of God, laid it on the donkey, and brought it back. So
> the old prophet came to the city to mourn, and to
> bury him.
> 30 Then he laid the corpse in his own tomb; and
> they mourned over him, *saying,* "Alas, my brother!"
> 31 So it was, after he had buried him, that he spoke
> to his sons, saying, "When I am dead, then bury me in
> the tomb where the man of God *is* buried; lay my
> bones beside his bones.
> 32 "For the saying which he cried out by the word
> of the LORD against the altar in Bethel, and against all
> the shrines on the high places which *are* in the cities
> of Samaria, will surely come to pass."
> 33 After this event Jeroboam did not turn from his
> evil way, but again he made priests from every class
> of people for the high places; whoever wished, he
> consecrated him, and he become *one* of the priests of
> the high places.
> 34 And this thing was the sin of the house of Jer-
> oboam, so as to exterminate and destroy *it* from the
> face of the earth.
>
> *1 Kings 13:1–34*

Prophets in the Old Testament were not only "king-makers" but also "king-breakers." Those the Lord sent to choose and anoint kings could also be sent to declare divine judgment and condemn them. This interesting narrative in chapter 13 is an example. Though nameless, this *"man of God"* courageously spoke out publicly against the sins of Jeroboam and shamed the disobedient king by his own exemplary obedience to God. It was the first time Jeroboam had been publicly condemned for his failures. Even though the miraculous withering and healing of the king's arm must have caught his attention, it did not cause him to change his ways.

Verse 6 might imply a royal change of heart when the king asked the prophet to intercede for him to the Lord. His literal request was, "stroke the face of God for me," or in other words, "smooth God's anger for me."[7] But whatever softening of the king's heart the request might imply, it was short-lived. He continued in disobedience until his death (v. 33).

Meanwhile, the obedient "man of God" met his own sad fate. He, who had refused so courageously to disobey God by accepting the king's invitation to eat and drink in Israel, was now deceived by a false prophet (vv. 11–34). It may seem somehow unfair that Jeroboam would be allowed to live on in gross disobedience, while this brave man of God died simply because he was deceived by a false prophet. But perhaps God expects more from the people He calls into His prophetic service. They must not only be alert to obvious temptations but also be careful to resist those more subtle as well.

Three hundred years later, in 2 Kings 23:16, the predictions of the man of God are fulfilled. Josiah, as verse 2 predicted, destroyed the altars of Jeroboam and burned bones on the pagan site to defile it, just as he said. We are also told in that chapter that good king Josiah noticed the gravestone nearby and asked its identity. He was told it was the grave of the man of God who came from Judah and foretold what Josiah would do three hundred years later. Josiah honored the brave man of God and ordered his grave protected. Even though he was anonymous as far as Scripture is concerned, his influence for God had been a lasting one. In his *Antiquities* (7.9.1), Josephus details additional exploits of this prophet and declares his name to be Yadon.[8]

The Conclusion of Jeroboam's Reign

14:1 At that time Abijah the son of Jeroboam became sick.

2 And Jeroboam said to his wife, "Please arise, and disguise yourself, that they may not recognize you as the wife of Jeroboam, and go to Shiloh. Indeed, Ahijah the prophet *is* there, who told me *I would be* king over this people.

3 "Also take with you ten loaves, *some* cakes, and a jar of honey, and go to him; he will tell you what will become of the child."

4 And Jeroboam's wife did so; she arose and went to Shiloh, and came to the house of Ahijah. But Ahijah could not see, for his eyes were glazed by reason of his age.

5 Now the LORD had said to Ahijah, "Here is the wife of Jeroboam, coming to ask you something

about her son, for he *is* sick. Thus and thus you shall say to her; for it will be, when she comes in, that she will pretend *to be* another *woman.*"

6 And so it was, when Ahijah heard the sound of her footsteps as she came through the door, he said, "Come in, wife of Jeroboam. Why do you pretend *to be* another *person?* For *I have been* sent to you *with* bad *news.*

7 "Go, tell Jeroboam, 'Thus says the LORD God of Israel: "Because I exalted you from among the people, and made you ruler over My people Israel,

8 "and tore the kingdom away from the house of David, and gave it to you; and *yet* you have not been as My servant David, who kept My commandments and who followed Me with all his heart, to do only *what was* right in My eyes;

9 "but you have done more evil than all who were before you, for you have gone and made for yourself other gods and molded images to provoke Me to anger, and have cast Me behind your back—

10 "therefore behold! I will bring disaster on the house of Jeroboam, and will cut off from Jeroboam every male in Israel, bond and free; I will take away the remnant of the house of Jeroboam, as one takes away refuse until it is all gone.

11 "The dogs shall eat whoever belongs to Jeroboam and dies in the city, and the birds of the air shall eat whoever dies in the field; for the LORD has spoken!"'

12 "Arise therefore, go to your own house. When your feet enter the city, the child shall die.

13 "And all Israel shall mourn for him and bury him, for he is the only one of Jeroboam who shall come to the grave, because in him there is found something good toward the LORD God of Israel in the house of Jeroboam.

14 "Moreover the LORD will raise up for Himself a king over Israel who shall cut off the house of Jeroboam; this is the day. What? Even now!

15 "For the LORD will strike Israel, as a reed is shaken in the water. He will uproot Israel from this good land which He gave to their fathers, and will scatter them beyond the River, because they have

made their wooden images, provoking the LORD to
anger.
16 "And He will give Israel up because of the sins
of Jeroboam, who sinned and who made Israel sin."
17 Then Jeroboam's wife arose and departed, and
came to Tirzah. When she came to the threshold of
the house, the child died.
18 And they buried him; and all Israel mourned
for him, according to the word of the LORD which He
spoke through His servant Ahijah the prophet.
19 Now the rest of the acts of Jeroboam, how he
made war and how he reigned, indeed they *are* written in the book of the chronicles of the kings of Israel.
20 The period that Jeroboam reigned *was* twenty-
two years. So he rested with his fathers. Then Nadab
his son reigned in his place.

1 Kings 14:1–20

For twenty-two years the unrepentant Jeroboam ruled the young Northern Kingdom, first from his early capital at Shechem and apparently in later years from the city of Tirzah about seven miles to the northeast of Shechem. But the wages of sin is death, even for a king, and Jeroboam's tragic reign came to a pathetic end.

His son Abijah, described as seriously ill in verse 1, is not mentioned elsewhere in Scripture. The king's concern for his recovery leads some interpreters to believe Abijah was the oldest son and therefore the heir to the throne. Isn't it telling that it took the illness of his son to finally persuade Jeroboam to turn to the word of the Lord? Ahijah, the prophet who had first proclaimed Jeroboam to be God's choice for king, had been in Shiloh all these years. The king knew his address, but only now did he turn to the prophet for spiritual guidance. It was too late.

Unwilling to approach Ahijah directly, Jeroboam conceived a scheme that called for his wife, the queen, to go in disguise to meet the prophet to ask for what the king hoped would be a favorable oracle. It was a traditional practice for the person making such a request of a man of God to take appropriate gifts. Those the queen took in verse 3 were not what one would expect from royalty and may have been intentionally played down as part of the disguise.

There are two interesting features in the description of the gifts.

The word translated *"cakes"* is linked to the Hebrew word for "spotted sheep" and may refer to a large sweet roll with raisins or seeds sprinkled on the crust.[9]

The other interesting word is the one used for the jar in which the honey was carried. The Hebrew word *baqbūq* is an onomatopoeic word; that is, it imitates the natural sound of the object it names—like our words "tinkle" and "buzz." This onomatopoeic Hebrew word sounds like the gurgling sound made when pouring a liquid out of a bottle with a narrow neck.[10]

Jeroboam's devious scheme failed because God forewarned the prophet Ahijah. He greeted the surprised queen with the announcement that even though his eyesight was nearly gone, he knew who she was (v. 6). After predicting the death of the king's son, Ahijah then delivered a scorching condemnation of Jeroboam and foretold not only the end of his reign but the end of his dynasty as well. The one referred to in verse 14 who would be raised up to put an end to Jeroboam's final heir to the throne was king Baasha, who is introduced much later in 15:25.

Instead of an encouraging oracle from the man of God, Jeroboam received one of the most scathing rebukes in the entire book (vv. 7–16). He had made God angry (v. 9). Anger ascribed to God in the Scriptures is not the sudden passionate emotion of which men are guilty but is anger in the sense of a steady, reasoned antagonism against evil. It describes God's settled attitude toward sin and unrepentant sinners.

In this case, God's anger brought *"disaster on the house of Jeroboam"* (v. 10). Every male in the house of Jeroboam would be taken out like garbage (v. 10). None of his heirs, except Ahijah, would be given a respected burial, but they would be devoured by scavengers (v. 11). Eventually, Israel would be uprooted from their good land and scattered beyond the River (v. 15). *"The River"* refers to the Euphrates, obviously a reference to the future captivity of Israel.

Why this severe judgment on the reign of Jeroboam? In verses 8–9, the prophet Ahijah listed six reasons: (1) Jeroboam had not obeyed God as David had done. (2) He had done more evil than any before him. (3) He had made other gods. (4) He had fashioned graven images. (5) He had made God angry. (6) He had cast God behind his back. This last reason implies a neglect, a scorning of God. It is the same figure of speech used to describe God's forgiveness of our sins.

He puts them behind His back, or in other words, He forgets them. That is good news when it describes God's treatment of our sins, but it is tragically bad news when it describes a person's treatment of God.

What might have been a memorable reign by the man chosen of God to rule His people is summed up in routine fashion in verses 19–20. Before returning to his report of Rehoboam in Judah, the author announced that Nadab, Jeroboam's son, took over the throne of Israel. But we already know from the prophecy in verse 14 what will happen to him.

THE REIGN OF REHOBOAM IN JUDAH

> 14:21 And Rehoboam the son of Solomon reigned in Judah. Rehoboam *was* forty-one years old when he became king. He reigned seventeen years in Jerusalem, the city which the LORD had chosen out of all the tribes of Israel, to put His name there. His mother's name *was* Naamah, an Ammonitess.
>
> 22 Now Judah did evil in the sight of the LORD, and they provoked Him to jealousy with their sins which they committed, more than all that their fathers had done.
>
> 23 For they also built for themselves high places, *sacred* pillars, and wooden images on every high hill and under every green tree.
>
> 24 And there were also perverted persons in the land. They did according to all the abominations of the nations which the LORD had cast out before the children of Israel.
>
> 25 It happened in the fifth year of King Rehoboam *that* Shishak king of Egypt came up against Jerusalem.
>
> 26 And he took away the treasures of the house of the LORD and the treasures of the king's house; he took away everything. He also took away all the gold shields which Solomon had made.
>
> 27 Then King Rehoboam made bronze shields in their place, and committed *them* to the hands of the captains of the guard, who guarded the doorway of the king's house.

28 And whenever the king entered the house of the
LORD, the guards carried them, then brought them
back into the guardroom.
29 Now the rest of the acts of Rehoboam, and all
that he did, *are* they not written in the book of the
chronicles of the kings of Judah?
30 And there was war between Rehoboam and
Jeroboam all *their* days.
31 So Rehoboam rested with his fathers, and was
buried with his fathers in the City of David. His
mother's name *was* Naamah, an Ammonitess. Then
Abijam his son reigned in his place.

1 Kings 14:21–31

Not much time nor space is wasted in narrating the remaining years of King Rehoboam. His weak, vacillating performance as king led Judah into sins far more severe than those of Israel to the north. Jeroboam built a couple of golden bulls, but Rehoboam, not to be outdone, built *"high places, sacred pillars, and wooden images on every high hill and under every green tree"* (v. 23). He also allowed *"perverted persons,"* male and female prostitutes, to practice their cultic religions with court approval (v. 24). Within five years after he assumed the throne of his powerful father Solomon, Judah fell under the oppression of Egypt.

Shishak, the pharaoh, had been watching the developments in Solomon's kingdom. He had given sanctuary to Jeroboam after his abortive rebellion against Solomon, and now his ally had taken ten of the twelve tribes in Solomon's kingdom away, leaving only Judah, along with tiny Benjamin, in the South. When it became obvious that Rehoboam had none of the strengths of the great Solomon and was instead a thoughtless weakling, Shishak marched on Jerusalem. His invasion, not detailed here, has been found by archaeologists recorded on inscribed stones in the ruins of the Egyptian temple of Amun at Karnak.

There apparently was not much resistance. As far as the record shows, Shishak did not even have to besiege the once-powerful capital of Solomon and David. The fortress cities that Solomon had established to protect the land had toppled like dominoes. All that remained was for Shishak to threaten the weakling Rehoboam in order to win his abject capitulation.

Those beautiful golden shields that Solomon had hung in the House of the Cedars of Lebanon as symbols of his wealth were now given to Shishak as tribute along with other golden treasures from the temple. *"He took away everything"* (v. 26), leaving Rehoboam to quickly commission substitute shields of bronze to take the place of the treasures of his father.

What a contrast! From mighty Solomon with all his wisdom, wealth, and power to spineless Rehoboam with his shallow judgment, his cheap bronze shields, and a kingdom subjected to Egypt. The only good thing the writer can say about Rehoboam is that he reigned *"in Jerusalem, the city which the Lord had chosen out of all the tribes of Israel, to put His name there"* (v. 21).

The account ends with the note that Rehoboam's mother was Naamah, an Ammonitess. Is this not the writer's way of reminding us that it was Solomon's marriage to foreign wives that started the precipitous decline in the first place?

NOTES

1. Norman H. Snaith, Ralph W. Sockman, and Raymond Calkins, "The First and Second Books of Kings," in *The Interpreter's Bible,* vol. 3 (Nashville: Abingdon, 1954), 114.
2. Karl Chr. W. F. Bähr, *The Books of the Kings,* Commentary on the Holy Scriptures, ed. John Peter Lange (Grand Rapids: Zondervan, 1960), 150.
3. Ibid.
4. I. W. Slotki, *Kings* (London: Soncino Press, 1950), 90.
5. Bernhard W. Anderson, *Understanding the Old Testament* (Englewood Cliffs, NJ: Prentice-Hall, 1958), 190.
6. Gwilym H. Jones, *1 and 2 Kings,* New Century Bible Commentary, ed. Ronald E. Clements (Grand Rapids: Eerdmans, 1984), 257.
7. M. Pierce Matheney and Roy Honeycutt, "1-2 Kings," in *The Broadman Bible Commentary,* ed. Clifton J. Allen, vol. 3 (Nashville: Broadman, 1970), 196.
8. John Gray, *I and II Kings,* Old Testament Library (Philadelphia: Westminster, 1963), 295.
9. Jones, 269.
10. Snaith, Sockman, and Calkins, 126.

CHAPTER SEVEN

The Reigns of Two Kings in Judah and Five Kings in Israel

1 Kings 15:1–16:28

INTRODUCTION

Whatever method God used to inspire the writers of Scripture, it seems to have included a certain amount of freedom on the part of the author to research existing sources and to employ his own unique literary style as he composed his work. The reader is made aware of this in Luke's reference to his sources in Luke 1:1–4 and in Luke's distinctive writing style compared to the other Gospels. The writer reveals his individuality in the Books of Kings as well.

Several sources that the author of Kings used are identified by name in his book: "The Book of the Acts of Solomon" (1 Kings 11:41), "The Book of the Chronicles of the Kings of Israel" (1 Kings 14:19), and "The Book of the Chronicles of the Kings of Judah" (1 Kings 14:29). These last two sources were apparently well known in the author's day, but are not to be identified with the Books of Chronicles in our Bible. They were written earlier and were probably collections of brief records in the form of public annals. Additional sources used by the author of Kings came from certain eyewitness accounts of individual prophets (referred to in 2 Chron. 9:29) and various recorded court histories. No copies of these source documents are extant, but present-day interpreters of Kings and Chronicles can guess some of their content by the manner in which the inspired author of Kings used them.

Under the guidance of the Holy Spirit, and based on these and other sources, the gifted historian employed his own writing techniques to convey the message God wanted preserved. His distinctive style is reflected in a number of places in the book, particularly where he introduces a new king into the narrative and where he ends one reign before beginning another. His standard introductory formula for the kings of Judah runs as follows:

> In the ______ year of ______, king of Israel, ______ the son of ______, became king over Judah. He was ______ years old when he began to reign, and he reigned ______ years in ______. His mother's name was ______. And he did what was evil (or right) in the sight of the Lord.

For the kings of Israel, the formula is similar but omits the age of the new king and the name of his mother. The typical format utilized for writing the conclusion of a king's reign is illustrated in 1 Kings 16:5–6:

> Now the rest of the acts of ______, what he did, and his might, are they not written in the book of the chronicles of the kings of Israel? So ______ rested with his fathers and was buried in ______. Then ______ his son reigned in his place.

Throughout the books, with some variations, the author employed these standard outlines as a literary technique for recording his message.

Since there was no official calendar reference (such as B.C. or A.D.) which would allow him to date the kings, the author also devised an ingenious dating mechanism to synchronize his account and to keep the history of the two kingdoms in step with each other. Having begun, for example, his history of a king of Judah, he takes it to its conclusion and follows it with the reigns of all the kings of Israel who came to the throne during that Judean king's reign. After completing the account of the last Israelite king of that period, he then switches back to the Judean king who had by that time come to power in Judah, and so on.[1]

In the present section, for instance, the author discusses the forty-one years of Asa's reign in Judah and then turns to present the reigns of the Israelite kings who came to the throne during this period. Additionally, throughout the book, interspersed in their proper places, are the activities of the prophets.

It was an ingenious dating scheme in the light of such limited calendaring in ancient days, but it is very difficult for modern interpreters, separated from these events by so many intervening centuries, to unravel the clever dating exactly. Consequently, the chronology of Kings is a continuing challenge for current biblical scholars.

In order to examine the entire scriptural record of this period in biblical history, one must study not only 1 and 2 Kings, but the parallel passages in Chronicles and Samuel, as well as related passages in the prophets. There are "harmonies" of these books similar to a "harmony of the Gospels," which are very helpful in coordinating the separate accounts.

ABIJAM REIGNS IN JUDAH

15:1 In the eighteenth year of King Jeroboam the son of Nebat, Abijam became king over Judah.

2 He reigned three years in Jerusalem. His mother's name *was* Maachah the granddaughter of Abishalom.

3 And he walked in all the sins of his father, which he had done before him; his heart was not loyal to the LORD his God, as was the heart of his father David.

4 Nevertheless for David's sake the LORD his God gave him a lamp in Jerusalem, by setting up his son after him and by establishing Jerusalem;

5 because David did *what was* right in the eyes of the LORD, and had not turned aside from anything that He commanded him all the days of his life, except in the matter of Uriah the Hittite.

6 And there was war between Rehoboam and Jeroboam all the days of his life.

7 Now the rest of the acts of Abijam, and all that he did, *are* they not written in the book of the chronicles of the kings of Judah? And there was war between Abijam and Jeroboam.

8 So Abijam rested with his fathers, and they buried him in the City of David. Then Asa his son reigned in his place.

1 Kings 15:1–8

Solomon's son, King Rehoboam, was buried with his fathers in the City of David, and his son Abijam (spelled Abijah in 2 Chron. 12:16ff.) now begins what will be a brief three-year reign over Judah. As the grandson of the great Solomon, he presided over a shrunken kingdom, only a fraction of the vast domain of his grandfather. Likewise, Abijam possessed only a fraction of Solomon's wisdom. Of course for seventeen years, his father Rehoboam's poor example of statesmanship clouded any good influence Solomon might have had on Abijam. So perhaps it should be no surprise that his tenure as king was not only brief but weak.

In fact, verse 3 traces his failure directly to the influence of his father: *"He walked in all the sins of his father, which he had done before him. . . ."* From the previous chapter we know what those sins were: (1) his clumsy, insensitive handling of the complaints of the Northern tribes, which led to the division of the kingdom (1 Kings 12:1–16); (2) his futile attempt to force his leadership on the rebel tribes (1 Kings 12:18–24); (3) his installation of pagan high places, sacred pillars, and wooden images, which he built "on every hill and under every green tree" (1 Kings 14:23); (4) his sanction of "perverted persons," male and female prostitutes, who practiced their cultic abominations with court approval (1 Kings 14:24); and (5) his squandering of the royal treasures, including Solomon's priceless gold shields, which he paid as tribute to Shishak of Egypt (1 Kings 14:25–28). Apparently, Abijam was guilty of similar sins so that he is condemned in verse 3 as *"not loyal to the Lord his God, as was . . . his father David."*

The king's mother is identified in verse 2 as Maachah, the granddaughter of Abishalom. Abishalom is an alternate spelling of Absalom, David's son. (Josephus says her mother was Tamar, the daughter of Absalom.[2]) In the parallel passage in 2 Chron. 11:20–22, we are told that because Maachah was Rehoboam's favorite among his sixty concubines and eighteen wives, he elevated her son Abijam, rather than his oldest son, to the position of crown prince. So, although she was not a "foreign wife" like Solomon's who brought idolatry into the land, Maachah nevertheless had as much negative influence on Abijam as his father did. In verse 13, she is censured as a worshiper of Asherah and as an idolater who built and worshiped an *"obscene image."*

It is impossible throughout the Book of Kings to overlook the strong implications of parental influence over the lives of children. When a king is described as reversing the pattern of his father and mother before him, it is a rare exception to the rule. In almost every case, the king "walked in the ways of his father before him," or as in Abijam's case the ways of his father *and* mother. There were other noble role models he could have followed: namely David, and to a lesser extent, Solomon. But Abijam followed instead the example of the two he knew the best, his mother and father.

A gardener knows that ripe fruit never falls very far from the tree where it grew, and the keen observer of history knows that children seldom stray very far from the example of their parents. The German proverb expresses it well, *"Was die Alten sungen, das zwitshern die Jungen."* "Whatever the old sing, the young chirp."

Is there an indirect insight into this king's moral decline in the diverse spelling of his name? Chronicles spells his name Abijah, which means "Yahweh is my father." Kings spells the name Abijam, which means "my father is Yam." Yam was a Canaanite sea-god. Could it be he started out as Abijah, a follower of Yahweh, and ended up as Abijam, a follower of a false god? Obviously, he was not all bad. For example, verse 15 indicates he dedicated to the house of the Lord silver and gold treasures, which his son Asa later installed in the temple. Perhaps the young king had a good beginning that eventually, under so many contrary influences, declined into moral bankruptcy.

Why would God allow such a sinful man to remain as king over His people in Judah? One answer is given in verse 4. It was for David's sake. Because his heart was loyal, God promised David a continuing posterity on the throne in Jerusalem, or a *"lamp"* as it is expressed in verse 4. (See comments on 1 Kings 11:36.) So, as a descendant of David, the wicked Abijam was permitted to rule and to have his son follow him on the throne as a divine concession for David's sake.

The honesty of scriptural history is reflected in verse 5, where David's otherwise noble life is qualified by the mention of his sin against Uriah the Hittite. Not even David was perfect. While perfection is God's ultimate goal for His people, He will accept and love us as sinners if we trust Him. David's faith in Yahweh was strong despite his failures, and by God's grace, his great-grandson was allowed to continue the Davidic dynasty.

Brief mention is given in this section to the continuing war between the North and the South (vv. 6, 7). The more detailed account in Chronicles describes a military victory Abijam won against Jeroboam in which the city of Bethel and parts of southern Ephraim fell temporarily into the hands of Judah.

Thus the inspired biographer of the kings seals up his testimony of Abijam with the traditional formula in verses 7 and 8. His purpose is to teach Judah, Israel, and us the lessons drawn from the facts and events of the passage.

ASA REIGNS IN JUDAH

15:9 In the twentieth year of Jeroboam king of Israel, Asa became king over Judah.

10 And he reigned forty-one years in Jerusalem. His grandmother's name *was* Maachah the granddaughter of Abishalom.

11 Asa did *what was* right in the eyes of the LORD, as *did* his father David.

12 And he banished the perverted persons from the land, and removed all the idols that his fathers had made.

13 Also he removed Maachah his grandmother from *being* queen mother, because she had made an obscene image of Asherah. And Asa cut down her obscene image and burned *it* by the Brook Kidron.

14 But the high places were not removed. Nevertheless Asa's heart was loyal to the LORD all his days.

15 He also brought into the house of the LORD the things which his father had dedicated, and the things which he himself had dedicated: silver and gold and utensils.

16 Now there was war between Asa and Baasha king of Israel all their days.

17 And Baasha king of Israel came up against Judah, and built Ramah, that he might let none go out or come in to Asa king of Judah.

18 Then Asa took all the silver and gold *that was* left in the treasuries of the house of the LORD and the treasuries of the king's house, and delivered them into

the hand of his servants. And King Asa sent them to
Ben-Hadad the son of Tabrimmon, the son of Hezion,
king of Syria, who dwelt in Damascus, saying,
19 *"Let there be* a treaty between you and me, as
there was between my father and your father. See, I
have sent you a present of silver and gold. Come and
break your treaty with Baasha king of Israel, so that
he will withdraw from me."
20 So Ben-Hadad heeded King Asa, and sent the
captains of his armies against the cities of Israel.
He attacked Ijon, Dan, Abel Beth Maachah, and all
Chinneroth, with all the land of Naphtali.
21 Now it happened, when Baasha heard *it,* that
he stopped building Ramah, and remained in Tirzah.
22 Then King Asa made a proclamation throughout
all Judah; none *was* exempted. And they took away
the stones and timber of Ramah, which Baasha had
used for building; and with them King Asa built Geba
of Benjamin, and Mizpah.
23 The rest of all the acts of Asa, all his might, all
that he did, and the cities which he built, *are* they not
written in the book of the chronicles of the kings of
Judah? But in the time of his old age he was diseased
in his feet.
24 So Asa rested with his fathers, and was buried
with his fathers in the City of David his father. Then
Jehoshaphat his son reigned in his place.

1 Kings 15:9–24

Under the careful examination of the inspired writer, only two kings in the entire book are given a clean record. Most are condemned as wicked. Six others pass his final examination, but with only mediocre grades. Asa, the son of Abijam, is one of the better examples of this last category. He managed to reverse the godless trend of his father and grandfather before him and is praised in verse 11 as one who *"did what was right in the eyes of the Lord, as did his father David."*

But there were failures too. He did not complete the task of destroying pagan influences in the land, and he made a short-sighted nonaggression treaty with Ben-Hadad of Syria. The Syrians were always ready to play the double game in Palestinian politics, aligning themselves now with Judah and now with Israel according to the changing advantage of the hour. Abijam's Syrian pact was foolish enough, but when the prophet Hanani rebuked him for relying on Syria instead of the Lord, the king became angry and imprisoned him (2 Chron. 16:7–10).

Furthermore, in order to fortify the cities of Geba and Mizpah, he drafted forced labor, even though this practice always aroused rebellion. Finally, according to Chronicles, instead of seeking the Lord when he became ill, Abijam sought the help of physicians (2 Chron. 16:12). These may appear to be minor faults, but they were considered serious enough by the writer to drop his grade from "A" to "C."

But the commendable accomplishments of King Asa were so refreshing in the company of so much apostasy that they earned him the praise of the author as a successful reformer. Asa's reign in Judah was a long one, beginning while Jeroboam was still king in Israel and lasting an unprecedented forty-one years. Eight petty kings came and went in the land of Israel while Asa ruled in Judah.

His reforms were impressive. First, he banished the *"perverted persons"* from the land (v. 12). The Hebrew word is *qĕdēšîm,* which refers to both men and women who practiced sodomy and prostitution in religious rituals.[3] Second, he removed all the idols his fathers had made (v. 12). *"Fathers"* refers to those who reigned before him all the way back to Solomon. The word for idols comes from the Hebrew word "to roll" and literally means "idol blocks." Some believe the idols were doll-like images rolled or wrapped in cloth or dressed up in clothing. Most agree it was a term of derision or scorn for these ugly objects of pagan worship.[4]

Third, he removed his own grandmother, Maachah, from the position of queen mother because of her idolatry (v. 13). This must have been an impressive public statement to the entire population. Fourth, he cut down and burned the well-known *"obscene image"* which the queen mother had built (v. 13). This image is described as "obscene" in our English translation, but the Hebrew word is closer in meaning to "frightening," "horrible," or "abominable."[5] Some commentators believe it was some sort of phallic symbol consistent with the fertility cult of Asherah. The destruction of this famous image, and its public burning by the Brook Kidron, must also have made a profound impression on the people.

Fifth, Asa began to replenish the treasures of the temple, which had been squandered by his grandfather, King Rehoboam, when he paid tribute to Shishak of Egypt (v. 15). Sixth, he strengthened Judah by repelling Israel's invading army and fortifying the cities of Geba and Mizpah (v. 22).

The Book of Chronicles adds two more praiseworthy accomplishments of King Asa. He repaired the great altar of sacrifice in front of the temple, and he gathered all the people to the temple to praise the Lord in a revival of Yahweh worship (2 Chron. 15:8–10).

Baasha, king of Israel, is introduced in verse 16. This gets ahead of the upcoming story of the kings in the Northern Kingdom. We will meet Baasha in his proper place in the order in chapter 16. His significance here is to tell us that the war between Judah and Israel had gone against Judah to such an extent that King Baasha could build an Israelite fortress at Ramah, just five miles north of Judah's capital, Jerusalem. It was only by bribing Ben-Hadad to attack Israel from the north, that Asa was able to drive Baasha from Ramah and actually use the stones of the Israelite fortress to fortify his own military outposts at Geba and Mizpah (vv. 16–22).

Except for an interesting reference to Asa's foot disease (some believe it was gout from the rich diet of the royal palace), the concluding remarks of the author are standard. Asa stands as a reminder that a godly leader can have a powerful impact for good over an entire nation.

Even though a person may not be a king, that person's single influence can have a similar vast impact today. Martin Marty tells about Anne Sabine Halle, a German Quaker who outlasted Hitler during the Nazi regime. He wondered if all the sufferings and sacrifices during that time made any difference. The courageous heroine, now in her sixties, believed it did. She referred to a quotation from Albert Schweitzer that encouraged her people often during those dark days:

> Not one of us knows what effect we may be having or what we may be giving to other persons. It is hidden from us and shall remain so. Often we are permitted to see a very little portion of this, so that we may not become discouraged. Power works in mysterious ways.[6]

The quiet power of those who courageously stand by convictions, speak the truth, and protest in silence during dark days of oppression is indeed immeasurable and continues to bear its influence long after the courageous believer is gone.

NADAB REIGNS IN ISRAEL

15:25 Now Nadab the son of Jeroboam became king
over Israel in the second year of Asa king of Judah,
and he reigned over Israel two years.
26 And he did evil in the sight of the LORD, and
walked in the way of his father, and in his sin by
which he had made Israel sin.
27 Then Baasha the son of Ahijah, of the house of
Issachar, conspired against him. And Baasha killed
him at Gibbethon, which *belonged* to the Philistines,
while Nadab and all Israel laid siege to Gibbethon.
28 Baasha killed him in the third year of Asa king
of Judah, and reigned in his place.
29 And it was so, when he became king, *that* he
killed all the house of Jeroboam. He did not leave to
Jeroboam anyone that breathed, until he had destroyed him, according to the word of the LORD which
He had spoken by His servant Ahijah the Shilonite,
30 because of the sins of Jeroboam, which he had
sinned and by which he had made Israel sin, because
of his provocation with which he had provoked the
LORD God of Israel to anger.
31 Now the rest of the acts of Nadab, and all that
he did, *are* they not written in the book of the chronicles of the kings of Israel?
32 And there was war between Asa and Baasha
king of Israel all their days.

1 Kings 15:25–32

Consistently following his literary plan, the author of Kings now goes back to pick up the royal succession of five rulers in Israel (six if Tibni is counted) during the forty-one years of Asa's reign in Judah. The brevity of the tenure of the Northern kings illustrates the instability of the kingdom of Israel. That instability is explained in part by the fact that Israel was made up of ten competing tribes and that the nation's political center was moved from capital to capital. Judah, on the other hand, consisted of only one tribe (along with tiny Benjamin) and had one political capital, Jerusalem. The Southern Kingdom, therefore, was more stable than the Northern Kingdom.

The writer had left the story of Israel at 14:20 with the death of Jeroboam, mentioning that Nadab his son succeeded him. Now the Israel narrative continues with a fuller discussion of Nadab's short reign.

Nadab was king little more than one year, but since it covered parts of two years, Hebrew time measurement reckons his reign as two years (15:25). We know nothing whatever about Nadab except what is found in these eight verses. Showing some military prowess, he besieged the city of Gibbethon, a Levitical town on the frontiers of the tribe of Dan that had been captured by the Philistines. Apparently Nadab's campaign was unsuccessful, because Gibbethon, still a Philistine possession, continued under siege by Israel twenty-four years later when Omri became king.

Verse 26 reproves Nadab for imitating the sins of his father Jeroboam and doing evil in the sight of the Lord. This must imply that Nadab continued the calf-worship his father had introduced (12:28). As a result, he was judged by God, and the divine warning recorded earlier in 14:14 took effect. Baasha, probably a military commander in Nadab's army, assassinated the king and claimed the throne for himself. To secure his coup, Baasha also wiped out all the descendants of Nadab (v. 29), thereby erasing Jeroboam's royal dynasty as predicted in 14:14.

Normally, the author of Kings concluded his story of a king by saying, "he slept with his fathers," but an exception was made when the king did not die a natural death. Since Nadab was struck down by an act of treason, the usual phrase is omitted as this king's brief story is terminated.

Baasha Reigns in Israel

> 15:33 In the third year of Asa king of Judah, Baasha the son of Ahijah became king over all Israel in Tirzah, and *reigned* twenty-four years.

34 He did evil in the sight of the LORD, and walked
in the way of Jeroboam, and in his sin by which he
had made Israel sin.
16:1 Then the word of the LORD came to Jehu the son
of Hanani, against Baasha, saying:
2 "Inasmuch as I lifted you out of the dust and
made you ruler over My people Israel, and you have
walked in the way of Jeroboam, and have made My
people Israel sin, to provoke Me to anger with their
sins,
3 "surely I will take away the posterity of Baasha
and the posterity of his house, and I will make your
house like the house of Jeroboam the son of Nebat.
4 "The dogs shall eat whoever belongs to Baasha
and dies in the city, and the birds of the air shall eat
whoever dies in the fields."
5 Now the rest of the acts of Baasha, what he did,
and his might, *are* they not written in the book of the
chronicles of the kings of Israel?
6 So Baasha rested with his fathers and was
buried in Tirzah. Then Elah his son reigned in his
place.
7 And also the word of the LORD came by the
prophet Jehu the son of Hanani against Baasha and
his house, because of all the evil that he did in the
sight of the LORD in provoking Him to anger with
the work of his hands, in being like the house of
Jeroboam, and because he killed them.

1 Kings 15:33–16:7

Baasha's father, Ahijah, is not identified. He was from the tribe of Issachar and was obviously not the prophet by the same name, who is called a Shilonite in chapter 14. Since he was at Gibbethon with the army, Baasha was probably an army official with no royal lineage. Implying that he was elevated from a very low position, verse 2 says he was *"lifted . . . out of the dust"* to become ruler.[7]

In spite of his modest roots, Baasha must have been a clever and powerful monarch, since he remained in office twenty-four years against the recurring pattern of treasonous plots and frequent assassinations. He himself had helped establish the pattern by murdering King Nadab, and his own son would quickly be cut down by the same murderous treachery, but Baasha survived for a considerable time.

The mention of Tirzah in verse 33 has led most interpreters to assume that it was Baasha who established the capital of Israel in that city, where it remained until Omri moved it to Samaria.[8]

Another of the many prophets in Israel during this period is introduced in 16:1. Jehu is his name. He had a long tenure as God's spokesman in Israel, since he is apparently the same man who fifty years later condemned Jehoshaphat after the death of Ahab.[9] Jehu was also the author of a history book that was incorporated into the Books of the Kings (2 Chron. 20:34). Transmitting the words of the Lord, Jehu scathingly rebuked Baasha for his sin, quoting the same grisly description Ahijah had used against Jeroboam in 14:11: "The dogs shall eat whoever belongs to Baasha and dies in the city, and the birds of the air shall eat whoever dies in the fields."

Baasha's evil is referred to in three places: 15:34, 16:2, and 16:7. Basically, he was guilty of the sins of Jeroboam and Nadab in leading Israel to worship the calf images, but another crime is mentioned in 16:7, *"he killed them."* This is a reference to Baasha's killing of the descendants of Jeroboam, and it raises a question. Why was Baasha condemned for wiping out the house of Jeroboam, since this was a part of God's providential judgment on the wicked king? The answer seems to be that if Baasha had been righteous, his acts would have been regarded as a divine mission; but since he was obviously motivated by personal ambition and since as king he perpetuated the same evil patterns of Jeroboam, his acts were judged as sinful.

Another question arises from this story. Why would Baasha, who saw how God punished his predecessors for allowing calf-worship and who actually participated in the divine punishment himself, so quickly turn and commit the same sin?

The identical question arises regarding tragic and senseless sins today. Why would an otherwise intelligent person knowing full well the dangers of drugs begin to experiment with cocaine or heroin? Why would informed individuals who read every day the tragic stories of alcohol-related traffic deaths get behind the wheel of a car after taking a drink? In spite of repeated media coverage of an epidemic of sexually transmitted diseases in our country, and in spite of God's clear prohibition, why would a person continue to be involved in sexual promiscuity?

The answer lies in Satan's ability to blind his victims to obvious truth. Personal ambition, physical lust, desire for popularity and thrills become satanic smoke screens clouding man's reason and permitting Satan to deceive his victims.

That's what happened in Israel. Spiritual blindness caused the kings to repeat the same mistakes of their predecessors and to execute each other in turn in a tragic cycle of destruction. And that's what is driving the same cyclical pattern of sin today.

Baasha rested with his fathers and was buried in his new capital of Tirzah (v. 6). This is the first time a burial place for a Northern king is mentioned in the account.

Elah Reigns in Israel

16:8 In the twenty-sixth year of Asa king of Judah,
Elah the son of Baasha became king over Israel, *and*
reigned two years in Tirzah.
9 Now his servant Zimri, commander of half *his*
chariots, conspired against him as he was in Tirzah
drinking himself drunk in the house of Arza, steward of *his* house in Tirzah.
10 And Zimri went in and struck him and killed
him in the twenty-seventh year of Asa king of Judah,
and reigned in his place.
11 Then it came to pass, when he began to reign,
as soon as he was seated on his throne, *that* he killed
all the household of Baasha; he did not leave him one
male, neither of his relatives nor of his friends.
12 Thus Zimri destroyed all the household of
Baasha, according to the word of the LORD, which He
spoke against Baasha by Jehu the prophet,
13 for all the sins of Baasha and the sins of Elah
his son, by which they had sinned and by which they
had made Israel sin, in provoking the LORD God of
Israel to anger with their idols.
14 Now the rest of the acts of Elah, and all that he
did, *are* they not written in the book of the chronicles
of the kings of Israel?

1 Kings 16:8–14

The next king on the historian's stage is Elah, again one about whom we know very little and one whose reign was very brief, only a few months. Guilty of the same national sins of his father, Elah added another personal weakness as well, drunkenness. While his army was enduring the hardships and dangers of battle in the field against the Philistines, Elah was *"drinking himself drunk"* in the house of Arza, the manager of his royal palace in Tirzah (v. 9). The words are literally "drinking drunk."[10]

Taking advantage of Elah's weakness, a military officer named Zimri devised a plot to eliminate the king and assume the crown himself. (The word *"servant"* in verse 9 means officer.[11]) More than likely, the king's steward, Arza, was in on the plot too and may have lured the king to his house. When he was sufficiently drugged by alcohol, Arza let in Zimri to carry out the assassination.

"As soon as he was seated on his throne" in Tirzah, Zimri killed all the family of Elah as well as the families of the king's friends. This was to make sure there was no heir to claim succession nor friend to avenge his death.[12]

The author condemns Elah's brief term as sinful. In addition to the usual failures, there is added in verse 13 the sin of idolatry. Until now, the kings had been guilty of making graven images of Yahweh like the golden calves of Jeroboam, but now the nation had been led to worship idols or false Gods. The word translated *"idols"* in verse 13 is literally "vanities" or "vapor."[13] It is sometimes used adverbially to mean "to no purpose." The word appears here for the first time for idols, and emphasizes the "nothingness" of alien gods. (Compare comments on 2 Kings 17:15.)

ZIMRI REIGNS IN ISRAEL

> 16:15 In the twenty-seventh year of Asa king of Judah, Zimri had reigned in Tirzah seven days. And the people *were* encamped against Gibbethon, which *belonged* to the Philistines.
>
> 16 Now the people *who were* encamped heard it said, "Zimri has conspired and also has killed the king." So all Israel made Omri, the commander of the army, king over Israel that day in the camp.

17 Then Omri and all Israel with him went up from
Gibbethon, and they besieged Tirzah.
18 And it happened, when Zimri saw that the city
was taken, that he went into the citadel of the king's
house and burned the king's house down upon himself with fire, and died,
19 because of the sins which he had committed in
doing evil in the sight of the LORD, in walking in the
way of Jeroboam, and in his sin which he had committed to make Israel sin.
20 Now the rest of the acts of Zimri, and the treason he committed, *are* they not written in the book of
the chronicles of the kings of Israel?

1 Kings 16:15–20

Zimri lasted only seven days as Israel's new king. Having wrested the power from Elah and totally exterminated the opposition, he felt secure on the throne. But when his fellow soldiers still encamped at Gibbethon heard what their upstart, low-ranking officer had done in Tirzah, they promptly rallied behind their commander, Omri, and proclaimed him the true king over Israel (v. 16). Then with their new ruler at the head of the troops, the army temporarily lifted their siege of Gibbethon and marched to surround King Zimri in his palace in Tirzah.

Realizing the hopelessness of his situation, Zimri set fire to the royal palace and died in the flames. He is one of the rare cases of suicide recorded in the Old Testament (cf. Judg. 9:54; 1 Sam. 31:4; 2 Sam. 17:23).

Although he ruled only seven days and spent most of those days murdering people, the author gives Zimri the full biographical treatment, including his traditional introductory and closing formulas. He also accuses Zimri of perpetrating the same evils as the previous kings (v. 19). How, in just seven days, could the king have deserved such inclusive condemnation? It must be that he was guilty of these sins while he served as a commander in the army before his brief reign, or maybe in one short week he demonstrated that he fully supported the religious policies of his predecessors Baasha and Jeroboam.

Omri (and Tibni) Reigns in Israel

16:21 Then the people of Israel were divided into two
parts: half of the people followed Tibni the son of
Ginath, to make him king, and half followed Omri.
22 But the people who followed Omri prevailed
over the people who followed Tibni the son of
Ginath. So Tibni died and Omri reigned.
23 In the thirty-first year of Asa king of Judah,
Omri became king over Israel, *and reigned* twelve
years. Six years he reigned in Tirzah.
24 And he bought the hill of Samaria from Shemer
for two talents of silver; then he built on the hill, and
called the name of the city which he built, Samaria,
after the name of Shemer, owner of the hill.
25 Omri did evil in the eyes of the LORD, and did
worse than all who *were* before him.
26 For he walked in all the ways of Jeroboam the
son of Nebat, and in his sin by which he had made
Israel sin, provoking the LORD God of Israel to anger
with their idols.
27 Now the rest of the acts of Omri which he did,
and the might that he showed, *are* they not written in
the book of the chronicles of the kings of Israel?
28 So Omri rested with his fathers and was buried
in Samaria. Then Ahab his son reigned in his place.

1 Kings 16:21–28

Even though it was one of the most important periods in Israel's history, the author uses only eight verses to describe this next reign, leaving some tantalizing questions unanswered. After a week of bloody violence in which (1) King Baasha, his family, and his closest friends were killed by Zimri, who then assumed the throne, (2) a military countercoup named Commander Omri king in opposition to Zimri, (3) King Omri and his troops besieged the capital city, and (4) King Zimri committed suicide by burning down the palace—it is no surprise that a full-scale civil war broke out.

That seems to be the situation in verse 21. Half the people followed the newly proclaimed military ruler, Omri, and the other half followed a man named Tibni, who also claimed the throne. Tibni may have been a member of a civilian party who had supported Zimri in his brief reign. It appears that at least for a while, Israel had two kings reigning simultaneously, maybe in different parts of the country.

Some believe this situation lasted only a few days, after which Omri claimed uncontested rights to the monarchy.[14] Others believe the civil division lasted four or five years.[15] Verse 15 suggests that Omri took over from Zimri in the twenty-seventh year of Asa's reign in Judah, and verse 23 suggests that he did not assume full royal control until the thirty-first year of Asa's reign. During how much of this interlude Tibni also claimed to be king of Israel, competing with Omri for national support, is not clear.

What do we know about Tibni? Very little. He was the son of an unknown man named Ginath. His name may be a nickname meaning "man of straw" in contrast to Omri, which means "man of the sheaf."[16] Tibni, not formally presented as the other kings, is not reckoned in the author's scheme to be a legitimate ruler in Israel; but verse 21 implies that, for a while at least, he was named king by his followers. We also know that the followers of Tibni eventually lost out to the more powerful followers of Omri and that, mysteriously, *"Tibni died"* (v. 22).

That haunting sentence at the close of verse 22 deserves some attention. Did he die of natural causes? It would be unlikely that Tibni just happened to die at precisely the moment his followers were overcome by Omri's, or that Omri, having achieved this victory, would have delayed his official rule until Tibni's natural death at some later date. Did he commit suicide as Zimri had done? Was he assassinated as were Nadab and Elah? Or did he die in battle? Had any of these been the case one would expect the passage to have given some details of such a death as it did in the other cases. However, the author simply states he "died."

One interesting theory has been proposed by J. Max Miller in an article in *Vetus Testamentum.*[17] He cites evidence of a practice in the ancient Near East in which literary accounts speak of a king's loss of authority as his "death" even though he remained physically alive. In at least one case cited, a prince was said to have been "killed" when actually he was only prevented from ascending to the throne. If that were the approach taken by the author in this passage, then when verse 22 says, *"So Tibni died,"* it merely means he was divested of whatever royal authority he previously held.

Whatever the interpretation of its difficult elements, the clear implication of this passage is that, after some struggle for control, Omri eventually won the right to be king and ruled for twelve years. And he became one of Israel's most significant rulers.

One notable accomplishment of his reign was the establishment of the nation's capital in Samaria, where it remained until Israel was taken away captive by Assyria in 722 B.C. After the death of Tibni, Omri felt free to relocate the capital wherever he pleased, and he made what strategists call a wise choice. The hill of Samaria, rising about three hundred feet above the surrounding fertile plain, is located not far from the important coastal highway. This location afforded easy access to Megiddo and Jezreel in the north, Shechem and Tirzah in the east, and Jerusalem in the south.[18]

Omri bought the site for the city personally, just as David had purchased the site for Jerusalem. Consequently he could pass on the property to his children and thus begin a new dynasty in his own capital city. Excavations in 1924 verified the biblical report, showing that Omri's city was the first to occupy the site. He paid the previous owner, Shemer, two talents of silver (about $8,448 at today's silver prices) and kept the name of the hill as the name of the new town.

Omri's fame as a monarch, while downplayed by the author of Kings, was widely recognized in other places. The Moabite stone, discovered in 1868, refers to him as the conqueror of Moab. Assyrian inscriptions make mention of him as a great warrior.[19] For years the Assyrians referred to Israel as "the house of Omri."[20] His strength earned for him the title, "The David of Israel."[21]

Why then does the author of Kings pass over his accomplishments so casually as having little to do with the destiny of Israel? Conceivably because the author's purpose was not to write a purely secular history of this period but to tell the story from the perspective of Israel's place in God's plan. These inspired narratives then are more than just accurate chronicles of events. The author was interested in one angle of Israel's history and wanted to draw spiritual lessons from the occurrences that would guide his readers in every generation. (For this reason, some call the author of Kings a "Deuteronomist.") Under the guidance of the Holy Spirit, he accordingly chooses as important certain events a purely secular historian might consider trivial. Contrarily, he omits some significant items as unimportant to his spiritual purpose.

Omri's report card in verse 25 carries not only a failing grade but an "F minus." The grading curve by which the author appraises the moral quality of the kings puts Omri at the bottom of the class—*"worse than all who were before him."* He was the first king to be buried in the new capital of Samaria.

Conclusion

These severely condensed records of seven kings may appear to be nothing more than dull, routine historical annals. But they point to some valuable and timely lessons. "All Scripture is given by inspiration of God, and is profitable for doctrine, for reproof, for correction, for instruction in righteousness" (2 Tim. 3:16).

One "instruction in righteousness" from this passage is that, in the final analysis, the one thing that counts in life is one's relationship to God. All the impressive accomplishments of Israel's great king Omri finally boil down to one judgment only: "Omri did evil in the eyes of the Lord" (v. 25). What about his military victories against Moab, his imposing building projects, his international reputation for wealth and power? In the end they count for nothing. The king's relation to God is the only thing that counts.

Inviable records of financial expertise, scholarship, beauty, or celebrity status may dazzle and impress the twentieth century, but what does it matter if God's hand should write silently across those records, "He did evil in the eyes of the Lord"?

Another truth to which this segment of Scripture points is the progressive momentum of evil. Even the smallest departure from God inevitably intensifies into gigantic proportions unless God intervenes with forgiveness and renewal. Jeroboam's sin was not so serious. He was not guilty of idolatry but merely of setting up images of Yahweh to help the people visualize God's power and virility. However, this small departure from God's will gradually widened until fifty years later there was rampant, unblushing idolatry in Israel. Jeroboam sowed the wind, and Omri and Ahab reaped the whirlwind (Hos. 8:7). From Solomon on, the momentum of evil in Israel and Judah gathered velocity—each dynasty more wicked than the last—and swept like an avalanche over the land. To those who boast, "I will step this far into disobedience and no farther," this passage issues a warning: there is no stopping on the slippery, glazed ice of sin's slopes. Only repentance and divine forgiveness can reverse moral decline in the life of a nation or of an individual.

NOTES

1. E. W. Heaton, *The Hebrew Kingdoms,* The New Clarendon Bible, vol. 3 (London: Oxford University Press, 1968), 62.
2. I. W. Slotki, *Kings* (London: Soncino Press, 1950), 110.
3. Charles F. Burney, *Notes on the Hebrew Text of the Books of Kings* (Oxford: Clarendon Press, 1903), 193.
4. Ibid., 197.
5. Slotki, 110.
6. Martin E. Marty, "The Hope that Outlived Hitler," *Context* 18, no. 10 (15 May 1986): 5.
7. C. F. Keil, *The Books of the Kings,* Biblical Commentary on the Old Testament, ed. C. F. Keil and F. Delitzsch, vol. 4 (Grand Rapids: Eerdmans, 1950), 223.
8. Gwilym H. Jones, *1 and 2 Kings,* New Century Bible Commentary, ed. Ronald E. Clements (Grand Rapids: Eerdmans, 1984), 290.
9. Norman H. Snaith, Ralph W. Sockman, and Raymond Calkins, "The First and Second Books of Kings," in *The Interpreter's Bible,* vol. 3 (Nashville: Abingdon, 1954), 138.
10. Burney, 200.
11. Slotki, 117.
12. Burney, 200.
13. Jones, 292.
14. Ibid., 294.
15. John Gray, *I and II Kings,* Old Testament Library (Philadelphia: Westminster, 1963), 330.
16. Jones, 294.
17. J. Max Miller, "So Tibni Died (1 Kings xvi 22)," *Vetus Testamentum* 18 (1968): 392.
18. Simon J. DeVries, *1 Kings,* Word Biblical Commentary, ed. John D. W. Watts, vol. 12 (Waco, TX: Word Books, 1985), 202.
19. Slotki, 119.
20. Gray, 330.
21. M. Pierce Matheney and Roy Honeycutt, "1-2 Kings," in *The Broadman Bible Commentary,* ed. Clifton J. Allen, vol. 3 (Nashville: Broadman, 1970), 206.

CHAPTER EIGHT

The Early Reign of Ahab of Israel and the Early Ministry of Elijah

1 Kings 16:29–18:46

INTRODUCTION

The biographer's spotlight now encircles the next personality on the stage of Israel's history. He is Ahab, the son of King Omri. He reigned in Samaria for twenty-two years. After what appears to be a routine introductory formula and recital of Ahab's sins, the author interrupts his typical narrative pattern to insert a long and interesting segment about the prophet Elijah. It is not until 1 Kings 22:39 that the author concludes the story of Ahab's reign with his traditional closing formula.

The extensive account of Elijah's escapades, sandwiched between the opening and closing of Ahab's reign, has been rightly reckoned among the finest pieces of prose writing in the Old Testament.[1]

AHAB AND HIS EVIL REIGN IN ISRAEL

16:29 In the thirty-eighth year of Asa king of Judah, Ahab the son of Omri became king over Israel; and Ahab the son of Omri reigned over Israel in Samaria twenty-two years.

30 Now Ahab the son of Omri did evil in the sight of the LORD, more than all who *were* before him.

31 And it came to pass, as though it had been a trivial thing for him to walk in the sins of Jeroboam the son of Nebat, that he took as wife Jezebel the

> daughter of Ethbaal, king of the Sidonians; and he
> went and served Baal and worshiped him.
> 32 Then he set up an altar for Baal in the temple of
> Baal, which he had built in Samaria.
> 33 And Ahab made a wooden image. Ahab did
> more to provoke the LORD God of Israel to anger than
> all the kings of Israel who were before him.
> 34 In his days Hiel of Bethel built Jericho. He laid
> its foundation with Abiram his firstborn, and with his
> youngest *son* Segub he set up its gates, according to
> the word of the LORD, which He had spoken through
> Joshua the son of Nun.
>
> *1 Kings 16:29–34*

In Judah, Asa was in his thirty-eighth year of a long and stable administration when, in Israel, Ahab began another cycle of that nation's stormy, unpredictable royal dominions. Ahab would be the seventh contender for the Northern throne, while Asa, Judah's durable king, outlasted them all.

"Like father, like son." Seldom has that proverb been more convincingly illustrated than it is here in the story of Ahab, who inherited his father's propensity for immoral excesses. The author has already mentioned twice in verse 29 that Ahab was the son of Omri, and now in verse 30 he repeats it, making sure his readers catch the paternal connection. Furthermore, the author echoes for the son the condemnation he used earlier in verse 25 for the father, Omri: he *"did evil in the sight of the Lord, more than all who were before him."* Reinforcing this father-son relationship is the name *Ahab,* which can be translated "brother of the father" or "resembling the father."[2] The very name suggests that Ahab "took after" Omri (he had his father's lies!).

In his description of Omri, the author was content to generalize his sins, but with Ahab, the list of failures is specific. Ahab was guilty of: (1) marrying the Baalist daughter of a Baalist king, (2) worshiping Baal and bowing down to him, (3) building a temple for Baal-Melkart in Samaria, (4) erecting in the same temple an image of the goddess Asherah, "the earth-mother." (He also set up a golden pillar in the temple of Baal similar to the one Hiram set up in Baal's temple in Tyre [2 Kings 3:2].[3])

They were all bad, but Ahab's worst crime, according to this passage, was his marriage to Jezebel. She was the daughter of Ethbaal, the king of the Sidonians. From one of Josephus's records (*Against Apion,* 1.18.8), we learn he was called Ithobal I, a priest of Astarte, who at the age of thirty-six murdered his brother, King Phelles, and took over the kingdom of Tyre and Sidon where he reigned for thirty-two years. His name means "with Baal." Ethbaal's god was Baal-Melkart, whose worship was similar to that of the Baal of the Ras Shamra texts, and who in later years was identified with Hercules.[4] The name *Baal* means "lord" or "owner" and is sometimes used as a title in connection with the proper name of a deity, such as Baal-Melkart.[5]

Jezebel's name may come from a cultic cry used in the worship of Baal meaning "Where is Baal?" Translated into Hebrew the name was also a verbal pun that the Israelites must have relished. *Zebel* in Hebrew means dung![6] Years earlier, Solomon was condemned because he married an Egyptian princess who brought pagan influences to Jerusalem, and now Ahab takes a Phoenician princess as his queen. (If Omri was called "the David of the North," Ahab could be called "the Solomon of the North.") Because she was more assertive, however, Jezebel was more dangerous. None of Solomon's foreign wives had the missionary zeal of the Sidonian princess. It would not be long before her religious influence would be felt all over Israel.

Had a secular historian been recording these events, the marriage of Ahab and Jezebel would likely have been applauded as a prudent political move. Both Phoenicia and Israel were being threatened by Syria, and the marriage gave Ahab a powerful military ally at a crucial time. It also allowed Ahab to regain the region around Mount Carmel, which the Phoenicians had held. But for his writing of the history, the author of Kings had a more focused purpose. Under divine inspiration, his purpose was to report the story from the standpoint of its spiritual and religious impact. Therefore, he ignores the political implications of the marriage and deals with its religious implications alone, condemning the king for a union secular historians might have regarded as wise.

Since he named his sons after Yahweh, Ahab apparently remained primarily a Yahweh worshiper. But international courtesy demanded that his foreign queen should have a sanctuary for her own religion in her adopted country. So, following Solomon's example, he built in Samaria a temple to Baal with an altar, an *ʾăšērâ* (image), and a golden pillar. And in due time, the king himself began to participate in the new cult along with his worship of Yahweh. Verse 31 says, *"and he went and served Baal and worshiped him."*

Idol worship still lives today. In Thailand's modern capital of Bangkok, we saw the Buddhist "spirit houses" on busy corners throughout the city. Most businesses, office buildings, and hotels had their own "spirit houses" nearby. Some are crude wooden structures shaped like a birdhouse; others are elaborate miniature duplications of Buddhist temples. Manufactured "spirit houses" are for sale in shops similar to those in America that sell birdbaths and concrete statues for the lawn. The elegant and modern Dusit Thani hotel in downtown Bangkok, where we stayed, had its own "spirit house" in the parking lot.

On a regular basis, devotees bring fresh flowers, fruit, food, or other gifts and leave them at one of the little shrines. Noticing that some "spirit houses" had more than their share of gifts while others seemed deserted, I asked a missionary friend, "Why?" His explanation was that at some locations, following the leaving of a gift, the worshiper had received from the spirits of that house good luck or an answer to his wish. That story would get around and, because of its enhanced reputation, that particular "spirit house" would become very popular. "The superstitious worship of idols is basically a selfish worship," he explained. "You bring your gifts in order to receive good luck."

Ahab's motivation must have been similar. Unwilling to give up his worship of Yahweh, he pragmatically adopted idol worship as a superstitious attempt to buy good luck and success. Unfortunately, under the guise of a "theology of prosperity," some Christian worshipers are making the same mistake today.

Verses 33 and 34 blame another transgression on Ahab—the rebuilding of the fortress of Jericho. Although the building contractor was an unknown man named Hiel of Bethel, the work was obviously done under the authority of the king and probably at his command. The adding of the phrase *"in his days"* (v. 34) lays the blame at Ahab's feet.

What was wrong with rebuilding Jericho? Years earlier, following the destruction of Jericho by the children of Israel, Joshua had forbidden its reconstruction with a curse: "'Cursed be the man before the Lord who rises up and builds this city Jericho; he shall lay its foundation with his firstborn, and with his youngest he shall set up its gates'" (Josh. 6:26). But Ahab needed Jericho as a protected passageway across the Jordan, so Hiel was apparently commissioned by the king to proceed. The curse of Joshua took effect, however, and Hiel lost both his firstborn and his youngest sons.

While the general intention of verse 34 is clear, the exact meaning is difficult. Some interpreters believe that at the beginning of the project Hiel lost Abiram his firstborn, and then as the work progressed, one by one, his other sons died also. Finally, when he completed the gates of Jericho, Segub his youngest son died.[7] It is suggested by others that the two sons, or perhaps the whole family, were wiped out because of a contaminated spring inside the city which, according to tradition, Elisha later purified.[8]

Others see the possibility that Hiel intentionally sacrificed his two sons because of his superstitious belief that it would guarantee the project's success. Archaeological excavations have uncovered evidence of a practice in ancient biblical times called "foundation sacrifices" in which children were buried, maybe alive, in the foundations of buildings.[9] Whatever the exact meaning of the verse, it is clear that Hiel paid a high price for violating Joshua's ban on fortifying Jericho.

Elijah and the Widow of Zarephath

17:1 And Elijah the Tishbite, of the inhabitants of Gilead, said to Ahab, "*As* the LORD God of Israel lives, before whom I stand, there shall not be dew nor rain these years, except at my word."

2 Then the word of the LORD came to him, saying,

3 "Get away from here and turn eastward, and hide by the Brook Cherith, which flows into the Jordan.

4 "And it will be *that* you shall drink from the brook, and I have commanded the ravens to feed you there."

5 So he went and did according to the word of the LORD, for he went and stayed by the Brook Cherith, which flows into the Jordan.

6 The ravens brought him bread and meat in the morning, and bread and meat in the evening; and he drank from the brook.

7 And it happened after a while that the brook
dried up, because there had been no rain in the land.
8 Then the word of the LORD came to him, saying,
9 "Arise, go to Zarephath, which *belongs* to Sidon,
and dwell there. See, I have commanded a widow
there to provide for you."
10 So he arose and went to Zarephath. And when
he came to the gate of the city, indeed a widow *was*
there gathering sticks. And he called to her and said,
"Please bring me a little water in a cup, that I may
drink."
11 And as she was going to get *it*, he called to her
and said, "Please bring me a morsel of bread in your
hand."
12 So she said, "As the LORD your God lives, I do
not have bread, only a handful of flour in a bin, and
a little oil in a jar; and see, I *am* gathering a couple of
sticks that I may go in and prepare it for myself and
my son, that we may eat it, and die."
13 And Elijah said to her, "Do not fear; go *and* do
as you have said, but make me a small cake from it
first, and bring *it* to me; and afterward make *some* for
yourself and your son.
14 "For thus says the LORD God of Israel: 'The bin
of flour shall not be used up, nor shall the jar of oil
run dry, until the day the LORD sends rain on the
earth.'"
15 So she went away and did according to the
word of Elijah; and she and he and her household ate
for *many* days.
16 The bin of flour was not used up, nor did the jar
of oil run dry, according to the word of the LORD
which He spoke by Elijah.
17 Now it happened after these things *that* the son
of the woman who owned the house became sick.
And his sickness was so serious that there was no
breath left in him.
18 So she said to Elijah, "What have I to do with
you, O man of God? Have you come to me to bring
my sin to remembrance, and to kill my son?"
19 And he said to her, "Give me your son." So he
took him out of her arms and carried him to the

upper room where he was staying, and laid him on
his own bed.
20 Then he cried out to the LORD and said, "O
LORD my God, have You also brought tragedy on the
widow with whom I lodge, by killing her son?"
21 And he stretched himself out on the child three
times, and cried out to the LORD and said, "O LORD my
God, I pray, let this child's soul come back to him."
22 Then the LORD heard the voice of Elijah; and the
soul of the child came back to him, and he revived.
23 And Elijah took the child and brought him down
from the upper room into the house, and gave him to
his mother. And Elijah said, "See, your son lives!"
24 Then the woman said to Elijah, "Now by this I
know that you *are* a man of God, *and* that the word
of the LORD in your mouth *is* the truth."

1 Kings 17:1–24

Elijah's name is a combination of two names for God, Elohim and Yahweh (or Jehovah). It means literally *"Yah* is *El"* and could be translated "Yahweh is God." Elijah has been called the most important leader of Yahweh worship since Moses and Samuel.[10] Although he is one of the best-known prophets in the Old Testament, we know very little about his early life. According to verse 1 he was born in Tishbeh, an unidentified village probably in the vicinity of Gilead, where he was living when he appears on the scene.

And appear he does, with remarkable suddenness. Dramatically, without any introduction, Elijah leaps into the arena. He and the royal couple had apparently never met. Without preface or introduction, he appeared before Ahab and Jezebel in Samaria and with startling bravado abruptly announced the drought. No personal credentials. No reasons for the drought. No conditions for mercy. He delivered his message and just as suddenly disappeared.

Can you imagine how Hollywood would stage this scene? Elijah crashes into Ahab's private chambers like an intruding thunderbolt. Jezebel is shocked at this wild man from the other side of Jordan with his long hair, rough robe, and flashing eyes. The striking effect of the sudden appearance of such a heroic personality is what real-life dramas are made of, and Hollywood would have a field day with such a story.

His emergence is so unexpected that the ancient rabbis felt compelled to explain it with a legend. They wanted to create a smoother literary transition from the incident at the close of chapter 16. The legend goes like this. Ahab and Elijah went to Jericho to comfort Hiel on the loss of his sons. Ahab refused to see the hand of God in Hiel's punishment. His reasoning was that Hiel's curse must not have been from God, because all Israel was worshiping idols, and God was doing nothing to punish them. The heavens had not been shut up. The rain was still falling on the land, and Israel's crops and flocks still flourished. Whereupon Elijah stood in righteous indignation and proclaimed, *"As the Lord God of Israel lives, before whom I stand, there shall not be dew nor rain these years, except at my word"* (17:1).

Dew and rain were the two main sources of moisture in ancient Israel. The rains came regularly from about October to March. The dew condensed on the mountains in the hot season, sometimes as heavily as a drizzle, especially around the higher elevations about Jerusalem, Hebron, and Bethel.[11] To cut off both sources of moisture would mean an absolute drought of extreme proportions. Since Baal was supposed to be the god of fertility, the god of the storm, present in the dew and rain, the drought was a direct challenge to this alien deity.

After an extended rainless period of record-breaking temperatures, our newspapers in the summer of 1986 headlined a severe drought in the southeast states. Its effect on crops, grazing land, orchards, and farm animals, to say nothing of landscaping and drinking supplies, was devastating. Lakes were so low that people were searching dry lake beds never before accessible for rings or other valuables lost on past boating trips. But even worse, the drought infected the population with an attendant mood of depression. A mile-long train filled with hay donated by farmers in other unaffected parts of the country helped provide for starving cattle, but it did little to lift the depressed spirits of the people. That dry mood can only be alleviated by the return of cool, refreshing rain. One can imagine similar impacts on ancient Israel during the severe drought that lasted three and a half years.

Little wonder Elijah had to flee from the angry presence of King Ahab. Not only was he escaping the king's wrath but also what surely would have been his constant pressure on Elijah to call off the drought. After all, Elijah had said rain would come only at his word.

If he could have found Elijah, can you imagine how often in three and a half years he would have pestered him to bring the rain? So God sent him to a safe hiding place beside a stream flowing into the east bank of the Jordan, where there would be ample drinking water and where God would miraculously provide him bread and meat delivered twice a day by ravens.

Interpreters with antisupernatural presuppositions are uncomfortable with the miraculous element in passages like this. Some have gone to extremes to provide natural explanations for the ravens. For example, some suggest that the Hebrew word for "ravens," *ʿōrĕbîm,* could be changed a little to stand for "Arabs" or "Orebites," natives of an imaginary city called "Oreb."[12] Others say the word means "steppe-dwellers," suggesting Elijah was fed by friendly bedouins or itinerant traders.[13] But the supernatural miracles belong in the passage and are acceptable to persons of faith, who see them as consistent with the omnipotent power of the Lord who made the universe.

Since there were more comfortable places where Elijah could have hidden (friendly Obadiah hid and fed two caves full of fleeing prophets [18:4]), why did God protect Elijah in such an unusual manner? Perhaps to weld his faith into courageous determination for the challenges ahead. With the mental image of black ravens delivering food on schedule twice a day imbedded in his memory, Elijah could never doubt again that God would take care of him. After seeing how His word about the drought had come to pass, he could never again doubt God's promises. Elijah would soon need this reinforced faith to face the awesome challenge of powerful kings and entrenched religious cults.

In time, the drought worsened. The Brook Cherith dried up, and God sent Elijah some one hundred miles north to the home of a widow in the Phoenician coastal city of Zarephath, about seven miles south of Sidon. Here he witnessed the God of miracles at work again.

What a hopeless situation he encountered at Zarephath. A poverty-stricken widow suffering the deprivation of the drought with a son she was struggling to feed. And Elijah was supposed to ask her for—of all things—water and something to eat. The hopelessness served to intensify the approaching miracle. Even though she lived in a Gentile city, the widow was probably a believer in Yahweh. Verse 12 indicates that she knew the name of the Lord and that she recognized Elijah as an Israelite—even as a man of God. Jesus' reference to her in Luke 4:26 implies she was a believer. But her immature faith was as small as a mustard seed. Because of this experience with Elijah, however, it opened into full bloom. When the prophet asked her to bake him a cake from her last supply of oil and flour, it was a severe test of her faith. She passed with flying colors. Believing God, she gave up the certain for the uncertain and obediently trusted His word. The miracle of the unending supply of oil and flour was her reward.

The next miracle was even more spectacular. The resurrection of her dead son brought her faith to its highest point. Seeing her boy alive again, she exclaimed, *"Now by this I know that you are a man of God, and that the word of the Lord in your mouth is the truth"* (v. 24).

Noting several differences in the account, some commentators believe the widow in this passage is different from the one in verses 8–16, but most believe it is a continuation of the story of the same widow. Although the passage does not actually say her son died, that is the obvious implication. Her immature faith struggles with the tragedy, and she assumes the death is God's punishment for some unknown sin in her life. She believed Elijah's saintly presence in her home had somehow drawn God's attention to her. If he had not come, God would have continued to overlook her sin, and her son would not have died. It is sad to see the same distorted belief expressed today in the midst of suffering. "What did I do to deserve this?" is a question pastors and counselors hear too often from confused people facing tragedy.

In the upper chamber, Elijah stretched himself over the body of the child in the same manner of Elisha in 2 Kings 4:34 and Paul in Acts 20:10; and the boy came back to life. Not only was the woman's faith undergirded, but Elijah's catalogue of remembered miracles had one more added to reinforce his faith. It would give him boldness when he stood again before Ahab. The mighty king would be only a poor puppet in the hands of the miracle-working God who held the keys of life and death. And it was before that God Elijah stood. *"As the Lord God of Israel lives, before whom I stand. . . ."* That perspective was the secret of the prophet's courage.

On a recent spring day in Moscow, we met a courageous Baptist preacher who serves in one of the large cities of the Soviet Union. Under unlikely circumstances, he has succeeded in planting a dozen new Baptist congregations throughout his city, each well-established with pastoral leadership and modest buildings. He told us how on one occasion he approached the Soviet minister of religious affairs for permission to build a Baptist church on an attractive piece of property. The Soviet official refused, saying, "As long as I am alive, there will never be a Baptist church on that location!"

As the preacher turned to leave the office, he replied, "Mr. Minister, I respect the fact that you serve as a minister of the Supreme Soviet. But I serve as a minister of the Most High God, and I will pray that God will spare you and not take your life so His church can be built in this place."

He said the Soviet official was obviously taken aback. "You're serious aren't you?" he said quietly, calling the Baptist preacher back into his office. That incident led to a series of ardent conversations, which eventually resulted in the acquiring of the property and the building of the church. Our Baptist friend smiled and said, "The minister of religious affairs even came to the dedication service!"

Elijah would have been proud of this twentieth-century prophet, unafraid to stand before a powerful leader with the courage that comes from faith in the God of miracles.

ELIJAH AND OBADIAH

18:1 And it came to pass *after* many days that the word of the LORD came to Elijah, in the third year, saying, "Go, present yourself to Ahab, and I will send rain on the earth."

2 So Elijah went to present himself to Ahab; and *there was* a severe famine in Samaria.

3 And Ahab had called Obadiah, who *was* in charge of *his* house. (Now Obadiah feared the LORD greatly.

4 For so it was, while Jezebel massacred the prophets of the LORD, that Obadiah had taken one hundred prophets and hidden them, fifty to a cave, and had fed them with bread and water.)

5 And Ahab had said to Obadiah, "Go into the land to all the springs of water and to all the brooks; perhaps we may find grass to keep the horses and mules alive, so that we will not have to kill any livestock."

6 So they divided the land between them to ex-
plore it; Ahab went one way by himself, and Obadiah
went another way by himself.
7 Now as Obadiah was on his way, suddenly Elijah met him; and he recognized him, and fell on his
face, and said, "*Is* that you, my lord Elijah?"
8 And he answered him, "*It is* I. Go, tell your
master, 'Elijah *is here.*' "
9 So he said, "How have I sinned, that you are
delivering your servant into the hand of Ahab, to kill
me?
10 "*As* the LORD your God lives, there is no nation
or kingdom where my master has not sent someone
to hunt for you; and when they said, '*He is* not *here,*'
he took an oath from the kingdom or nation that they
could not find you.
11 "And now you say, 'Go, tell your master, "Elijah
is here"'!
12 "And it shall come to pass, *as soon as* I am gone
from you, that the Spirit of the LORD will carry you
to a place I do not know; so when I go and tell Ahab,
and he cannot find you, he will kill me. But I your
servant have feared the LORD from my youth.
13 "Was it not reported to my lord what I did when
Jezebel killed the prophets of the LORD, how I hid
one hundred men of the LORD's prophets, fifty to a
cave, and fed them with bread and water?
14 "And now you say, 'Go, tell your master, "Elijah
is here"' He will kill me!"
15 Then Elijah said, "*As* the LORD of hosts lives,
before whom I stand, I will surely present myself to
him today."
16 So Obadiah went to meet Ahab, and told him;
and Ahab went to meet Elijah.

1 Kings 18:1–16

Despite the fact that the drought was severe in Samaria (v. 2 literally says it "had a firm hold on Samaria"), Ahab did not change his ways. There was only one thing to do. Elijah must lay before the people a convincing proof that Yahweh was the true God. So after about three years in Zarephath, Elijah was sent to face Ahab and lay down the challenge.

At this point we are introduced to an interesting and inspiring character named Obadiah, not the canonical prophet with the same name, but a God-fearing high official in Ahab's court. That Ahab would pick him for the task in verse 6 shows the high position he held and the respect Ahab had for him. He was the immediate representative of the king and likely bore the royal seal to certify decisions he made on the king's behalf. He was probably second in command in Israel. And yet, in this unlikely and highly visible position in Ahab's court, Obadiah maintained a brave loyalty to the true faith. Neither Jezebel's flatteries nor her frowns had moved him.

His brave protection of the prophets of Yahweh described in verse 4 was apparently necessitated by Jezebel's campaign to eliminate the worship of Yahweh in Israel. These one hundred hapless men of God were young pupils of the prophets whom Obadiah shielded in limestone caves very likely located in the region of Mount Carmel.[14] It was a risky venture for anyone, especially one so close to the royal couple.

In his typical manner, Elijah "suddenly" met Obadiah, who recognized the prophet immediately. Because of his high position in the palace, Obadiah might even have been present when Elijah first appeared before Ahab three and a half years earlier. He not only recognized Elijah; he knew him well enough to predict his usual behavior. His reason for not telling Ahab he had found Elijah was that he feared the mercurial prophet would suddenly disappear and anger Ahab further. That fear was justified. Elijah had a way of doing just that. But after securing an oath from the prophet, Obadiah informed the king, and the fateful meeting between the two men was arranged.

Obadiah has been described as a good man in a bad place. His firmness and religious zeal did not prevent him from retaining his place of honor and dignity in the royal court. Should godly Obadiah have resigned his post in the wicked court in protest? That is the action some righteous people take as they confront evil situations, but the New Testament makes it clear that at times disciples are to remain in an imperfect environment in order to be salt and leaven for good. Jesus prayed, "I do not pray that You should take them out of the world, but that You should keep them from the evil one" (John 17:15). Sometimes Christian boldness necessitates a costly withdrawal, the resignation from a high-paying job, the cancellation of a contract, the refusal to join a certain organization. But sometimes Christ-like valor means sweetening the sour situation by staying. Like Obadiah, some are called to be "good people in a bad place."

ELIJAH AND THE PROPHETS OF BAAL

18:17 Then it happened, when Ahab saw Elijah, that Ahab said to him, "*Is that* you, O troubler of Israel?"
18 And he answered, "I have not troubled Israel, but you and your father's house *have,* in that you have forsaken the commandments of the LORD and have followed the Baals.
19 "Now therefore, send *and* gather all Israel to me on Mount Carmel, the four hundred and fifty prophets of Baal, and the four hundred prophets of Asherah, who eat at Jezebel's table."
20 So Ahab sent for all the children of Israel, and gathered the prophets together on Mount Carmel.
21 And Elijah came to all the people, and said, "How long will you falter between two opinions? If the LORD *is* God, follow Him; but if Baal, follow him." But the people answered him not a word.
22 Then Elijah said to the people, "I alone am left a prophet of the LORD; but Baal's prophets *are* four hundred and fifty men.
23 "Therefore let them give us two bulls; and let them choose one bull for themselves, cut it in pieces, and lay *it* on the wood, but put no fire *under it;* and I will prepare the other bull, and lay *it* on the wood, but put no fire *under it.*
24 "Then you call on the name of your gods, and I will call on the name of the LORD; and the God who answers by fire, He is God." So all the people answered and said, "It is well spoken."
25 Now Elijah said to the prophets of Baal, "Choose one bull for yourselves and prepare *it* first, for you *are* many; and call on the name of your god, but put no fire *under it.*"
26 So they took the bull which was given them, and they prepared *it,* and called on the name of Baal from morning even till noon, saying, "O Baal, hear

us!" But *there was* no voice; no one answered. Then
they leaped about the altar which they had made.
27 And so it was, at noon, that Elijah mocked them
and said, "Cry aloud, for he *is* a god; either he is
meditating, or he is busy, or he is on a journey, *or*
perhaps he is sleeping and must be awakened."
28 So they cried aloud, and cut themselves, as was
their custom, with knives and lances, until the blood
gushed out on them.
29 And when midday was past, they prophesied
until the *time* of the offering of the *evening* sacrifice.
But *there was* no voice; no one answered, no one paid
attention.
30 Then Elijah said to all the people, "Come near
to me." So all the people came near to him. And he
repaired the altar of the LORD *that was* broken down.
31 And Elijah took twelve stones, according to the
number of the tribes of the sons of Jacob, to whom
the word of the LORD had come, saying, "Israel shall
be your name."
32 Then with the stones he built an altar in the
name of the LORD; and he made a trench around the
altar large enough to hold two seahs of seed.
33 And he put the wood in order, cut the bull in
pieces, and laid *it* on the wood, and said, "Fill four
waterpots with water, and pour *it* on the burnt sacrifice and on the wood."
34 Then he said, "Do *it* a second time," and they
did *it* a second time; and he said, "Do *it* a third time,"
and they did *it* a third time.
35 So the water ran all around the altar; and he
also filled the trench with water.
36 And it came to pass, at *the time of* the offering of
the *evening* sacrifice, that Elijah the prophet came
near and said, "LORD God of Abraham, Isaac, and Israel, let it be known this day that You *are* God in Israel
and I *am* Your servant, and *that* I have done all these
things at Your word.
37 "Here me, O LORD, hear me, that this people
may know that You *are* the LORD God, and *that* You
have turned their hearts back *to You* again."
38 Then the fire of the LORD fell and consumed the

burnt sacrifice, and the wood and the stones and
the dust, and it licked up the water that *was* in the
trench.
39 Now when all the people saw *it,* they fell on
their faces; and they said, "The LORD, He *is* God! The
LORD, He *is* God!"
40 And Elijah said to them, "Seize the prophets of
Baal! Do not let one of them escape!" So they seized
them; and Elijah brought them down to the Brook
Kishon and executed them there.
41 Then Elijah said to Ahab, "Go up, eat and
drink; for *there is* the sound of abundance of rain."
42 So Ahab went up to eat and drink. And Elijah
went up to the top of Carmel; then he bowed down
on the ground, and put his face between his knees,
43 and said to his servant, "Go up now, look toward the sea." So he went up and looked, and said,
"*There is* nothing." And seven times he said, "Go
again."
44 Then it came to pass the seventh *time,* that he
said, "There is a cloud, as small as a man's hand, rising out of the sea!" So he said, "Go up, say to Ahab,
'Prepare *your chariot* and go down before the rain
stops you.'"
45 Now it happened in the meantime that the sky
became black with clouds and wind, and there was a
heavy rain. So Ahab rode away and went to Jezreel.
46 Then the hand of the LORD came upon Elijah;
and he girded up his loins and ran ahead of Ahab to
the entrance of Jezreel.

1 Kings 18:17–46

"Then the Pharisees and Sadducees came, and . . . asked that He would show them a sign from heaven" (Matt. 16:1). "So the Jews answered and said to Him, 'What sign do You show to us . . . ?'" (John 2:18). "Then Jesus said to him, 'Unless you people see signs and wonders, you will by no means believe'" (John 4:48). There is embedded in the consciousness of humankind an almost irrepressible desire for rational, visible proofs on which to base beliefs. "Reason before faith" is the order of unregenerate skepticism. But Jesus reversed the order. Faith comes first; then reason follows to undergird and confirm. But the yearning for evidence, so deeply embedded in human experience, has been reinforced in our day by reverence for the scientific method with its quest for demonstrated certainty. The desire for convincing signs dies slowly.

That desire was very much alive in Elijah's day. The people wanted some visible proof that Yahweh was the true God. And this time God was willing to give them a spectacular sign.

The conversation between the king and the prophet beginning in verse 17 confirms that Ahab still blamed the drought on Elijah's arbitrary stubbornness, not on his own idolatry. Like Nathan's "Thou art the man," Elijah sets the record straight. Israel is troubled because Ahab has replicated his father Omri's disobedience and added to it his own idolatry. He has *"followed the Baals."* The plural form is used in derision, contrasting the multiple village shrines across the land with the awesome ideal of one God. A great national contest will settle once and for all who is the true God.

Carmel, the location of Elijah's "contest," means "the garden land."[15] It is a low range of mountains running northwest to southeast from the Mediterranean Sea to the fertile Plain of Esdraelon. After years of Sunday school lessons about this event, in which I pictured Mount Carmel as a tall snow-capped peak like Mount McKinley, I was somewhat disappointed to see it for myself on our first trip to Israel. But I came to realize how much better the real mountain fit the passage than did my imagined peak. Today, tour guides show modern travelers the spot where tradition claims the contest took place. And of all the historical sites in Israel, this one seems most believable. The location is called "El Muhraka," literally, "the place of burning." It is a level plateau halfway up Mount Carmel where a large crowd could have easily gathered. One cannot see the Mediterranean from here, but a short climb higher up the mountain opens up a dramatic view (cf. vv. 42–44). Just below the plateau the Brook Kishon still flows, and beside it is a huge rock mound called "Tel el Qassis" or "Priest's Mound" where tradition says the slaughter of the prophets of Baal took place (cf. v. 40). There are springs in the area from which the water to douse the altar could have been drawn without traveling to the brook (cf. vv. 33–35). Standing on the site helps one to visualize the dramatic scene described by our author.

It was decision time. No one could avoid it. Ahab was mistaken. One cannot serve Yahweh and Baal together. *"If the Lord is God, follow*

Him; but if Baal, follow him" (v. 21). The phrase, *"How long will you falter between two opinions?"* is difficult to translate clearly. Therefore, every translation of this phrase is someone's interpretation of what it means. "Falter" means "to limp, halt, hop, dance, or leap." It is the same word used in verse 26 where the prophets of Baal "leaped" about the altar. There it probably refers to the typical ritual dance used in the worship of Baal, similar to the low, squatting dance of the Cossacks. It may explain the term "bending the knee to Baal."[16]

The word translated "opinions" speaks of "clefts, branches, forks in a tree limb or in a road."[17] So, even though an exact translation is difficult, the obvious meaning is: "How long will you keep on dancing from one leg to the other, like a bird trying to straddle a widening branch or a man trying to take both forks of a road at the same time?" In other words, "How long will you try to worship both Yahweh and Baal at the same time?" The statement is clearly a metaphor to condemn half-hearted, double-minded indecision.

In order to forestall any accusations of unfairness, Elijah set the conditions of the contest to give every possible concession to the prophets of Baal: (1) They could be first to choose the sacrifice. (2) They could pray first and for as long as they wished. (3) The proof-sign was to be fire. Since Baal was supposed to be the god of the sun, the god of the storm, they could not object. So they set up their altar and called on their god to answer.

Elijah's taunts were classic sarcasms. One slur was especially abrasive. The phrase translated *"he is busy"* has been translated in other versions: "he is pursuing," "he is gone aside," "he is engaged," "he has business to transact," or "he hath an occasion to retire." Most commentators believe the phrase is a euphemism for "turning aside for a call of nature," or "going to the privy." The mockery incited the Baalists to accelerate their frenzies as they carried on until the evening sacrifice.

The word *"evening"* is not in the Hebrew text and has been added by translators. The Hebrew word *minḥâ* probably refers to the traditional ninth hour of prayer at about three o'clock in the afternoon.[18] That gave Elijah time for his own calm and deliberate preparations.

How composed and self-assured he is in contrast to the wild acrobatics of the Baal worshipers. There must have been nearby a previous altar to Yahweh which had been torn down, maybe by Jezebel's followers. From the old altar Elijah took twelve stones from which to symbolically form the base of a new altar. The trench, as big as the square area of field in which two seahs (about five gallons) of grain might be planted, was dug. Then, symbolically, twelve jars of water were poured over it all.

After his simple and dignified prayer, the mighty fire of God fell and consumed sacrifice, altar, stones, water, everything. The people, now convinced, cried out, *"The Lord, He is God!"* "Yahweh is Elohim!" Those words in Hebrew were actually Elijah's name! "Yah is El!"

Verse 40 describes the execution of the prophets of Baal near the Brook Kishon at the base of Carmel. It flows toward Phoenicia, implying that the blood of the false prophets should flow back to where it belongs.[19]

The humble entreaty of the lonely prophet of Yahweh on the mountain is moving. His servant, who is not mentioned before now, climbed higher to see the first small approaching cloud, and Elijah warned Ahab to start his chariot ride back to Jezreel. Jezebel was waiting for him there. Then, with the hand of the Lord upon him in renewed strength, Elijah outruns the chariot to Jezreel, about seventeen miles cross country.

Among many lessons in the passage, one is primary: the impossibility of neutrality in relationship to God. Our English word "neutral" comes from two roots, "ne" and "uter," meaning "not either." In many realms of life neutrality has been exalted as a virtue. Judicious calmness, open-mindedness, and suspended judgment are often honored as sophisticated.

In an interview just before his retirement, John Chancellor remarked that he and other reporters worked hard to make their presentations neutral. He even practiced in front of a mirror to make sure he didn't exercise "eyebrow power" (that is, report the news with even a trace of doubt or shock on his face). No matter how startling the news, anchormen are expected to be unflappable, impartial, objective on camera. "It's a skill," Chancellor said, "and we ought to be good at it."[20]

Maybe it is appropriate to give the news without a flicker of emotion, without declaring which side we are on; but such neutrality in matters of faith is a sin. Jesus said:

> No one can serve two masters; for either he will hate the one and love the other, or else he will be loyal

to the one and despise the other. You cannot serve
God and mammon.

Matt. 6:24

NOTES

1. I. W. Slotki, *Kings* (London: Soncino Press, 1950), 122.
2. John Gray, *I and II Kings,* Old Testament Library (Philadelphia: Westminster, 1963), 29.
3. C. F. Keil, *The Books of the Kings,* Biblical Commentary on the Old Testament, ed. C. F. Keil and F. Delitzsch, vol. 4 (Grand Rapids: Eerdmans, 1950), 228.
4. Norman H. Snaith, Ralph W. Sockman, and Raymond Calkins, "The First and Second Books of Kings," in *The Interpreter's Bible,* vol. 3 (Nashville: Abingdon, 1954), 144.
5. Gwilym H. Jones, *1 and 2 Kings,* New Century Bible Commentary, ed. Ronald E. Clements (Grand Rapids: Eerdmans, 1984), 298.
6. Ibid.
7. Slotki, 121.
8. Jones, 298.
9. Snaith, Sockman, and Calkins, 144.
10. M. Pierce Matheney and Roy Honeycutt, "1-2 Kings," in *The Broadman Bible Commentary,* ed. Clifton J. Allen, vol. 3 (Nashville: Broadman, 1970), 208.
11. Gray, 335.
12. Keil, 236.
13. Matheney and Honeycutt, 208.
14. Gray, 346.
15. Snaith, Sockman, and Calkins, 152.
16. Gray, 349.
17. Snaith, Sockman, and Calkins, 152.
18. Ibid., 156.
19. Jones, 325.
20. Daniel Henninger, *Wall Street Journal,* 30 March 1982, 24.

CHAPTER NINE

The Account of Elijah's Confrontation with Ahab

1 Kings 19:1–22:40

ELIJAH ESCAPES FROM JEZEBEL

19:1 And Ahab told Jezebel all that Elijah had done, also how he had executed all the prophets with the sword.

2 Then Jezebel sent a messenger to Elijah, saying, "So let the gods do *to me,* and more also, if I do not make your life as the life of one of them by tomorrow about this time."

3 And when he saw *that,* he arose and ran for his life, and went to Beersheba, which *belongs* to Judah, and left his servant there.

4 But he himself went a day's journey into the wilderness, and came and sat down under a broom tree. And he prayed that he might die, and said, "It is enough! Now, LORD, take my life, for I *am* no better than my fathers!"

5 Then as he lay and slept under a broom tree, suddenly an angel touched him, and said to him, "Arise *and* eat."

6 Then he looked, and there by his head *was* a cake baked on coals, and a jar of water. So he ate and drank, and lay down again.

7 And the angel of the LORD came back the second time, and touched him, and said "Arise *and* eat, because the journey *is* too great for you."

8 So he arose, and ate and drank; and he went in the strength of that food forty days and forty nights as far as Horeb, the mountain of God.

9 And there he went into a cave and spent the
night in that place; and behold, the word of the LORD
came to him, and He said to him, "What are you doing here, Elijah?"
10 So he said, "I have been very zealous for the
LORD God of hosts; for the children of Israel have
forsaken Your covenant, torn down Your altars, and
killed Your prophets with the sword. I alone am left;
and they seek to take my life."
11 Then He said, "Go out, and stand on the mountain before the LORD." And behold, the LORD passed
by, and a great and strong wind tore into the mountains and broke the rocks in pieces before the LORD,
but the LORD *was* not in the wind; and after the wind
an earthquake, *but* the LORD *was* not in the earthquake;
12 and after the earthquake a fire, *but* the LORD
was not in the fire; and after the fire a still small
voice.
13 So it was, when Elijah heard *it*, that he wrapped
his face in his mantle and went out and stood in the
entrance of the cave. Suddenly a voice *came* to him,
and said, "What are you doing here, Elijah?"
14 And he said, "I have been very zealous for the
LORD God of hosts; because the children of Israel
have forsaken Your covenant, torn down Your altars,
and killed Your prophets with the sword. I alone am
left; and they seek to take my life."

1 Kings 19:1–14

Apparently Ahab and Jezebel had a second home in Jezreel. When the king's chariot arrived there from Carmel, Elijah, having outrun him, waited to see what would happen when Jezebel heard the report. If he expected Ahab to force Jezebel to give up her campaign against Yahweh-worship, Elijah had overestimated the king's courage. If he expected Jezebel to admit defeat and give up her opposition, Elijah had underestimated the queen's determination. Whichever was the case, the prophet seemed surprised and disappointed when Jezebel sent her messenger with the threat in verse 2. The Septuagint adds a phrase to Jezebel's warning, "As surely as you are Elijah and I am Jezebel."[1] It is as though the queen were pitting her name, meaning "Where is Baal?" against the prophet's name, meaning "Yahweh is God."

It was obviously not Jezebel's intent to kill Elijah or she would have done so quickly in Jezreel without the benefit of a warning. She simply wanted him out of the country. Elijah obliged her, leaving immediately for Beersheba. How could the high-flying Elijah, fresh from his spectacular victory, so suddenly appear frightened, running for his life from the Phoenician princess he had so recently challenged? Some interpreters see a different meaning in verse 3.

"He arose and ran for his life" can also be translated "he arose and went for his soul." Since in the next verse Elijah pleads with God to take away his life, he obviously was not afraid to die. He may have fled to the wilderness not so much to escape Jezebel's threat as to engage in a spiritual retreat for the benefit of his soul. He wanted to be alone with God in order to pour out his troubles, recommit his soul to the Lord, and see what God would say to him.[2] It is difficult to believe that the man who a few hours earlier had witnessed God's convincing fire at Carmel, who could vividly remember the miraculous drought, the providential ravens, the widow's oil and her risen son, could so quickly melt before Jezebel and retreat in cowardice. This alternate interpretation of verse 3 may explain the inconsistent behavior of our hero.

Of course, being afraid is no sign of weakness; it is the response to fear that reveals character. Even courageous heroes are often afraid. So perhaps we should not be surprised that even this super-prophet had moments of fear, disappointment, and self-pity.

Beersheba was a hundred miles from Jezreel on the extreme southern border of Judah's territory. "From Dan to Beersheba" was the biblical phrase used to describe the entire territory of Palestine. So as far as Elijah was concerned, he was going as far away as possible out of Ahab and Jezebel's jurisdiction. But that was still not remote enough for Elijah's purpose of undisturbed contemplation. He left his servant in Beersheba and went still deeper into the wilderness. The servant, who first appeared with Elijah on Mount Carmel, was, according to legend, the son of the widow of Zarephath who was raised from the dead.[3]

Exhausted physically and emotionally, and unable to go any farther, Elijah sat down under a broom bush to rest. The *Retama roetam* is a shrub that still grows in the wilderness areas south of the Dead

Sea. It has a delicate white blossom that appears in February in advance of tiny foliage. The plant often reaches a height of ten to twelve feet and affords grateful shade in the heat of the desert.[4] Here, under his lonely shelter, Elijah finally gave in to the weariness of his soul and cried out for death. He did not contemplate suicide, for he believed God was the Lord of life. Though a man might wish to die, he was not at liberty to take his life. Only God had the right to do that.[5]

Twice the bone-weary man of God fell asleep only to be awakened by an angel with food and water. The word translated *"cake baked on coals"* is the name for the round flat bread that Arabs in this part of the desert still bake on hot stones in the ashes.[6] After rest and miraculous nourishment, Elijah was able to travel for forty days and nights into the Sinai desert as far as Mount Horeb (or Mount Sinai), over a hundred fifty miles further south.

Since the Hebrew definite article is used in verse 9, "the" cave, it may be that it was the same cave in which Moses hid when God appeared to him on this same mountain.[7] Here God addressed a question to the prophet, which He repeated again in verse 13: *"What are you doing here, Elijah?"* Though it contains the sting of a divine rebuke, it seems to have been God's gracious way of inviting Elijah to speak, to pour out his heart. When Jesus appeared to the disciples on the Emmaus Road, they were depressed about the things that had happened in Jerusalem; and the Lord asked them, "What things?" Of course Jesus knew "what things." He had asked not for information, but to encourage them to unload the burden of their hearts. God did the same for Elijah.

Elijah's whining tone of complaining self-pity in verse 10 is out of character for someone like Elijah, who had so recently experienced such dramatic evidences of God's care. If the earlier miracles were not sufficient to encourage him, the more recent angelic meals should have convinced him that God still loved him and cared for him. God obviously still needed him and wanted to preserve him for future tasks. But Elijah's despondency blinded him. The correct answer to God's question, "What are you doing here?" would have been, "I was afraid of Jezebel and ran to hide in this cave." Instead, like a martyr, he felt compelled to piously remind God about his zeal, his commitment, and his lonely suffering.

Despondency has a way of selectively focusing on certain facts from life and conveniently overlooking others. As he gushed out his lonely complaint about being the only faithful one left, he forgot about the great multitudes at Carmel who acknowledged that Yahweh was God. He forgot about the one hundred prophets protected by courageous Obadiah. "Despair is always color-blind; it can only see the dark tints."[8]

Of the several theophanies in the Old Testament, the one described in the next section is perhaps the most famous. God sent the wind, earthquake, and fire, but His presence was not found in these spectacular demonstrations of destruction. Instead, it was in the "still small voice" that followed them. Others translate this phrase, "a gentle, little breeze,"[9] "a sound of thin silence," "a light whisper."[10]

The message of the theophany seems to be that Elijah should not always expect God to break into history in such spectacular manifestations as wind, earthquake, and fire. God also reveals Himself in clear, intelligible communication. This message may be an anticipation of the coming of Jesus Christ who would be God's ultimate Word to His creation.

Typical of his fiery temperament, Elijah wanted vengeance. He wanted God to send the windstorm, the earthquake, and the fire upon Jezebel and her idolaters, but God was reminding him that He is in control, not Elijah. He has other ways of dealing with the problems of history. The poet, Heine, half in jest, described his notion of happiness:

> My wishes are a humble dwelling with a thatched roof, a good bed, good food, flowers at my windows, and some fine tall trees before my door. And if the good God wants to make me completely happy, he will grant me the joy of seeing six or seven of my enemies hanging from the trees.[11]

Elijah needed to restore his faith in God, his faith in himself, and his faith in others. This experience in the wilderness addressed all three. God was still there, as powerful and loving as ever. Elijah could still trust Him. He could believe in himself because he was still important to God. There was work for him to do. His faith in others was renewed when God reminded him that he was not alone in the battle after all. There were the prophets in the caves; there was brave Obadiah. There were the multitudes who proclaimed their renewed faith at Carmel, and, as he will be told in verse 18, seven thousand others who have remained faithful to Yahweh. In reverence and humility, Elijah wrapped his mantle about his face and returned to his cave. He had learned his lesson.

Discouragement is a devastating experience. In a recent issue of a national news magazine, discouragement was labeled "the social disease of the 1980s in America." The article went on to describe how the disillusioned 1960s college generation has become the "big chill" generation of the 1980s. Listlessness, despair, and resignation are crippling people all across the country in a wave of chronic cynicism. As evidence of this national mood one can see an alarming increase in teenage suicides and an exploding drug epidemic.

The Bible has a great deal to say about discouragement, fainting, falling away, and losing heart. Even the apostle Paul had to struggle with Elijah's malady himself, and he mentions it in 2 Corinthians 4. "Therefore, since we have this ministry . . . , we do not lose heart." Paul overcame discouragement and discovered strength for endurance by becoming involved in a significant ministry. He could not give up or disengage, because his task was too important. Like Nehemiah building his wall around Jerusalem, Paul could say, "I'm doing a great work, I cannot come down." It was the significance of his task that kept Paul traveling, witnessing, and preaching in spite of persecution and disheartening opposition. In like manner Elijah was aroused out of his despair by being given another important task by God. That significant task helped him overcome his negative mood (v. 15).

Paul also found the power to see it through in his sensitive compassion for the needs of others. In that same chapter in 2 Corinthians the apostle's deep concern for others is obvious as he describes the lost people of his day as "perishing, blinded by Satan." In Romans he cried, "My heart's desire for Israel is that they may be saved." It was his genuine compassion for others that kept Paul going when he was tempted to give up. On Horeb's mountain, God turned Elijah's eyes away from his own problem and refocused them on others. The prophet needed to begin thinking about the faithful remnant who had not bowed the knee to Baal; he needed to be concerned with Hazael, Jehu, and Elisha, who were waiting for his prophetic word. The vision of need injected the prophet with new enthusiasm for the task.

But Paul's ultimate weapon against discouragement was his certainty of God's power in his life. In 2 Cor. 4:7ff., Paul said:

> But we have this treasure in earthen vessels, that the excellence of the power may be of God and not of us. We are hard pressed on every side, yet not crushed. . . . Therefore we do not lose heart. Even though our outward man is perishing, yet the inward man is being renewed day by day . . . while we do not look at the things which are seen, but at the things which are not seen. For the things which are seen are temporary, but the things which are not seen are eternal.

Power to overcome discouragement comes ultimately from the presence of the Holy Spirit within a believer's life, supernaturally reinforcing that life and enabling it to overcome anything. When a person looks at transient circumstances, that person will sink like Peter did when he took his eyes off Jesus and began to look at the waves. But when one's eyes are focused on the Eternal One, there is courage to see it through. For a while at least, Elijah had forgotten the eternal and had focused his vision on the discouraging circumstances surrounding him. No wonder he was down. But when God revealed Himself in the power and stillness of His presence, Elijah focused his perspective on the eternal. Then his crippling wave of depression passed.

On one of Albuquerque's cloudless summer days, we drove just outside the city to ride the famous tram to the top of Sandia Peak. It is one of the longest tram rides in North America, rewarding the rider with a spectacular view from the top of the twelve-thousand-foot-high peak. Getting on the tram car with us at the bottom of the mountain was a young man with a huge canvas bag, so big we had to help him drag it on the cable car. At the top we helped him unload it and watched with curiosity as he dragged it across the top of the mountain to a preselected spot beside a sheer drop-off to the valley below. He unzipped the bag and pulled out pieces of aluminum tubing and nylon cloth; and there on the top of Sandia, the young stranger pieced together a hang glider! It was fascinating.

We watched as he assembled the glider and then walked around it a couple of times checking every joint and connection, making sure every guy wire was tight. (If it had been me, I would still be on top of Sandia Peak checking every connection and guy wire!) Satisfied it was all secure, he went to the edge of the precipice, tied a yellow ribbon on a branch to check the direction of the wind, put on his helmet, and strapped on the hang glider. And as we literally caught our breath, he ran as fast as he could and jumped from the top of the mountain!

He fell a few feet as the wind caught the sails of the glider, and then gracefully and quietly he glided across the valley until he encountered what aeronautical experts call a "thermal," an invisible column of hot air that spirals upward like a minitornado. Having found his thermal, our young pilot circled over it like a giant bird and began to gain altitude. He was soon lifted back to our eye level as we stood on top of Sandia. Before long he was gliding silently, effortlessly, gracefully, two thousand feet above us, upheld by his invisible column of air.

A loud roar distracted our attention back down to Albuquerque. At the airport just beyond the city, a 727 jet was lumbering at full power down the runway for a takeoff. The sound of its huge engines, burning hundreds of pounds of fuel, was echoing all the way to the top of Sandia. We could see and hear the plane as it struggled to lift its load off the concrete, inching its way higher, reaching to clear the mountains. All the while, our hang-glider friend was circling effortlessly, silently, gracefully, fifteen thousand feet in the air lifted by his invisible column of support.

We had seen a graphic reminder of the power to soar above the discouragements of life made available by depending not on the visible but on the invisible and eternal. We don't have to rely on our own cleverness, courage, or endurance. As believers we have the invisible power of the Holy Spirit to lift us. We can be more than conquerors through Him.

Elijah Receives a New Task

19:15 Then the LORD said to him: "Go, return on your
way to the Wilderness of Damascus; and when you
arrive, anoint Hazael *as* king over Syria.
16 "Also you shall anoint Jehu the son of Nimshi *as*

> king over Israel. And Elisha the son of Shaphat of Abel Meholah you shall anoint *as* prophet in your place.
> 17 "It shall be *that* whoever escapes the sword of Hazael, Jehu will kill; and whoever escapes the sword of Jehu, Elisha will kill.
> 18 "Yet I have reserved seven thousand in Israel, all whose knees have not bowed to Baal, and every mouth that has not kissed him."
> 19 So he departed from there, and found Elisha the son of Shaphat, who *was* plowing *with* twelve yoke *of oxen* before him, and he was with the twelfth. Then Elijah passed by him and threw his mantle on him.
> 20 And he left the oxen and ran after Elijah, and said, "Please let me kiss my father and my mother, and *then* I will follow you." And he said to him, "Go back again, for what have I done to you?"
> 21 So *Elisha* turned back from him, and took a yoke of oxen and slaughtered them and boiled their flesh, using the oxen's equipment, and gave it to the people, and they ate. Then he arose and followed Elijah, and became his servant.
>
> *1 Kings 19:15–21*

One cure for depression is to get busy. So the first word from God to Elijah after the dramatic demonstration on Mount Horeb is "Go." The anointing of Hazael, Jehu, and Elisha would ensure that the campaign against Baal worship would continue, and a faithful remnant of Yahweh worshipers would survive. Jehu was actually the grandson of Nimshi, not his son. The Hebrew word for son, *bēn,* can be used for both son and grandson.[12] Nowhere else in the Bible is there mention of a prophet being anointed, and there is no record that such an anointing ceremony for Elisha ever took place. It may be that the word here represents an "appointment" of Elisha rather than a ceremonial anointing with oil.

Elisha, whose name means "God is salvation," was apparently from a wealthy family. Otherwise there would not have been servants behind twelve pair of oxen pulling twelve plows lined up in an echelon formation across the field. Casting the mantle on this young farmer was Elijah's ceremonial way of drafting him for the prophetic task to which God had called him. Elisha obviously knew what it meant. *"He left the oxen and ran after Elijah"* (v. 20).

Like the reluctant followers in Jesus' parable, Elisha asked for the privilege of first saying goodbye to his parents (cf. Matt. 8:21; Luke 9:61). It is not exactly clear whether Elijah willingly granted his petition or not. What did Elijah mean when he said, *"Go back again, for what have I done to you"*? Seeing it as a favorable response to Elisha's request, one commentator translates the comment: "Go (kiss your parents). Then come back, for (remember) what I have done to you (i.e. casting my mantle on you)."[13] Elisha must have understood it this way. Not only did he go back to tell his parents farewell but he also symbolically put his entire past life behind him by sacrificing his oxen and burning them with a fire kindled from the wooden plow. The plow was probably the simple run-rig type still common among Palestinian peasants today.

We will hear more from Elisha later when he appears again during Elijah's translation scene in 2 Kings 2:1–14.

Ahab Defeats the Syrians

20:1 Now Ben-Hadad the king of Syria gathered all his forces together; thirty-two kings were with him, with horses and chariots. And he went up and besieged Samaria, and made war against it.

2 Then he sent messengers into the city to Ahab king of Israel, and said to him, "Thus says Ben-Hadad:

3 'Your silver and your gold *are* mine; your loveliest wives and children are mine.'"

4 And the king of Israel answered and said, "My lord, O king, just as you say, I and all that I have *are* yours."

5 Then the messengers came back and said, "Thus speaks Ben-Hadad, saying, 'Indeed I have sent to you, saying, "You shall deliver to me your silver and your gold, your wives and your children";

6 'but I will send my servants to you tomorrow about this time, and they shall search your house and the houses of your servants. And it shall be, *that* whatever is pleasant in your eyes, they will put *it* in their hands and take *it*.'"

7 So the king of Israel called all the elders of the land, and said, "Notice, please, and see how this *man* seeks trouble, for he sent to me for my wives, my children, my silver, and my gold; and I did not deny him."
8 And all the elders and all the people said to him, "Do not listen or consent."
9 Therefore he said to the messengers of Ben-Hadad, "Tell my lord the king, 'All that you sent for to your servant the first time I will do, but this thing I cannot do.'" And the messengers departed and brought back word to him.
10 Then Ben-Hadad sent to him and said, "The gods do so to me, and more also, if enough dust is left of Samaria for a handful for each of the people who follow me."
11 So the king of Israel answered and said, "Tell *him,* 'Let not the one who puts on *his armor* boast like the one who takes *it off.*'"
12 And it happened when *Ben-Hadad* heard this message, as he and the kings *were* drinking at the command post, that he said to his servants, "Get ready." And they got ready to attack the city.
13 Suddenly a prophet approached Ahab king of Israel, saying, "Thus says the LORD: 'Have you seen all this great multitude? Behold, I will deliver it into your hand today, and you shall know that I *am* the LORD.'"
14 So Ahab said, "By whom?" And he said, "Thus says the LORD: 'By the young leaders of the provinces.'" Then he said, "Who will set the battle in order?" And he answered, "You."
15 Then he mustered the young leaders of the provinces, and there were two hundred and thirty-two; and after them he mustered all the people, all the children of Israel—seven thousand.
16 So they went out at noon. Meanwhile Ben-Hadad and the thirty-two kings helping him were getting drunk at the command post.
17 The young leaders of the provinces went out first. And Ben-Hadad sent out *a patrol,* and they told him, saying, "Men are coming out of Samaria!"
18 So he said, "If they have come out for peace, take

them alive; and if they have come out for war take them alive."

19 Then these young leaders of the provinces went out of the city with the army which followed them.

20 And each one killed his man; so the Syrians fled, and Israel pursued them; and Ben-Hadad the king of Syria escaped on a horse with the cavalry.

21 Then the king of Israel went out and attacked the horses and chariots, and killed the Syrians with a great slaughter.

22 And the prophet came to the king of Israel and said to him, "Go, strengthen yourself; take note, and see what you should do, for in the spring of the year the king of Syria will come up against you."

23 Then the servants of the king of Syria said to him, "Their gods *are* gods of the hills. Therefore they were stronger than we; but if we fight against them in the plain, surely we will be stronger than they.

24 "So do this thing: Dismiss the kings, each from his position, and put captains in their places;

25 "and you shall muster an army like the army that you have lost, horse for horse and chariot for chariot. Then we will fight against them in the plain; surely we will be stronger than they." And he listened to their voice and did so.

26 So it was, in the spring of the year, that Ben-Hadad mustered the Syrians and went up to Aphek to fight against Israel.

27 And the children of Israel were mustered and given provisions, and they went against them. Now the children of Israel encamped before them like two little flocks of goats, while the Syrians filled the countryside.

28 Then a man of God came and spoke to the king of Israel, and said, "Thus says the LORD: 'Because the Syrians have said, "The LORD *is* God of the hills, but He *is* not God of the valleys," therefore I will deliver all this great multitude into your hand, and you shall know that I *am* the LORD.'"

29 And they encamped opposite each other for seven days. So it was that on the seventh day the battle was joined; and the children of Israel killed

one hundred thousand foot soldiers *of* the Syrians in one day.

30 But the rest fled to Aphek, into the city; then a wall fell on twenty-seven thousand of the men *who were* left. And Ben-Hadad fled and went into the city, into an inner chamber.

31 Then his servants said to him, "Look now, we have heard that the kings of the house of Israel *are* merciful kings. Please, let us put sackcloth around our waists and ropes around our heads, and go out to the king of Israel; perhaps he will spare your life."

32 So they wore sackcloth around their waists and *put* ropes around their heads, and came to the king of Israel and said, "Your servant Ben-Hadad says, 'Please let me live.'" And he said, "*Is* he still alive? He *is* my brother."

33 Now the men were watching closely to see whether *any sign of mercy would come* from him; and they quickly grasped *at this word* and said, "Your brother Ben-Hadad." So he said, "Go, bring him." Then Ben-Hadad came out to him; and he had him come up into the chariot.

34 So *Ben-Hadad* said to him, "The cities which my father took from your father I will restore; and you may set up marketplaces for yourself in Damascus, as my father did in Samaria." Then *Ahab said,* "I will send you away with this treaty." So he made a treaty with him and sent him away.

35 Now a certain man of the sons of the prophets said to his neighbor by the word of the LORD, "Strike me, please." And the man refused to strike him.

36 Then he said to him, "Because you have not obeyed the voice of the LORD, surely, as soon as you depart from me, a lion shall kill you." And as soon as he left him, a lion found him and killed him.

37 And he found another man, and said, "Strike me, please." So the man struck him, inflicting a wound.

38 Then the prophet departed and waited for the king by the road, and disguised himself with a bandage over his eyes.

39 Now as the king passed by, he cried out to the king and said, "Your servant went out into the midst

of the battle; and there, a man came over and brought a man to me, and said, 'Guard this man; if by any means he is missing, your life shall be for his life, or else you shall pay a talent of silver.'

40 "While your servant was busy here and there, he was gone." Then the king of Israel said to him, "So *shall* your judgment *be;* you yourself have decided *it.*"

41 And he hastened to take the bandage away from his eyes; and the king of Israel recognized him as one of the prophets.

42 Then he said to him, "Thus says the LORD: 'Because you have let slip out of *your* hand a man whom I appointed to utter destruction, therefore your life shall go for his life, and your people for his people.'"

43 So the king of Israel went to his house sullen and displeased, and came to Samaria.

1 Kings 20:1–43

The tone of this section of the story shifts considerably. Elijah has been the central character up to this point, but now the focus is on Ahab. Neither Elijah nor Elisha appears again until chapter 21. In this section, the attitude toward Ahab seems more forgiving. He is presented as a more righteous and courageous leader whom the Lord's prophets support with favorable predictions.

Ben-Hadad may be the same king Asa enlisted against Baasha in 15:18, or he may be that king's son or grandson by the same name. His allies, the thirty-two *"kings"* mentioned in verse 1, were likely heads of satellite states and tribal chieftains from the territory around the capital. Damascus was the natural center to which the tribes in the North Arabian desert were drawn and around which some of them settled.[14]

Ahab's readiness to submit to Ben-Hadad's demands after only a brief siege of Samaria may be explained by the fact that he was already a semivassal of Syria. Or it may be he understood Ben-Hadad's first demand in 2–4 as no more than a general demand for the usual form of tribute, which he was willing to pay in order to spare the city. But when the second, more specific demand was delivered (vv. 5–6) Ahab realized the terms were too extreme. Ben-Hadad was asking for total subjection and immediate possession of all of Samaria.

Having received the unanimous agreement of his elders, Ahab politely rejected the enemy's offer, still using the self-effacing language of a vassal. With the brash self-confidence of a bully, Ben-Hadad responded with the boastful threat of total destruction in verse 10. Another interesting translation (Lucian's recension of the Septuagint) expresses it, "There will not be enough dust left of Samaria for foxes to build their holes there."

But Ahab had a way with words, too, and answered the taunt with what was probably a well-known proverb in that day. *"Let not the one who puts on his armor boast like the one who takes it off"* (v. 11). It was an ancient version of "Don't count your chickens before they hatch," or "He who laughs last, laughs best."

So confident of victory was the Syrian monarch that he was prematurely celebrating with his troops in drunken abandon when Ahab's clever proverb was delivered. The "command post" was a field hut constructed from tree branches similar to the booths built by Hebrew worshipers when they celebrated the Feast of the Tabernacles. In fact, the only other place this noun is used is to describe the ceremonial booths. Incensed, Ben-Hadad issued an immediate order for full military mobilization in preparation for an assault on Samaria. The command in verse 12 can also be translated, "Prepare the battering-rams!"[15]

Meanwhile, an unknown prophet delivered to Ahab the divine plan whereby God would deliver Samaria from the surrounding armies. None of the three prophets mentioned here and in verses 28 and 35 is identified. They may well be the same person. The 232 *"young leaders of the provinces"* were probably skilled assault commandoes who would precede the standing army in an initial surprise attack. In order to show that the victory belonged to God, Ben-Hadad's vast army of experienced military veterans would be humiliated, overpowered by a few young neophytes from Samaria.

Caught off guard, their leaders drunk, their ranks divided among thirty-two competitive kings, each more interested in the safety of his own ranks than in the success of the overall objective, Ben-Hadad's army panicked. They retreated in confusion before the fierce Israeli counterattack, their king fleeing on horseback to Damascus before them.

Some interpreters link the seven thousand Israelite soldiers in verse 15 with the seven thousand in 19:18 who had not worshiped

Baal. Such an interpretation would add strength to the idea that it was God who gave the victory, this time by using His righteous band of faithful followers.[16]

There is a revealing insight into pagan theology in verse 23. We have already been told that Samaria was built by Omri on a high hill rising three hundred feet above the surrounding plain (16:24). So as they rehearsed the battle, Ben-Hadad's advisers drew the conclusion that Israel's gods must be "mountain gods," giving Israel a military advantage when they fought on higher elevations such as the hill of Samaria. Since their own gods were gods of the plain, the Syrians concluded they had been unfairly matched in the Samaritan campaign. They wanted a rematch on level terrain where their army would have the advantage.

So the Syrian strategy was to challenge Israel again in the spring, this time on the flat plains surrounding the city of Aphek. There are several Old Testament towns with that name, making it difficult to decide precisely where this second engagement took place. Most likely, it was at the Aphek located east of the Sea of Galilee on the direct route from Israel to Damascus.[17]

Verse 17 is difficult to translate, but its obvious purpose is to contrast the enormous number of Ben-Hadad's troops with a grossly outnumbered Israeli army. Up against Syria's vast host, Ahab's army looked *"like two little flocks of goats"* (v. 27). For the second time an unknown prophet reminded Ahab that he would prevail, but only because of Yahweh's miraculous intervention (v. 28). An unusually large number of Syrian troops were killed that day, both on the battle field and in a collapsing city wall at Aphek where survivors had fled. The wall may have been deliberately sabotaged by Israeli guerrillas, a strategy frequently used in ancient warfare.[18]

Ben-Hadad's baseless bravado had now been reduced to groveling subservience. With no hope of survival apart from the compassion of Ahab, Ben-Hadad and his hapless survivors donned sackcloth, a traditional symbol of submission and repentance, and prepared to throw themselves on the mercy of their captors. For added effect they put ropes around their heads. The ropes probably represented halters by which their captors could lead them around. Or perhaps the ropes were symbols that their surrender was so complete that they were even ready to be hanged.[19]

Ahab's reference to Ben-Hadad as "my brother" in verse 32 is a polite expression of Eastern hospitality expressing big-hearted congeniality rather than kinship. When the terms of the peace treaty are described in verse 32, it is the first time we learn that King Omri, Ahab's father, had lost territory to Syria and had granted the enemy access to "markets" in the capital city of Samaria. The "markets" were bazaars surrounded by residential neighborhoods similar to the ethnic quarters or "barrios" found in large cities today. Examples of such "markets" in recent years are the Jewish and Armenian quarters in the city of Jerusalem.[20]

The closing episode in chapter 20 is another illustration of the style of historical writing that is unique to the Books of Kings. A traditional historian would probably have portrayed Ahab's Syrian-Israeli peace treaty as a stroke of diplomatic genius. The king would be praised for the national security and power his shrewd political negotiations had guaranteed. But not the biblical writer. Interested only in interpreting these historical events from the perspective of God's purpose for Israel, he denounced Ahab's treaty as a serious violation of Yahweh's will. Instead of being praised for what he did, Ahab would be punished by the loss of his life (v. 42).

Although he is not named, Josephus believed the anonymous "man of God" introduced in verse 35 was Micaiah who figures so prominently in the next story.[21] He suggested it was in retaliation for Micaiah's prophetic condemnation that the king put him in prison.

Acting out the part of a wounded soldier, the prophet cleverly led Ahab to judge his own case, a technique similar to the one Nathan the prophet had employed when he induced King David to judge the fictional rich man who slaughtered a poor man's lamb. In like manner the nameless prophet in verse 35 let Ahab hang himself with his own judicious logic; then he unleashed his stern condemnation on the chagrined king. It was clearly his way of saying, "Thou art the man." Predictably, Ahab reacted like a spoiled child, *"sullen and displeased"* (v. 43).

Ahab Takes Naboth's Vineyard

21:1 And it came to pass after these things *that*
Naboth the Jezreelite had a vineyard which *was* in
Jezreel, next to the palace of Ahab king of Samaria.
2 So Ahab spoke to Naboth, saying, "Give me

your vineyard, that I may have it for a vegetable garden, because it *is* near, next to my house; and for it I will give you a vineyard better than it. *Or,* if it seems good to you, I will give you its worth in money."

3 But Naboth said to Ahab, "The LORD forbid that I should give the inheritance of my fathers to you!"

4 So Ahab went into his house sullen and displeased because of the word which Naboth the Jezreelite had spoken to him; for he had said, "I will not give you the inheritance of my fathers." And he lay down on his bed, and turned away his face, and would eat no food.

5 But Jezebel his wife came to him, and said to him, "Why is your spirit so sullen that you eat no food?"

6 He said to her, "Because I spoke to Naboth the Jezreelite, and said to him, 'Give me your vineyard for money; or else, if it pleases you, I will give you *another* vineyard for it.' And he answered, 'I will not give you my vineyard.'"

7 Then Jezebel his wife said to him, "You now exercise authority over Israel! Arise, eat food, and let your heart be cheerful; I will give you the vineyard of Naboth the Jezreelite."

8 And she wrote letters in Ahab's name, sealed *them* with his seal, and sent the letters to the elders and the nobles who *were* dwelling in the city with Naboth.

9 She wrote in the letters, saying, "Proclaim a fast, and seat Naboth with high honor among the people;

10 "and seat two men, scoundrels, before him to bear witness against him, saying, 'You have blasphemed God and the king.' *Then* take him out, and stone him, that he may die."

11 So the men of his city, the elders and nobles who were inhabitants of his city, did as Jezebel had sent to them, as it *was* written in the letters which she had sent to them.

12 They proclaimed a fast, and seated Naboth with high honor among the people.

13 And two men, scoundrels, came in and sat

before him; and the scoundrels witnessed against
him, against Naboth, in the presence of the people,
saying, "Naboth has blasphemed God and the king!"
Then they took him outside the city and stoned him
with stones, so that he died.
14 Then they sent to Jezebel, saying, "Naboth has
been stoned and is dead."
15 And it came to pass, when Jezebel heard that
Naboth had been stoned and was dead, that Jezebel
said to Ahab, "Arise, take possession of the vineyard
of Naboth the Jezreelite, which he refused to give
you for money; for Naboth is not alive, but dead."
16 So it was, when Ahab heard that Naboth was
dead, that Ahab got up and went down to take possession of the vineyard of Naboth the Jezreelite.

1 Kings 21:1–16

It is impossible for me to read the biblical account of Ahab and Naboth without remembering the dramatic sermon regarding this Scripture by R. G. Lee, the legendary Baptist preacher from Memphis, Tennessee. He preached it hundreds of times before conventions, pastors' conferences, and evangelistic rallies, always with the same timeless appeal. Audiences were always moved by this story's classic theme of the triumph of right over wrong. Lee called his sermon, "Payday Someday!" Its textual subtitle could have been, "Be sure your sins will find you out."

Verse 1 sets the scene in Jezreel where the king and queen apparently had another royal residence as a winter retreat from the colder elevations of Samaria. Naboth refused to release his vineyard to his next-door neighbor not because Ahab's offer was unfair but because he considered the sale a violation of the biblical law of inherited land. His response in verse 3 is literally, "a profanation to me from the Lord should I give the inheritance of my fathers to you!"[22] Naboth probably had in mind the prohibition found in Num. 27:8–11.

Since Ahab was motivated by wealth and material possessions, he could not understand why Naboth would turn down such a profitable offer. Surely a handful of silver would sway anybody. But the brusque, flat refusal of sturdy Naboth, showing there was still some independence in Israel, sent Ahab into another of his childish pouting moods. He is described in verse 4 with the same words used in 20:43, *"sullen and displeased."* The *"bed"* in verse 4 was a couch beside the eating table where diners, in the traditional Eastern style, lounged while they ate. So the scene is a vivid picture of peevish Ahab turning his face to the wall and refusing to eat. He was like a sulking child who could not get his own way.

When the king explained to Jezebel why he was upset, he conveniently left out the legitimate reason Naboth gave for not selling his property and thereby makes his refusal seem harsher and more unreasonable than it really was. Ahab implied Naboth stubbornly and arbitrarily told him "no" with the same petulant spirit so characteristic of his own temperament. According to Ahab, Naboth rudely said: *"I will not give you my vineyard"* (v. 6).

Attempting to lift his spirits, Jezebel goaded Ahab with the statement in verse 7, which literally means "you now, do kingdom over Israel." It could be a positive affirmation from the queen to her dejected husband, "You are the one who exercises authority over Israel!" Or it could be taken as a sarcastic parody of his weakness, "Look at you! The mighty ruler of Israel!" Jones believes the statement is a question, "Don't you now govern Israel? Is this the way for the king of Israel to act?"[23] All three possibilities indicate Jezebel thought Ahab was weak. Because of her upbringing in the absolutist monarchy of the Phoenician court, she was used to a dictatorial leadership style. She decided to take matters into her own hands and show Ahab how her strong father, King Ethbaal, would have handled such a matter in Tyre.

Her scheme involved the bribing of false witnesses to frame Naboth with a capital crime, getting him legally prosecuted and finally executed. Since the property of public criminals in the ancient East reverted to the crown, Ahab would have his vineyard.[24] The fabricated story, substantiated by paid witnesses, must have been that Naboth had legally agreed to sell Ahab his vineyard for a fair price, then welshed on the deal and withdrew from the agreement. Her case was reinforced with forged letters and documents that perhaps contained Naboth's written promise to sell and maybe a false deed of sale—all sealed with the royal signet. It was an airtight case. So the elders and nobles of the city, out of dread for Jezebel, went along with the plot, and Naboth was summarily tried and stoned.

Two interesting words are found in this section. The *"seal"* in verse 8 was the wax imprint of the king's ring or signet similar to several from this time period that archaeologists have uncovered in Israel. One is inscribed with the name "Yotham," probably belonging to Jotham the son of Azariah. Another has the phrase "Belonging to Gedaliah, the royal chamberlain" and was found in the ruins of the Judean city of Lachish.[25] Ancient letters were usually written by a scribe or amanuensis in the name of the writer who was depicted as speaking in the third person. The letter would then be sealed in clay or wax stamped with the official symbol of the sender. Like a distinctive signature, that symbol from a seal or a ring would authenticate the letter as genuine. So Ahab's complicity in the vicious plot must have at least involved his permission for Jezebel to use his personal seal to legitimize her forged letters.

The other interesting word is in verse 10, translated *"scoundrels."* Its literal translation is "sons of *Bĕliyyaʿal."* It comes from two words: *bĕlî,* "without," and *yaʿal,* "worth." An alternative spelling, *bĕlî-yaʿăleh,* would carry the meaning, "not going up," or in other words "not successful or ne'er-do-wells."[26] Popularized, the term is "Sons of Belial" or "Sons of Worthlessness."

Maclaren notes there are three types of dangerous characters in this story: (1) Ahab, who is wicked and weak, (2) Jezebel, who is wicked and strong, and (3) the Elders of Jezreel, who are wicked and subservient. He believes the latter of the three are the most reprehensible. Wickedness is always odious, and cowardice is always contemptible. When the two come together and a person has no other reason for his sin than "I was afraid," each makes the other blacker. "Better to be lying dead beneath a heap of stones like the sturdy Naboth who could say no to a king, than be one of his stoners who killed their innocent neighbor to pleasure Jezebel."[27]

Even though Jezebel did the dirty work, Ahab was guilty. This grave and contemptible sin was the last drop in the full cup of the king's sins. It brought down the judgment of God on him and his house.

ELIJAH CONDEMNS AHAB

21:17 Then the word of the LORD came to Elijah the Tishbite, saying,
18 "Arise, go down to meet Ahab king of Israel, who

lives in Samaria. There *he is,* in the vineyard of Naboth, where he has gone down to take possession of it.

19 "You shall speak to him, saying, 'Thus says the LORD: "Have you murdered and also taken possession?"' And you shall speak to him, saying, 'Thus says the LORD: "In the place where dogs licked the blood of Naboth, dogs shall lick your blood, even yours."'"

20 So Ahab said to Elijah, "Have you found me, O my enemy?" And he answered, "I have found *you,* because you have sold yourself to do evil in the sight of the LORD:

21 'Behold, I will bring calamity on you. I will take away your posterity, and will cut off from Ahab every male in Israel, both bond and free.

22 'I will make your house like the house of Jeroboam the son of Nebat, and like the house of Baasha the son of Ahijah, because of the provocation with which you have provoked *Me* to anger, and made Israel sin.'

23 "And concerning Jezebel the LORD also spoke, saying, 'The dogs shall eat Jezebel by the wall of Jezreel.'

24 "The dogs shall eat whoever belongs to Ahab and dies in the city, and the birds of the air shall eat whoever dies in the field."

25 But there was no one like Ahab who sold himself to do wickedness in the sight of the LORD, because Jezebel his wife stirred him up.

26 And he behaved very abominably in following idols, according to all *that* the Amorites had done, whom the LORD had cast out before the children of Israel.

27 So it was, when Ahab heard those words, that he tore his clothes and put sackcloth on his body, and fasted and lay in sackcloth, and went about mourning.

28 And the word of the LORD came to Elijah the Tishbite, saying,

29 "See how Ahab has humbled himself before Me? Because he has humbled himself before Me, I will not bring the calamity in his days. In the days of his son I will bring the calamity on his house."

1 Kings 21:17–29

Elijah, the colorful prophet from Tishbeh, enters the picture again after the long interlude since chapter 18 when he was last mentioned. In this passage God sends him to Jezreel to confront the wicked King Ahab for the second time. *"There he is,"* God said, *" in the vineyard of Naboth, where he has gone down to take possession of it"* (v. 18). God wanted Elijah to catch Ahab red-handed, in the very act of confiscating the murdered Naboth's property. Without the slightest tinge of guilt, Ahab had rushed next door to claim his new toy. Instead he found there, standing by the vineyard gate, waiting for him—dark-browed, motionless, grim—the prophet whom he had not seen for years. As usual, Elijah had appeared with dramatic suddenness, this time like an incarnate conscience, to judge the king for the last time. Elijah's words are harsh: *"In the place where dogs licked the blood of Naboth, dogs shall lick your blood, even yours."* Their grammatical form reinforced their harshness: literally, "your own blood, yes yours!" Then he added the conventional scavenger-saying repeated already in 14:11 and 16:4.

The macabre prophecy came true all right, but not in Jezreel where Naboth's blood had been spilt (v. 19). Instead it was in Samaria that dogs licked Ahab's blood as described in 22:38. It could be that Elijah did not intend for the exact location to be taken as a literal part of the prophecy. Or perhaps the prophet intended for the fulfillment to be literally completed with the death of Ahab's son Joram, whose blood was spilled in Naboth's field (2 Kings 9:26). This would be consistent with verse 29, where God promised to postpone His judgment on Ahab because of his repentance. One commentator explains that the words in verse 19 "in the place" could be understood as "instead of" or "because of," expressing the idea that Ahab's blood would be shed as a retribution in the place of Naboth's.[28]

After two verses of editorial comment about Ahab's evil reign, the writer then tells us that Ahab, convicted by Elijah's condemnation, repented. His repentance was exhibited by four customary actions: (1) He tore his clothes. "Rending a garment" historically meant ripping off a broad strip of the robe from the neck down.[29] (2) He wore sackcloth next to his body. The uncomfortable scratchy material would irritate the skin and constantly remind the penitent of his sin. (3) He fasted. (4) He *"went about mourning."* The word is variously translated: "went about quietly," "went about creaking like a leather saddle," "went about moaning like a camel," or "went about barefoot."

All the translations vividly portray the humility and heartbreak of a sinner who is sorry for his transgressions. The repentance was apparently genuine, if not long-lasting, so God tempered His wrath with mercy by delaying the total destruction of Ahab's dynasty until Jehu killed his sons in 2 Kings 9:1–10:28.

The last time they met, Ahab had called Elijah "O troubler of Israel" (18:17). Now Elijah is *"O my enemy."* Actually, Elijah was the best friend Ahab had in his kingdom. Jezebel, who had just spoiled him with his new toy, was certainly not his friend. She was the worst enemy that hell could have sent him. But Elijah, by whose guidance Ahab could have been a great king, was the best friend heaven could have given him. Sin always blinds the sinner to the true identity of friends and enemies, and often causes the sinner to be ashamed of the best things in life.

Beatrix Potter was featured in a newspaper article recently. She is famous for her classic childhood stories, particularly the ones about Peter Rabbit. Who can forget hearing those tales of Flopsy, Mopsy, Cottontail, and Mr. MacGregor's cabbage patch, or who hasn't read them to children or grandchildren? They were well-written and entertaining, but Beatrix Potter didn't think so. According to the newspaper article, she was intensely ashamed of the stories she had written. After becoming a proud member of stuffy British aristocracy, she wouldn't let anyone mention the fact that she had written Peter Rabbit. She considered the stories somehow beneath the dignity of her new social status and was embarrassed to be identified as the author. Ironically, she became an expert rabbit hunter, winning awards for her marksmanship! However, in history's appraisal of her life, the little stories were the best things Beatrix did. She had become ashamed of the best thing in her life.

When Simon Peter with a curse said to the maiden by the fire, "I never knew him!" he was at that moment ashamed of the very best thing that had ever come into his life. Ahab made this same mistake when he despised Elijah. He saw his best ally as his worst enemy. He was ashamed of the best.

Ahab Is Warned by Micaiah

22:1 Now three years passed without war between
Syria and Israel.

2 Then it came to pass, in the third year, that
Jehoshaphat the king of Judah went down to *visit* the
king of Israel.
3 And the king of Israel said to his servants, "Do
you know that Ramoth in Gilead *is* ours, but we hesitate to take it out of the hand of the king of Syria?"
4 So he said to Jehoshaphat, "Will you go with me
to fight at Ramoth Gilead?" Jehoshaphat said to the
king of Israel, "I *am* as you *are,* my people as your
people, my horses as your horses."
5 Also Jehoshaphat said to the king of Israel,
"Please inquire for the word of the LORD today."
6 Then the king of Israel gathered the prophets
together, about four hundred men, and said to them,
"Shall I go against Ramoth Gilead to fight, or shall I
refrain?" So they said, "Go up, for the LORD will deliver *it* into the hand of the king."
7 And Jehoshaphat said, "*Is there* not still a prophet
of the LORD here, that we may inquire of Him?"
8 So the king of Israel said to Jehoshaphat, "*There
is* still one man, Micaiah the son of Imlah, by whom
we may inquire of the LORD; but I hate him, because
he does not prophesy good concerning me, but evil."
And Jehoshaphat said, "Let not the king say such
things!"
9 Then the king of Israel called an officer and
said, "Bring Micaiah the son of Imlah quickly!"
10 The king of Israel and Jehoshaphat the king
of Judah, having put on *their* robes, sat each on his
throne, at a threshing floor at the entrance of the gate
of Samaria; and all the prophets prophesied before
them.
11 Now Zedekiah the son of Chenaanah had made
horns of iron for himself; and he said, "Thus says the
LORD: 'With these you shall gore the Syrians until
they are destroyed.'"
12 And all the prophets prophesied so, saying, "Go
up to Ramoth Gilead and prosper, for the LORD will
deliver *it* into the king's hand."
13 Then the messenger who had gone to call Micaiah spoke to him, saying, "Now listen, the words of the
prophets with one accord encourage the king. Please,

let your word be like the word of one of them, and
speak encouragement."
14 And Micaiah said, "*As* the LORD lives, whatever
the LORD says to me, that I will speak."
15 Then he came to the king; and the king said to
him, "Micaiah, shall we go to war against Ramoth
Gilead, or shall we refrain?" And he answered him,
"Go and prosper, for the LORD will deliver *it* into the
hand of the king!"
16 So the king said to him, "How many times shall
I make you swear that you tell me nothing but the
truth in the name of the LORD?"
17 Then he said, "I saw all Israel scattered on the
mountains, as sheep that have no shepherd. And the
LORD said, 'These have no master. Let each return to
his house in peace.'"
18 And the king of Israel said to Jehoshaphat, "Did
I not tell you he would not prophesy good concerning me, but evil?"
19 Then *Micaiah* said, "Therefore hear the word of
the LORD: I saw the LORD sitting on His throne, and
all the host of heaven standing by, on His right hand
and on His left.
20 "And the LORD said, 'Who will persuade Ahab
to go up, that he may fall at Ramoth Gilead?' So one
spoke in this manner, and another spoke in that
manner.
21 "Then a spirit came forward and stood before
the LORD, and said, 'I will persuade him.'
22 "The LORD said to him, 'In what way?' So he
said, 'I will go out and be a lying spirit in the mouth of
all his prophets.' And *the LORD* said, 'You shall persuade *him*, and also prevail. Go out and do so.'
23 "Therefore look! The LORD has put a lying spirit
in the mouth of all these prophets of yours, and the
LORD has declared disaster against you."
24 Now Zedekiah the son of Chenaanah went near
and struck Micaiah on the cheek and said, "Which
way did the spirit from the LORD go from me to
speak to you?"
25 And Micaiah said, "Indeed, you shall see on
that day when you go into an inner chamber to hide!"

> 26 So the king of Israel said, "Take Micaiah, and
> return him to Amon the governor of the city and to
> Joash the king's son;
> 27 "and say, 'Thus says the king: "Put this *fellow* in
> prison, and feed him with bread of affliction and
> water of affliction, until I come in peace."'"
> 28 But Micaiah said, "If you ever return in peace,
> the LORD has not spoken by me." And he said, "Take
> heed, all you people!"
>
> *1 Kings 22:1–28*

In the zig-zag pattern used to switch his story back and forth between Israel and Judah, the writer left Judah at 15:24, after outlining the reign of Asa, and then jumped to Israel to tell the story of the kings of the Northern Kingdom. Next he picks up the story of Judah again at 22:41 with the reign of Jehoshaphat, Asa's son. But before coming to that, he is forced to introduce Jehoshaphat prematurely in this section in order to complete the account of Ahab. In so doing, he postpones any details about his life until verse 41, giving here only his name and the details of his military alliance with Ahab.

The three-year period in verse 1 is measured from the second defeat of Ben-Hadad at Aphek, described in chapter 20. It appears that the two kings had already established some kind of alliance or at least a detente. 2 Kings 8:18 confirms that Ahab's daughter Athaliah had married Jehoshaphat's son Jehoram.

Because of his ingratiating attitude toward Ahab in this chapter, some suggest that Jehoshaphat was a vassal of Israel's king. It does seem clear that he had yielded to Ahab's request when he came to Samaria, but later he is obviously free to decide whether he will participate in Ahab's campaign against Ben-Hadad. This would indicate he was more of a "junior partner" than a vassal (v. 4).

Ramoth Gilead, Ben-Hadad's fortress commanding the approach to Israel and Judah from Transjordan, had been ceded to Israel by treaty following Syria's surrender at Aphek. Presumably, Ben-Hadad had treacherously refused to give up the city, and it was still in Syrian hands. Jehoshaphat, the ruler of the Southern Kingdom, agreed to help Ahab regain the fortress.

Curiously, after making his decision, Jehoshaphat then requested that an inquiry be made about God's will in the matter. The order should have been reversed. He should have sought the will of God first. The tragic consequences that follow (vv. 29–40) should be a warning to anyone who would make the same mistake. First, we should pray with Paul that we "may be filled with the knowledge of His will in all wisdom and spiritual understanding" (Col. 1:9). Then, armed with divine knowledge, we can wisely make critical choices. That is better than making our own decision and then piously seeking God's sanction on our choice.

A few commentaries associate the four hundred prophets in verse 6 with Jezebel's prophets of Baal, some of whom might have survived the massacre at Mount Carmel.[30] But more than likely they were prophets of Ahab's adulterated version of Yahweh worship, which held that Baal and Asherah could be worshiped along with Yahweh and that calf-images were permissible worship-aids symbolizing Yahweh's power and virility. They obviously saw their profession as a trade rather than a divine calling.[31]

Jehoshaphat, who was more at home with the traditional form of Yahweh worship, was not satisfied with the authenticity of Ahab's four hundred courtesans. He did not trust their "poly-anna" good news report and asked if there were not a true spokesman of Yahweh around. (It is never difficult, in any age, to find prophets who will pat the leader on the back, curry his favor, and tell him to "do whatever you think is best.") Ahab reluctantly mentioned Micaiah as an exception to the popular trend in prophets.

Both the kings had flawed concepts of prophecy. Ahab thought of prophets as agents of magic who, with the use of dramatic symbolism, could give moral support to the king and the people when called upon. Their magic, he believed, could influence God by autosuggestion. On the other hand, Jehoshaphat correctly saw prophets as agents of divine revelation, but he erred in his mistaken belief that the revelation was primarily intended to confirm decisions he had already made and that prophetic warnings could be ignored without danger.[32]

Apart from what is related here, nothing is known about Micaiah. Some identify him with the unnamed prophet in 20:35. His meeting with the two kings in the wide-open arena of the threshing floor at the gate of Samaria must have been a dramatic scene. The two kings in their splendid regalia, the four hundred crowd-pleasing prophets of Ahab, the false prophet Zedekiah wearing bull's horns to act out his reassurance that Ahab would *"gore the Syrians,"* the curious spectators taking it all in (v. 11). And then, suddenly, Micaiah, a rugged individualist reminiscent of Elijah, erupted on the scene to confront them all.

At first it appeared that Micaiah had yielded to their plea not to make waves by giving a negative report to the king. When asked for his advice, he repeated the same ingratiating encouragement the other four hundred prophets had given the king in verse 6: *"Go and prosper, for the Lord will deliver it into the hand of the king!"* (v. 15). But even Ahab recognized that Micaiah was mocking them all with biting irony and sarcasm. He was mimicking the baseless optimism of the smooth-talking court preachers of Samaria.

After a royal reprimand, Micaiah unleashed the painful truth on the two kings and their followers. Just as Ahab expected, the truth was bad news. *"I saw all Israel scattered on the mountains, as sheep that have no shepherd"* (v. 17). Then Micaiah related another vision that God had let him see of a curious scene in heaven. *"The host of heaven"* in verse 19 probably consists of angels and other spiritual beings around God's throne. In the vision God asked for a volunteer from among the host to go to Ahab and influence him to disregard Micaiah's prophecy and attack Syria so *"that he may fall at Ramoth Gilead"* (v. 20). After a brief discussion, one of the group around the throne volunteered a plan. The volunteer is identified in verse 21 as *"a spirit," rûah* in Hebrew. This is not satan, nor an evil spirit, but an angelic being, perhaps a prophetic spirit who was also responsible for calling the prophets, inspiring them, authenticating their predictions, and distinguishing them from lying prophets.[33] The volunteer's plan was to go to earth and put *"a lying spirit in the mouth of all his prophets"* so Ahab would believe them and go to war (v. 22).

Micaiah declared that the vision had come true just as he had seen it. The spirit had put lies in the mouths of Ahab's advisers. Zedekiah, who must have been a spokesman for the four hundred false prophets, perhaps still wearing his foolish manmade bull horns, rushed forward, incensed, and slapped Micaiah. God's prophet retaliated only in word. *"Indeed, you shall see on that day when you go into an inner chamber to hide!"*—that is, to hide from the victorious Syrian army or from the people in the audience whom he had just misled by his false prophecy.

Micaiah is then returned to the custody of Amon and Joash, where he apparently was being held under some kind of arrest. Amon is identified as the governor of Samaria, but Joash is not known. The name may not be a proper one, but a formal title denoting a high-ranking official.[34] The phrase *"bread of affliction and water of affliction"* may be translated "bread and water of scant measure."[35]

AHAB IS SLAIN IN BATTLE

22:29 So the king of Israel and Jehoshaphat the king
of Judah went up to Ramoth Gilead.
30 And the king of Israel said to Jehoshaphat, "I
will disguise myself and go into battle; but you put
on your robes." So the king of Israel disguised himself and went into battle.
31 Now the king of Syria had commanded the
thirty-two captains of his chariots, saying, "Fight
with no one small or great, but only with the king of
Israel."
32 So it was, when the captains of the chariots saw
Jehoshaphat, that they said, "Surely it *is* the king of
Israel!" Therefore they turned aside to fight against
him, and Jehoshaphat cried out.
33 And it happened, when the captains of the
chariots saw that it *was* not the king of Israel, that
they turned back from pursuing him.
34 Now a *certain* man drew a bow at random, and
struck the king of Israel between the joints of his
armor. So he said to the driver of his chariot, "Turn
around and take me out of the battle, for I am
wounded."
35 The battle increased that day; and the king was
propped up in his chariot, facing the Syrians, and
died at evening. The blood ran out from the wound
onto the floor of the chariot.
36 Then, as the sun was going down, a shout went
throughout the army, saying, "Every man to his city,
and every man to his own country!"
37 So the king died, and was brought to Samaria.
And they buried the king in Samaria.
38 Then *someone* washed the chariot at a pool in
Samaria, and the dogs licked up his blood while the

harlots bathed, according to the word of the LORD
which He had spoken.
39 Now the rest of the acts of Ahab, and all that he
did, the ivory house which he built and all the cities
that he built, *are* they not written in the book of the
chronicles of the kings of Israel?
40 So Ahab rested with his fathers. Then Ahaziah
his son reigned in his place.

1 Kings 22:29–40

Flying in the face of Micaiah's warning, the two kings rallied their two armies for an assault on Ramoth Gilead. Even though he despised Micaiah, Ahab knew better than to totally disregard his words. He decided to take some precautions as the better part of wisdom. So the king devised a plan to disguise himself and go into battle as a common charioteer. While it must have been a plan for self-protection, some believe the plan was a military strategy intended to deceive the Syrians. According to this view, Ahab's military surveillance had given him advance notice of Ben-Hadad's strategy to concentrate his attack on the king's personal position on the battlefield (v. 31). With the king disguised, they would mistakenly attack the wrong position. While being distracted by their mistake, Ahab would surround them in a surprise attack.

The plan might have worked had not an anonymous Syrian archer shot an arrow at random, striking the disguised Ahab in a tiny, vulnerable seam in his armor. Propped up in his chariot, his life's blood flowing from the fatal wound, the king bravely remained throughout the day on the margin of the battlefield with his troops. As the sun was going down, the cry went up that the king was dead. Israel retreated, bearing their slain leader back to Samaria.

As Elijah had predicted, when Ahab's bloody chariot was washed at a pool in Samaria, the dogs were there to lick his blood. The unusual phrase *"while the harlots bathed"* (v. 38) does not suggest a pagan practice of bathing in the blood of slain heroes, as some suggest. Instead it is the writer's method of identifying the particular pool where the incident took place. It was at the pool where harlots were accustomed to bathing.[36] *"The ivory house"* mentioned in verse 39 refers to the palace in Samaria, built by Omri, but upgraded by Ahab with ivory decorations and furnishings.[37] Archaeologists have located the pool mentioned here as well as numerous pieces of ivory carving and inlaid furniture.[38]

CONCLUSION

How can one determine who is right when two prophets, both claiming to speak for God, give conflicting reports? Zedekiah and Micaiah both called themselves prophets of Yahweh. They both defended their messages as authentic. Both claimed they were inspired by the spirit of the Lord (v. 24). When someone says "God told me," is that the last word? How is the ultimate authority of the Supreme God communicated and understood so that it can become a norm or standard of belief and practice? Where is the final court of appeal in religion?

Ecclesiastical tradition has historically answered that the church is the ultimate authority. Human reason is proposed by certain philosophers as the final arbiter. Creeds as authoritative norms have the increasing support of a number of legalists today. Certain mystics and Christian enthusiasts through the years have held the view that final religious authority is found in the Holy Spirit's direct communication in the believer's heart. Rejecting any external or objective authority, they make personal experience the final court of appeal in matters of faith.

Admittedly, the principle of a self-authenticating, inward, divine witness is a vital part of any adequate statement of religious authority. The danger lies, however, in making religious experience the primary, or worse, the only source of authority. To trust the subjective feelings of imperfect humanity, even redeemed humanity, as absolute authority does not take human sin seriously. Many a tragic error in Christian history has been committed because someone said, "God told me to do it," or "This is God's will." Ahab and Jehoshaphat were victims of just such a trust in a false prophet's unauthenticated, subjective authority.

Ideally, religious authority must be both objective and subjective, grounded in the witness both of the Word and the Spirit. John Calvin made a valuable contribution to Christian thought with his emphasis on the relationship between the Scriptures (objective authority) and the inner witness of the Holy Spirit (subjective authority). He taught that the Holy Spirit's inward voice is always consistent with the objective word of revelation, and conversely, that the authority of the word is affirmed through the Holy Spirit's witness in the heart of the believer.

This balanced view avoids the weaknesses of the mechanical, legalistic approach to authority, while at the same time it rejects the unsound conclusions of extreme individualism. There is a mutual check and balance: the Scriptures serving as a corrective to unbridled experience, while spiritual experience gives meaning and vitality to the Scriptures lest they become a wooden, legalistic rule book.

Ahab should have verified his prophet's subjective claim of spiritual authenticity by referring to the objective record of Scripture. He had very little of God's revealed word available to him in that day, but the little he had would have helped him "test the spirits" and avoid being misled by false prophets who claimed God had spoken to them.

NOTES

1. Simon J. DeVries, *1 Kings,* Word Biblical Commentary, ed. John D. W. Watts, vol. 12 (Waco, TX: Word Books, 1985), 235.
2. C. F. Keil, *The Books of the Kings,* Biblical Commentary of the Old Testament, ed. C. F. Keil and F. Delitzsch, vol. 4 (Grand Rapids: Eerdmans, 1950), 252.
3. I. W. Slotki, *Kings* (London: Soncino Press, 1950), 136.
4. Charles F. Burney, *Notes on the Hebrew Text of the Books of Kings* (Oxford: Clarendon Press, 1903), 228.
5. John Gray, *I and II Kings,* Old Testament Library (Philadelphia: Westminster, 1963), 361.
6. Ibid.
7. Keil, 256.
8. Alexander Maclaren, *Second Samuel and the Books of Kings,* Expositions of Holy Scripture, vol. 2 (Grand Rapids: Eerdmans, 1952), 261.
9. DeVries, 235.
10. Robert C. Dentan, *Kings and Chronicles,* Layman's Bible Commentary, vol. 7 (Richmond: John Knox Press, 1964), 63.
11. Norman H. Snaith, Ralph W. Sockman, and Raymond Calkins, "The

First and Second Books of Kings," in *The Interpreter's Bible,* vol. 3 (Nashville: Abingdon, 1954), 160.

12. J. Rawson Lumby, *I and II Kings,* The Cambridge Bible, ed. J. J. S. Perowne (Cambridge: Cambridge University Press, 1889), 203.

13. Gwilym H. Jones, *1 and 2 Kings,* New Century Bible Commentary, ed. Ronald E. Clements (Grand Rapids: Eerdmans, 1984), 334.

14. Ibid., 336.

15. Slotki, 141.

16. Keil, 263.

17. Jones, 336.

18. Ibid., 338.

19. Slotki, 142.

20. Gray, 368.

21. Lumby, 217.

22. Slotki, 150.

23. Jones, 355.

24. Gray, 245.

25. Ibid.

26. Burney, 278.

27. Maclaren, 278.

28. Slotki, 153.

29. Gray, 392.

30. Slotki, 156.

31. Keil, 274.

32. Gray, 398.

33. M. Pierce Matheney and Roy Honeycutt, "1–2 Kings," in *The Broadman Bible Commentary,* ed. Clifton J. Allen, vol. 3 (Nashville: Broadman, 1970), 221.

34. Jones, 369.

35. Burney, 252.

36. Ibid., 256.

37. Gray, 406.

38. Matheney and Honeycutt, 224.

CHAPTER TEN

The Reigns of Jehoshaphat of Judah and Ahaziah of Israel and the Conclusion of Elijah's Ministry

1 Kings 22:41–2 Kings 2:14

JEHOSHAPHAT'S REIGN SUMMARIZED

22:41 Jehoshaphat the son of Asa had become king over Judah in the fourth year of Ahab king of Israel.

42 Jehoshaphat *was* thirty-five years old when he became king, and he reigned twenty-five years in Jerusalem. His mother's name *was* Azubah the daughter of Shilhi.

43 And he walked in all the ways of his father Asa. He did not turn aside from them, doing *what was* right in the eyes of the LORD. Nevertheless the high places were not taken away, *for* the people offered sacrifices and burned incense on the high places.

44 Also Jehoshaphat made peace with the king of Israel.

45 Now the rest of the acts of Jehoshaphat, the might that he showed, and how he made war, *are* they not written in the book of the chronicles of the kings of Judah?

46 And the rest of the perverted persons, who remained in the days of his father Asa, he banished from the land.

47 *There was* then no king in Edom, only a deputy of the king.

48 Jehoshaphat made merchant ships to go to Ophir for gold; but they never sailed, for the ships were wrecked at Ezion Geber.

49 Then Ahaziah the son of Ahab said to Jehoshaphat, "Let my servants go with your servants in the ships." But Jehoshaphat would not.
50 And Jehoshaphat rested with his fathers, and was buried with his fathers in the City of David his father. Then Jehoram his son reigned in his place.

1 Kings 22:41–50

Having concluded his long narrative of Israel's king Ahab, including the stories of the prophet Elijah, the writer in typical fashion now switches his story back to Judah, picking up where he left off in 1 Kings 15:24 with Asa's death. While waiting to come back to Judah, he has told of Israel's suffering through the turbulent reigns of seven kings and one pretender: Jeroboam, Nadab, Baasha, Elah, Zimri, Omri (and Tibni), and Ahab. Now Ahab is dead, and the writer returns to Judah's history. Asa's forty years on the throne in Jerusalem came to an end with his death from natural causes, and his son Jehoshaphat was crowned in his place (v. 41).

The writer of Kings is consistent in following his pattern of switching back and forth between the two kingdoms, but occasionally the pattern has to be broken and the two separate national accounts merged for a short time. An example of such an exception is seen here. Because of his involvement in Ahab's war against the Syrians, Jehoshaphat had to be introduced ahead of time in 1 Kings 22:2. However, the writer, following his outline, still wanted to complete the story of Ahab before beginning the account of another southern king. So he withheld the usual introductory information about Jehoshaphat until he reached the proper position in the sequence.

Several interesting features appear in Jehoshaphat's introduction in verses 41–42. This is the first time a king's age has been noted at the beginning of his reign. From now on this is the usual pattern in the stories of the kings of Judah. Another feature commonly associated with the accounts of Judah's kings is the mention of the mother's name. Because of the widespread practice of polygamy, readers would want to know which of Asa's wives was the mother of the new king, Jehoshaphat. Identifying *"Azubah the daughter of Shilhi"* as the mother was also a way of indicating which of the royal wives held the important post of queen mother, the first lady of the state.[1] The name "Azubah" is not known apart from this verse. Its meaning is also unclear. Its probable connotation is "abandoned," or "divorced." But the name might have come from Arabic roots meaning "sweet" or Ugaritic roots meaning "prepared."[2]

A third unusual feature of the story of Jehoshaphat is its brevity. Even though he was an important historical figure and continued the long and stable dynasty of his father Asa by reigning for twenty-five years, Jehoshaphat is given only ten verses for his story. By way of contrast, notice the much longer section given to King Jehoshaphat in 2 Chronicles 17–20. No doubt a technical historian would have spent a great deal more time on the crucial reign of Jehoshaphat. This is one of several places where it seems evident that the author is more interested in telling about the kings of Israel than the kings of Judah. With special glee he catalogues the sins of Israel's rulers in embarrassing detail, while only hitting the high spots of the transgressions of the southern monarchs.

Even though Asa's moral reforms were impressive, they were not absolute. Asa had not destroyed all the "high places" (1 Kings 15:14). Now Jehoshaphat was also guilty of this same shortcoming (v. 43). From earliest times, cultures have tended to locate their worship centers on high elevations. It seems to be inherent in human nature to identify deity with hills and mountains. Because the Canaanites had practiced their pagan rituals (including human sacrifices) on the mountain tops of Palestine, God had ordered the children of Israel to destroy these abominable shrines on the high places:

> You shall drive out all the inhabitants of the land from before you, destroy all their engraved stones, destroy their molded images, and demolish all their high places.
>
> (Num. 33:52)

Obviously, they did not follow that command completely, because throughout the period of the judges there were instances in which the Israelites were still worshiping Baal and Asherah on the high places (Judg. 2:11–13; 6:25).

Later, after most of these pagan shrines had been destroyed, the people of Israel built altars on top of the ruins of the pagan high places, where they then began to worship Yahweh. While not approving such a practice, God apparently permitted it temporarily

(1 Kings 3:2). For example, before Solomon built the temple, the tabernacle or "tent of meeting" was located on the high place at Gibeon. It was there that Solomon went to offer sacrifices to Yahweh, who heard his prayer at that altar and granted him miraculous wisdom (1 Kings 3:4–15).

Even though they were worshiping Him and not idols, and even though He had overlooked the practice on occasion, God was not pleased when His people chose the pagan high places for their altars. In later years, each king was judged on the basis of how thoroughly he had ruled out this practice. Therefore, while it may not have been his worst failure, Jehoshaphat's report card is marked down because he, like his father, allowed the people to worship Yahweh on the *"high places"* (v. 43).

Jehoshaphat is also condemned because he *"made peace with the king of Israel"* (v. 44). This could refer in a general way to his peaceful relations with all the kings in Israel during his reign: Ahab, Ahaziah, and Jehoram. But the writer probably had in mind the specific alliance Jehoshaphat made with Ahab of Israel during his war with Syria (1 Kings 22:2). This was the first such alliance between Israel and Judah since the divided kingdom in the days of Rehoboam.[3] God's displeasure with this alliance is mentioned in 2 Chron. 18:1 where the marriage of Jehoshaphat's son to the daughter of Ahab and Jezebel is identified as the main complaint.

Are there times when peace is not necessarily what God desires of us in a particular situation? "Blessed are the peacemakers" and "let us pursue the things that make for peace" must surely be normative ideals for those who seek to carry out the will of God. But are there some occasions when making peace is wrong, contrary to the divine will? That appears to be the case here when the author condemns Jehoshaphat because he *"made peace with the king of Israel"* (v. 44).

Jesus may have been pointing to such a possibility when He said, "Do not think that I came to bring peace on earth. I did not come to bring peace but a sword" (Matt. 10:34). There were other occasions when in righteous indignation He fiercely confronted evil situations with anything but peaceful intentions (Matt. 12:34; 21:12–19; 23:13–33). Furthermore, the Old Testament prophets, who usually held up the principle of peace as an ideal, did not plead for peace at any cost. They called for peace with justice and righteousness. These and other scriptures seem to teach that there are times when evil should be confronted bravely; when going along just to preserve peace is a sinful option.

In the 1930s, churches in Germany were faced with just such a situation. Would they support the semipagan, nationalistic Nazi regime? The Nazis applied social, political, and economic pressure. Some church members succumbed to the pressure and either went along with the new political movement or, for the sake of peace, simply refused to protest. Other Christians took a strong stand against the Nazis. One such protest came from a former submarine commander in the German navy who had become a prominent Protestant pastor. Martin Niemöller made a costly choice. He decided it was wrong to make peace with the Nazi movement. So one Sunday he preached on the subject "God Alone Is My *Führer* [Leader]." The storm troopers were present in his church that Sunday to take Niemöller to prison.

Sometimes, in church or denominational controversies, there is a tendency on the part of peace-loving Christians to avoid confrontation, debate, or struggles for control. They are tempted to remain silent, or to "rise above the strife." But when grave issues of truth are at stake, is it not wrong to "go along" or ignore the issues just for the sake of peace? Is it not better to take a costly stand for truth and justice in the spirit of love, even when such action tends to prolong the strife and postpone peace? This seems to be the biblical choice. God's condemnation of Jehoshaphat for making peace with Israel may be explained on this basis. Instead of making peace with the Northern Kingdom, Jehoshaphat should have confronted Ahab and Jezebel and rebuked their evil ways.

With the exception of his lax attitude toward the high places and his peace treaty with Ahab, Jehoshaphat is given good marks by the writer. *"He walked in all the ways of his father Asa,"* who also ranked high in the writer's judgment, and he did *"what was right in the eyes of the Lord"* (v. 43). Jehoshaphat banished the sacred prostitutes who remained after his father's incomplete campaign against them (v. 46). Furthermore, he is commended for his military efforts (v. 45), his continued subjection of Edom (v. 47), and his ill-fated attempt to reestablish Judah's trade routes to Ophir (vv. 48–49).

In verse 47, the nation of Edom is mentioned for the first time since 1 Kings 11:14–17. Since David's conquest of their territory years earlier, the Edomites had been denied the right to have a regular king.

Jehoshaphat apparently reestablished this policy, ruling Edom through his appointed deputy.[4] Later, during the reign of Jehoram, the Edomites revolted against Judah and appointed their own king.

Here is another example of the writer's unique approach to recording history. He does not mention what must have been a significant military operation on the part of Jehoshaphat in securing Edom's subjection. A secular historian would certainly have given information about such an important event. But the author of 1 Kings has another purpose, and he unapologetically omits events such as this one which he does not consider germane to it. So here he skips the important details of Edom's subjection and lumps this event together with other miscellaneous accomplishments under the category *"the rest of the acts of Jehoshaphat"* (v. 45).

Because Edom was under his subjection and no longer posed a threat to Judah, Jehoshaphat could renew the shipping trade to the south that Solomon had established years earlier. So he built a fleet of merchant ships for this purpose. (Jones suggests that he may have simply renovated the fleet Solomon had built.[5]) The word translated *"merchant ships"* in verse 48 is literally "Tarshish ships," a term given to the large oceangoing vessels that sailed to the mines of the far west.[6] According to 2 Chron. 20:36, Jehoshaphat built his ships at the port of Ezion Geber, so they apparently never left the harbor where they were launched. How the ships were wrecked is not described, but in 2 Chron. 20:35–37 we are told that the shipping accident was a punishment from God because He was displeased with Jehoshaphat's alliance with Ahaziah, Ahab's son. Later, Ahaziah tried to establish another coalition with Jehoshaphat, offering him assistance in the form of better ships and experienced sailors. Because of Israel's ties to Phoenicia, Ahaziah was in a position to provide these advantages to Jehoshaphat. But his setback at Ezion Geber had taught Jehoshaphat a lesson. Having been properly rebuked by the prophet Eliezer (2 Chron. 20:35–37), he refused to cooperate with Israel this time.[7]

Like his father Asa, Jehoshaphat died of natural causes and was buried in Jerusalem following a long and, for the most part, godly reign. After the usual concluding formula, the writer mentions that Jehoshaphat's son Jehoram took his place on the throne of Judah (v. 50). However, he does not continue with the account of the new king here. He must now switch back to Israel and catch up with what has happened in the Northern Kingdom during Jehoshaphat's rule in Judah.

Ahaziah's Reign Summarized

> 22:51 Ahaziah the son of Ahab became king over Israel in Samaria in the seventeenth year of Jehoshaphat king of Judah, and reigned two years over Israel.
> 52 He did evil in the sight of the LORD, and walked in the way of his father and in the way of his mother and in the way of Jeroboam the son of Nebat, who had made Israel sin;
> 53 for he served Baal and worshiped him, and provoked the LORD God of Israel to anger, according to all that his father had done.
>
> *1 Kings 22:51–53*

In 1 Kings 16:29, the writer began his story of Ahab, king of Israel, with a brief opening statement. Then he abruptly inserted a long section dealing with the life of Elijah before concluding the history of Ahab in chapter 22. Now in telling the story of Ahab's son Ahaziah, the writer follows the same pattern. He introduces Ahaziah briefly in the last three verses of 1 Kings and then turns aside to describe an incident in the life of Elijah before returning to conclude Ahaziah's story in 2 Kings 1:17–18.

In a departure from his usual style, the writer mentions Ahaziah's mother (Jezebel) when he lists the influences that predisposed the new king toward evil (v. 52). As a rule, only the mothers of Judah's kings are mentioned. A credible explanation is that Jezebel's wickedness was so legendary that it could hardly be omitted as a factor in the character of her son. Few historical figures have grown up in a more unpromising family environment than the son of Ahab and Jezebel.

Here, at what most scholars believe is an awkward place, the book of 1 Kings ends, and the rest of the story of Ahaziah is arbitrarily pushed forward into 2 Kings. In the introductory material at the beginning of the commentary, it was pointed out that 1 and 2 Kings were originally a single unit in the Hebrew Bible. The book was not divided into 1 and 2 Kings until the fifteenth century under the influence of the Greek and Latin versions. The division was made at 1 Kings 22:53, probably in order to fit the book equally on two scrolls.[8] A division at 1 Kings 22:50 or at 2 Kings 1:18 would have avoided the awkwardness of splitting Ahaziah's reign.

AHAZIAH'S REIGN JUDGED BY ELIJAH

1:1 Moab rebelled against Israel after the death of
Ahab.
2 Now Ahaziah fell through the lattice of his upper room in Samaria, and was injured; so he sent messengers and said to them, "Go, inquire of Baal-Zebub,
the god of Ekron, whether I shall recover from this
injury."
3 But the angel of the LORD said to Elijah the
Tishbite, "Arise, go up to meet the messengers of
the king of Samaria, and say to them, '*Is it* because
there is no God in Israel *that* you are going to inquire
of Baal-Zebub, the god of Ekron?'
4 "Now therefore, thus says the LORD: 'You shall
not come down from the bed to which you have gone
up, but you shall surely die.'" So Elijah departed.
5 And when the messengers returned to him, he
said to them, "Why have you come back?"
6 So they said to him, "A man came up to meet
us, and said to us, 'Go, return to the king who sent
you, and say to him, "Thus says the LORD: '*Is it* because *there is* no God in Israel *that* you are sending to
inquire of Baal-Zebub, the god of Ekron? Therefore
you shall not come down from the bed to which you
have gone up, but you shall surely die.'"'"
7 Then he said to them, "What kind of man *was it*
who came up to meet you and told you these words?"
8 So they answered him, "A hairy man wearing a
leather belt around his waist." And he said, "It *is* Elijah
the Tishbite."
9 Then the king sent to him a captain of fifty
with his fifty men. So he went up to him; and there
he was, sitting on the top of a hill. And he spoke to
him: "Man of God, the king has said, 'Come down!'"
10 So Elijah answered and said to the captain of

fifty, "If I *am* a man of God, then let fire come down
from heaven and consume you and your fifty men."
And fire came down from heaven and consumed him
and his fifty.
11 Then he sent to him another captain of fifty with
his fifty men. And he answered and said to him: "Man
of God, thus has the king said, 'Come down quickly!'"
12 So Elijah answered and said to them, "If I *am* a
man of God, let fire come down from heaven and
consume you and your fifty men." And the fire of
God came down from heaven and consumed him and
his fifty.
13 Again, he sent a third captain of fifty with his
fifty men. And the third captain of fifty went up,
and came and fell on his knees before Elijah, and
pleaded with him, and said to him: "Man of God,
please let my life and the life of these fifty servants
of yours be precious in your sight.
14 "Look, fire has come down from heaven and
burned up the first two captains of fifties with their
fifties. But let my life now be precious in your sight."
15 And the angel of the LORD said to Elijah, "Go
down with him; do not be afraid of him." So he arose
and went down with him to the king.
16 Then he said to him, "Thus says the LORD: 'Because you have sent messengers to inquire of Baal-
Zebub, the god of Ekron, *is it* because *there is* no God
in Israel to inquire of His word? Therefore you shall
not come down from the bed to which you have gone
up, but you shall surely die.'"
17 So *Ahaziah* died according to the word of the
LORD which Elijah had spoken. Because he had no
son, Jehoram became king in his place, in the second
year of Jehoram the son of Jehoshaphat, king of Judah.
18 Now the rest of the acts of Ahaziah which he
did, *are* they not written in the book of the chronicles
of the kings of Israel?

2 Kings 1:1–18

The Moabites were the descendants of Lot's grandson Moab (Gen. 19:30–38). Their land was immediately east of the Dead Sea and shared an indefinite border with Israel to the north at approximately the point where the Jordan River enters the Dead Sea. Moab was a powerful enemy of Israel until the time of the judges, when, under the leadership of Ehud, it was subdued (Judg. 3:30). It continued under Israel's subjection until Ahab was defeated at Ramoth Gilead. At that time, taking advantage of Israel's temporary weakness, Moab rebelled. This rebellion, led by Moab's king Mesha, is described in 2 Kings 3. Here in chapter 1 the event is mentioned only briefly in order to place it chronologically within the reign of Ahaziah.

Ahaziah died of injuries received in an accidental fall. The lattice through which he fell may have been a wooden railing around the flat roof of his house in Samaria. Or, more likely, since the royal palace in Samaria was a very substantial dwelling, the lattice was a wooden screen shielding the window of an upper-story room. Outside the window, there was probably a balcony closed in by a screen that let in air but excluded light and public gaze.[9] The king apparently leaned against the wooden screen and fell through from the second-floor balcony to the ground below.

The word "messenger" in verse 2 is *mal'āk* and is the same word used for "angel" in verse 3.[10] Ahaziah *"sent messengers"* to a pagan shrine in Ekron, a city in Philistia fifteen miles south of Joppa. There they were to *"inquire of Baal-Zebub,"* a localized version of the great Baal of Syria, whether his injuries were fatal. Why did Ahaziah select this particular shrine? Maybe he had heard popular rumors of a miraculous cure at Ekron that gave that particular altar a reputation for success.

Baal-Zebub is an interesting name. *Zĕbūb* means "a fly," so the name literally is "lord of the flies." This could suggest that Baal-Zebub was a god who warded off plagues that were brought on by flies. There are numerous references to "fly gods" in classical literature. For example, Herakles was also known as Zeus Apomuios, indicating his power over plagues.[11]

Other commentators offer an interesting alternative explanation. They believe that the original spelling of the name was Baal-Zebul or Beelzebul (Matt. 10:25), which means "lord of earth." Later, they believe, orthodox Hebrews intentionally changed the spelling to Baal-Zebub, "lord of the flies," in order to make this god appear as ridiculous as the pesky insects.[12]

Previously, God had spoken to Elijah directly, but on this occasion He spoke through an angel (v. 3). Elijah, following the instructions of the angel, intercepted the messengers and sent them back to Samaria with a prophecy of Ahaziah's impending death. Then, in typical fashion, Elijah abruptly disappeared. Ahaziah was surprised that the messengers had returned so quickly from what should have been a long journey (v. 5) and demanded an explanation. They reported that an unexpected encounter with the prophet, whom they identified only as *"a man,"* had cut short their trip to Ekron.

Apparently the royal messengers had not recognized Elijah. If that was the case, if they regarded him as a total stranger, what an overwhelming impression Elijah must have made on them. This official delegation from the king would certainly not have turned back from their royal assignment just because some anonymous wayfarer asked them to. There must have been an irresistible quality to Elijah's personality, a forceful spiritual presence, that compelled them to obey this stranger even though they didn't know who he was.

In response to the king's inquiry, they described the man who had sent the message, and His Royal Highness knew immediately that it must have been Elijah. How did he know? Growing up as a child in the household of Ahab and Jezebel, Ahaziah must have heard his distressed parents speak often of their dreaded nemesis Elijah. It may be that Ahaziah, as a youth, had actually seen the rugged prophet at the palace in Samaria.

But it is more likely that the king identified the stranger as Elijah because of his appearance. He was *"a hairy man wearing a leather belt around his waist"* (v. 8). The Hebrew words translated "hairy man" are *baʿal sēʿār,* literally "an owner of hair." This description more than likely refers to the hairy animal skins he wore cinched around his waist with a leather belt, or it could indicate that Elijah himself had long hair. Elijah apparently had adopted this unique clothing style as a mark of his prophetic calling. When Ahaziah heard the description given by his messengers, he responded unhesitatingly, *"It is Elijah the Tishbite"* (v. 8).

Centuries later, John the Baptist lived as a Nazirite in the desert, eating locusts and wild honey. As he called the people to repentance in preparation for the coming Messiah, he exhibited the same rugged characteristics as Elijah. He even wore camel's-hair robes and a leather belt (Matt. 3:4). Since the scribes believed that Elijah would return to prepare the way for the Messiah, it is no surprise that the priests and Levites, seeing John's hairy garments, asked him, "What then? Are you Elijah?" (John 1:21). Jesus acknowledged that John did indeed fulfill symbolically the expectation that Elijah would precede the Messiah. He said of John:

> "But I say to you that Elijah has come already, and they did not know him but did to him whatever they wished. Likewise the Son of Man is also about to suffer at their hands."
>
> (Matt. 17:12)

Why Ahaziah sent the soldiers to the spot where the messengers had last seen Elijah is not indicated, but the large detachment of armed soldiers is evidence that he intended to use force to bring the prophet back to the palace, dead or alive. Having found him on a hilltop not far from Samaria, the king's captain confidently commanded Elijah, *"Man of God, the king has said, 'Come down!'"* The man of God didn't, but the fire of God did! And the fifty-one soldiers were consumed (v. 10).

Half a hundred armed men is a powerful force to send against one prophet. But military might shrivels before the power of God. Elijah's response to the cold command of the captain in verse 10 is given in such a way as to emphasize the word *"if,"* as though to say, "You glibly call me a man of God while overlooking the power of God to withstand the king's command. *If* I am a man of God, then . . . "[13]

The same scene was repeated twice more at verse 11 and verse 13. The reader can notice a rising crescendo in the three repeated occurrences by comparing the orders of each captain. The first captain said curtly, *"Come down!"* (v. 9). The second captain said even more urgently, *"Come down quickly!"* (v. 11). But the third captain, perhaps casting an anxious glance at the two blackened spots of scorched earth nearby, fell on his knees and pleaded: *"Please let my life and the life of these fifty servants of yours be precious in your sight. Look, fire has come down from heaven and burned up the first two captains of fifties with their fifties. But let my life now be precious in your sight"* (vv. 13–14).

In Luke 9:54–56, when Samaritan villagers refused to receive Jesus, James and John suggested that He repeat Elijah's miracle and call down fire on them. But Jesus refused, saying, "You do not know what manner of spirit you are of. For the Son of Man did not come to destroy men's lives but to save them." Jesus did not condemn Elijah; He simply indicated that destruction was not His plan.

Elijah followed the captain back to Samaria and delivered his message in person to Ahaziah. Soon afterwards, the king died *"according to the word of the Lord"* (v. 17). Since he had no son, his brother Jehoram became king in his place (v. 18). Jehoram is not identified here as Ahaziah's brother, but in 2 Kings 3:1 he is called "the son of Ahab." Ahaziah's unspectacular reign lasted only two years. It was not only an evil reign but a weak one as well. Once the powerful hand of Ahab was removed, his inept son let the kingdom fall apart. Everything he did was weak, faithless, and miserable; he achieved nothing but ruin and failure. He let Moab rebel. He hurt himself in a clumsy accident. He foolishly attempted to use military force against Elijah. And worse, he sought help in the wrong place—in Philistia at the altar of a pagan god.

Ruskin said that a nation's history is written not by its wars but by its homes. We see a clear illustration of that truth here. Ahaziah, cursed with evil parents, was raised in a house of cruelty and paganism. We expect him to do evil and fail. It is the exception to the rule when, later, a king like Josiah breaks the pattern and follows a noble path of righteousness in spite of evil parents.

One reason so many in contemporary society are miserable is that they have repeated Ahaziah's worst mistake: seeking help in the wrong place. They are searching for strength, fulfillment, and comfort in the wrong places. Some look for help in chemical reinforcement, mistakenly assuming that a prescription, a pill, a bottle, or an injection can provide life's missing ingredient. The worldwide epidemic of heroin and cocaine addiction has shocked us. Alcoholism continues to take its toll in traffic deaths and broken homes. These are painful reminders that the remedy for personal emptiness is not a chemical substance.

A popular black preacher in America warns his congregation from time to time: "Some of you think you can drown your troubles in drink. But I want to remind you, 'Troubles can swim!'" Those who seek help in drugs are, like Ahaziah, looking in the wrong place.

Paul pointed to the only source that can fill man's emptiness. He said that God is the "God of *all* comfort" (2 Cor. 1:3; italics added). Genuine comfort comes only through faith in God. It cannot be found anywhere else. Ahaziah failed to understand this basic truth.

ELIJAH'S MINISTRY ENDED

2:1 And it came to pass, when the LORD was about to take up Elijah into heaven by a whirlwind, that Elijah went with Elisha from Gilgal.

2 Then Elijah said to Elisha, "Stay here, please, for the LORD has sent me on to Bethel." But Elisha said, "*As* the LORD lives, and *as* your soul lives, I will not leave you!" So they went down to Bethel.

3 Now the sons of the prophets who *were* at Bethel came out to Elisha, and said to him, "Do you know that the LORD will take away your master from over you today?" And he said, "Yes, I know; keep silent!"

4 Then Elijah said to him, "Elisha, stay here, please, for the LORD has sent me on to Jericho." But he said, "*As* the LORD lives, and *as* your soul lives, I will not leave you!" So they came to Jericho.

5 Now the sons of the prophets who *were* at Jericho came to Elisha and said to him, "Do you know that the LORD will take away your master from over you today?" So he answered, "Yes, I know; keep silent!"

6 Then Elijah said to him, "Stay here, please, for the LORD has sent me on to the Jordan." But he said, "*As* the LORD lives, and *as* your soul lives, I will not leave you!" So the two of them went on.

7 And fifty men of the sons of the prophets went and stood facing *them* at a distance, while the two of them stood by the Jordan.

8 Now Elijah took his mantle, rolled *it* up, and struck the water; and it was divided this way and that, so that the two of them crossed over on dry ground.

9 And so it was, when they had crossed over, that Elijah said to Elisha, "Ask! What may I do for you, before I am taken away from you?" Elisha said, "Please let a double portion of your spirit be upon me."

10 So he said, "You have asked a hard thing. *Nevertheless,* if you see me *when I am* taken from you, it shall be so for you; but if not, it shall not be *so.*"

11 Then it happened, as they continued on and talked, that suddenly a chariot of fire *appeared* with horses of fire, and separated the two of them; and Elijah went up by a whirlwind into heaven.

> 12 And Elisha saw *it*, and he cried out, "My father, my father, the chariot of Israel and its horsemen!" So he saw him no more. And he took hold of his own clothes and tore them into two pieces.
>
> 13 He also took up the mantle of Elijah that had fallen from him, and went back and stood by the bank of the Jordan.
>
> 14 Then he took the mantle of Elijah that had fallen from him, and struck the water, and said, "Where *is* the LORD God of Elijah?" And when he also had struck the water, it was divided this way and that; and Elisha crossed over.
>
> *2 Kings 2:1–14*

Rosey Grier is a retired professional football player who gained fame in the 1960s as a member of the Los Angeles Rams' "Fearsome Foursome" defensive line. Since giving up football he has devoted his life to spiritual ministry. The six-five, three-hundred-pound Grier has also written an autobiography appropriately titled *The Gentle Giant.* A modern biography of Elijah could well use the same title. This rugged prophet who marched like a spiritual Goliath through this era in Israel's history also had a gentle nature. Robert Young, in his famous *Analytical Concordance to the Bible,* called Elijah "The grandest and most romantic character that Israel ever produced."[14]

Up to this point in Kings we have seen mostly the grandeur of Elijah—his sudden appearances, abrupt speeches, spectacular miracles, and fiery condemnations. We have seen him as the fearless and forceful personification of God's wrath. But here in 2 Kings 2 the writer shows us the romantic Elijah, the tender side of this "gentle giant."

Elijah was aware that God was about to take him home in a whirlwind. Keeping that final earthly appointment a secret, Elijah headed toward Bethel and Jericho for one last visit with the *"sons of the prophets"* who lived in those cities. Unknown to Elijah, God had also told Elisha and the sons of the prophets that this was the day He would take up Elijah to heaven. Assuming that Elisha and the young prophets were uninformed about what was about to happen, Elijah tried to leave them behind at each stop along the way. *"Stay here, please"* he said to Elisha at Samaria, *"for the Lord has sent me on to Bethel"* (v. 2). But Elisha insisted that he would not leave Elijah alone. *"Stay here, please,"* he said to Elisha and the prophets at Bethel, *"for the Lord has sent me on to Jericho"* (v. 4). But the young prophets and Elisha continued to follow Elijah. *"Stay here, please,"* he pleaded with Elisha and the prophets in Jericho, *"for the Lord has sent me on to the Jordan"* (v. 6). But a third time Elisha and the other prophets refused and accompanied Elijah to the Jordan.

Why did Elijah want them to stay behind? It must have been that little touch of tenderness from the tough old prophet. He wanted to spare Elisha and the young men the pain of seeing him leave. Furthermore, he didn't want his departure to be a self-aggrandizing spectacle. He knew God was going to perform some kind of miracle to bring his earthly life to an end, and he didn't want to "show off" in this final event. So the gentle giant and his faithful friend Elisha, trailed at a distance by their fifty young colleagues, came to the Jordan for the dramatic closing event in Elijah's life.

Rolling up his mantle into a kind of rod, Elijah struck the water, and the Jordan divided itself as it had done for the children of Israel (Josh. 3:17). Then, while the young prophets waited respectfully at the shore, he and Elisha crossed over on dry ground (v. 8). Even at this climactic moment, Elijah thought not of himself but of Elisha who would be left behind. *"What may I do for you, before I am taken away from you?"* Elisha answered without hesitation, *"Please let a double portion of your spirit be upon me"* (v. 9).

Although it has often been interpreted in this way, Elisha was not asking for twice as much of the prophetic spirit as Elijah had possessed. He was not asking to be twice as powerful as his predecessor. Instead, his request relates to the custom in Deut. 21:17 where the firstborn son was entitled to a double share of the father's estate, while the younger sons received only a single share. Elisha wanted to be designated as Elijah's rightful heir, receiving double what the other prophets would get as a signal that he would now be their "lead prophet."[15]

Elijah acknowledged that only God could grant such a request. If Elisha was permitted by God to see Elijah when he was taken away, that would be a sign that God had granted his request to become the successor to Elijah (vv. 10–11). *"Elisha saw it,"* verse 12 tells us, so we assume that Elisha did receive the double portion he had requested.

Elijah's departure was even more spectacular than expected. The prophet knew there would be a whirlwind (v. 1), but the chariot and horses of fire were apparently a surprise. The great prophet, like Enoch, did not die but was translated directly into heaven, leaving behind for Elisha his mantle and a double portion of his spirit. Returning to the Jordan and striking the waters of the river with the mantle again, Elisha made a statement that was not so much a question as a solemn invocation. *"Where is the Lord God of Elijah?"* The implied answer, dramatized by the miraculous opening up of the river, was: "He has not abandoned us; He is now with Elisha as He was with Elijah."

NOTES

1. John Gray, *I and II Kings,* Old Testament Library (Philadelphia: Westminster, 1963), 407.
2. Gwilym H. Jones, *1 and 2 Kings,* New Century Bible Commentary, ed. Ronald E. Clements (Grand Rapids: Eerdmans, 1984), 373.
3. I. W. Slotki, *Kings* (London: Soncino Press, 1950), 163.
4. Gray, 407.
5. Jones, 373.
6. Gray, 407.
7. C. F. Keil, *The Books of the Kings,* Biblical Commentary on the Old Testament, ed. C. F. Keil and F. Delitzsch, vol. 4 (Grand Rapids: Eerdmans, 1950), 281.
8. Brevard S. Childs, *Introduction to the Old Testament as Scripture* (Philadelphia: Fortress Press, 1979), 287.
9. Gray, 412.
10. M. Pierce Matheney and Roy Honeycutt, "1–2 Kings," in *The Broadman Bible Commentary,* ed. Clifton J. Allen, vol. 3 (Nashville: Broadman, 1970), 225.
11. Jones, 375.
12. Norman H. Snaith, Ralph W. Sockman, and Raymond Calkins, "The First and Second Books of Kings," in *The Interpreter's Bible,* vol. 3 (Nashville: Abingdon, 1954), 187.
13. Charles F. Burney, *Notes on the Hebrew Text of the Books of Kings* (Oxford: Clarendon Press, 1903), 261.
14. Robert Young, *Analytical Concordance to the Bible* (New York: Funk and Wagnalls, 1936), 295.
15. Keil, 290.

CHAPTER ELEVEN

The Beginning of Elisha's Ministry and the Reign of Jehoram of Israel

2 Kings 2:15–3:27

ELISHA BEGINS HIS MIRACULOUS MINISTRY

2:15 Now when the sons of the prophets who *were* from Jericho saw him, they said, "The spirit of Elijah rests on Elisha." And they came to meet him, and bowed to the ground before him.

16 Then they said to him, "Look now, there are fifty strong men with your servants. Please let them go and search for your master, lest perhaps the Spirit of the LORD has taken him up and cast him upon some mountain or into some valley." And he said, "You shall not send anyone."

17 But when they urged him till he was ashamed, he said, "Send *them!*" Therefore they sent fifty men, and they searched for three days but did not find him.

18 And when they came back to him, for he had stayed in Jericho, he said to them, "Did I not say to you, 'Do not go'?"

19 Then the men of the city said to Elisha, "Please notice, the situation of this city *is* pleasant, as my lord sees; but the water *is* bad, and the ground barren."

20 And he said, "Bring me a new bowl, and put salt in it." So they brought *it* to him.

21 Then he went out to the source of the water, and cast in the salt there, and said, "Thus says the

LORD: 'I have healed this water; from it there shall be
no more death or barrenness.'"
22 So the water remains healed to this day, according to the word of Elisha which he spoke.
23 Then he went up from there to Bethel; and as
he was going up the road, some youths came from
the city and mocked him, and said to him, "Go up,
you baldhead! Go up, you baldhead!"
24 So he turned around and looked at them, and
pronounced a curse on them in the name of the
LORD. And two female bears came out of the woods
and mauled forty-two of the youths.
25 Then he went from there to Mount Carmel, and
from there he returned to Samaria.

2 Kings 2:15–25

Everyone who has had the experience of following in a position of service a person who was considered "a legend," a giant heroic personality, can sympathize with Elisha. He had to assume the responsibilities of the illustrious Elijah, one of the brightest lights in the constellation of Israel's great heroes. Elijah has been called "God's answer to Baal." His celebrated distinction was unprecedented. One of two men in Scripture who had the privilege of being taken from this life without passing through death, Elijah was also one of two granted the honor of standing on the Mount of Transfiguration with Jesus. It must have been intimidating to try to fill the place of one of the most imposing figures in history.

At an evangelism conference in South Carolina, guest speakers and listeners alike were amused by one country preacher in the audience who was a world class "amener." Every time a speaker paused at a key place in his sermon, this "amener" shouted encouragement and approval. He went beyond the traditional "Amen!" or "Preach on!" or "Praise the Lord!" His responses were creative. "You're about to say something now!" he would shout. Or "You got it right that time!" People in the congregation couldn't wait to hear what his next interjection would be. Then we came to the final, climactic message from the keynote speaker, Dr. John Bisagno, pastor of the giant First Baptist Church in Houston, Texas. Having arrived just before he was to bring the message, Dr. Bisagno was unaware of the "amen champion" on the front row as he began one of his famous sermon introductions.

In addition to being an eloquent preacher, Dr. Bisagno is also a talented impersonator—a kind of Baptist Rich Little—who can mimic famous personalities, especially evangelists and preachers. Since he frequently is the last speaker on a program of big-name preachers, he sometimes employs these impersonations to introduce his message and warm up his audience. He will say, for example:

> I really feel intimidated having to follow all these great preachers on the program. What can I say? Here I am trying to preach after you've listened to some of the best communicators in the country. How can I preach after them? Well, maybe I'll just preach like Billy Graham.

And then he breaks into an impersonation of the great evangelist that is so realistic the audience can't believe it. Next he imitates Dr. W. A. Criswell of the First Baptist Church of Dallas and other well-known evangelical leaders, and by then his audience is laughing and ready to listen to his sermon.

So in the South Carolina Evangelism Conference, with the "amener" poised on the front row ready to punctuate the unwary preacher's message, Dr. Bisagno started his famous introduction.

> I really feel intimidated having to follow all these great preachers on the program. What can I say? Here I am trying to preach after you've listened to some of the best communicators in the country. How can I preach after them?

But before he could get into his impersonations, the country preacher on the front row interrupted the talented Dr. Bisagno by shouting: "Just do the best you can, brother. Just do the best you can." John Bisagno was speechless. He never got around to his imitations. When the laughter in the hall died down, he just announced his text and "did the best he could" with the sermon.

Elisha must have felt like that. How could he hold a candle to Elijah, the physical, spiritual, moral giant of God? He had to do the best he could.

On his way out of the wilderness where he had hidden from Jezebel's wrath, Elijah had stopped by Abel Meholah in the Jordan valley to find a young plowboy named Elisha the son of Shaphat. Elijah had placed his mantle on the young man's shoulders, symbolizing

God's choice of him as Elijah's successor. For several years Elisha followed Elijah as an apprentice (1 Kings 19:16–21). Now the time had come for the transfer of responsibility. As the dust of the miraculous whirlwind settled, and the chariot of fire bearing Elijah disappeared, Elisha picked up not only Elijah's mantle, but also his position as *the* prophet of Yahweh.

In verse 15, the sons of the prophets, having witnessed Elisha's first miracle, the dividing of the Jordan, acknowledged that he was indeed Elijah's successor: *"The spirit of Elijah rests on Elisha."* He was now their teacher, the president of that ancient seminary for prophets. That they still needed a teacher is evident from the account in verse 16. Although they saw the whirlwind, they did not perceive it as the miraculous vehicle for Elijah's translation. It appeared to them that a mighty "dust devil," a natural whirlwind, had picked up Elijah and no doubt had dropped him as a helpless victim on the side of a rugged mountain or a hidden canyon.

Others interpret verse 16 to mean that the sons of the prophets believed that Elijah, in a spiritual trance, had accidentally fallen from a precipice. *"Perhaps the Spirit of the Lord has taken him up and cast him upon some mountain or into some valley."*

Still others hold that these seminarians understood that the soul of Elijah had been taken up into heaven but thought that his body was left somewhere in the wilderness and should be found and properly buried.[1] Whatever the explanation, the sons of the prophets, who were used to seeing Elijah suddenly disappear, volunteered a search party. Contrary to the advice of Elisha, and with his reluctant permission, they began to scour the countryside for their former leader.

When they returned empty-handed, their confidence in Elisha was strengthened. He had told them so. He was right. *"Did I not say to you, 'Do not go'?"* (v. 18).

There follows in our text the account of two more miracles that seem intended to further accredit Elisha in the eyes of the people as a man endowed with the Spirit and power of God as Elijah had been. The first is the miracle of the purification of Jericho's water source.

Most biblical geographers agree that the spring referred to in this passage is the Ain es Sultan, the only spring near ancient Jericho. It begins near the foot of the mound of the old city and still spreads its water over the plain of Jericho. It is popularly known today as "the Spring of Elisha."[2]

Some contamination of the spring not only made it unpalatable, but caused infertility in the soil, the herds, and the population. *"The water is bad,"* the men of the city complained, *"and the ground barren"* (v. 19). A more literal translation would be "and the land casts her young."[3] This seems to suggest that as a result of the contaminated spring water, women miscarried, cattle dropped their young prematurely, and trees shed their fruit before it was ripe.[4] Some scholars believe the water may have come in contact with radioactive geographical strata as it flowed underground to the spring at Jericho, thereby causing the tragic circumstances.[5] Another explanation links the contaminated spring to the curse placed on Jericho many years earlier (Josh. 6:26; 1 Kings 16:34).

Calling for a new bowl filled with salt, Elisha went to the source of the spring and ceremonially poured the salt into the water. The spring was miraculously purified. The purification was not a result of some natural chemical reaction triggered by the salt. Rather, the salt, representing preservation from corruption, was used by Elisha as a symbol of divine cleansing.[6] The writer of 2 Kings added: *"So the water remains healed to this day, according to the word of Elisha which he spoke"* (v. 22).

In July 1987, newspapers reported a serious contamination of the water supply of Mineral Wells, a city in west Texas. Since the city is noted for the quality of its drinking water, the situation was particularly ironic. An underground pipe sprang a leak and hundreds of gallons of gasoline flowed into the municipal water supply before it was noticed. Officials declared an emergency, and citizens were told to turn off the water in their homes. It was unfit for drinking, cooking, or even bathing or watering plants. The people of Mineral Wells were forced to used bottled water for several weeks. First, the gasoline leak had to be located and repaired. Next, the source of their water had to be treated and purified. Finally, the lines had to be flushed, and the people had to drain their own water pipes. Only then was palatable water available again in Mineral Wells.

In Mineral Wells, as in Jericho, the unhappy situation had to be dealt with at the source. It would have done no good to try to treat the water where it was being consumed, or—even worse—to add deodorants to make it smell better or sweeteners to improve the taste. The supply had to be purified.

Reading this account, one can hardly resist the impulse to relate it allegorically to the moral situation in our own cities. Many of the wells of human thought, action, and influence today have become polluted. The public springs of literature, drama, and entertainment have become so poisoned by pornography that they are, like the water at Jericho, foul and unpalatable, creating moral barrenness in the land. But too many are offering superficial solutions to the problem, nothing more than adding sweeteners or perfumes to make the situation appear better. The only answer to such moral pollution is to treat the source. Humanity's sinful condition must be dealt with first.

Elisha purified the springs of Jericho with salt. Jesus said that we who follow Him are to be the salt of the earth. The influence of our lives in the midst of a polluted society is to lead the lost to Jesus, the only Savior. He alone can save sinners, stop the decay, and "heal the springs" of this crooked and perverse generation at the source.

The second miracle, the punishment of the young boys of Bethel who jeered at and humiliated the prophet of Yahweh, indicated that the Lord would not allow His servants to be ridiculed with impunity. The young boys made fun of Elisha's baldness: *"Go up* (perhaps referring to Elijah's translation into heaven), *you baldhead! Go up, you baldhead!"* (v. 23).

It is the suggestion of some commentaries that Elisha's baldness was actually a special tonsured hair style similar to that of some monastic orders. More than likely Elisha was simply prematurely bald. The lack of hair was not a result of old age; since he lived about fifty years after this incident, he was at the time a relatively young man. Elisha's baldness must have been in striking contrast to Elijah's hairy appearance. Could it be that Elisha was ridiculed in part because he was different?

The severe punishment—the boys were attacked by two female bears—for what appears to be nothing more than lighthearted, childish behavior has led some to attempt to soften this incident by various explanations. It has been pointed out, for example, that since the Hebrew word translated "little children" in the King James Version may also be applied to older youths, the revilers of Elisha may have been dangerous teenaged "punks" deserving such punishment. The New King James Version translates the word "youths." It is true that the word *nĕʿārim* does not necessarily refer to little children. For example, the same word is used in 1 Kings 3:7 by Solomon, a young adult, when he assumed the throne: "But I am a little child [*naʿar*]; I do not know how to go out or come in." Most translations, however, use "young boys," "little children," or similar designations.

Another attempt to soften the harshness of the punishment proposes that it was the parents of the young offenders who actually instigated the verbal attack, sending their children to do their dirty work. So the children were punished for their parents' sin as a lesson to the whole town to respect the prophet whom they would not accept despite his miracles. This is Augustine's explanation.[7]

Since the details of the account are sketchy, we should not presume to call the punishment unjust or "pre-moral," nor try to rearrange the passage to make it more acceptable. It is helpful to remember, however, that the attack on Elisha may have been a more serious threat to his safety than that posed by a few mischievous playmates. Since forty-two of the boys were struck by the bears, the group may have been quite large and therefore dangerously out of control. Elisha may have needed miraculous intervention to escape. Also, verse 24 does not say that the victims were killed. The Hebrew word translated "mauled" might indicate less serious injuries. The ultimate outcome of the miracle was to break up the gang, frighten the offenders and the entire village, and punish them not so much for insulting Elisha as for their impiety.[8]

Here, at the beginning of Elisha's ministry, it is obvious that he is not as outstanding a personality as Elijah. With Elisha there are no stupendous, dramatic scenes, no outstanding achievements, no exhibitions of grandeur of soul. Elisha is not an originator. He brings no fresh revelations. As a secondary character, he primarily carries on what Elijah began, without the spectacular dimensions of Elijah's ministry. Elijah battled murderous kings and queens singlehandedly. He stopped an entire nation's headlong rush to destruction. He walked as confidently in the courts of royalty as he did in the lonely wilderness. The same Spirit was upon Elisha, but his gifts were different. The life of Elisha is therefore an encouraging reminder to us that even without huge capacities, even without heroic qualities, an ordinary, average person can do much good in the world. One does not have to be a headline maker to be effective for God.

Here and in other places, history teaches us that when God lays aside one tool He quickly takes up another. He has inexhaustible resources. The work of the Lord goes on even though the workers change. None of God's great heroes is indispensable. He sometimes does His best work with unlikely instruments. That's why Paul said, "But we have this treasure in earthen vessels, that the excellence of the power may be of God and not of us" (2 Cor. 4:7).

Elisha calls to mind the compliment the crowds paid to John the Baptist when they said: "John performed no sign, but all the things that John spoke about this Man were true" (John 10:41). We must remember that when Moses the great lawgiver died, God passed over many a "star" in Israel's ranks and chose Joshua, the servant, the valet of Moses, as the leader. He was not a superior, multitalented headliner, but he was faithful. So was Elisha.

Jehoram Makes an Alliance and Seeks Elisha's Prophecy

3:1 Now Jehoram the son of Ahab became king over Israel at Samaria in the eighteenth year of Jehoshaphat king of Judah, and reigned twelve years.

2 And he did evil in the sight of the LORD, but not like his father and mother; for he put away the *sacred* pillar of Baal that his father had made.

3 Nevertheless he persisted in the sins of Jeroboam the son of Nebat, who had made Israel sin; he did not depart from them.

4 Now Mesha king of Moab was a sheepbreeder, and he regularly paid the king of Israel one hundred thousand lambs and the wool of one hundred thousand rams.

5 But it happened, when Ahab died, that the king of Moab rebelled against the king of Israel.

6 So King Jehoram went out of Samaria at that time and mustered all Israel.

7 Then he went and sent to Jehoshaphat king of Judah, saying, "The king of Moab has rebelled against me. Will you go with me to fight against Moab?" And he said, "I will go up; I *am* as you *are,* my people as your people, my horses as your horses."

8 Then he said, "Which way shall we go up?" And he answered, "By way of the Wilderness of Edom."

9 So the king of Israel went with the king of

Judah and the king of Edom, and they marched on that roundabout route seven days; and there was no water for the army, nor for the animals that followed them.

10 And the king of Israel said, "Alas! For the LORD has called these three kings together to deliver them into the hand of Moab."

11 But Jehoshaphat said, "*Is there* no prophet of the LORD here, that we may inquire of the LORD by him?" So one of the servants of the king of Israel answered and said, "Elisha the son of Shaphat *is* here, who poured water on the hands of Elijah."

12 And Jehoshaphat said, "The word of the LORD is with him." So the king of Israel and Jehoshaphat and the king of Edom went down to him.

13 Then Elisha said to the king of Israel, "What have I to do with you? Go to the prophets of your father and the prophets of your mother." But the king of Israel said to him, "No, for the LORD has called these three kings *together* to deliver them into the hand of Moab."

14 And Elisha said, "*As* the LORD of hosts lives, before whom I stand, surely were it not that I regard the presence of Jehoshaphat king of Judah, I would not look at you, nor see you.

15 "But now bring me a musician." Then it happened, when the musician played, that the hand of the LORD came upon him.

16 And he said, "Thus says the LORD: 'Make this valley full of ditches.'

17 "For thus says the LORD: 'You shall not see wind, nor shall you see rain; yet that valley shall be filled with water, so that you, your cattle, and your animals may drink.'

18 "And this is a simple matter in the sight of the LORD; He will also deliver the Moabites into your hand.

19 "Also you shall attack every fortified city and every choice city, and shall cut down every good tree, and stop up every spring of water, and ruin every good piece of land with stones."

20 Now it happened in the morning, when the

> grain offering was offered, that suddenly water came
> by way of Edom, and the land was filled with water.
>
> *2 Kings 3:1–20*

Going back to pick up the thread of royal descent in Israel after his long section on Elijah and Elisha, the writer now begins the story of King Jehoram of Israel. For twenty-two years wicked Ahab reigned in Israel with his even more wicked queen, Jezebel. When Ahab died in battle, his son Ahaziah became king. After a reign of only two years Ahaziah was killed in a freak fall through a balcony lattice screen in his palace in Samaria (2 Kings 1:2–18). Since he had no sons to rule in his place, the throne reverted to his brother Jehoram (another son of Ahab and Jezebel). The evil Jezebel was still living and no doubt still exerting her pernicious influence, so it is no surprise to read here the writer's condemnation of King Jehoram: *"He did evil in sight of the Lord . . . he persisted in the sins of Jeroboam the son of Nebat, who had made Israel sin; he did not depart from them"* (2 Kings 3:2–3).

The "sins of Jeroboam" that Jehoram perpetuated were not related to the worship of Baal but to the false worship of Yahweh under the calf (or ox) images that Jeroboam set up at Dan and Bethel. This was primarily a political strategy rather than a religious one. It was intended to keep the people of the Northern Kingdom from going to Jerusalem to worship in the temple. Jeroboam was fearful that such religious pilgrimages to Jerusalem would tempt his subjects in the North to shift their political allegiance to the house of David and would thereby encourage rebellion. Successive kings, including Jehoram, continued the practice for the same reason.[9]

However, Jehoram is condemned less severely than his parents, Ahab and Jezebel, and he is given some credit for putting away the *"pillar of Baal that his father had made"* (v. 2). This pillar was some sort of cultic object used in the worship of Baal. This act, while commendable, hardly indicates that the worship of Baal was eradicated from Israel—not with Jezebel's influence still overshadowing the land. Later, Jehu found in Israel a thriving Baalism which he had to destroy (2 Kings 10:10ff.).

Like John Bunyan's Mr. Facing-both-ways, Jehoram represents a man who is neither all bad nor all good. He reminds us of some pragmatic opportunists today who try to play it safe, especially in confronting crucial controversial issues. Afraid of offending those who may end up as the winners in a struggle, they refuse to take sides, to take a stand. They work hard at maintaining a safe neutrality, constantly monitoring which way the winds are blowing, hoping that at the propitious moment they can jump on the winning side.

Such a man, during the War Between the States, had friends on both sides and refused to give allegiance to either the blue or the gray. Instead he opted to wear a uniform with gray pants and a blue jacket. But he ended up getting shot in both parts of his uniform!

People who are not all that bad, but who cannot decide to break entirely with the world, will never be happy. One cannot be at peace when a civil war is going on within the heart. James said that a double-minded man is "unstable in all his ways" and "like a wave of the sea driven and tossed by the wind" (James 1:8, 6).

There was a henpecked husband whose domineering wife made his life miserable. Even when he was drafted during World War II and found himself on the battlefield in Europe, her nagging letters followed him. One day he had taken her abuse as long as he could, and he wrote her a scorching reply: "Leave me alone so I can fight this war in peace!"

But those are contradictory terms: war and peace. A person with a divided heart, a divided allegiance, cannot be at peace. The Lord said, "So then, because you are lukewarm, and neither cold nor hot, I will vomit you out of My mouth" (Rev. 3:16).

In verse 4 we are introduced to Mesha, king of Moab. The kingdom of Moab, just east of the Dead Sea, had long been under the subjection of Israel, paying an annual tribute as described in verse 4. Taking advantage of the temporary military weakness following Israel's defeat at Ramoth Gilead and the nation's distraction over the death of King Ahab, Moab had rebelled and fortified the cities on her northern boundary with Israel. King Ahaziah, with only a short reign, had been unable to do anything to renew the subjection of Moab.

Now Jehoram wanted to regain control of what his brother had neglected. Since Ahaziah's weak reign in Israel had given Moab two years to grow strong, Jehoram knew he would need help. Furthermore, since Moab's military forces were concentrated on her northern border, he needed help from the south. That meant Judah and her vassal neighbor, Edom.

Verse 9 mentions the king of Edom, but we have already been told in 1 Kings 22:47 that there was no king in Edom at this time. So "king" here must refer to a vice-regent appointed by the king of Judah.[10]

There were only two ways to invade Moab: cross the Jordan above the Dead Sea to enter from the north, or go around the southern end of the Dead Sea and advance through the mountains of Edom to enter from the south. The latter way was longer and more difficult and dangerous, but the allied kings decided on this strategy. Taking the southern route, they would not have to worry about the Syrians in the north, and, because the Moabites would not expect them from this more difficult direction, they might be caught off guard. The southern assault through Edom would also force the Edomites to go with them. Otherwise they might be tempted to join Moab in rebelling against Israel and Judah.

Verse 9 calls the approach a *"roundabout route."* The King James Version translates more literally "they fetched a compass." This means they traveled in a circular fashion eventually following each of the points of the compass in turn.[11] The detour then was through Edom, in a complete circle around the southern border of Moab in a giant fishhook pattern to attack from the east. (This explains how the Moabite defenders looked eastward to spot the invading allied troops in verse 22.)

The long journey exhausted the water supply of the three armies, and the oases where they had expected to find water were dry. It was such a serious crisis that they despaired, sounding like the disgruntled children of Israel during the Exodus, *"Alas! For the Lord has called these three kings together to deliver them into the hand of Moab"* (v. 10).

How Elisha happened to be in the area of the Edomite wilderness is not explained. Perhaps the Spirit of the Lord had led him there anticipating this opportunity to demonstrate the power of Yahweh.[12] He is identified here as the one *"who poured water on the hands of Elijah"* (v. 11). This picturesque phrase was used to identify a servant who held the jar of water while his master washed his hands.[13] It means that Elisha was known as the servant of the great prophet Elijah, and therefore, *"the word of the Lord is with him"* (v. 12).

Echoing Elijah's sarcastic taunts on Mount Carmel, Elisha said to the wicked king of Israel, *"Go to the prophets of your father and the prophets of your mother"* (v. 13). He was of course referring to Ahab and Jezebel and the prophets of Baal, whom Elijah's contest of fire had exposed as pitifully impotent. Nevertheless Elisha agreed to help.

Why did Elisha call for a musician before giving his prophetic word (v. 15)? It is not made clear, but it may be that the purpose of music was to help Elisha collect his thoughts, turning his mind away from the distractions of the outer world and subduing selfish concerns so he could become absorbed in the intuition of divine things.[14] The soothing sounds of the instrument would make him more receptive to spiritual inspiration. Remember the effect music had on the troubled mind of King Saul? It soothed his spirit (1 Sam. 16:16). Verse 15 says, *"it happened, when the musician played, that the hand of the Lord came upon him [Elisha]."* In the Old Testament, the hand is the symbol of power, so this verse means that the power of God came upon Elisha.[15]

This nameless musician was endowed with God-given talents and he used them for the good of others. Surely it never occurred to him that by his music he would help win a military victory and have a dramatic effect on history. But when he shared his God-given ability, the power of God came upon the prophet. How important music is to the kingdom of God. It not only provides believers with a medium for expressing worship; it not only communicates the gospel; it also warms the heart to God's presence, opens the life to God's will, and establishes an atmosphere in which the word of God may be more clearly discerned. To be such a spiritual minstrel is to be able to lift a burdensome cloud from someone's soul, to let light into a dark and troubled heart. Thank God He still has His gifted musicians ready to serve Him in times of great need.

The miracle involved the appearance of water without the sound of wind or the presence of rain. Perhaps God brought a great thunderstorm high in the mountains out of sight of the thirsty troops and sent the water gushing into the dry valley at exactly the right time.

Traveling in dry west Texas, one crosses numerous dry arroyos where the warning signs are posted, "Be Careful of Unexpected Water." One can be driving in bright sunshine with no cloud in the sky and suddenly come upon an arroyo filled with water. Like a flash flood it has rushed across the desert from a distant storm which may already have dissipated. Within a few minutes the water is gone, but for the moment it is a miracle of God's providence in a dry land. (As well as a threat to the unsuspecting driver!)

The army was to exhibit faith in the prophecy by digging trenches in the dry sand to catch the water. Sure enough, in the morning, *"suddenly water came by way of Edom, and the land was filled with water"* (v. 20). It may not have been as spectacular as Elijah's calling down fire from heaven on the water-soaked altar, but the message was clear: Yahweh reigns, and Elisha is His prophet.

Jehoram Quells the Moabite Rebellion

3:21 And when all the Moabites heard that the kings had come up to fight against them, all who were able to bear arms and older were gathered; and they stood at the border.

22 Then they rose up early in the morning, and the sun was shining on the water; and the Moabites saw the water on the other side *as* red as blood.

23 And they said, "This is blood; the kings have surely struck swords and have killed one another; now therefore, Moab, to the spoil!"

24 So when they came to the camp of Israel, Israel rose up and attacked the Moabites, so that they fled before them; and they entered *their* land, killing the Moabites.

25 Then they destroyed the cities, and each man threw a stone on every good piece of land and filled it; and they stopped up all the springs of water and cut down all the good trees. But they left the stones of Kir Haraseth *intact.* However the slingers surrounded and attacked it.

26 And when the king of Moab saw that the battle was too fierce for him, he took with him seven hundred men who drew swords, to break through to the king of Edom, but they could not.

27 Then he took his eldest son who would have reigned in his place, and offered him *as* a burnt offering upon the wall; and there was great indignation against Israel. So they departed from him and returned to *their own* land.

2 Kings 3:21–27

How could the Moabite defenders have been so easily deceived? An explanation is given in verses 22 and 23. As the Moabites looked eastward in the early morning dawn, the reflection in the pools of water gathering on the dry plain glowed bright red. The Moabites, who never saw standing water in that area, could only assume that what they saw was blood—the result of a fierce battle.

No doubt another factor that reinforced their faulty conclusions was the wild disarray of the enemy troops and their animals. Imagine the disorganized bedlam of parched soldiers, horses, and cattle suddenly inundated with a deluge of fresh water, running in every direction quenching their thirst, filling up empty animal skins and canteens, probably even splashing in the pools in happy abandon. From a distance, the Moabite leaders assumed that what they were witnessing was a vicious battle between the three kings and their troops. After all, Israel and Judah were not the best of friends, and Edom was a subject nation waiting for an opportunity to throw off her Judean yoke. The three nations were really enemies allied in a loose coalition for their own survival. The idea that they were killing each other made sense. The Moabites simply put two and two together and thought the answer was five!

Now was the time to attack the invaders. By the time the Moabites discovered their mistake it was too late. They had already left the safety of their fortresses on the high ground, and their soldiers now stood vulnerable on the open plains. When the three kings saw this, they quickly regrouped their armies and routed the Moabites as Elisha had predicted (vv. 24–25).

An interesting glimpse of Semitic culture is recorded in verse 21. "*All who were able to bear arms and older*" is literally "everyone girdling himself with a girdle and upwards." Instead of using numbers to designate ages of persons, the Semites often used descriptive phrases. An activity or a feature characteristic of a certain age would therefore represent how old a person was. For example, a very young child under five years old was described as "chasing the hens from the door of the house." A girl of ten or eleven years of age was "one who gathers sticks and carries water." One of thirteen or fourteen years was "marriageable." So here in this passage a young boy was considered old enough for military service if he had given up running around in a childish loose shirt and had started wearing a girdle or belt like a grown-up.[16]

Apparently Moab's capital city was Kir Haraseth (v. 25). Gray prefers the spelling "Kir Heres," which means "Fortification of the Watch," or in German "Wartburg."[17] Some suggest that the name of the city was actually Kir Hedasa, meaning "New Castle," but the Jewish invaders nicknamed it Kir Haraseth, meaning "Sherd Wall." It was their way of disdaining the fortress by calling it "Sherdsville!" But the walls of Kir Haraseth were not like pottery sherds. They were built of stones so large they could not be easily destroyed, so the allied armies were content to besiege the city and bombard its inhabitants with huge slingshots.

Mesha, the king of Moab, made one desperate attempt to break through the siege lines with seven hundred swordsmen. He aimed at the battle line held by the army of Edom because he considered it the weakest of the nations and the least concerned with the success of the attack. He also hoped he might persuade the Edomites to switch sides and join him in a counterattack on the remaining armies of Israel and Judah.[18] But the attempt failed, and the Moabites were driven back into the beleaguered city.

The worshipers of Chemosh, the god of the Moabites, regularly practiced human sacrifices. (It was to please his Moabite wives that Solomon introduced the worship of Chemosh into his capital city of Jerusalem; for this abomination he was chastised by Yahweh.) So the sacrifice on the city wall of Kir Haraseth was not unexpected behavior. However, when Mesha chose as his sacrifice his own son, the heir to the Moabite throne, both the citizens of the capital city and the allied attackers were shocked. What happened next is difficult to determine. Verse 27 says: *"There was great indignation against Israel. So they departed from him and returned to their own land."*

That could mean that the Moabite defenders were so indignant because the enemy had in a sense taken their prince from them that they rose up with renewed determination and threw off the besieging armies, sending them home in defeat. It also may mean that the Israelites were shocked by the sacrifice and somehow felt that they themselves were partly to blame. They assumed that Yahweh's displeasure with human sacrifices would likely bring His wrath down on them as well as the Moabites, so they turned and voluntarily gave up the siege without subjugating the people of Moab.[19] Whatever happened, verse 27 seems to indicate that although Elisha's prophecy was fulfilled to the letter, the Israelites were not totally successful in regaining Moab as a vassal state.

An unusual archaeological discovery sheds some interesting light on the incidents of this section of 2 Kings. In 1868 F. A. Klein, a Church of England missionary, was traveling through the territory east of the Dead Sea where ancient Moab once existed. An Arab sheik told him of a remarkable stone he had seen inscribed with mysterious writing. It was located at nearby Dibon, so Klein persuaded the sheik to take him to see it. About four feet tall by two feet wide, the bluish basalt monument was artfully curved at the top. A raised rim formed a neat border enclosing the inscription. The discovery generated unbridled excitement in the archaeological world, and European scholars began to bargain with the Turks to purchase the stone. When the Arabs realized it was so valuable, they reasoned that several pieces of such a stone could be sold to different bidders and would therefore be worth more than the single monument. So they built a fire around it and then poured cold water on it to break it into pieces. They nearly destroyed one of biblical history's most important archaeological discoveries. However, the broken fragments were eventually purchased, and because Klein had made a copy of the inscription, the pieces were accurately fitted together again. The restored stone monument can be seen today at the Louvre Museum in Paris.

It is called the Moabite Stone or the Mesha Stele. The forty-two lines of the inscription are in the Moabite language, which is so similar to Hebrew that the stone has been called the earliest Hebrew inscription.[20] (Since Moab and Jacob were both descendants of Terah, it is not strange that the nations spoke similar languages.) Offering an account of the wars between King Mesha and the Israelites, it confirms the story in 2 Kings but also leaves unanswered other questions.

The inscription is a war report obviously meant to enhance the reputation of Moab and her national deity, Chemosh. What we have in the Moabite Stone is an ancient example of political and religious propaganda. No Moabite defeats are mentioned. Nothing that would tarnish the national image is included. It tells instead how their great king build a high place in honor of victories given him by their god Chemosh. Admitting that Moab was under the oppression of Israel for forty years, the writing describes how Mesha threw off the foreign yoke and "Israel perished utterly forever." Mesha tells how he refortified the cities on his northern border, confirming the biblical account of Israel's expansion into the Transjordan and the control Israel exercised over that area after the time of David.[21]

Since Moab came out the loser in the invasion of the three allied kings in our passage, this event would be out of place on the propaganda stone. However, one part of the inscription mentions an emergency in the south which caused Mesha to move to the southern border and deal with it. According to the Moabite account, he was successful. This could have been the invasion of the three kings.[22]

NOTES

1. C. F. Keil, *The Books of the Kings,* Biblical Commentary on the Old Testament, ed. C. F. Keil and F. Delitzsch, vol. 4 (Grand Rapids: Eerdmans, 1950), 299.
2. Norman H. Snaith, Ralph W. Sockman, and Raymond Calkins, "The First and Second Books of Kings," in *The Interpreter's Bible,* vol. 3 (Nashville: Abingdon, 1954), 196.
3. Charles F. Burney, *Notes on the Hebrew Text of the Books of Kings* (Oxford: Clarendon Press, 1903), 266.
4. I. W. Slotki, *Kings* (London: Soncino Press, 1950), 173.
5. Gwilym H. Jones, *1 and 2 Kings,* New Century Bible Commentary, ed. Ronald E. Clements (Grand Rapids: Eerdmans, 1984), 387.
6. Keil, 299.
7. M. Pierce Matheney and Roy Honeycutt, "1-2 Kings," in *The Broadman Bible Commentary,* ed. Clifton J. Allen, vol. 3 (Nashville: Broadman, 1970), 231.
8. Slotki, 173.
9. Keil, 300.
10. Jones, 394.
11. Matheney and Honeycutt, 233.
12. Keil, 300.
13. Matheney and Honeycutt, 233.
14. Keil, 300.
15. T. R. Hobbs, *2 Kings,* Word Biblical Commentary, ed. John D. W. Watts, vol. 13 (Waco, TX: Word Books, 1985), 36.

16. John Gray, *I and II Kings*, Old Testament Library (Philadelphia: Westminster, 1963), 438.

17. Ibid., 438.

18. Matheney and Honeycutt, 234.

19. Ibid., 234.

20. Merrill C. Tenney, ed., *The Zondervan Pictorial Bible Dictionary* (Grand Rapids: Zondervan, 1963), 550.

21. Hobbs, 39.

22. Ibid.

CHAPTER TWELVE

The Account of Elisha's Miracles

2 Kings 4:1–6:7

INTRODUCTION

Here is another place in 2 Kings where it is clear that Elisha and Elijah were very different persons. Elijah was the prophet of the desert. He would suddenly appear from the lonely wilderness when a religious or political crisis developed. Then, when the problems were resolved, he would dramatically disappear again into some remote dwelling place. Elisha, on the contrary, was more gregarious, spending his time surrounded by people. For him, "the top of the news" included not only national headline events but also human interest features. He was at home with the daily experiences of common folks. His miracles were less spectacular than Elijah's but more humane, characterized by small kindnesses, courtesies, and individual considerations of ordinary persons. This compassionate quality in his miracles gave greater charm and appeal to his personality. To that extent, Elisha was more like Jesus who "went about doing good."

Those of us who consider ourselves less than extraordinary should find Elisha's approach very encouraging. Most of us will never confront kings, threaten governments, or influence international developments as Elijah did. However, we can imitate the caring, personal style of Elisha, and in so doing become more like Jesus too. And isn't it true that those who concentrate on the everyday needs of people often do more good in the world than those who aim only at spectacular accomplishments? History is more often moved forward by peripheral figures than by headline makers.

Robert Browning said, "Would you have your songs endure? Build on the human heart." We need such an emphasis on the personal today, when people live crowded together in mass population centers.

They lose their individual worth, becoming little more than numbers on somebody's records. Automation intensifies this process of depersonalization. Automatic teller machines dispense money. Synthesized voices remind automobile drivers that their seat belts need fastening. Using a computer, we can receive medical diagnoses, make airline reservations, buy stock shares, and receive letters without ever seeing or hearing a "real, live person." The result is a loss of personal worth.

A service station operator in Houston has humorous evidence of the disappearance of the personal dimension in daily life. He placed a plastic container beside his cash register, like the ones you see beside cash registers everywhere to collect money for good causes. Customers have become conditioned to drop their change in the containers to support the Red Cross or to fight muscular dystrophy. But the plastic container beside my friend's cash register has a label in big red letters: "Help free me from financial worry!" It was a joke, of course, but he was surprised at how many people in this mechanical, depersonalized society of ours, without thinking, dropped their change automatically into the plastic receptacle. They never took time to read the label. And I suppose my friend uses the money precisely for the purpose plainly displayed on his collection box!

An anonymous cynic with poetic gifts expressed it like this:

The fellows up in personnel,
  They have a set of cards on me,
Whose sprinkled perforations tell
  My individuality.

And what am I? I am a card,
  Within the files of IBM,
The secret places of my heart
  Hold little secrecy with them.

It matters not how much I prate,
  They punch with punishment the scroll.
The cards are the captain of my fate,
  The files are the masters of my soul.

Monday my brain began to buzz,
  I was in agony all night.

I found out what the trouble was:
They had my paper clip too tight!

So Elisha as an example of a person-centered minister is a man whose time has come. Helping others is still the best measure of the degree to which one fulfills the prophetic calling. A study of his miracles will be a timely one.

Elisha and the Widow's Oil

4:1 A certain woman of the wives of the sons of
the prophets cried out to Elisha, saying, "Your servant my husband is dead, and you know that your
servant feared the LORD. And the creditor is coming
to take my two sons to be his slaves."
2 So Elisha said to her, "What shall I do for you?
Tell me, what do you have in the house?" And she
said, "Your maidservant has nothing in the house but
a jar of oil."
3 Then he said, "Go, borrow vessels from everywhere, from all your neighbors—empty vessels; do
not gather just a few.
4 "And when you have come in, you shall shut
the door behind you and your sons; then pour it into
all those vessels, and set aside the full ones."
5 So she went from him and shut the door behind
her and her sons, who brought *the vessels* to her; and
she poured *it* out.
6 Now it came to pass, when the vessels were full,
that she said to her son, "Bring me another vessel."
And he said to her, "*There is* not another vessel." So
the oil ceased.
7 Then she came and told the man of God. And
he said, "Go, sell the oil and pay your debt; and you
and your sons live on the rest."

2 Kings 4:1–7

While they generally occurred during the reign of Jehoram, the miracles in this section of 2 Kings are not easily dated nor necessarily listed in chronological order. With very little connecting language to indicate sequence, the writer has loosely grouped them by category. The first group includes miracles performed for individuals in need. The second group includes miracles that are more political and national in purpose.

The first miracle, reminiscent of Elijah's miracle in 1 Kings 17:16, provided help for the family of one of the sons of the prophets. The sons of the prophets were disciples of great prophets like Elijah and Elisha. They were prophets-in-training, seminary students in a sense, who lived together in small communities that Elijah and Elisha visited from time to time. This passage gives us some insight into the customs of such communities. They were not monastic. The student prophets were married and lived in family groups. Apparently they had limited resources and economic obligations from which the larger community did not relieve them.

Times really haven't changed that much. In every age seminary students always seem to have financial difficulty. On our campus, most seminarians are married, many have families. The challenge of going to school and making a living is sometimes more than they can handle. Our student aid office frequently hears from students with financial problems very similar to the ones described here in chapter four.

A particular young prophet had to borrow money for some purpose and died before he could pay back the debt. Credit life insurance had not yet been invented, so the creditor had a right to make a claim against the family, a claim which today would be unthinkable. The Mosaic law allowed the creditor to take the debtor's children as slaves in payment for the debt. They would have to work for the creditor until the year of Jubilee when the law required him to free them (Lev. 25:39–40; Exod. 21:7; cf. Neh. 5:4–5). So, even though his actions sound harsh to our ears, this creditor was acting responsibly according to the law.

The young prophet whose family was in trouble is unnamed, but the Targum of Jonathan suggests he was Obadiah, who hid the prophets of Yahweh from King Ahab. The same tradition identifies the creditor as Jehoram, the son of Ahab, who lent Obadiah money to maintain the hidden prophets (1 Kings 18:3–4).[1] Josephus (*Antiquities* 9.4.2) also links the prophet with Obadiah because 1 Kings 18 calls him a "God-fearing" man, and in this passage the same term is used (v. 1). Josephus adds that the wife herself was in danger of being sold into slavery with her children.

The Hebrew word for *"jar"* in verse 2 comes from a verb meaning "anoint," and therefore refers to a small container like those used to hold ceremonial oil. Some translators consequently use the phrase, "Your maidservant has nothing in the house but a single anointing of olive oil."[2]

Elisha intentionally added an important detail to his instructions: *"Do not gather just a few"* (v. 3). Later it becomes clear that the amount of miraculous oil she received was limited only by the number of vessels she was willing to collect (v. 6). So the extent of the resolution of her crisis was directly proportionate to the degree of her faith.

In verse 4 he added another detailed instruction typical of his miracles: *"Shut the door behind you."* The theme of a closed door is repeated often (4:5, 21, 33; 5:9; 6:32; 9:2) and seems to indicate the prophet's preference for privacy. For some reason he wanted to avoid publicity about his miracles. Maybe he thought that a miracle performed in his absence would not draw attention to himself. It would therefore be clearly an act of God and not a magic sleight-of-hand trick.

The literal translation of the last part of verse 5 expresses in a graphic way the hectic excitement of the family as they realized what was happening, "They were bringing the vessels to her and she was pouring out."[3]

The spiritual lesson of the miracle seems to focus on the limited number of jars she collected thereby showing what little faith she had. If only she had gathered more containers, she would have had more oil. One remembers the words of our Lord, "O you of little faith, why did you doubt?" (Matt. 14:31).

The reader must notice, however, the final instructions of *"the man of God"* in verse 7. She was to sell the oil she had collected and use the money to pay their debts. After that, there would still be enough money left for an endowment on which she and her family could live. The number of jars she and her sons borrowed must have been significant! It might be, in fact, that the family had borrowed all the jars in the village and ran out simply because there were no more vessels available! If so, then the passage is a spiritual example of great faith.

Certainly one lesson is that God keeps giving Himself to us as long as we bring to Him that into which He can pour Himself. When we stop bringing, He stops giving. Of course God can give many things whether we want them or not, but His best gift can only be given if we desire it. That gift is Himself, His saving presence within us. God will not force Himself on anyone who will not in earnest faith open his heart like an empty vessel to Him. So the lesson here is that we have as much of God as we are willing to take in. He will not make us wise or holy or powerful unless we really desire these gifts and bring Him our empty lives for His filling. "You do not have because you do not ask" (James 4:2). Feeble wishing for things is one thing, but the intense, steadfast desire of faith is another. Wish for anything else and you may or may not get it, but come to God with empty vessels of expectant faith, earnestly desiring His gifts, and He will fill them.

Remember, though, spiritual vessels are not fixed in shape and capacity like those in this story. They are flexible and elastic. They can expand and contract. Therefore, the more we allow God to pour into them, the bigger they expand and the more they can hold. When it comes to receiving God's gifts, there are no bounds or capacities except our faith. He "is able to do exceedingly abundantly above all that we ask or think, according to the power that works in us" (Eph. 3:20).

Of course the vessel must be empty if we are to receive the fullness of God. If our hearts are already crowded with lesser concerns or sinful values when we bring them to the source of supply, there will be no room for the oil. So the miracle not only teaches the importance of desire, expectation, and faith; it teaches obedience also.

Elisha and the Shunammite's Son

4:8 Now it happened one day that Elisha went to Shunem, where there *was* a notable woman, and she persuaded him to eat some food. So it was, as often as he passed by, he would turn in there to eat some food.

9 And she said to her husband, "Look now, I know that this *is* a holy man of God, who passes by us regularly.

10 "Please, let us make a small upper room on the wall; and let us put a bed for him there, and a table and a chair and a lampstand; so it will be, whenever he comes to us, he can turn in there."

11 And it happened one day that he came there,
and he turned in to the upper room and lay down
there.
12 Then he said to Gehazi his servant, "Call this
Shunammite woman." When he had called her, she
stood before him.
13 And he said to him, "Say now to her, 'Look, you
have been concerned for us with all this care. What
can I do for you? Do you want me to speak on your
behalf to the king or to the commander of the army?'"
She answered, "I dwell among my own people."
14 So he said, "What then *is* to be done for her?"
And Gehazi answered, "Actually, she has no son, and
her husband is old."
15 So he said, "Call her." When he had called her,
she stood in the doorway.
16 Then he said, "About this time next year you
shall embrace a son." And she said, "No, my lord.
Man of God, do not lie to your maidservant!"
17 But the woman conceived, and bore a son when
the appointed time had come, of which Elisha had
told her.
18 And the child grew. Now it happened one day
that he went out to his father, to the reapers.
19 And he said to his father, "My head, my head!"
So he said to a servant, "Carry him to his mother."
20 When he had taken him and brought him to his
mother, he sat on her knees till noon, and *then* died.
21 And she went up and laid him on the bed of the
man of God, shut *the door* upon him, and went out.
22 Then she called to her husband, and said,
"Please send me one of the young men and one of the
donkeys, that I may run to the man of God and come
back."
23 So he said, "Why are you going to him today? *It
is* neither the New Moon nor the Sabbath." And she
said, "*It is* well."
24 Then she saddled a donkey, and said to her
servant, "Drive, and go forward; do not slacken the
pace for me unless I tell you."
25 And so she departed, and went to the man of
God at Mount Carmel.

So it was, when the man of God saw her afar off, that he said to his servant Gehazi, "Look, the Shunammite woman!
26 "Please run now to meet her, and say to her, '*Is it* well with you? *Is it* well with your husband? *Is it* well with the child?'" And she answered, "*It is* well."
27 Now when she came to the man of God at the hill, she caught him by the feet, but Gehazi came near to push her away. But the man of God said, "Let her alone; for her soul *is* in deep distress, and the LORD has hidden *it* from me, and has not told me."
28 So she said, "Did I ask a son of my lord? Did I not say, 'Do not deceive me'?"
29 Then he said to Gehazi, "Get yourself ready, and take my staff in your hand, and be on your way. If you meet anyone, do not greet him; and if anyone greets you, do not answer him; but lay my staff on the face of the child."
30 And the mother of the child said, "*As* the LORD lives, and *as* your soul lives, I will not leave you." So he arose and followed her.
31 Now Gehazi went on ahead of them, and laid the staff on the face of the child; but *there was* neither voice nor hearing. Therefore he went back to meet him, and told him, saying, "The child has not awakened."
32 When Elisha came into the house, there was the child, lying dead on his bed.
33 He went in therefore, shut the door behind the two of them, and prayed to the LORD.
34 And he went up and lay on the child, and put his mouth on his mouth, his eyes on his eyes, and his hands on his hands; and he stretched himself out on the child, and the flesh of the child became warm.
35 He returned and walked back and forth in the house, and again went up and stretched himself out on him; then the child sneezed seven times, and the child opened his eyes.
36 And he called Gehazi and said, "Call this Shunammite woman." So he called her. And when she came in to him, he said, "Pick up your son."

37 So she went in, fell at his feet, and bowed to the
ground; then she picked up her son and went out.
2 Kings 4:8–37

This second miracle is very similar to the one in 1 Kings 17:17 where Elijah raises the son of the widow of Zarephath. In both accounts a prominent woman provides hospitality for the prophet, her son dies, he is brought to an upper room kept for the prophet and placed on the bed, the prophet lies prostrate on the dead body, and the boy is miraculously brought to life again. But certain features of Elisha's miracle are different, and it is recounted with some appealing details that give it a winsome human quality not found in the Elijah passage.

For example, verse 8 says that the woman *"persuaded"* (KJV: "constrained") Elisha to eat the food she had prepared. What preacher has not had an identical experience—a talented cook in the church family who delights in frustrating every good intention of pastoral weight control by "constraining" him to eat a second helping of her prize-winning coconut pie? No wonder Elisha *"as often as he passed by, . . . would turn in there to eat some food."*

The wife's plea to her husband to build a special room for the prophet, the details of the furniture, the open invitation to stop by any time, all give the story an authentic charm (v. 9).

In a Mississippi town where I preached recently, I was the guest of a retired couple who regularly extended this "Shunammite" brand of hospitality for special guests of their church. They had added a comfortable apartment above their garage, had it decorated and comfortably furnished by a professional designer, kept it stocked with fruit and snacks, and made it available free of charge to visiting preachers and other church guests. Their ministry was a valuable contribution to the church budget and a thoughtful gesture to the fortunate ones who stayed there. The couple enjoyed it too, because they were able to get acquainted with some very interesting people over the years. Christian hospitality always brings this reciprocal blessing.

Shunem was a village on the southwestern slopes of lesser Hermon, about twenty miles southeast of Mount Carmel where Elisha lived. His house was likely on the very site where Elijah had challenged the prophets of Baal.[4] On his frequent trips to Jezreel, Elisha would regularly pass through the village of Shunem.

Shunem was also known as the home of Abishag, the beautiful girl who was brought to King David in his old age in an attempt to revive him (1 Kings 1:3). It is interesting to note that rabbinic tradition identifies the Shunammite woman in this miracle as the sister of Abishag and the wife of the prophet Iddo. If the tradition is true, she would have been over one hundred years old.[5]

According to verse 10 the upper room was built *"on the wall."* This probably refers to a room added to the roof of the house with access by an outside stairway or ladder.[6] Unlike Ahaziah's open-air room with lattices in 2 Kings 1:2, this one was more permanent, with walls. Its furnishings were sparse but adequate: a bed, a table, a chair, and a lampstand. This lamp was probably not a candlestick, but a saucer lamp fashioned from clay. The Hebrew word *mĕnôrâ* indicates a shallow pottery bowl with a pinched nozzle. Some of these from the Israelite period had seven nozzles at which seven flames could be lighted.[7]

In verse 12 we meet Gehazi, a servant of Elisha just as Elisha had been the servant of Elijah. His name may be from the Arabic word *jahida,* meaning "to be avaricious, covetous, greedy."[8] If so, then his name accurately depicted his character. Every time he is mentioned in the story, his materialistic nature comes out, especially in 2 Kings 5:20 when he runs after Naaman to get the reward that Elisha had waived.

Here Elisha used Gehazi as a go-between in his conversation with the woman. Why did Elisha not speak to her directly? It was not in order to protect his dignity or because it was forbidden for a prophet to talk to a woman. Later, in verse 15, he did talk to her directly. Perhaps he remained at a distance because he knew she stood in awe of the *"man of God"* and he respected her respect.

Elisha was impressed by her insistent hospitality, her "concern for his care." The words are literally, "you have trembled" or "you have been in panic for our care." In other words, "you have been so anxious for our welfare."[9] The word "concerned" is from an Arabic word for "bashful" and may also refer to her genial humility.[10] Elisha wanted to do something to repay her, and through Gehazi he asked for some suggestions. Since her husband was very old and she was childless, did she perhaps need the protection of the king or the military commander (v. 13)? No, she lived among her own people, that is, with her relatives who looked after her. She needed neither royal nor military protection. What then? Gehazi had a suggestion. (He always seemed to be an expert on gifts and rewards!) She needed a son. So Elisha prophesied that even though she had been childless so long, she would conceive and bear a son (v. 16).

Her surprised response, *"No, my lord. Man of God, do not lie to your maidservant,"* is equivalent to our modern, "You're kidding!" It expressed polite skepticism. But in spite of her incredulity, the prophecy of Elisha came true, and the son was born (v. 17).

Verse 18 picks up the story some time later, when the miracle baby had grown up to be a young boy, perhaps seven or eight years old. While accompanying his father in the field, the boy suffered an illness that sounds like a heatstroke (v. 19). This would be consistent with the fact that harvesting was done during the warm season of the year.

When it was obvious to the heartbroken mother that her only son was dead, she set about a plan of action while maintaining a remarkable composure. Step by step her calm, resolute steps are indicative of a strong faith in the midst of crisis. She placed the body on Elisha's bed, closed the door so no one would find him and be alarmed, and called for her husband to prepare a donkey for a quick trip to see Elisha. Without revealing their son's death, she bravely sidestepped his questioning curiosity and headed straight to Mount Carmel, about twenty miles away. Her answer to her husband's question in verse 23, *"It is well,"* is the Hebrew word for "peace," *šālôm.* It was probably the common form of "good-bye" given curtly to avoid answering her husband's question. He was obviously worried about her sudden trip; so she calmly answered *šālôm* to reassure him. "Don't worry, I'll be back soon."

In her instruction to her servant, one can sense the tension and urgency of her frantic dash for help, *"Drive, and go forward; do not slacken the pace for me unless I tell you"* (v. 24). The servant was to follow beside and beat the donkey to make it run faster.

Once again, Gehazi was the communicator between Elisha and the Shunammite. She answered all three of Gehazi's questions, even the one about her son's health, with a polite, *"It is well."* This is the same word, *šālôm,* that she used with her husband in verse 23. She knew it would take too long to explain the situation to Gehazi first. She wanted to make her appeal directly to Elisha without the delay of an intercessor.

Actually, the death of the boy is never mentioned in their conversation. Her anguish communicates the unspeakable tragedy clearly to the understanding man of God. This time, God has not miraculously revealed the situation to Elisha as He did at other times. The prophet naturally deduces from the circumstances that the boy is dead (v. 27).

Elisha knew Gehazi's character well. He was vainglorious. He lived for praise and recognition. He loved to be the first to know inside information. So knowing he would probably stop and tell everyone he met along the way where he was going and why, Elisha sent Gehazi ahead with pointed advice, *"If you meet anyone, do not greet him; and if anyone greets you, do not answer him"* (v. 29).

Several explanations have been given for Elisha's instruction to lay his staff on the boy's body until he arrived. The action may have been designed to allay the mother's impatience by giving her a pledge that even though it would take some time for Elisha to get to Shunem, he was doing something about the situation.[11] Or perhaps he thought his staff lying on the body would prevent the unsuspecting family from burying the boy before he arrived. Since it would be the next day before Elisha and the mother could make it to Shunem, he feared that the family might search for the missing boy, discover his body, and bury it, preventing the miracle.[12]

Is there a suggestion in verse 31 that presumptuous Gehazi had tried to raise the child using Elisha's rod? It fits with what we know of his character, and the declaration that nothing happened, *"neither voice nor hearing,"* and that *"the child has not awakened,"* sounds like the report of an attempt that failed.[13] If so, then the spiritual truth here is that a rod in the hands of a weak bearer cannot work miracles. Even the mightiest instruments are weak when selfishness, coldness, and faithlessness wield them.

At least this passage about Elisha's rod demonstrates that the miracle that was about to happen was not some sorcerer's cheap trick associated with a magic rod. The miracle must wait for the man of God Himself. It also teaches that some responsibilities in life cannot be delegated. We must attend to them ourselves. A church cannot expect a paid professional staff to carry out the great commission for them. Even if he works hard, a pastor cannot make all the evangelistic calls for the membership. They must go themselves. Neither can a minister remain remote in the church office, sending out others and expecting them to witness in his place. The minister must also be involved. There are some kingdom tasks we cannot entirely delegate.

Following the example set by his great predecessor, Elijah, in a similar situation in 1 Kings 17:17, Elisha first shut the door of the room and prayed. Then, as Elijah had done, he prostrated his body over that of the child. This was not a mouth-to-mouth resuscitation as some have suggested. The child was dead. Rather the act symbolized the fact that God often uses human mediation for His miracles. It is often not enough to send a servant or offer a staff; one must give oneself in spiritual work. Life gives life. As the supreme example of this, Jesus stretched Himself on the cross in order to offer eternal life to men and women who were dead in trespasses and sins.

Alexander Maclaren calls this passage "one of the tenderest and sweetest pages in the history [of the kings]."[14] Who would not be touched by reading about the courage of the mother who hurries across the plain of Jezreel to Carmel while her poor son, so lately won and so early lost, lies pale and lifeless on the prophet's cot in Shunem? The questions in verse 26 inscribed the entire range of this godly woman's chief concerns. Her husband, her son, herself—these were the concentric circles of concern within which her heart moved. If these were well, nothing could be very wrong. If these were not well, nothing could be very right. Her great faith opened the door for miracles that otherwise would never have occurred.

The passage also reveals much about the character of Elisha. We can see his gentleness and sensitive concern for human suffering. Approachable as always, when he recognized her from a distance, he took the initiative and reached out to her (v. 25). With admirable empathy, he sensed her problem without the need for her to say it.

She was angry and bitter, but Elisha did not rebuke her. She even accused him and God of deceit. They had given her a son and then suddenly and capriciously taken him away. *"Did I ask a son of my lord? Did I not say, 'Do not deceive me?'"* (v. 28). But instead of rebuking her, Elisha wisely discerned beneath her wild words and rough approach an aching misery. Sometimes, because of a tragedy or disappointment, we get angry with God; but if we cling to Him in faith, He will translate our rough words and bitter thoughts into petitions and will be swift to overlook our anger and answer us.

The Shunammite's persistent faith throughout this passage is similar to that of the importunate widow whom Jesus commended. *"As the Lord lives, and as your soul lives, I will not leave you,"* she announced to Elisha (v. 30). The Scriptures promise, "Those who wait on the Lord shall renew their strength; they shall mount up with wings like eagles, they shall run and not be weary, they shall walk and not faint" (Isa. 40:31).

Here we also see Elisha's humility. When the news came of the child's death, some proud prophets would have said, "Of course I knew about it already. What kind of prophet do you think I am? I can foresee the future, and God hides nothing from me." But Elisha readily admitted his limitations. He was surprised at the death of the miraculous son and confessed, *"The Lord has hidden it from me, and has not told me"* (v. 27). How much better it would be for the church today if more of its teachers and preachers were willing to copy Elisha's modesty and admit their limited knowledge.

Because secular science has idealized experimental precision and intellectual certainty, some believers today are not willing to admit that human intellect is limited. They cannot live with ambiguity. They are unwilling to accept the great mysteries of life that our sinful minds cannot comprehend. Of course it is possible and appropriate to possess experiential certainty, to know that we are saved, that our sins are forgiven, and that we will spend eternity in heaven. Intellectual certainty, however, is something entirely different. We are sinful humans whose intellectual grasp of reality is limited. We can only know in part. Therefore, the quest for absolute intellectual certainty can be idolatry. We need to copy the modesty of Elisha and say about a great many things, *"The Lord has hidden it from me."*

ELISHA AND THE MIRACULOUS FOOD

4:38 And Elisha returned to Gilgal, and *there was* a famine in the land. Now the sons of the prophets *were* sitting before him; and he said to his servant, "Put on the large pot, and boil stew for the sons of the prophets."

39 So one went out into the field to gather herbs, and found a wild vine, and gathered from it a lapful of wild gourds, and came and sliced *them* into the pot of stew, though they did not know *what they were.*

40 Then they served it to the men to eat. Now it happened, as they were eating the stew, that they

cried out and said, "Man of God, *there is* death in the
pot!" And they could not eat *it*.
41 So he said, "Then bring some flour." And he put
it into the pot, and said, "Serve *it* to the people, that
they may eat." And there was nothing harmful in the
pot.
42 Then a man came from Baal Shalisha, and
brought the man of God bread of the firstfruits,
twenty loaves of barley bread, and newly ripened
grain in his knapsack. And he said, "Give *it* to the
people, that they may eat."
43 But his servant said, "What? Shall I set this before one hundred men?" He said again, "Give it to
the people, that they may eat; for thus says the LORD:
'They shall eat and have *some* left over.'"
44 So he set *it* before them; and they ate and had
some left over, according to the word of the LORD.

2 Kings 4:38–44

The next two miracles of Elisha are grouped together at this point in the text because they both deal with food. This seems to be the historical style of the author of Kings. His interest in chronological sequencing is often secondary to his desire to tell the story topically. So without suggesting the order in which these two events occurred, the author relates first how Elisha purified a poisonous cauldron of stew and second how he fed one hundred men with twenty loaves of barley bread.

The first miracle, which a preacher friend of mine with a propensity for alliteration likes to call "The Prophet Purifies a Poisonous Pot of Porridge," took place in Gilgal. Although its exact location is not certain, this city was apparently near the Jordan above the Dead Sea about fifteen miles northeast of Jerusalem. Its name means "Circle of Stones." Joshua established his camp there after crossing the Jordan (Josh. 4:19). Gilgal was also the place where Saul was formally received as king by the united tribes of Israel (1 Sam. 11:15). At this time Gilgal was the site of another extension center for the School of the Prophets. Consequently, Elisha frequently visited there.[15]

The famine mentioned in verse 38 may be the seven-year famine alluded to in 2 Kings 8:1–3. Because of the famine, these young seminarians, circled about Elisha like pupils assembled before their teacher for instruction, must have appeared hungry. Out of typical concern for their needs, Elisha commanded *"his servant,"* probably Gehazi, to prepare a large pot of boiled stew for them. Again, Gehazi's performance fell short. In gathering herbs for the stew, he discovered a wild vine, and, using his robe to form a large bag, he brought back some *"gourds"* and sliced them into the stew.

The gourds were probably colocynth. Popularly called "wild cucumber," the vine still grows near the Dead Sea. When the gourds are cut open the pulp dries rapidly and forms a powder, which in that part of the world is still used as a cathartic medicine. It has a very bitter taste.[16] If eaten in enough quantity, it induces colic and can be fatal.[17]

As they tasted the bitter stew, they were afraid it was poisonous and cried out, *"Death in the pot!"* Gray has humorously suggested that perhaps these students were simply complaining sarcastically to the cooks. *"Death in the pot"* could then be taken as a witty description of the foul-tasting food.[18] (Since we sometimes hear similar remarks about the food from students in the seminary refectory, this theory sounds plausible!)

Some suggest that this was not really a miracle. They believe Elisha was merely an experienced cook who knew how to add special ingredients to improve the taste of the stew.[19] But the context of this passage suggests that what he did was supernatural, a miracle. Somehow the flour (or meal) added to the stew miraculously absorbed the bitter taste and the danger, and they were able to eat it.[20]

The second miracle, the feeding of one hundred men, reminds the reader of Jesus' feeding of the five thousand many centuries later. However, in this case, Elisha only predicted that the food would be more than enough, whereas Jesus actually multiplied the loaves Himself. The location was Baal Shalisha, mentioned only here in Scripture (v. 42). It has been identified with modern Khirbet Kefr Thilth, fourteen miles northwest of Gilgal.[21] Although he is not identified, the man in verse 42 was obviously a worshiper of Yahweh, conceivably one of the seven thousand who had not bowed the knee to Baal. He brought his firstfruits offerings: *"twenty loaves of barley bread, and newly ripened grain in his knapsack"* (v. 42). The Hebrew word for *"knapsack"* is an unfamiliar word used only here in the Bible. It can mean "husks," and thus the phrase might be translated, ". . . newly ripened grain in its husks."[22] The word for *"grain"* in verse 42 is *karmel,* sometimes used for corn still on the ear. So the ripened grain might have been something like roasted ears of corn.[23]

Elisha suggested that the food be given *"to the people."* The one hundred hungry men are not identified, but they may have been another group of young prophets. The loaves must have been small and obviously inadequate for such a large crowd or the servant would not have objected so incredulously (v. 43). If this doubting servant was Gehazi, as is probable, it illustrates once more his seeming inability to rise to the occasion.

ELISHA AND THE LEPER NAAMAN

5:1 Now Naaman, commander of the army of the king of Syria, was a great and honorable man in the eyes of his master, because by him the LORD had given victory to Syria. He was also a mighty man of valor, *but* a leper.

2 And the Syrians had gone out on raids, and had brought back captive a young girl from the land of Israel. She waited on Naaman's wife.

3 Then she said to her mistress, "If only my master *were* with the prophet who *is* in Samaria! For he would heal him of his leprosy."

4 And *Naaman* went in and told his master, saying, "Thus and thus said the girl who *is* from the land of Israel."

5 Then the king of Syria said, "Go now and I will send a letter to the king of Israel." So he departed and took with him ten talents of silver, six thousand *shekels* of gold, and ten changes of clothing.

6 Then he brought the letter to the king of Israel, which said,

> Now be advised, when this letter comes to you, that I have sent Naaman my servant to you, that you may heal him of his leprosy.

7 And it happened, when the king of Israel read the letter, that he tore his clothes and said, "*Am* I God, to kill and make alive, that this man sends a man to me to heal him of his leprosy? Therefore please consider, and see how he seeks a quarrel with me."

8 So it was, when Elisha the man of God heard
that the king of Israel had torn his clothes, that he
sent to the king, saying, "Why have you torn your
clothes? Please let him come to me, and he shall
know that there is a prophet in Israel."
9 Then Naaman went with his horses and chariot,
and he stood at the door of Elisha's house.
10 And Elisha sent a messenger to him, saying, "Go
and wash in the Jordan seven times, and your flesh
shall be restored to you, and *you shall* be clean."
11 But Naaman became furious, and went away
and said, "Indeed, I said to myself, 'He will surely
come out *to me,* and stand and call on the name of the
LORD his God, and wave his hand over the place, and
heal the leprosy.'
12 "*Are* not the Abanah and Pharpar, the rivers of
Damascus, better than all the waters of Israel? Could
I not wash in them and be clean?" So he turned and
went away in a rage.
13 And his servants came near and spoke to him,
and said, "My father, *if* the prophet had told you *to do*
something great, would you not have done *it?* How
much more then, when he says to you, 'Wash, and be
clean'?"
14 So he went down and dipped seven times in the
Jordan, according to the saying of the man of God;
and his flesh was restored like the flesh of a little
child, and he was clean.
15 And he returned to the man of God, he and all
his aides, and came and stood before him; and he
said, "Indeed, now I know that *there is* no God in all
the earth, except in Israel; now therefore, please take
a gift from your servant."
16 But he said, "*As* the LORD lives, before whom I
stand, I will receive nothing." And he urged him to
take *it,* but he refused.
17 So Naaman said, "Then, if not, please let your
servant be given two mule-loads of earth; for your
servant will no longer offer either burnt offering or
sacrifice to other gods, but to the LORD.
18 "Yet in this thing may the LORD pardon your
servant: when my master goes into the temple of

Rimmon to worship there, and he leans on my hand,
and I bow down in the temple of Rimmon—when I
bow down in the temple of Rimmon, may the LORD
please pardon your servant in this thing."
19 Then he said to him, "Go in peace." So he departed from him a short distance.
20 But Gehazi, the servant of Elisha the man of
God, said, "Look, my master has spared Naaman this
Syrian, while not receiving from his hands what he
brought; but *as* the LORD lives, I will run after him
and take something from him."
21 So Gehazi pursued Naaman. When Naaman
saw *him* running after him, he got down from the
chariot to meet him, and said, "*Is* all well?"
22 And he said, "All *is* well. My master has sent me,
saying, 'Indeed, just now two young men of the sons
of the prophets have come to me from the mountains
of Ephraim. Please give them a talent of silver and
two changes of garments.'"
23 So Naaman said, "Please, take two talents."
And he urged him, and bound two talents of silver in
two bags, with two changes of garments, and handed
them to two of his servants; and they carried *them* on
ahead of him.
24 When he came to the citadel, he took *them* from
their hand, and stored *them* away in the house; then
he let the men go, and they departed.
25 Now he went in and stood before his master.
Elisha said to him, "Where *did you go,* Gehazi?" And
he said, "Your servant did not go anywhere."
26 Then he said to him, "Did not my heart go *with*
you when the man turned back from his chariot to
meet you? *Is it* time to receive money and to receive
clothing, olive groves and vineyards, sheep and oxen,
male and female servants?
27 "Therefore the leprosy of Naaman shall cling to
you and your descendants forever." And he went out
from his presence leprous, *as white* as snow.

2 Kings 5:1–27

Naaman, whose name means "pleasant," is described as the commander of the army of Syria, great, honorable, victorious, mighty, and valorous. Because of his noble character the Lord had allowed the Syrian army to defeat wicked King Ahab of Israel. (This is the interpretation of Josephus in *Antiquities* 15.5. Josephus believed Naaman was the nameless archer who shot the arrow that killed Ahab.) This outstandingly favorable description nonetheless ends with a note of pathos: *"but [he was] a leper"* (v. 1). In the original Hebrew it is even more abrupt and pathetic. It says literally ". . . also a mighty man of valor—a leper." The word *"leprosy"* throughout this chapter is a generic term, *sāraʿat,* which covers a full range of skin diseases.[24]

Since Israel and Syria were officially at peace at this time, the military raids mentioned in verse 2 must have been minor border skirmishes.[25] As a matter of fact, the Hebrew word in this verse for *"raids"* is from a root meaning "to cut or penetrate." Its Greek translation is *monozōnos,* meaning "one-belted," and is used to describe the light armor a soldier might wear on a brief raiding expedition.[26]

In verse 3 the interjection uttered by the Hebrew maiden, *"If only . . . ,"* is found only in this verse and in Ps. 119:5, "Oh, that my ways were directed to keep Your statutes!" Her familiarity with Elisha, even to the point of knowing he had a house in Samaria, must mean that the prophet's reputation was widespread. It is encouraging that this anonymous Hebrew maiden did not hide her faith. She shared it with a comely naturalness, and, as a result, she was used for a major purpose, bringing miracles to pass of international significance.

Ben-Hadad, whose death is discussed in 2 Kings 8:7–15, was probably the Syrian king in verse 5, and the king of Israel to whom he wrote his letter was apparently Jehoram.[27] It is not easy to figure the rate of exchange between the silver and gold reported in verse 5 and present currency. A talent was approximately 70.4 pounds which is equivalent to 844.8 troy ounces. Therefore, *"ten talents of silver"* would be 8448 ounces of silver. At the current price of about $5.00 an ounce, that amounts to approximately $42,240. A shekel is equal to .033 pounds or .4 troy ounces. *"Six thousand shekels of gold,"* then, would be about 2400 ounces of gold. At the current price of about $500 an ounce, this comes to $1,200,000. If one gives a change of clothing the value of $500, *"ten changes of clothing"* would be worth about $5000. So Naaman took with him to Israel approximately $1,247,240!

"Now be advised . . ." introduces the letter in verse 6 and indicates that only a portion of the letter is quoted here. The formal introduction and other official elements are omitted. The letter, even though abbreviated, gives us some insight into the niceties of ancient international protocol. Ben-Hadad assumed that King Jehoram would know Elisha and would enlist him to carry out his royal request for Naaman's healing. Instead, Jehoram showed his lack of spiritual insight and faith. Forgetting about Elisha's miraculous powers, he overreacted violently. *"He tore his clothes"* and presumed Ben-Hadad was trying to seek a quarrel with him (v. 7). It was Elisha who took the initiative to contact the king and remind him that with God's help he could handle the situation.

The fact that Naaman and his large entourage of horses and chariots could drive up to the house of Elisha shows that the ancient city of Samaria was well laid out, with wide accessible streets. The prophet must have lived either in the commodious neighborhood surrounding the royal palace or out in the spacious suburbs, not in the congested quarters of the inner city.[28]

Elisha was not impressed by the pompous elegance of Naaman's caravan. He casually sent his messenger (Gehazi?) to meet the guests with his instructions. It was not because he feared contact with the leprous Naaman, nor because it was forbidden for a holy man. Elisha wanted to emphasize the fact that Yahweh was in charge of the miracle and would do it His way. Obviously, from his reaction in verse 11, Naaman had his own idea of how the cure should be handled. So by sending the servant with simple instructions, Elisha was making it clear that Naaman could not design his own cure. That was in God's hands, and He could do it any way He wished. Even though it required only a few dips in the Jordan, the amazing miracle included not only stopping the inevitable progress of Naaman's disease but actually restoring the flesh the disease had already eaten away and removing all symptoms (v. 10).

Today, people like Naaman will do anything spectacular to ensure their salvation. They will suffer, build churches, give money, sacrifice privileges. But the simple plan of God is for sinners to wash in the blood of Jesus Christ and receive by faith the eternal life He offers. And, because the plan is so simple, many turn away as Naaman did and refuse the greatest of all gifts.

The Abanah River in verse 12 is the Nahr Barada, which flows through the city of Damascus, and the Pharpar is the Nahr el-Awaj, which runs parallel to it a few miles to the south.[29] These clear rivers of legendary beauty made the ancient city of Damascus a beautiful oasis. The Arabs called it the Garden of the World.

One ancient story tells that in his youth the prophet Mohammed traveled to Damascus in a caravan, but when he came to the summit of the southern hills and saw the unexpected view of the oasis with its orchards and blossoms, he turned away, wrapping his face in his mantle, saying that man may enter but one paradise and his was above.

A valuable opportunity was offered to Naaman, but he flew into a rage and refused it, an action out of character with the noble qualities by which he is described in verse 1. However, eventually yielding to the gentle persuasion of his servants, Naaman reluctantly agreed to follow Elisha's instructions; and he was healed (v. 14).

Elisha was right. The simple method of this miracle, performed without the prophet there, did give God the credit. It was obvious that the healing came from Yahweh rather than from the sort of magical incantation that Naaman had anticipated. Naaman understood that and professed that Israel's God was the only God.

Out of overwhelming gratitude he offered a generous reward to Elisha. The word for *"gift"* here is *bĕrākâ,* translated in other places "blessing." It is possible for a person to politely refuse a generous gift in such a way that he is actually saying, "I really want the gift, but I don't want to appear grasping, so please, keep on insisting until I take it." But Elisha's refusal was not just polite; it was genuine, expressed with firm resolve. He wanted to make sure Naaman understood he could not buy God's blessings. *"As the Lord lives, before whom I stand, I will receive nothing"* (v. 16). Even after Naaman urged him to accept the rich gifts, Elisha turned him down. (You can imagine greedy Gehazi standing nearby biting his tongue and grimacing in disbelief!)

It seems clear that Naaman became a convert to the faith of Israel, a worshiper of Yahweh. He assumed that Yahweh could only be worshiped properly on the sacred soil of the land of Israel, so he asked Elisha for two mule-loads of soil to take back to Syria. Presumably he would build a site from that soil on which to erect an altar to Yahweh. In similar incidents, the Jewish synagogue in Neharda, Persia, is said to have been built from stone and earth brought from

Jerusalem, and the empress Helena is said to have brought holy soil from Jerusalem to Rome.[30]

Naaman then begged Elisha to excuse one pragmatic exception to his exclusive worship of Yahweh. When the king of Syria leaned on him in the temple of Rimmon, the national deity of Syria, he also would have to bow down before the idol. He was the king's right-hand man, and had little choice. But this act of obeisance would not be out of reverence for Rimmon, but out of deference to the king (v. 18). Rimmon, whose name is sometimes spelled "Ramman," was the god of storm, thunder, and rain. He is also identified in the Book of Kings by the name Hadad.[31]

The writer now gives us the final chapter in the life of Gehazi, the opportunistic servant of Elisha. He couldn't stand to see the caravan with its rich treasures disappear over the horizon. (The *"short distance"* referred to in verse 19 was the distance the eye could see to the horizon.) Consequently, he conceived a sad story about two penniless seminary students from the rural area around Mount Ephraim who needed financial aid. Grateful Naaman was more than happy to grant what he thought was Elisha's reasonable request for a student scholarship and even doubled the amount of money desired (v. 23).

If that scenario sounds familiar, it may be because of the proliferation of pseudoreligious hucksters who have fine-tuned Gehazi's scam into an art form. Recent exposés of television fund-raisers who appeal for contributions on the pretext of giving aid to needy persons or religious causes, only to squander the receipts on themselves, prove that the sinful world hasn't advanced very far beyond the ancient deception of Gehazi.

In order to keep his newly acquired treasure a secret, Gehazi dismissed Naaman's two servants who were sent to carry the gifts. The *"citadel"* in verse 24 must have been a well-known hill near where Elisha and Gehazi lived. Meaning "a swelling mound," the name may have designated a section of the royal fortification near the king's palace.[32] Having hidden his wealth, and thinking he had deceived Elisha, Gehazi boldly went into Elisha's house. At once the prophet of the Lord confronted him with an embarrassing quiz about his whereabouts.

Some believe Elisha was reading Gehazi's mind when he spoke of buying *"olive groves and vineyards, sheep and oxen, male and female servants."* Gehazi must have been thinking at that very moment about what he was going to do with Naaman's gifts.[33] Obviously Elisha had been given supernatural information on which to base his charge. It is interesting to note that Elisha's gift of supernatural knowledge was intermittent. He did not know the Shunammite's son had died, but here the treachery of Gehazi is revealed to him in full detail.

The Jerusalem Bible translates verse 26: "Now you have taken the money, you can buy gardens with it, and olive groves, sheep and oxen, and male and female slaves. But Naaman's leprosy will cling to you and to your descendants forever." A pitiful character, Gehazi. Like Judas, he lived in the presence of God and great men, but he was fatally infected with materialism and worldliness. Ironically, we see here a pagan who by an act of faith is cured of leprosy and an Israelite who by an act of dishonor is cursed with it.

A number of practical lessons can be drawn from this miraculous incident in Elisha's life. All men must come to God humbly, whether they are great or small. The ground around the cross is level. No matter what one's station may be in life, the gift of salvation must be received the same way, by repentance and faith. "All have sinned and fall short of the glory of God" (Rom. 3:23).

There is another lesson in Elisha's characteristic style of ministry. He was a spokesman, not a high and mighty priest. He did not dispense esoteric incantations as though he were responsible for the miracles. Elisha simply gave the instructions; he faithfully delivered God's message. The healing was from God, not man.

Similarly, our business is to deliver God's message of hope and salvation today. We are responsible for declaring how sick humanity can be divinely healed. Our commission is to preach, not to perform rites or administer sacraments. We are not to argue or defend. We are neither priests nor professors, but preachers who are to make the message plain. Our calling is not to dress up the message with man-made ornaments nor rephrase it to make it more palatable. We are to be faithful heralds, messengers and nothing more.

John the Baptist understood the model of Elisha when he said, "I am a voice." Elisha didn't even come out of his house to pass his hands over the leprosy of Naaman and thereby take some credit for the miracle. He stayed in the background in order to give glory to God. Modern ministers need to be reminded that we are called, not to be media stars, but to be minister-servants of the most high God.

Elisha and the Floating Ax Head

6:1 And the sons of the prophets said to Elisha,
"See now, the place where we dwell with you is too
small for us.
2 "Please, let us go to the Jordan, and let every
man take a beam from there, and let us make there
a place where we may dwell." So he answered,
"Go."
3 Then one said, "Please consent to go with your
servants." And he answered, "I will go."
4 So he went with them. And when they came to
the Jordan, they cut down trees.
5 But as one was cutting down a tree, the iron *ax
head* fell into the water; and he cried out and said,
"Alas, master! For it was borrowed."
6 So the man of God said, "Where did it
fall?" And he showed him the place. So he cut off a
stick, and threw *it* in there; and he made the iron
float.
7 Therefore he said, "Pick *it* up for yourself." So
he reached out his hand and took it.

2 Kings 6:1–7

Now we come to the last of the miracles in this collection of six: the widow's oil, the Shunammite's son, the purified stew, the feeding of one hundred, the cure of Naaman's leprosy, and now the floating ax head. The occasion is a building program at one of the prophetic seminary extension centers, perhaps either Gilgal or Jericho. Dormitory space had become limited, so a cooperative program of capital expansion was launched (v. 2). Everybody pitched in to help.

The word *"ax head"* is not actually in the text. Verse 5 literally says, "But as one was cutting down a tree, the iron fell into the water." "Ax head" has been inserted by the translators as the logical meaning. *"Borrowed"* is too mild a translation in verse 5. "It was begged" is better.

Even though Elisha tossed a floating stick into the water first, the incident was not an example of imitative magic, but another miracle from the hand of the prophet. The floating stick was merely a symbol of what Elisha wanted the ax head to do. The text says, "*. . . and he made the iron float.*"[34]

NOTES

1. I. W. Slotki, *Kings* (London: Soncino Press, 1950), 182.
2. C. F. Keil, *The Books of the Kings,* Biblical Commentary on the Old Testament, ed. C. F. Keil and F. Delitzsch, vol. 4 (Grand Rapids: Eerdmans, 1950), 307.
3. Slotki, 182.
4. Keil, 310.
5. T. R. Hobbs, *2 Kings,* Word Biblical Commentary, ed. John D. W. Watts, vol. 13 (Waco, TX: Word Books, 1985), 50.
6. Slotki, 183.
7. John Gray, *I and II Kings,* Old Testament Library (Philadelphia: Westminster, 1963), 444.
8. Ibid., 441.
9. Slotki, 183.
10. Gray, 441.
11. Robert C. Dentan, *Kings and Chronicles,* Layman's Bible Commentary, vol. 7 (Richmond: John Knox Press, 1964), 58.
12. Gwilym H. Jones, *1 and 2 Kings,* New Century Bible Commentary, ed. Ronald E. Clements (Grand Rapids: Eerdmans, 1984), 404.
13. Ibid.
14. Alexander Maclaren, *Second Samuel and the Books of Kings,* Expositions on Holy Scripture, vol. 2 (Grand Rapids: Eerdmans, 1952), 352.
15. Charles F. Pfeiffer, *Baker's Bible Atlas* (Grand Rapids: Baker Book House, 1961), 132.
16. Slotki, 189.
17. Gray, 448.
18. Ibid., 448.
19. Ibid.
20. Keil, 314.
21. Slotki, 189.
22. Ibid.
23. Jones, 410.
24. M. Pierce Matheney and Roy Honeycutt, "1-2 Kings," in *The Broadman Bible Commentary,* ed. Clifton J. Allen, vol. 3 (Nashville: Broadman, 1970), 239. See also E. V. Hulse, "The Nature of Biblical 'Leprosy' and the

Use of Alternative Medical Terms in Modern Translations of the Bible," *Palestine Exploration Quarterly* 107 (1975): 87.

25. Slotki, 190.
26. Hobbs, 62.
27. Keil, 316.
28. Gray, 451.
29. Slotki, 190.
30. Matheney and Honeycutt, 239.
31. Ibid.
32. Gray, 451.
33. Slotki, 190.
34. Dentan, 62.

CHAPTER THIRTEEN

The Account of Elisha's Role in the Syrian Wars

2 Kings 6:8–8:15

The Blinded Syrians Are Captured

6:8 Now the king of Syria was making war against
Israel; and he consulted with his servants, saying,
"My camp *will be* in such and such a place."
9 And the man of God sent to the king of Israel,
saying, "Beware that you do not pass this place, for
the Syrians are coming down there."
10 Then the king of Israel sent *someone* to the place
of which the man of God had told him. Thus he
warned him, and he was watchful there, not just once
or twice.
11 Therefore the heart of the king of Syria was
greatly troubled by this thing; and he called his servants and said to them, "Will you not show me which
of us *is* for the king of Israel?"
12 And one of his servants said, "None, my lord, O
king; but Elisha, the prophet who *is* in Israel, tells
the king of Israel the words that you speak in your
bedroom."
13 So he said, "Go and see where he *is,* that I may
send and get him." And it was told him, saying,
"Surely *he is* in Dothan."
14 Therefore he sent horses and chariots and a
great army there, and they came by night and surrounded the city.
15 And when the servant of the man of God arose
early and went out, there was an army, surrounding

the city with horses and chariots. And his servant
said to him, "Alas, my master! What shall we do?"
16 So he answered, "Do not fear, for those who *are*
with us *are* more than those who *are* with them."
17 And Elisha prayed, and said, "LORD, I pray, open
his eyes that he may see." Then the LORD opened the
eyes of the young man, and he saw. And behold,
the mountain *was* full of horses and chariots of fire all
around Elisha.
18 So when *the Syrians* came down to him, Elisha
prayed to the LORD, and said, "Strike this people, I
pray, with blindness." And He struck them with blindness according to the word of Elisha.
19 Now Elisha said to them, "This *is* not the way,
nor *is* this the city. Follow me, and I will bring you to
the man whom you seek." But he led them to Samaria.
20 So it was, when they had come to Samaria, that
Elisha said, "LORD, open the eyes of these *men,* that
they may see." And the LORD opened their eyes, and
they saw; and there *they were,* inside Samaria!
21 Now when the king of Israel saw them, he said
to Elisha, "My father, shall I kill *them?* Shall I kill
them?"
22 But he answered, "You shall not kill *them.*
Would you kill those whom you have taken captive
with your sword and your bow? Set food and water
before them, that they may eat and drink and go to
their master."
23 Then he prepared a great feast for them; and
after they ate and drank, he sent them away and they
went to their master. So the bands of Syrian *raiders*
came no more into the land of Israel.

2 Kings 6:8–23

The national scene in Israel has drastically changed since the stormy days of Elijah's bloody confrontations with King Ahab and Queen Jezebel. A more sensible king, Jehoram, now sits on the throne of Ahab, and the prophet of the Lord is no longer a dreaded antagonist, but the king's trusted counselor. Elijah was a fugitive constantly on the run from a wrathful king, but now Elisha is a welcome visitor in Jehoram's court. What a contrast! Furthermore, unlike King Ahab, Jehoram has given up the worship of Baal and turned to Yahweh. Even though he has retained the forbidden images of Yahweh at Dan and Bethel, King Jehoram has brought Israel back to the faith, and Elisha and the other prophets now enjoy the respect of the entire nation.

In this narrative of Israel's skirmish with Syrian troops, the author focuses on four miracles of the prophet Elisha: his supernatural knowledge of the enemy's plans, the opening of his servant's eyes to see the heavenly hosts, the blinding of the Syrians, and the restoration of their sight.

The king of Syria referred to in verse 8 is probably Ben-Hadad. Inasmuch as the history of 2 Kings is not always given in chronological order, it is not possible to give the events an exact date. There was no formal war between Israel and Syria during this period, so the military conflict reported here must have been an intermittent campaign carried on by marauding bands of Syrian guerrilla fighters with the approval of the king.

"My camp" in verse 8 does not necessarily imply that Ben-Hadad would himself be with his soldiers; it was simply the location that he, as commander in chief, had chosen for the camp where the troops would secretly lie in wait for Israel's army. Some ancient versions of the passage describe the situation more clearly, "Let us make an ambush in such and such a place."[1]

In verse 9, *"the man of God"* is Elisha, who had been miraculously informed of the Syrian plan for ambush. Immediately the prophet sent a warning to King Jehoram to change any plans he had for travel in that area. Jones understands the clause *"Beware that you do not pass this place"* to mean "Don't overlook this place and leave it unfortified or unprotected."[2] In either case, verse 10 indicates that Jehoram took the prophet's warning seriously and on several occasions sent out military patrols to verify it. It may be that Israel's troops preceded Ben-Hadad's to the spot and set up a fortified camp there themselves, frustrating the Syrian plan.[3]

The king of Syria was understandably *"troubled by this thing"* (v. 11). Actually, the phrase says the king was "storm-tossed" (according to Slotki) or "in a whirlwind" (according to Gray). Suspecting that some traitor among his troops was relaying private information to the enemy, he asked for an explanation and was told that it was Elisha's fault. The great prophet's reputation as a miracle worker was known even among the soldiers of Ben-Hadad! Apparently, his supernatural knowledge was legendary. *"Elisha, the prophet who is in Israel, tells the king of Israel the words that you speak in your bedroom,"* they told Ben-Hadad (v. 12).

Since they were aware of Elisha's telepathic gifts, it is strange that they did not assume that the prophet would see through their new strategy too. It seemingly never occurred to these Syrians that the prophet who knew miraculously where they were planning their ambush would also know when and where they were planning to come for him.

Dothan, in verse 13, was about eleven miles north of Samaria. Near there Joseph's brothers had held him captive in a cistern and had subsequently sold him into slavery. This is the only reference that associates Elisha with this city. Obviously he moved around a lot, knew the countryside well, and enjoyed a variety of contacts in cities throughout the land.[4]

Because Dothan was only eleven miles from the capital with its strong military defenses, it is unlikely that the army Ben-Hadad sent to capture Elisha was very large, even though it is described as *"a great army"* in verse 14. That could mean an army that was powerful even though small—perhaps a force of crack commandos.[5] They marched at night, and before dawn they surrounded the unsuspecting city where Elisha was staying. The archaeological site of ancient Dothan is a hill surrounded by a flat plain, indicating that such a siege would be possible, even by an army of modest size.

Elisha's frantic and faithless servant in verse 15 sounds like Gehazi, but if this incident follows chronologically after the healing of Naaman and the punishment of Gehazi, this is not likely. Of course it could be that Gehazi was healed of his leprosy and was once again serving Elisha (cf. 2 Kings 8:1–6). Opening the servant's eyes to see, in the distant mountains surrounding Dothan, the horses and chariots of fire ready to defend them was the second miracle in this passage. Notice how regularly the miracles of Elisha were preceded by his prayers. "Elisha prayed, and then . . ." is an often-repeated formula just before the prophet performs some great supernatural act.

Verse 16 is one of the memorable, unforgettable words of Scripture. It emphasizes the importance of seeing things from God's point of view, with spiritual insight, with faith. After a trip to France, a pastor described the disappointment he felt on first seeing the famous cathedral of Chartres. The old building was dirty and gray; its windows looked dark and dreary. The church had no charm or appeal. He wondered what there was about this ordinary structure that had drawn medieval pilgrims there by the thousands and still attracted tourists today. Then he went inside, and the transformation was dramatic. It was magnificent. Streaming through the stained-glass windows, the sunlight set the sanctuary aglow with the deepest hues of the rainbow. The inside of the old church was totally different from its outside. It was a place of rare, incomparable beauty.

Looking at the Christian faith from the outside, many critics describe it as dull, legalistic, unintelligent, unappealing; but from the inside it is something else altogether. Through the eyes of faith, the Christian life is beautiful, majestic, powerful, full of joy and meaning.

Similarly, through the eyes of fear and unbelief, the situation at Dothan looked hopeless. No wonder the unbelieving servant sighed, *"Alas my master! What shall we do?"* (v. 15). But Elisha, facing the identical situation, saw things differently. He said, *"Do not fear, for those who are with us are more than those who are with them"* (v. 16). He was viewing the situation from inside the cathedral of faith. Through the eyes of God, the horses and chariots of divine protection were clearly visible. Elisha asked God to give his servant the same 20/20 vision on the spiritual eye-chart, so he too would not be afraid. "Seeing is believing" is the motto of the secular world. "Believing is seeing" is the motto of faith.

> Open my eyes, that I may see,
>   Glimpses of truth Thou hast for me;
> Place in my hands the wonderful key,
>   That shall unclasp, and set me free.
>
> Silently now I wait for Thee,
>   Ready, my God, Thy will to see;
> Open my eyes, illumine me,
>   Spirit divine![6]

Elisha prayed again, and the Syrian warriors lost their eyesight. The word for "blind" here is *sanwērîm,* which occurs again only in Gen. 19:11. In addition to a total lack of sight, the word *sanwērîm* can denote a condition of confused vision, that is, seeing objects that are not there and not seeing those that are.[7] Since the soldiers could see well enough to drive their horses and chariots behind Elisha directly into Israel's fortress of Samaria, it appears that the miracle was one of confused sight, a supernatural impediment that deceived them. They were miraculously blocked from recognizing Elisha and, in their ignorance, willingly trusted him when he offered to guide them to *"the man whom you seek."* Furthermore, they were miraculously prevented from recognizing the great walled city of Samaria until they were already inside, surrounded by the enemy (v. 19).

Once inside Samaria, Elisha prayed still again, and the fourth miracle of this passage took place. *"The Lord opened their eyes, and they saw; and there they were, inside Samaria!"* (v. 20). There is a touch of humor in verse 21 when the king of Israel suddenly realized Ben-Hadad's *"great army"* had just been deposited helpless within the very walls of his royal capital. One can almost see the dignified monarch, his royal composure shattered, waving his arms and shouting excitedly, *"My father, shall I kill them? Shall I kill them?"* (v. 21).

Elisha wanted to embarrass his foes with kindness and impress them with the all-sufficient power of Yahweh, so he advised the king to give them food and water and send them back to Ben-Hadad. If they had been killed or, according to normal procedures of war, made slaves, the effect of Elisha's miracle would have been lost. As it was, with their release, Yahweh's power was glorified, and peace was ensured, at least for a while.

Some believe there should be a "not" inserted in verse 22 so that it would read, *"Would you kill those whom you have [not] taken captive with your sword and bow?"* Still others remove the question in the sentence so that it reads, "You may kill those you have taken captive by sword and bow, but as for these men, set food and water before them."[8]

A far worse army surrounds us in these days of spiritual warfare; we face demonic foes incomparably more evil than the human soldiers whose armor glittered in the morning sunshine around Dothan. As Paul said, "We do not wrestle against flesh and blood, but against principalities, against powers, against the rulers of the darkness of this age, against spiritual hosts of wickedness in the heavenly places" (Eph. 6:12). Realizing the enormity of Satan's hosts, we wonder with the apostle, "Who is sufficient for these things?" (2 Cor.

2:16). In spiritual warfare it is not sufficient to whistle in the dark and try to lift discouraged hearts with a cheery "Fear not!" Human words of encouragement are not sufficient. We must have eyes of faith to see the evidence of God's powerful presence.

Elisha's servant personifies the despair and fear that come when we depend on human judgment and common sense. But Elisha personifies the confidence that comes from faith, when we depend on God's power. Notice that Elisha did not pray that God would send help; it was already there. He simply prayed for open eyes to see it.

There is a popular story being circulated about a man whose house was in a low area threatened by rising flood waters. As the water rose right up to his door, the National Guard came by in a four-wheel-drive vehicle to pick him up, but he refused to go, saying, "God will take care of me." When the water was three feet deep inside the house, a Red Cross motorboat came by to rescue him, but he again refused, saying, "God will save me." Finally the rising water drove him to the roof of his house, where a military helicopter hovered overhead and lowered a rope ladder to pluck him to safety. But he refused, saying, "God will rescue me." The man soon slipped from the roof and drowned, and when he went through the pearly gates to heaven, he complained to the Lord, "Why didn't you rescue me?" The Lord answered, "Who do you think sent the jeep, the motorboat, and the helicopter?"

Sometimes the appropriate prayer is not "O God, rescue me," but "O God, open my eyes that I may see Your providential presence."

The City of Samaria Is Besieged

6:24 And it happened after this that Ben-Hadad king of Syria gathered all his army, and went up and besieged Samaria.

25 And there was a great famine in Samaria; and indeed they besieged it until a donkey's head was *sold* for eighty *shekels* of silver, and one-fourth of a kab of dove droppings for five *shekels* of silver.

26 Then, as the king of Israel was passing by on the wall, a woman cried out to him, saying, "Help, my lord, O king!"

27 And he said, "If the LORD does not help you,

where can I find help for you? From the threshing floor or from the winepress?"

28 Then the king said to her, "What is troubling you?" And she answered, "This woman said to me, 'Give your son, that we may eat him today, and we will eat my son tomorrow.'

29 "So we boiled my son, and ate him. And I said to her on the next day, 'Give your son, that we may eat him'; but she has hidden her son."

30 Now it happened, when the king heard the words of the woman, that he tore his clothes; and as he passed by on the wall, the people looked, and there underneath *he had* sackcloth on his body.

31 Then he said, "God do so to me and more also, if the head of Elisha the son of Shaphat remains on him today!"

32 But Elisha was sitting in his house, and the elders were sitting with him. And *the king* sent a man ahead of him, but before the messenger came to him, he said to the elders, "Do you see how this son of a murderer has sent someone to take away my head? Look, when the messenger comes, shut the door, and hold him fast at the door. *Is* not the sound of his master's feet behind him?"

33 And while he was still talking with them, there was the messenger, coming down to him; and then *the king* said, "Surely this calamity *is* from the LORD; why should I wait for the LORD any longer?"

2 Kings 6:24–33

Since verse 23 ends with the message, "So the bands of Syrian raiders came no more into the land of Israel," it is difficult to understand how the next verse could go immediately into an account of a Syrian military siege of Samaria. Probably the explanation lies in the fact already mentioned that the author of Kings did not always write his accounts in chronological order. On the other hand, the answer may be that Syria no longer dared to bother Israel with small groups of guerrilla raiders (v. 23) and that the result was the complete mobilization of the Syrian army described in verse 24—maybe in revenge for the humiliation of the preceding event in which their soldiers were deceived.[9]

Several Syrian kings carried the name Ben-Hadad. Like the term "Pharaoh," it is a throne name as well as a proper name.[10] So the king here may be the Ben-Hadad son of Hazael mentioned in 2 Kings 13:25 rather than the Ben-Hadad whom Hazael murdered to take the throne (2 Kings 8:7–15). If so, then the king in Israel would be Jehoash, not Jehoram, and the incident must have been inserted here in order to group certain acts of Elisha together thematically.[11]

The famine in verse 25 seems to be restricted to the city of Samaria, and therefore does not have to coincide with a calamity of national proportions like the one in 2 Kings 8:1. It may have resulted from a double cause, a poor harvest in the fields around Samaria and a military siege that stopped the flow of food into the city. However, since the king held Elisha responsible for the famine (v. 31), and since prophets were known to withhold rain, and since 7:2 refers to "windows in heaven," some believe the famine must have resulted from a severe drought.[12]

Whatever the cause, the famine was serious. Gruesome details of the conditions it brought about are given in verses 25–29. Food scalpers were asking scandalous black market prices for the most nauseating dishes. The most revolting garbage was worth its weight in gold. Even though a donkey was considered unclean for human consumption, and the animal's head the most repulsive cut of meat for eating, a donkey's head was still being sold for approximately $160.

Various explanations have been given for the *"dove droppings"* in verse 25. Some believe it was actually pigeon dung and the fact that the Samaritans were willing to eat it shows how desperate they were.[13] Substantiating this interpretation is an incident in 2 Kings 18:27 in which starving people actually consumed human waste. Other interpreters believe the word was a popular botanical term for a plant that was sometimes used for fuel or, crushed, as a substitute for salt.[14] There is such a plant called *Ornithogalum umbellatum* or the Star of Bethlehem, a species of the soap plant, which the Arabs call Sparrow's Dung. It is not normally used for food, but it is edible.[15] The Jerusalem Bible translates the term "wild onions." Whatever it was, it was another very unappetizing food, and *"one-fourth of a kab"* or about one-half of a quart of it cost $10.

By far the most shocking occurrence in the starving city is depicted in verses 28–29. The complaining mother seemed to have no feeling for her dead son, but only for the unfairness of the neighbor woman who refused to keep her word and let her son also be boiled for food. Cannibalism is not unknown in the Old Testament (cf. Deut. 28:56; Ezek. 5:10; Lam. 2:20; 4:10), but the horror of the situation in Samaria reaches its deepest level here. Burney cites a Spanish record of a similar famine in England in the fourteenth century: "In 1316 so great a famine distressed the English that men ate their own children, dogs, mice, and pigeon's dung."[16]

Faced with this hopeless situation, the king admitted his helplessness (v. 27). The threshing floor and the winepress here are both symbols of divine judgment. The King was saying, "We are between a rock and a hard place. If God can't help us, then what can a mere king do!"

His frustration mounting, the king, wearing scratchy sackcloth under his torn royal robe as a mark of mourning, angrily blamed Elisha for the situation (v. 31). Maybe he was angry because he thought Elisha had not asked God to break the siege, or because he thought Elisha had inspired the people to hold out against the enemy instead of surrendering. Their prolonged resistance had therefore brought on the terrible suffering. If Jehoram is the king in this passage, then he was probably angry also that Elisha's decision to release the blinded Syrian troops instead of letting him kill them when they were captured had not succeeded in keeping peace with Syria. Whatever the cause of his irrational anger, the king decided to take out his frustration on Elisha and ordered the royal executioner to find Elisha and behead him.

Once more, Elisha's supernatural knowledge allowed him to predict the coming of the king's executioner (v. 32). *"Son of a murderer"* is a Hebrew idiom tantamount to saying simply "murderer." It is similar to "son of Belial" or "son of exhortation."[17] However, it may actually refer to the fact that the king was a descendent of Ahab, who massacred prophets and killed Naboth.

With his miraculous vision Elisha could also see that the king was not far behind the executioner, running toward the prophet's house. Apparently, realizing he had acted in haste, the king was rushing to cancel his rash order before the executioner could carry it out. Elisha asked the elders of the city, who had apparently come to his house for consultation, to hold the door and block the executioner's entrance until the king could arrive.

It seems clear that the statement in verse 33 came from the king, *"Surely this calamity is from the Lord; why should I wait for the Lord any longer?"* These are words of despair, but they contain a flickering glimmer of hope. "Is there any reason to wait on the Lord before I surrender the city to the enemy?" His cry of anguish is answered by the message of hope delivered by Elisha in the next chapter. The king's question reminds us again of the words of another prophet, "Those who wait on the Lord shall renew their strength; they shall mount up with wings like eagles, they shall run and not be weary, they shall walk and not faint" (Isa. 40:31).

The City of Samaria Is Delivered

7:1 Then Elisha said, "Hear the word of the LORD. Thus says the LORD: 'Tomorrow about this time a seah of fine flour *shall be sold* for a shekel, and two seahs of barley for a shekel, at the gate of Samaria.'"

2 So an officer on whose hand the king leaned answered the man of God and said, "Look, *if* the LORD would make windows in heaven, could this thing be?" And he said, "In fact, you shall see *it* with your eyes, but you shall not eat of it."

3 Now there were four leprous men at the entrance of the gate; and they said to one another, "Why are we sitting here until we die?

4 "If we say, 'We will enter the city,' the famine *is* in the city, and we shall die there. And if we sit here, we die also. Now therefore, come, let us surrender to the army of the Syrians. If they keep us alive, we shall live; and if they kill us, we shall only die."

5 And they rose at twilight to go to the camp of the Syrians; and when they had come to the outskirts of the Syrian camp, to their surprise no one *was* there.

6 For the LORD had caused the army of the Syrians to hear the noise of chariots and the noise of horses—the noise of a great army; so they said to one another, "Look, the king of Israel has hired against us the kings of the Hittites and the kings of the Egyptians to attack us!"

7 Therefore they arose and fled at twilight, and left

the camp intact—their tents, their horses, and their
donkeys—and they fled for their lives.

8 And when these lepers came to the outskirts of
the camp, they went into one tent and ate and drank,
and carried from it silver and gold and clothing, and
went and hid *them;* then they came back and entered
another tent, and carried *some* from there *also,* and
went and hid *it.*

9 Then they said to one another, "We are not doing
right. This day *is* a day of good news, and we remain
silent. If we wait until morning light, some punishment will come upon us. Now therefore, come, let us
go and tell the king's household."

10 So they went and called to the gatekeepers of
the city, and told them, saying, "We went to the Syrian camp, and surprisingly no one *was* there, not a
human sound—only horses and donkeys tied, and
the tents intact."

11 And the gatekeepers called out, and they told *it*
to the king's household inside.

12 So the king arose in the night and said to his
servants, "Let me now tell you what the Syrians have
done to us. They know that we *are* hungry; therefore
they have gone out of the camp to hide themselves in
the field, saying, 'When they come out of the city, we
shall catch them alive, and get into the city.'"

13 And one of his servants answered and said,
"Please, let several *men* take five of the remaining
horses which are left in the city. Look, they *may either become* like all the multitude of Israel that are
left in it; or indeed, *I say,* they *may become* like all
the multitude of Israel left from those who are consumed; so let us send them and see."

14 Therefore they took two chariots with horses;
and the king sent them in the direction of the Syrian
army, saying, "Go and see."

15 And they went after them to the Jordan; and indeed all the road *was* full of garments and weapons
which the Syrians had thrown away in their haste. So
the messengers returned and told the king.

16 Then the people went out and plundered the
tents of the Syrians. So a seah of fine flour was *sold*

for a shekel, and two seahs of barley for a shekel, according to the word of the LORD.

17 Now the king had appointed the officer on whose hand he leaned to have charge of the gate. But the people trampled him in the gate, and he died, just as the man of God had said, who spoke when the king came down to him.

18 So it happened just as the man of God had spoken to the king, saying, "Two seahs of barley for a shekel, and a seah of fine flour for a shekel, shall be *sold* tomorrow about this time in the gate of Samaria."

19 Then that officer had answered the man of God, and said, "Now look, *if* the LORD would make windows in heaven, could such a thing be?" And he had said, "In fact, you shall see *it* with your eyes, but you shall not eat of it."

20 And so it happened to him, for the people trampled him in the gate, and he died.

2 Kings 7:1–20

Probably more missionary sermons have been preached from this text than from any other in the Bible except Matt. 28:18–20 and Acts 1:8. The dramatic text resonates with the great evangelistic theme that those who know the good news are under an inescapable obligation to pass on that news to those who do not know it.

With a reverent introduction, the prophet begins his prediction: *"Hear the word of the Lord. Thus says the Lord . . ."* (v. 1). This is the first time in the Elisha account that he uses this classic introduction to prophetic speech. It emphasizes the importance of what Elisha is about to say. These are not the prophet's words, but God's. What follows will be direct inspiration, revelation straight from the mouth of Yahweh. The message is one of unbelievable joy. Tomorrow, conditions in Samaria will once again be normal. Proper food will be plentiful and available at regular prices.

Elisha's message of hope came just in the nick of time. Women were boiling their children for food; the citizens were eating dung; the frustrated king was in a murderous rage. Things could not have been worse. All hope was lost. God's promise of deliverance was desperately needed. The prophet probably knew as little as anyone about how the miracle would come to pass. It would have been easier for the people to believe it if some indication of how it could be accomplished had been shared. But faith is "the evidence of things not seen" (Heb. 11:1).

We should never be too concerned about how God will do things; we are simply to trust Him and believe His promises. Even the first-class passengers are not allowed to sit in the flight deck with the crew of an airliner. Nor do travelers participate in flight planning, fuel management, meteorology, or navigation. Without much regard for details, passengers simply trust the captain to take them to their destination. As a certain bus company advertisement puts it, "Sit back and leave the driving to us." In our relationship with God, we are to believe His promises and sit back and leave the details of methods and timing to Him.

So incredible was Elisha's optimistic prediction that the king's aide-de-camp, his right-hand man, refused to believe it and even sarcastically belittled the message. "Even if it should pour down rain, there would be no relief by tomorrow" (v. 2). As a punishment for his unbelief, Elisha predicted that the officer would not live to enjoy the divine deliverance. *"You shall see it with your eyes, but you shall not eat of it"* (v. 2). The fulfillment of this prophecy is recorded in verses 19–20.

Living in a small building erected for them near the city gate were four leprous men. One rabbi identifies them as Gehazi, the hapless servant of Elisha, and his three sons.[18] Having weighed their options and assessed the outcomes of various alternatives, they voted to throw themselves on the mercy of the Syrians and take their chances. Just before dark, *"at twilight"* (v. 5), they left the beleaguered capital city, crossed the no-man's-land, and entered the enemy camp, only to find it empty.

The same God who caused one Syrian army to see things that weren't there (2 Kings 6:18) now caused another Syrian army to hear things that weren't there. Does God have a sense of humor? The psalmist said, "He who sits in the heavens shall laugh; the Lord shall hold them in derision" (Ps. 2:4). There must be some divine humor in deceiving a mighty military power twice in such a short time!

Hearing the supernaturally generated noise of approaching armies, the Syrians feared the worst. Rumors swept through the camp. Had the Hittites in the north and the Egyptians in the south been enlisted by Israel to catch Ben-Hadad and his troops in a trap? The Syrian soldiers stampeded, leaving behind all their provisions in order to retreat more rapidly. They even left their horses and donkeys, believing there was no time to hitch them up. (It may be that the horses were left behind lest the sound of galloping give away their departure in the darkness of the night.) Obviously, Ben-Hadad and his troops had never studied Proverbs. God's word describes their predicament precisely: "The wicked flee when no one pursues" (Prov. 28:1). The entire army fled out the back door as four helpless, hungry lepers entered through the front door.

At first the diseased men gorged themselves and hid the loot they gathered from the empty tents, but then they "came to themselves." Conscience-stricken, they admitted that their selfishness was not right and that they must share the good news of their discovery with the starving Samaritans. Reinforcing their guilt was a fear of punishment by God or the king or both (v. 9).

"Punishment" here is the Hebrew word *ʿāwôn,* a comprehensive word that includes not only iniquity but also the consequences of that iniquity. The word suggests that it is not possible to separate the sin from its punishment. In fact, this same word can be used for both. The verb *"come upon us"* is literally "overtake us" or "catch up with us."[19] Did they remember the words of Moses in Num. 32:23, "Be sure your sin will find you out"?

With determined resolve, they returned to the city gate while it was still night and shared the good news (v. 10). The gatekeepers then relayed the information to others, one herald to another, until the chain of communication brought it to the king's servants at the royal palace. Today the best way to share the eternal good news is still by this same method, by a human chain that links each person to another. Mass communication, as important as it may be to the spread of the gospel, will never replace the traditional evangelistic method of one person sharing with another the good news of salvation.

His paranoia in high gear, the king suspected a Syrian plot; but he was willing to risk a reconnaissance patrol to see if the lepers' report was true (v. 14). There was no need to be concerned about the fate of the men who were sent to investigate. Their position was no more precarious than that of the people who remained in the starving city. If the Syrians killed them, they would still be no more dead than the other casualties (v. 13). So two chariots, presumably with two men in each one, went out to verify the incredible news. Then all the city ran out to claim God's deliverance, and Elisha's prediction came true. *"A seah of fine flour was sold for a shekel, and two seahs of barley for a shekel, according to the word of the Lord"* (v. 16).

To have any great gift—wealth, education, freedom—and not share it is evil. Using such gifts only for selfish purposes without regard for the needs of others is a serious sin. Never is that more true than with the gift of salvation. Do we think we are important enough that we are the ultimate end of God's mercy? Do we dare assume that God loved us enough that He sent Jesus to die for *our* sins alone? No, He saves us and empowers us so that we can become channels through which His blessings may flow to others. Paul wrote, "[God] comforts us . . . that we may be able to comfort those who are in any trouble, with the comfort with which we ourselves are comforted by God" (2 Cor. 1:4). We are to become links in His great chain of transmission, passing on our experience with the Lord to others.

As witnesses, we should also remember it is the message, not the messenger, that is important. God does not always choose great people to be His messengers. The Samaritan lepers were weak and unlikely instruments for God. They could only tell what they had seen and tasted, but that was enough. Just because you consider yourself ordinary and inadequate doesn't mean you are therefore excused from the responsibility of personal witnessing. God never requires His witnesses to be walking encyclopedias of theological knowledge, or champion debaters, or persuasive salesmen. He only expects us to be faithful conveyers of the message, the good news. No matter how weak or untalented you consider yourself to be, this passage reminds you, it is a sin to remain silent.

Survivalists have become a cult in this country in recent years. Persuaded that unavoidable calamity will soon befall the United States, that law and order will collapse, that our monetary system will become worthless, these gloomy pessimists organize to survive. They have retreats where they practice arranging their motor homes and campers like covered wagons in the Old West and circling them to ward off unnamed enemies. One advertiser on television in our city sells a year's supply of freeze-dried food for each member of the family as a survival strategy. The company promises to deliver your food supply in plain, unmarked containers, at night, under cover of darkness, so your neighbors will not be aware that you have a stockpile of supplies. That's shocking! Imagine having a secret storage closet full of food while your neighbors are starving.

The spiritual equivalent of this disturbing scenario is the Christian who, in full possession of the secret of eternal life, remains silent while millions are dying without Christ.

> Behold how many thousands still are lying,
> Bound in the darksome prison house of sin,
> With none to tell them of the Savior's dying,
> Or of the life He died for them to win?[20]

The Shunammite's Land Is Restored

8:1 Then Elisha spoke to the woman whose son he had restored to life, saying, "Arise and go, you and your household, and stay wherever you can; for the LORD has called for a famine, and furthermore, it will come upon the land for seven years."

2 So the woman arose and did according to the saying of the man of God, and she went with her household and dwelt in the land of the Philistines seven years.

3 It came to pass, at the end of seven years, that the woman returned from the land of the Philistines; and she went to make an appeal to the king for her house and for her land.

4 Then the king talked with Gehazi, the servant of the man of God, saying, "Tell me, please, all the great things Elisha has done."

5 Now it happened, as he was telling the king how he had restored the dead to life, that there was the woman whose son he had restored to life, appealing to the king for her house and for her land. And Gehazi said, "My lord, O king, this *is* the woman, and this *is* her son whom Elisha restored to life."

6 And when the king asked the woman, she told him. So the king appointed a certain officer for her, saying, "Restore all that *was* hers, and all the proceeds of the field from the day that she left the land until now."

2 Kings 8:1–6

When the woman from Shunem extended her generous hospitality to Elisha, she was making an investment that yielded a pretty good return! In 2 Kings 4:8–37 Elisha offered to secure royal favors for her, she miraculously bore a child in spite of her barrenness, and her son was raised from the dead. This passage tells us about two additional benefits that came to her because of her kindness to the prophet. First, Elisha warned her of an approaching famine and advised her to take prudent action (v. 1). Second, when the famine was over, Gehazi told the king who she was, and the king restored the property she had abandoned when she fled the famine.

It is difficult for those of us who have grown up in the midst of prosperity and plenty to imagine the serious consequences of a famine. In a country where our chief concern seems to be trying the latest fad diet to see if it will help us lose weight, it is hard to identify with the suffering of hunger. In this case the famine was serious enough to cause the woman and her household to leave everything behind and migrate to Philistia, the closest place unaffected by the lack of food. It was to this same country that Isaac had gone when famine struck Canaan in Gen. 26:1. The Shunammite's husband had been very old when she built the guest quarters for Elisha. Apparently he had died, and the woman was now in charge of the family.

During her seven-year absence, her house and property had been confiscated and occupied by strangers or possessive relatives who now refused to relinquish them. Or perhaps the king's officers had taken over her land under some legal arrangement. Once the famine was over, she began to take the steps necessary to reclaim her property.

There are several possible explanations for the appearance here of Gehazi, the servant of Elisha, evidently living in Samaria and engaging in relaxed and friendly conversation with the king of Israel. It could be that this event took place before Naaman was healed of his leprosy and Gehazi cursed with it. This is possible since the author of Kings doesn't always organize his material chronologically. Another explanation is that the king was so eager to know about Elisha that he was willing to risk his own health by talking to a leper. If Gehazi was one of the lepers in the preceding account of the siege of Samaria, then this conversation probably took place in the open market near the city gate, where public and judicial matters were often settled.[21] A third possibility is that since the word for leprosy in the Old Testament can be used for a wide variety of skin diseases, Gehazi's disease was not too serious, and he was now healed and back at work as Elisha's servant.[22]

The miracle in the story is the timing of the Shunammite's appeal to the king at the very moment when Gehazi was telling him about her (v. 5). Graciously, the king appointed a chamberlain to carry out his ruling to restore her land and to refund any money the property might have earned in her absence. This act was in striking contrast to the notorious land-grabbing of Jehoram's father, Ahab. The story provides another illustration of Elisha's spirit. He was never too busy with international affairs to take time to think of an individual who needed help.

When you read so many accounts in Scripture of famines and droughts in Canaan, it makes you wonder why God chose this dry and thirsty place for His people. A few years ago I traveled with the youth choir of the First Baptist Church of Dallas on a mission trip to Israel. Dr. W. A. Criswell, the pastor, had become ill and was not able to accompany the group, so it was my responsibility to bring biblical messages at the conclusion of the choir's musical performances. After a couple of demanding weeks in Israel, our tour group stopped in Interlaken, Switzerland, for a few days of recuperation before returning to the States. One of the young choir members looked around at the spectacular beauty of the Swiss Alps and, remembering the stark, barren landscape of most of Israel, asked, "Preacher, do you think God knew about this place when He called that other country the Promised Land?"

Why did God choose Israel as the Promised Land? Perhaps it was to better train His people for their spiritual task. The lack of material comforts and physical beauty would make it easier to arouse within them a hunger and thirst for God. Studies show that cultures in tropical climates, where people face very little struggle with their environment, seldom produce as many leaders as cultures in the deserts and mountains, where people must constantly struggle to survive.

When a tourist was being shown through one of the barren, rocky sections of Great Britain, he asked his host, "What in the world can you grow here?" His British host answered, "We grow great men." The unlikely soil of Canaan, with God's help, produced some of the greatest personalities in history.

The King of Syria Is Replaced

8:7 Then Elisha went to Damascus, and Ben-Hadad
king of Syria was sick; and it was told him, saying,
"The man of God has come here."
8 And the king said to Hazael, "Take a present in
your hand, and go to meet the man of God, and inquire of the LORD by him, saying, 'Shall I recover
from this disease?'"
9 So Hazael went to meet him and took a present
with him, of every good thing of Damascus, forty
camel-loads; and he came and stood before him, and
said, "Your son Ben-Hadad king of Syria has sent me
to you, saying, Shall I recover from this disease?'"
10 And Elisha said to him, "Go, say to him, 'You
shall certainly recover.' However the LORD has shown
me that he will really die."
11 Then he set his countenance in a stare until he
was ashamed; and the man of God wept.
12 And Hazael said, "Why is my lord weeping?"
And he answered, "Because I know the evil that you
will do to the children of Israel: Their strongholds
you will set on fire, and their young men you will
kill with the sword; and you will dash their children,
and rip open their women with child."
13 So Hazael said, "But what *is* your servant—a
dog, that he should do this gross thing?" And Elisha
answered, "The LORD has shown me that you *will
become* king over Syria."
14 Then he departed from Elisha, and came to his
master, who said to him, "What did Elisha say to you?"
And he answered, "He told me you would surely recover."
15 But it happened on the next day that he took a
thick cloth and dipped *it* in water, and spread *it* over
his face so that he died; and Hazael reigned in his
place.

2 Kings 8:7–15

Maclaren calls this "a strange, wild story."[23] And it is indeed a fascinating and unusual account. Hazael was probably one of

Ben-Hadad's chief ministers, maybe even his commander in chief. He was the one God had ordered Elijah to anoint as the next king of Syria (1 Kings 19:15). Now Elisha is sent to Damascus to carry out that commission.[24] Remembering how Naaman had been healed by Elisha, King Ben-Hadad, now ill himself, appealed to Elisha for help. Josephus explains the illness as a punishment from God because of the cruel treatment of the inhabitants of Samaria during the siege.[25]

How could Elisha the prophet travel in an enemy land without being harmed? Because the Syrians respected and feared him. They knew he was the one who had foreseen their troop movements, blinded their army, delivered Samaria from their siege, and healed Naaman. And now their king had appealed to him for a miracle. No one would dare harm him.

What an impressive caravan of gifts Ben-Hadad sent to Elisha with his question—forty camel-loads *"of every good thing of Damascus."* That would have included such treasures as apricots, dates, other food, trade goods, arms, costly furniture, and wine.[26] Slotki suggests that not every camel was fully loaded. All the gifts could probably have been carried on a few camels, but the use of forty was an ostentatious way of exaggerating the royal act of generosity.[27] There is a similar incident in Gen. 32:16 where Jacob employed just such a deceptive strategy when he sent peace gifts to Esau. He ordered his servants to leave a big space between the successive droves of camels to make the train seem longer and more impressive. But even without such an enhancement, the royal offerings to Elisha were undoubtedly most impressive, though not incredible when one considers that they came from the king. He had the wealth of the city at his command, and he was desperate.

At first, it seems as though Elisha answered the king's question with an enormous contradiction. *"Shall I recover from this disease?"* (v. 9) was the question. Elisha's answer was, *"Go, say to him, 'You shall certainly recover.' However the Lord has shown me that he will really die"* (v. 10). Nevertheless, it was no contradiction. Both prophecies came true. The illness would not be fatal, but the king would die of other causes. He would recover from the illness, but he would suffer death at the hand of an assassin.

In verse 11, the Hebrew construction makes it very difficult to determine the subject of each of the verbs. Probably Elisha was the one who *"set his countenance,"* staring at Hazael until he, Hazael, was ashamed. However, some hold the view that Elisha fell into the sort of ecstatic, prophetic trance sometimes associated with ancient oracles.[28] Others believe it was Hazael who stared at Elisha, his features unmoved, so that Elisha would not detect any emotion nor read his thoughts.[29] But the best interpretation seems to be that Elisha knew Hazael wanted to be king and was already plotting Ben-Hadad's assassination. The prophet stared at Hazael until, embarrassed, the pretender to the throne turned away, ashamed that Elisha had read his thoughts. Verse 11 literally says, "He caused his face to stand and be put."

Elisha then recited the unthinkable atrocities that Hazael would later commit (2 Kings 10:32–33; 13:3; cf. Hos. 10:14; Amos 1:3, 13). But Hazael seemed unaware that such cruelty lurked in his personality, and he was insulted that Elisha had thus accused him. Isn't it true that none of us knows the depth of sin he or she has the potential of committing? The most horrendous evil may lie dormant in the most unlikely personality, and perhaps most people are good basically because they've never been tried and tested to see what the limits are. This fact should make us reluctant to judge and criticize others and make us humble about our own goodness. We should respond like the great saint who, seeing the condemned murderer, said, "There but for the grace of God go I."

Immediately, Hazael delivered Elisha's cryptic answer to the king, and then, the very next day, Ben-Hadad died a most mysterious death. Again, in verse 15, the subjects and verbs are difficult to match, but it appears that Hazael placed the thick wet cloth over the face of King Ben-Hadad and smothered him. The word for "cloth" here is *makbēr* from the Hebrew root meaning "intertwine or weave." It denotes a twisted bath cloth, woven so thick that when it was soaked in water no one could possibly breathe through it. Was Ben-Hadad's death an accident while he was bathing? If it was an accident, the cloth was spread on his face to cool his fever, and he died by suffocation accidentally. If it was murder, which seems more likely, then the cloth was intentionally held over the king's face by Hazael to kill him.

An ancient Assyrian inscription, called the Berlin inscription, says,

"Hazael, the son of nobody, seized the throne." This designation indicates that he was a usurper with no dynastic line.[30]

NOTES

1. Norman H. Snaith, Ralph W. Sockman, and Raymond Calkins, "The First and Second Books of Kings," in *The Interpreter's Bible,* vol. 3 (Nashville: Abingdon Press, 1954), 216.
2. Gwilym H. Jones, *1 and 2 Kings,* New Century Bible Commentary, ed. Ronald E. Clements (Grand Rapids: Eerdmans, 1984), 424.
3. C. F. Keil, *The Books of the Kings,* Biblical Commentary on the Old Testament, ed. C. F. Keil and F. Delitzsch, vol. 4 (Grand Rapids: Eerdmans, 1950), 324.
4. Jones, 424.
5. Keil, 324.
6. Clara H. Scott, "Open My Eyes that I May See," in *Baptist Hymnal* (Nashville: Convention Press, 1975), no. 358.
7. I. W. Slotki, *Kings* (London: Soncino Press, 1950), 198.
8. Jones, 424.
9. T. R. Hobbs, *2 Kings,* Word Biblical Commentary, ed. John D. W. Watts, vol. 13 (Waco, TX: Word Books, 1985), 78.
10. Jones, 429.
11. Slotki, 200.
12. Charles F. Burney, *Notes on the Hebrew Text of the Books of Kings* (Oxford: Clarendon Press, 1903), 287.
13. Hobbs, 79.
14. John Gray, *I and II Kings,* Old Testament Library (Philadelphia: Westminster, 1963), 467.
15. Slotki, 200.
16. Burney, 287.
17. Snaith, Sockman, and Calkins, 219.
18. Slotki, 203.
19. Gray, 472.
20. Mary Ann Thomson, "O Zion, Haste," *Baptist Hymnal,* no. 295.
21. Slotki, 208.
22. Hobbs, 100. See also E. V. Hulse, "The Nature of Biblical 'Leprosy' and the Use of Alternative Medical Terms in Modern Translations of the Bible," *Palestine Exploration Quarterly* 107 (1975): 87.

23. Alexander Maclaren, *Second Samuel and the Books of Kings*, Expositions of Holy Scripture, vol. 2 (Grand Rapids, Eerdmans, 1952), 352.
24. Keil, 334.
25. Hobbs, 101.
26. Jones, 443.
27. Slotki, 209.
28. M. Pierce Matheney and Roy Honeycutt, "1-2 Kings," in *The Broadman Bible Commentary*, ed. Clifton J. Allen, vol. 3 (Nashville: Broadman, 1970), 247.
29. Slotki, 209.
30. Matheney and Honeycutt, 246.

CHAPTER FOURTEEN

The Reigns of Jehoram and Ahaziah of Judah and Jehu of Israel

2 Kings 8:16–10:36

Jehoram Reigns in Judah

8:16 Now in the fifth year of Joram the son of Ahab,
king of Israel, Jehoshaphat *having been* king of Judah,
Jehoram the son of Jehoshaphat began to reign as
king of Judah.
17 He was thirty-two years old when he became
king, and he reigned eight years in Jerusalem.
18 And he walked in the way of the kings of Israel,
just as the house of Ahab had done, for the daughter
of Ahab was his wife; and he did evil in the sight of
the LORD.
19 Yet the LORD would not destroy Judah, for the
sake of his servant David, as He promised him to
give a lamp to him *and* his sons forever.
20 In his days Edom revolted against Judah's authority, and made a king over themselves.
21 So Joram went to Zair, and all his chariots with
him. Then he rose by night and attacked the Edomites
who had surrounded him and the captains of the
chariots; and the troops fled to their tents.
22 Thus Edom has been in revolt against Judah's authority to this day. And Libnah revolted at that time.
23 Now the rest of the acts of Joram, and all that
he did, *are* they not written in the book of the chronicles of the kings of Judah?
24 So Joram rested with his fathers, and was buried

with his fathers in the City of David. Then Ahaziah
his son reigned in his place.

2 Kings 8:16–24

Having suspended his story of the kings of Israel and Judah in order to insert the lengthy account of Elisha and his miracles, the author of Kings now returns to the familiar format of the royal biographies. In 1 Kings 22:50, Jehoshaphat the son of Asa ended his twenty-five-year reign in Judah, and his son Jehoram reigned in his place. That is all that is said about Jehoram there. It is not until we reach the passage before us, 2 Kings 8:16, that the story of Jehoram continues. He became king of Judah while Ahaziah the son of Ahab was still on the throne in Israel. Two years later, Ahaziah died; and since he had no son, his brother Jehoram, another son of Ahab, ascended to the throne of Israel.

So for a while, coincidentally, both Israel and Judah had kings named Jehoram. Because of the confusion this causes, some early manuscripts slightly altered the spelling of one or the other of the two names in order to tell them apart. For that reason, some translations use the spelling "Joram" for the king of Israel and "Jehoram" for the king of Judah—or vice versa—adding to the confusion. To make matters even worse, when Jehoram of Judah died, he was succeeded by his son Ahaziah. This Ahaziah must be carefully distinguished from Ahab's son Ahazlah, whom Jehoram of Israel followed on the throne. It is quite a challenge to keep this puzzle unraveled.

This passage deals with the reign of Jehoram the son of Jehoshaphat. He became king of Judah at the age of thirty-two. Verse 16 follows the usual formula for presenting the kings of Judah except that each of the other accounts mentions the name of the new king's mother, the queen mother of the land. The omission here probably indicates that Jehoram's mother was dead. Nevertheless, the Scriptures give great importance to the role of parental influence on the kings of Israel and Judah, especially the role of the king's mother.

Recently, in the historic city of Fredricksburg, Virginia, we visited the home of Mary Ball Washington, the mother of our first president. The main part of the house has been beautifully maintained, so the dwelling and the grounds appear almost exactly as they did when George moved his mother there in the eighteenth century. In fact, the boxwood plants in the backyard are the very ones Mary Washington planted two hundred years ago!

Our guide took us to the "bed-sitter," a combination bedroom and sitting room just off the main hallway, where Mrs. Washington spent most of her later years. There she reminded us that on the very wooden floors where we were standing, the first president of the United States stood in 1789. He stopped by this house on the way to his inauguration to greet his mother and seek her blessing for his new work.

Washington always felt he owed a great debt to his mother for what he had become and for the great accomplishments of his life. Perhaps no example has been used more often than that one of Mother's Day, when we remember the importance of maternal influence not only on great leaders, but on ordinary persons as well. The story of the kings reinforces that truth.

Apparently in order to make peace between his country and Israel, Jehoram's father, Jehoshaphat, had arranged a marriage between him and Athaliah, the daughter of Ahab of Israel. (She would therefore have been the sister of the other Jehoram. More confusion!) It was her wicked influence that led Jehoram astray. The parallel passage in Chronicles says Jehoram killed all his brothers and "others of the princes of Israel" to ensure that he would have no competition on the throne (2 Chron. 21:4). Josephus expands on this, indicating he committed the murders at the prompting of Athaliah.[1] Through her influence the worship of Baal pervaded the court of Jerusalem, leading to the condemnation of both her husband, Jehoram, and their son Ahaziah (v. 18; cf. 2 Kings 8:26). Her wickedness eventually angered the people of Judah, and after the deaths of her husband and her son, and after a brief reign herself as queen, Athaliah was executed in Jerusalem (2 Kings 11:16). Because of this widespread apostasy, had it not been for God's promise to "*give a lamp*" to David and his sons forever, the kingdom of Judah might have been destroyed (v. 19). This "Davidic covenant," described in 1 Kings 11:36, kept alive the hope of God's presence with the people through all the dark days of the nation's troubled history.

It was a similar hope, guaranteed by God's promise, that sustained Joshua in the days of the conquest. God had promised him, "As I was with Moses, so I will be with you. I will not leave you nor forsake you" (Josh. 1:5). That promise made all the difference in the world to this ordinary leader who showed such extraordinary courage when he guided the people of Israel into an unpredictable future. He and they had every reason to be afraid, but they knew God would not forsake them, and that assurance gave them courage to go forward.

Uncertain futures are always cause for fear and hesitation. When I came from the pastorate in Atlanta to the seminary presidency in Fort Worth, I experienced that uncertainty. It was all so new, so unfamiliar. Like the Israelites preparing to cross the Jordan, I had "never passed this way before" (Josh. 3:4). I learned anew how important prayer is and how it gives us the privilege of claiming God's promise that He will never forsake us.

Adding to the anxiety was a news report in the Southern Baptist news journal in Alaska. Like most of the other state denominational papers, the *Alaska Baptist Messenger* ran a story about the election of the new president of Southwestern Seminary, and with it they published my picture. In the same issue they printed a very interesting story about a rodeo star from the west Texas town of Silverton. Walter Arnold is a world champion steer roper who is also a dedicated Baptist layman with an inspiring testimony. They had his picture in the paper too. But the problem was, they got the stories and the pictures reversed. Under my picture the headline read, "World Champion Steer Roper Shares His Faith on the Rodeo Circuit." And under Walter Arnold's typical rodeo picture with cowboy hat and twirling lariat it said, "The New President of Southwestern Seminary!" When they sent me the clippings, I wondered what kind of job I was facing out there in west Texas!

It is always fearful to face an uncertain future, but when you know God personally and remember that He has promised, "I will never leave you nor forsake you," you can go forward with courage. So Israel remembered God's promise, His covenant: "My servant David will always have a lamp before Me in Jerusalem, the city which I have chosen for Myself." That gave them hope to go forward.

Since David's time, neighboring Edom had been ruled by a governor appointed by the king of Judah. Now, for some reason, the Edomites felt that it was a propitious time to rebel against Judah and set up *"a king over themselves"* (v. 20). Gray suggests that Edom's boldness was based on the incident in 2 Kings 3 when Israel and Judah drafted Edom to help them put down a rebellion in the nation of Moab. When Moab prevailed, Edom may have assumed that Israel and Judah were sufficiently weak to allow her own rebellion to succeed as well.[2]

Immediately, Jehoram dispatched his army to a city called Zair, where he intended to put down the Edomite revolt. The exact location of Zair is uncertain. The name means "crossed over" and may indicate it was just across the border into Edom.[3] Some suggest it may have been the town of Zior northeast of Hebron.[4] What happened there is not clear. The account in verse 21 suggests that a superior Edomite army surrounded Jehoram and his chariots. In a desperate counterattack during the night, Jehoram broke through the enemy lines and retreated back to Judah, leaving his infantry to disband in defeat. They fled *"to their tents,"* that is, to their homes.[5] The revolt was successful, therefore, and Edom continued to be free from Judah's dominance *"to this day"* (v. 22). This phrase indicates that the author of Kings wrote his book some time after the events took place.

Encouraged by Jehoram's humiliating defeat, another of his enemies revolted as well. Libnah, a royal city of the Canaanites on the frontier of Judah, also threw off Judean control (v. 22). So King Jehoram was remembered only for his apostasy and his military weakness. His death, barely mentioned here, is described in detail in 2 Chronicles 21. Elijah wrote him a letter condemning him for his sins and predicting that a calamitous disease would come upon his nation, and he himself would die a terrible death (2 Chron. 21:12–15). That prophecy was fulfilled when at the age of forty Jehoram was struck with a fatal intestinal disease. "His intestines came out because of his sickness; so he died in severe pain" (2 Chron. 21:19).

Jehoram was buried in Jerusalem, but the Chronicles passage clearly states that it was not in the tombs of the kings of Judah. His twenty-two-year-old son Ahaziah became king in his place and reigned over Judah only one year.

AHAZIAH REIGNS IN JUDAH

> 8:25 In the twelfth year of Joram the son of Ahab, king of Israel, Ahaziah the son of Jehoram, king of Judah, began to reign.

26 Ahaziah *was* twenty-two years old when he became king, and he reigned one year in Jerusalem. His mother's name *was* Athaliah the granddaughter of Omri, king of Israel.

27 And he walked in the way of the house of Ahab, and did evil in the sight of the LORD, like the house of Ahab, for he *was* the son-in-law of the house of Ahab.

28 Now he went with Joram the son of Ahab to war against Hazael king of Syria at Ramoth Gilead; and the Syrians wounded Joram.

29 Then King Joram went back to Jezreel to recover from the wounds which the Syrians had inflicted on him at Ramah, when he fought against Hazael king of Syria. And Ahaziah the son of Jehoram, king of Judah, went down to see Joram the son of Ahab in Jezreel, because he was sick.

2 Kings 8:25–29

The typical formula for introducing the kings of Judah is followed in verse 26. Ahaziah's mother Athaliah was the daughter of Ahab and the granddaughter of Omri. The King James translation "daughter of Omri" is explained by the fact that in Hebrew, daughter and granddaughter are used interchangeably.[6] Since Jehoram was forty years old when he died, his son Ahaziah must have been born when he was only twenty years old. And since Ahaziah was the youngest of several sons, Jehoram must have married Athaliah at a very early age. Chronicles adds that she counseled her son to do wickedly.

It was these complicated family entanglements that apparently led to Ahaziah's death. He agreed to accompany his uncle, the other Jehoram, king of Israel, in a joint military campaign against the Syrians at the city of Ramoth Gilead. This was the same disputed city where Ahab, Ahaziah's grandfather, had been mortally wounded by the Syrians. It may be, therefore, that the assault on Ramoth Gilead was motivated by revenge. Wounded in the battle, Jehoram retreated to his royal palace in the city of Jezreel. Later, King Ahaziah traveled to visit his recuperating ally, and while he was there, he and Jehoram were killed by Jehu (2 Kings 9:14ff.). It seems ironic that the story ends at Jezreel, in the very place where Ahab appropriated Naboth's vineyard, the very act that set in motion the events that culminated in the destruction of Ahab's apostate dynasty.

ELISHA ANOINTS JEHU OF ISRAEL

9:1 And Elisha the prophet called one of the sons of
the prophets, and said to him, "Get yourself ready,
take this flask of oil in your hand, and go to Ramoth
Gilead.
2 "Now when you arrive at that place, look there
for Jehu the son of Jehoshaphat, the son of Nimshi,
and go in and make him rise up from among his associates, and take him to an inner room.
3 "Then take the flask of oil, and pour *it* on his
head, and say, 'Thus says the LORD: "I have anointed
you king over Israel."' Then open the door and flee,
and do not delay."
4 So the young man, the servant of the prophet,
went to Ramoth Gilead.
5 And when he arrived, there *were* the captains of
the army sitting; and he said, "I have a message for
you, commander." Jehu said, "For which *one* of us?"
And he said, "For you, commander."
6 Then he arose and went into the house. And he
poured the oil on his head, and said to him, "Thus
says the LORD God of Israel: 'I have anointed you
king over the people of the LORD, over Israel.
7 'You shall strike down the house of Ahab your
master, that I may avenge the blood of My servants
the prophets, and the blood of all the servants of the
LORD, at the hand of Jezebel.
8 'For the whole house of Ahab shall perish; and I
will cut off from Ahab all the males in Israel, both
bond and free.
9 'So I will make the house of Ahab like the house
of Jeroboam the son of Nebat, and like the house of
Baasha the son of Ahijah.
10 'The dogs shall eat Jezebel on the plot *of ground*
at Jezreel, and *there shall be* none to bury *her.*'" And
he opened the door and fled.
11 Then Jehu came out to the servants of his master, and *one* said to him, "*Is* all well? Why did this
madman come to you?" And he said to them, "You
know the man and his babble."
12 And they said, "A lie! Tell us now." So he said,

"Thus and thus he spoke to me, saying 'Thus says the LORD: "I have anointed you king over Israel."'"

13 Then each man hastened to take his garment and put *it* under him on the top of the steps; and they blew trumpets, saying, "Jehu is King!"

2 Kings 9:1–13

Here the Israelite dynasty of Omri and his infamous descendants Ahab, Ahaziah, and Jehoram comes to an abrupt end, and a new dynasty begins under Jehu. What Elijah had prophesied in 1 Kings 19:16 and 21:19 against the house of Ahab is fulfilled.

The young prophet sent to anoint Jehu in verse 1 is identified in the *Seder ʿOlam* as Jonah.[7] Elisha instructed him, *"Get yourself ready"*—that is, "Put on your traveling clothes." The word for *"flask"* here is "pak," an onomatopoeic word imitating the gurgling sound of liquid being poured out of a bottle.[8] This is the only place where the narrator calls Elisha *"the prophet."* He is usually identified as "the man of God."

"Jehu" means "Yahweh is He." He was probably the commander of the army of Israel, which was still occupying the city of Ramoth Gilead while King Jehoram was recuperating in Jezreel. His father, Jehoshaphat, is not the same as the Judean king by that name. It appears that his grandfather Nimshi was more famous than his father because later Jehu is known as the son of Nimshi (2 Kings 9:20). "Nimshi" means "the weasel," which might be a nickname.[9]

Jehu is mentioned twice in the cuneiform inscriptions on the Black Obelisk of Shalmaneser III. This inscription, translated in 1851, tells how Jehu (called the son of Omri) brought tribute to the Assyrian king. There is even a picture of Jehu's entourage presenting the tribute to the Assyrian monarch. It may be that Jehu solicited the aid of Assyria to fight off the encroachments of Hazael of Syria.[10] The Shalmaneser inscriptions also give us an objective date for this period in Hebrew chronology, 841 B.C.[11]

Jehu was the only ruler of the Northern Kingdom to be anointed. This ceremonial application of olive oil was a symbol of the *bĕrākâ*, the blessing of God. Jehoram's failures showed that he no longer had that blessing; it now belonged to Jehu. Elisha's insistence that the anointing ceremony be secret would allow the new king to choose the right time to raise the standard of his revolt without alerting

Jehoram. The surprise would prevent the king from making preparation to oppose it.

When Elisha's messenger arrived, he found the captains of Israel's army sitting in a council with Jehu, their commander. Possibly they were already plotting a military overthrow of Jehoram's regime. If so, they were in a receptive mood for the announcement that Jehu was God's choice for the throne.[12] Verse 6 implies that the generals were holding their council in the outer courtyard of the house. So the servant, following Elisha's instructions, led Jehu inside to the privacy of a room before he poured the oil on his head and repeated to him the words of Elisha's prophecy. Actually, Elisha's prophecy was a precise restatement of Elijah's prediction years before (cf. 1 Kings 14:10; 21:23). The graphic and explicit language used by the King James Version in verse 8 is the literal translation of the Hebrew word for "male."

Elisha's messenger must have been well known by the military officers. They were obviously acquainted with his peculiarities, calling him a *"madman"* and saying, *"You know the man and his babble."* But even though they considered him something of a lunatic, they respected his message as divine proclamation. *"Servants of his master"* in verse 11 refers to those who served King Jehoram, who was Jehu's *"master."*

Why was Jehu so reluctant to reveal to his comrades what the messenger had said and done inside the house? It was probably not humility. More than likely Jehu was testing the loyalty of Jehoram's generals by revealing the facts a little at a time and watching carefully their reactions. One rash step, and he would be labeled a traitor and arrested. But as it turned out, he had nothing to fear. The men were obviously anxious to follow him as their new leader. Placing their cloaks under Jehu was a symbol of their submission to his authority, similar to the response of the people to Jesus as He entered Jerusalem before His crucifixion. Other interpreters believe the cloaks were used to make an improvised throne upon which the captains elevated Jehu above them.[13] They blew the shophar, the ram's horn, with its monotonous tone, which was used on occasions of warning or festivity. Then they raised the coronation shout, *mālak yēhûʾ*, meaning *"Jehu is King!"* (Compare the same activities when Solomon was proclaimed king in 1 Kings 1:34.) Israel now had a new leader and new hope for the future.

Surely this experience of God's call and Jehu's anointing was an encouragement to him in the years ahead. During dark days, the king would remember, "I didn't choose this task; God anointed me for it. He will surely, therefore, see me through." At the seminary, we make sure all our students are there because they believe God has called them to ministry and led them to this school. The ministry is not a profession to be chosen in the way that one chooses law, or medicine, or business. We believe no minister is likely to succeed without a firm conviction that God has taken the initiative in "anointing," or "calling," that minister for His service. Enormous confidence comes to those who know they are serving not because the ministry is profitable, or easy, or even fulfilling, but because God touched them in some providential experience and chose them for the task. When the going gets rough, such a person can say, "Lord, You got me into this, now I look to You to get me through." Surely, King Jehu came to such dark moments in his own life and remembered the anointing ceremony in Ramoth Gilead.

JEHU SLAYS JEHORAM OF ISRAEL AND CLAIMS THE THRONE

> 9:14 So Jehu the son of Jehoshaphat, the son of Nimshi, conspired against Joram. (Now Joram had been defending Ramoth Gilead, he and all Israel, against Hazael king of Syria.
>
> 15 But King Joram had returned to Jezreel to recover from the wounds which the Syrians had inflicted on him when he fought with Hazael king of Syria.) And Jehu said, "If you are so minded, let no one leave *or* escape from the city to go and tell *it* in Jezreel."
>
> 16 So Jehu rode in a chariot and went to Jezreel, for Joram was laid up there; and Ahaziah king of Judah had come down to see Joram.
>
> 17 Now a watchman stood on the tower in Jezreel, and he saw the company of Jehu as he came, and said, "I see a company of men." And Joram said, "Get a horseman and send him to meet them, and let him say, '*Is it* peace?'"
>
> 18 So the horseman went to meet him, and said,

"Thus says the king: '*Is it* peace?'" And Jehu said, "What have you to do with peace? Turn around and follow me." So the watchman reported, saying, "The messenger went to them, but is not coming back."

19 Then he sent out a second horseman who came to them, and said, "Thus says the king: '*Is it* peace?'" And Jehu answered, "What have you to do with peace? Turn around and follow me."

20 So the watchman reported, saying, "He went up to them and is not coming back; and the driving *is* like the driving of Jehu the son of Nimshi, for he drives furiously!"

21 Then Joram said, "Make ready." And his chariot was made ready. Then Joram king of Israel and Ahaziah king of Judah went out, each in his chariot; and they went out to meet Jehu, and met him on the property of Naboth the Jezreelite.

22 Now it happened, when Joram saw Jehu, that he said, "*Is it* peace, Jehu?" So he answered, "What peace, as long as the harlotries of your mother Jezebel and her witchcraft *are so* many?"

23 Then Joram turned around and fled, and said to Ahaziah, "Treachery, Ahaziah!"

24 Now Jehu drew his bow with full strength and shot Jehoram between his arms; and the arrow came out at his heart, and he sank down in his chariot.

25 Then *Jehu* said to Bidkar his captain, "Pick *him* up, *and* throw him into the tract of the field of Naboth the Jezreelite; for remember, when you and I were riding together behind Ahab his father, that the LORD laid this burden upon him:

26 'Surely I saw yesterday the blood of Naboth and the blood of his sons,' says the LORD, 'and I will repay you in this plot,' says the LORD. Now therefore, take *and* throw him on the plot *of ground,* according to the word of the LORD."

2 Kings 9:14–26

Using a parenthetical insertion, the author reminds us of the events that sent Jehoram, wounded in the battle of Ramoth Gilead, to Jezreel to recuperate (2 Kings 8:28–29). *"All Israel"* in verse 14 refers to the entire army of Israel, most of whom were still occupying Ramoth Gilead. It was with the commanders of this army that Jehu *"conspired"* to overthrow Jehoram (v. 14).

The success of the coup d'état depended on surprise and secrecy, so Jehu said to his fellow soldiers, "If you really are with me, then don't let anybody leave Ramoth Gilead to warn Jehoram in Jezreel" (v. 15). Ramoth Gilead was on the border between Israel and Syria, and Jezreel was forty miles west, across the Jordan, near Megiddo.

Scattered along Jezreel's city wall were a number of watchtowers. The one in verse 17 was obviously on the east side of the city where the plain falls away toward the valley.[14] What did the watchman see when he reported, *"I see a company of men"*? The word *"company"* means literally "dust" and may indicate that he first saw the dust cloud stirred up by Jehu's approaching troops. The Septuagint translates the passage this way.[15] Since it took such a long time for the approaching army to get close enough to Jezreel for the watchman to recognize the driving of Jehu, it makes more sense to understand that the watchman saw first the dust then later the army.

Two mounted horsemen were successively sent out to investigate, and each one, instead of returning, joined Jehu's rebels. Then when the guard in the watchtower recognized Jehu, Jehoram himself boldly rode out to meet him, driving his own chariot. He was so sure of Jehu's loyalty that he didn't even take a driver or a military escort. Ahaziah, the hapless king of Judah, who had traveled to Jezreel to visit the ailing Jehoram, also boldly drove his own chariot behind Jehoram's to see why Jehu was approaching the city in such haste. The two kings may have feared that a Syrian counterattack had broken Israel's occupation of Ramoth Gilead and had driven Jehu and the army back to Jezreel in retreat. It was a rash move on the part of the two rulers. By the time Jehoram realized what was happening and cried out, *"Treachery, Ahaziah!"* it was too late.

Verse 20 has been the basis of many a joke about wild driving. The reckless chariot driving of the commander in chief of Israel's army has become a legendary symbol of reckless automobile driving today. *"He drives furiously"* means "he drives with madness." In fact the word is from the same root as "madman" in verse 11. However, it is interesting to note that Josephus finds the root in another word, which means "quiet." Both his translation and the ancient

Targum indicate that Jehu drove "leisurely and in good order."[16] If this translation is correct, it would ruin the humorous interpretations of the verse which have become so popular.

It seemed a coincidence that the two kings met Jehu on the ground of Naboth's vineyard, now no longer cultivated, but a "portion" set aside for other use. But was it a coincidence? The location was actually a fulfillment of God's promised judgment. Just as God had said, Ahab's descendants were about to reap the whirlwind at the very site that symbolized Ahab's greed and apostasy.

Jehu sharply rebuked Jehoram for the sins of his mother Jezebel and the rest of the dynasty. *"Harlotries"* and *"witchcraft"* are figurative terms often used by the prophets for idolatry and faithlessness. The worship of Baal was essentially a fertility cult that featured cultic prostitution, so the terms were very appropriate here.[17] Having condemned and sentenced Jehoram, Jehu then drew his bow and carried out the execution of the wicked king himself. *"With full strength"* means literally "to the full stretch of his arm."[18]

The quotation from Elijah in verse 26 is one Jehu and his captain Bidkar had overheard when they were young soldiers in Ahab's army. At that time Jehu was not a commander, nor even a warrior, but merely a driver in a three-man chariot team: warrior, driver, and shield bearer.[19]

The swift and terrible retribution that overtook King Jehoram is one of many illustrations in Scripture of the principle that the wages of sin is death.

JEHU SLAYS AHAZIAH OF JUDAH AND JEZEBEL

9:27 But when Ahaziah king of Judah saw *this,* he fled by the road to Beth Haggan. So Jehu pursued him, and said, "Shoot him also in the chariot." *And they shot him* at the Ascent of Gur, which is by Ibleam. Then he fled to Megiddo, and died there.

28 And his servants carried him in the chariot to Jerusalem, and buried him in his tomb with his fathers in the City of David.

29 In the eleventh year of Joram the son of Ahab, Ahaziah had become king over Judah.

30 Now when Jehu had come to Jezreel, Jezebel heard *of it;* and she put paint on her eyes and adorned her head, and looked through a window.

31 Then, as Jehu entered at the gate, she said, "*Is it* peace, Zimri, murderer of your master?"

32 And he looked up at the window, and said, "Who *is* on my side? Who?" So two *or* three eunuchs looked out at him.

33 Then he said, "Throw her down." So they threw her down, and *some* of her blood spattered on the wall and on the horses; and he trampled her underfoot.

34 And when he had gone in, he ate and drank. Then he said, "Go now, see to this accursed *woman,* and bury her, for she was a king's daughter."

35 So they went to bury her, but they found no more of her than the skull and the feet and the palms of *her* hands.

36 Therefore, they came back and told him. And he said, "This *is* the word of the LORD, which He spoke by His servant Elijah the Tishbite, saying, 'On the plot of *ground* at Jezreel dogs shall eat the flesh of Jezebel;

37 'and the corpse of Jezebel shall be as refuse on the surface of the field, in the plot at Jezreel, so that they shall not say, "Here *lies* Jezebel."'"

2 Kings 9:27–37

Since King Ahaziah of Judah was a blood relative of Ahab, Jehu's purge included him too. (Ahab's daughter Athaliah was his mother, so he was Ahab's grandson.) Beth Haggan literally means "garden house" (v. 27). It was probably on the site of modern Jenin, about seven miles south of Jezreel on the road to Samaria and Jerusalem. Ibleam is modern Belameh, a mile south of Jenin.[20] According to Chronicles, Ahaziah escaped to Samaria and was hiding there when the soldiers found him and brought him to Jehu, who then had him killed. This account can be harmonized with the account here in verse 27.

He was buried in Jerusalem in the tomb which had been prepared for him during his lifetime. Chronicles adds that this royal burial of an otherwise undeserving king was allowed because he was the grandson (literally, "son") of the respected King Jehoshaphat (2 Chron. 22:9).

Next on Jehu's list of condemned enemies was Jezebel, who must have been quite elderly by this time. However, the years had not softened her brazen wickedness. Her eye make-up in verse 30 was antimony, or stibium, a black powder used by women of the East to darken the edges of their eyelids and eyebrows. (Ancient eye shadow and eye liner!) It had the effect of enlarging the appearance of the eyes and giving them added brilliance.[21] The Hebrew here is literally "she treated her eyes with antimony." The archaeologist Rosellini found such eye paint in early Egyptian graves.[22] Jezebel's reason for this adornment was not to entice Jehu but to prepare herself to die as a queen.[23] She showed icy composure, knowing she was about to be killed.

With typical sarcasm, Jezebel addresses Jehu as *"Zimri, murderer of your master."* Zimri was the one who murdered King Elah and those who remained in the family of Baasha (1 Kings 16:10). He managed to hold the throne only a few days and committed suicide. Jezebel was obviously reminding Jehu of Zimri's fate and perhaps even threatening him.[24]

"Who is on my side? Who?" was Jehu's way of saying, "Is there anybody else up there who is loyal to me?" Following her violent death, Jehu drove his horses and chariot over her body and then casually went inside to eat and drink, showing intentional disdain for the queen (v. 34). Later he relented a little and ordered her burial. *"She was a king's daughter"* is a reference to the fact that Jezebel was the daughter of Ethbaal, the king of the Sidonians. By then, however, the dogs had already devoured most of her body in fulfillment of the prophecy in 1 Kings 21:23.

Jehu Slays the Families of Ahab and Ahaziah

10:1 Now Ahab had seventy sons in Samaria. And Jehu wrote and sent letters to Samaria, to the rulers of Jezreel, to the elders, and to those who reared Ahab's *sons,* saying:

2 Now as soon as this letter comes to you, since your master's sons *are* with you, and you have chariots and horses, a fortified city also, and weapons.

3 choose the best qualified of your master's sons,

set *him* on his father's throne, and fight for your
master's house.

4 But they were exceedingly afraid, and said,
"Look, two kings could not stand up to him; how
then can we stand?"

5 And he who *was* in charge of the house, and he
who *was* in charge of the city, the elders also, and
those who reared *the sons,* sent to Jehu, saying, "We
are your servants, we will do all you tell us; but we
will not make anyone king. Do *what is* good in your
sight."

6 Then he wrote a second letter to them, saying:

> If you *are* for me and will obey my voice, take
> the heads of the men, your master's sons, and
> come to me at Jezreel by this time tomorrow.

Now the king's sons, seventy persons, *were* with the
great men of the city, *who* were rearing them.

7 So it was, when the letter came to them, that
they took the king's sons and slaughtered seventy
persons, put their heads in baskets and sent *them* to
him at Jezreel.

8 Then a messenger came and told him, saying,
"They have brought the heads of the king's sons."
And he said, "Lay them in two heaps at the entrance
of the gate until morning."

9 So it was, in the morning, that he went out and
stood, and said to all the people, "You *are* righteous.
Indeed I conspired against my master and killed him;
but who killed all these?

10 "Know now that nothing shall fall to the earth
of the word of the LORD which the LORD spoke concerning the House of Ahab; for the LORD has done
what He spoke by His servant Elijah."

11 So Jehu killed all who remained of the house of
Ahab in Jezreel, and all his great men and his close
acquaintances and his priests, until he left him none
remaining.

12 And he arose and departed and went to Samaria. On the way, at Beth Eked of the Shepherds,

13 Jehu met with the brothers of Ahaziah king of
Judah, and said, "Who *are* you?" So they answered,
"We *are* the brothers of Ahaziah; we have come down

to greet the sons of the king and the sons of the queen mother."

14 And he said, "Take them alive!" So they took them alive, and killed them at the well of Beth Eked, forty-two men; and he left none of them.

15 Now when he departed from there, he met Jehonadab the son of Rechab, *coming* to meet him; and he greeted him and said to him, "Is your heart right, as my heart is toward your heart?" And Jehonadab answered, "It is." *Jehu said,* "If it is, give *me* your hand." So he gave *him* his hand, and he took him up to him into the chariot.

16 Then he said, "Come with me, and see my zeal for the LORD." So they had him ride in his chariot.

17 And when he came to Samaria, he killed all who remained to Ahab in Samaria, till he had destroyed them, according to the word of the LORD which He spoke to Elijah.

2 Kings 10:1–17

Jehu's bloody annihilation of the descendants of Ahab was not over. Since Ahab had been dead about fourteen years, even his youngest sons would be at least fourteen and would not need foster parents or guardians. So the seventy sons of Ahab in verse 1 must include grandsons and perhaps great-grandsons too. The rulers of Jezreel must have fled their city when the king was killed and taken refuge in Samaria to plan their next move in the light of the revolt.

Here is another interesting example of an official letter from the ancient world (vv. 2–3). In typical fashion the writer of Kings omits the introductory words and begins with the body of the letter. The word *"now"* is the usual term for the beginning of the main message of such correspondence.[25] *"Your master"* in verse 2 is a reference to Ahab. Jehu, in other words, was throwing down the gauntlet, challenging them to choose the best of Ahab's descendants, declare him king, and defend him. If they did, the army, which was loyal to Jehu and which far outnumbered any troops in Samaria, would immediately attack the city and remove the new king. If they backed down, which they in fact did, then they were surrendering to Jehu. He had them in a cruel dilemma.

The elders' statement that even two kings could not withstand

Jehu referred to Jehoram and Ahaziah (v. 4). A second letter commanded the hapless leaders to behead all seventy of Ahab's descendants and to bring their heads to Jezreel. Some commentators make the last part of verse 6 a part of Jehu's letter, letting them know he knew how many heads to count.[26]

One explanation for the unusual statements of verse 9 is that the people of Jezreel were awed by the sight of the massacre and feared they might be blamed for it. Jehu put them at ease by saying, *"You are righteous."* Then he defended himself by saying, "I'm not a common murderer; I am obeying the command of the Lord. Even the great men of Jezreel and Samaria are a part of this judgment on the house of Ahab. In slaying his seventy sons, they have not acted as murderers, but as agents of God's prophecy." The phrase, *"nothing shall fall to the earth of the word of the Lord"* means nothing will remain unfulfilled of the word of the Lord.[27]

Jehu's campaign of retribution was unrelenting. On the way to Samaria from Jezreel, he met forty-two brothers of Ahaziah, king of Judah. "Brother" here is used in the generic sense of "relative." Unaware of what had happened, they had come to visit other relatives of Ahaziah and his mother Athaliah. They too were killed by Jehu's men at a place called Beth Eked of the Shepherds. This term can also be translated "shearing house," and may refer to a place where sheep were bound and sheared. The Targum understands it to mean a meeting house where shepherds habitually gathered.[28]

The success of Jehu's revolt ultimately depended on his ability to take Samaria, the capital. So he continued his march south to the city, the crown possession of the Omride dynasty. On the way he met a mysterious man named Jehonadab, the founder of a group called the Rechabites. This ascetic tribe lived a simple nomadic life, dwelling in tents, abstaining from wine, and refusing to settle down to raise crops. Jeremiah held them up as a model of people who had refused to bow their knees to Baal, who were obedient to God, and who were therefore exempted from the judgment of the Chaldeans (Jeremiah 35). So Jehonadab, the Rechabite sheik, was a distinguished man, highly respected, and therefore a valuable ally for Jehu.[29] According to Josephus, Jehu and Jehonadab were friends of long standing, and both detested the luxurious surroundings of the royal family.[30]

By inviting him into his chariot, Jehu was symbolically sealing their alliance. It was more than a chariot ride Jehu offered. It was a handshake, a gesture of honor. (Although with Jehu's driving record, Jehonadab was actually risking his very life!) So the two of them rode together to Samaria where together they would complete the final act of Jehu's bloody purge.

Jehu Slays the Worshipers of Baal and Dies

10:18 Then Jehu gathered all the people together, and said to them, "Ahab served Baal a little, Jehu will serve him much.

19 "Now therefore, call to me all the prophets of Baal, all his servants, and all his priests. Let no one be missing, for I have a great sacrifice for Baal. Whoever is missing shall not live." But Jehu acted deceptively, with the intent of destroying the worshipers of Baal.

20 And Jehu said, "Proclaim a solemn assembly for Baal." So they proclaimed *it.*

21 Then Jehu sent throughout all Israel; and all the worshipers of Baal came, so that there was not a man left who did not come. So they came into the temple of Baal, and the temple of Baal was full from one end to the other.

22 And he said to the one in charge of the wardrobe, "Bring out vestments for all the worshipers of Baal." So he brought out vestments for them.

23 Then Jehu and Jehonadab the son of Rechab went into the temple of Baal, and said to the worshipers of Baal, "Search and see that no servants of the LORD are here with you, but only the worshipers of Baal."

24 So they went in to offer sacrifices and burnt offerings. Now Jehu had appointed for himself eighty men on the outside, and had said, "*If* any of the men whom I have brought into your hands escapes, *whoever lets him escape, it shall be* his life for the life of the other."

25 Now it happened, as soon as he had made an end of offering the burnt offering, that Jehu said to the guard and to the captains, "Go in *and* kill them;

let no one come out!" And they killed them with the
edge of the sword; then the guards and the officers
threw *them* out, and went into the inner room of the
temple of Baal.
26 And they brought the *sacred* pillars out of the
temple of Baal and burned them.
27 Then they broke down the *sacred* pillar of Baal,
and tore down the temple of Baal and made it a refuse dump to this day.
28 Thus Jehu destroyed Baal from Israel.
29 However Jehu did not turn away from the sins
of Jeroboam the son of Nebat, who had made Israel
sin, *that is,* from the golden calves that *were* at Bethel
and Dan.
30 And the LORD said to Jehu, "Because you have
done well in doing *what is* right in My sight, *and*
have done to the house of Ahab all that *was* in My
heart, your sons shall sit on the throne of Israel to
the fourth *generation.*"
31 But Jehu took no heed to walk in the law of the
LORD God of Israel with all his heart; for he did not
depart from the sins of Jeroboam, who had made Israel sin.
32 In those days the LORD began to cut off *parts* of
Israel; and Hazael conquered them in all the territory
of Israel
33 from the Jordan eastward: all the land of
Gilead—Gad, Reuben, and Manasseh—from Aroer,
which *is* by the River Arnon, including Gilead and
Bashan.
34 Now the rest of the acts of Jehu, all that he did,
and all his might, *are* they not written in the book of
the chronicles of the kings of Israel?
35 So Jehu rested with his fathers, and they buried
him in Samaria. Then Jehoahaz his son reigned in his
place.
36 And the period that Jehu reigned over Israel in
Samaria *was* twenty-eight years.

2 Kings 10:18–36

Once in Samaria, Jehu and Jehonadab carried out a clever deception in order to identify and trap the worshipers of Baal. Years earlier, in order to please his wife Jezebel, Ahab had built a temple for the worship of Baal, her Phoenician deity (1 Kings 16:32). Since he named both his sons after Yahweh (Ahaziah and Jehoram), Ahab himself probably gave only lip service to Baal. Hence, Jehu was telling the truth when he said, *"Ahab served Baal a little"* (v. 18).[31] It seems the people knew that Jehu had taken over the kingdom but were unaware of his religious preference. They had no reason to disbelieve Jehu when he told them that he would be an enthusiastic worshiper of Baal and wanted to prove it by declaring a great celebration of sacrifice to Baal. The word translated *"deceptively"* in verse 19 comes from the same Hebrew root as the name "Jacob." It means "take by the heel, trip, or deceive."

Those who were assembled were the leaders of the cult, not all those who worshiped Baal from across the land. There were still large numbers of Baal worshipers active in the years following this purge. Verse 19 identifies those whom Jehu assembled as prophets, servants, and priests, the ones who really counted in the false religion. They came in great numbers, filling the temple enclosure *"from one end to the other"* (v. 21). The words are literally "from mouth to mouth," signifying from one entrance of the temple to the other. Just where in Samaria this temple of Baal was located is unknown. No evidence of it has been uncovered during excavations there. This could be explained, however, by the fact that the temple was totally destroyed as described in verse 27.

What a dramatic scene it must have been as the officials of Baal worship gathered in open celebration. They were excited that their new king, Jehu, and the famous sheik of the Rechabites, Jehonadab, were now distinguished converts and were joining them in a ceremonial sacrifice to Baal. Jehu was careful to observe all the appropriate rituals, including the use of proper vestments and implements (v. 22). Jehu himself offered the main sacrifice, to the approving applause of the people, then went out supposedly to receive the praise of the crowd gathered outside. But once outside, Jehu gave a sharp command to the eighty soldiers who had surrounded the temple. The command is literally just two stern words in Hebrew, "Go smite!" Soon the slaughter was complete.

The sacred pillars of Baal were probably stone or wooden images of the deity. According to verse 26, these were brought out and burned. If they were of stone, they would be heated in the fire and then shattered into pieces by pouring cold water on the stone. Verse 27 seems to repeat verse 26 but uses the singular for *"pillar."* It may be that verse 27 has reference to a stone base upon which the smaller pillars in verse 26 stood.[32] The destruction of the shrine was so complete that it was totally leveled and the site became a well-known *"refuse dump."* Literally, the word means "a latrine, cesspool, or privy." This was a consummate insult to the worshipers of the false god Baal.

Up to this time Jehu is presented as perfectly following the will of God in his purge of Baalism and his takeover of the kingdom. But verse 29 introduces a serious failure. He allowed the golden calves used in the worship centers at Bethel and Dan to remain. Jeroboam had built them there not as images of false gods but as images of Yahweh to encourage worshipers to go there instead of to Jerusalem. Even though the calves were not idols, they corrupted the worship of Yahweh and inclined the people toward idolatry. In the Ten Commandments, God had specifically forbidden this practice. Tragically, this same shortcoming brought God's judgment on other kings of Israel who otherwise had done what was good in the sight of God.

With God, it is all or nothing. We are to respond to Him with all our heart and all our mind and all our soul and all our strength. Halfhearted responses will not do.

With this one exception, Jehu had performed God's will obediently, and God gave His blessing to the new king, promising that his sons would sit on the throne of Israel for four generations. And they did. The succession was from Jehu to Jehoahaz, to Joash, to Jeroboam II, and then to Zechariah.

The last five verses summarize the reign of Jehu. It was a period when Syria dominated Israel. The entire Transjordan territory was lost to Hazael (vv. 32–33). This territory was not regained until the conquests of Jeroboam II in the middle of the eighth century B.C.[33] It was also during this time that Jehu paid tribute to Assyria, perhaps to buy their help in fighting Syria. The Black Obelisk of Shalmaneser III tells about this subjection. The obelisk carries the only pictorial representation of a Hebrew king ever discovered. It bears the following inscription:

> The tribute of Jehu son of Omri; I received from him silver, gold, a golden saplu-bowl, a golden vase with pointed bottom,

golden tumblers, golden buckets, tin, a staff for a king and wooden puruhtu.[34]

(The meanings of some of the terms are unknown.)

Jehu reigned twenty-eight years. He evidently died a natural death and was buried in the royal tombs of Samaria. Jehoahaz his son reigned in his place. Jehu had a strangely mingled character. He had a commendable zeal for the Lord, but there were many elements of selfishness in his life as well. Sometimes zeal tempts strong people to cross the line between God's will and personal ambition. It is true that power corrupts and absolute power corrupts absolutely.

This king obeyed the law of justice and the command of God commendably, even though the bloody rigidness of the ancient system seems contrary to the later law of love. We are now under a higher law of love, which has come to us through Jesus Christ. The New Testament calls it a better law. But we are challenged by the lives of people like Jehu to obey our better law as faithfully as they did their lesser law.

NOTES

1. T. R. Hobbs, *2 Kings,* Word Biblical Commentary, ed. John D. W. Watts, vol. 13 (Waco, TX: Word Books, 1985), 103.
2. John Gray, *I and II Kings,* Old Testament Library (Philadelphia: Westminster, 1963), 479.
3. Hobbs, 103.
4. Gwilym H. Jones, *1 and 2 Kings,* New Century Bible Commentary, ed. Ronald E. Clements (Grand Rapids: Eerdmans, 1984), 446.
5. C. F. Keil, *The Books of the Kings,* Biblical Commentary on the Old Testament, ed. C. F. Keil and F. Delitzsch, vol. 4 (Grand Rapids: Eerdmans, 1950), 336.
6. I. W. Slotki, *Kings* (London: Soncino Press, 1950), 213.
7. Ibid., 214.
8. Jones, 454.
9. Gray, 486.
10. Charles F. Burney, *Notes on the Hebrew Text of the Books of Kings* (Oxford: Clarendon Press, 1903), 296.

11. Norman H. Snaith, Ralph W. Sockman, and Raymond Calkins, "The First and Second Books of Kings," in *The Interpreter's Bible*, vol. 3 (Nashville: Abingdon, 1954), 231.
12. Jones, 454.
13. Slotki, 214.
14. Gray, 492.
15. Snaith, Sockman, and Calkins, 233.
16. Gray, 492.
17. M. Pierce Matheney and Roy Honeycutt, "1-2 Kings," in *The Broadman Bible Commentary*, ed. Clifton J. Allen, vol. 3 (Nashville: Broadman, 1970), 249.
18. Gray, 492.
19. Ibid.
20. Slotki, 220.
21. Ibid.
22. Keil, 344.
23. Ibid., 345.
24. Jones, 462.
25. Slotki, 222.
26. Ibid.
27. Keil, 346.
28. Slotki, 222.
29. Jones, 465.
30. Snaith, Sockman, and Calkins, 240.
31. Gray, 506.
32. Slotki, 226.
33. Matheney and Honeycutt, 252.
34. Ibid., 254.

CHAPTER FIFTEEN

The Reigns of Athaliah the Queen and Jehoash of Judah

2 Kings 11:1–12:21

Athaliah Assumes the Throne, but Jehoash Is Spared and Crowned

11:1 When Athaliah the mother of Ahaziah saw that her son was dead, she arose and destroyed all the royal heirs.

2 But Jehosheba, the daughter of King Joram, sister of Ahaziah, took Joash the son of Ahaziah, and stole him away from among the king's sons *who were* being murdered; and they hid him and his nurse in the bedroom, from Athaliah, so that he was not killed.

3 So he was hidden with her in the house of the LORD for six years, while Athaliah reigned over the land.

4 In the seventh year Jehoiada sent and brought the captains of hundreds—of the bodyguards and the escorts—and brought them into the house of the LORD to him. And he made a covenant with them and took an oath from them in the house of the LORD, and showed them the king's son.

5 Then he commanded them, saying, "This *is* what you shall do: One-third of you who come on duty on the Sabbath shall be keeping watch over the king's house,

6 "one-third *shall be* at the gate of Sur, and one-third at the gate behind the escorts. You shall keep the watch of the house, lest it be broken down.

7 "The two contingents of you who go off duty on
the Sabbath shall keep the watch of the house of the
LORD for the king.
8 "But you shall surround the king on all sides,
every man with his weapons in his hand; and whoever comes within range, let him be put to death.
You are to be with the king as he goes out and as he
comes in."
9 So the captains of the hundreds did according
to all that Jehoiada the priest commanded. Each
of them took his men who were to be on duty on the
Sabbath, with those who were going off duty on
the Sabbath, and came to Jehoiada the priest.
10 And the priest gave the captains of hundreds
the spears and shields which *had belonged* to King
David, that were in the temple of the LORD.
11 Then the escorts stood, every man with his
weapons in his hand, all around the king, from the
right side of the temple to the left side of the temple,
by the altar and the house.
12 And he brought out the king's son, put the
crown on him, and *gave him* the Testimony; they
made him king and anointed him, and they clapped
their hands and said, "Long live the king!"

2 Kings 11:1–12

Israel's King Jehu reigned for twenty-eight years after his bloody purge of the nation's Baalists. He had also slain Ahaziah, the king of Judah, who had become Jehoram's ally, but Jehu seemed to have no further interest in interfering with Judah's royal descent. Even though Ahaziah's mother, Athaliah, was the daughter of Ahab and Jezebel and was well known for her wicked influence, first over her husband, King Jehoram, and later over their son, King Ahaziah, Jehu exempted her in his extermination of Ahab's descendants. "Athaliah" means "Yahweh is exalted." Ahab, her father, had named all his children after Yahweh, indicating he had some loyalty to the Lord and hoped his children would be true to the faith of Israel. Her name made no difference, however, in the personality and character of Athaliah.[1]

Normally, following the death of a king like Ahaziah, one of his sons would have become the ruler in his place, but the devious queen mother had other plans. As soon as the news of Ahaziah's assassination reached her, she set about to wipe out all her son's descendants and claim the throne for herself. The heirs mentioned in verse 1 had to be the sons of Ahaziah, since all his brothers had been taken away by Arabs and put to death (2 Chron. 22:1) and all his other relatives had been slain by Jehu (2 Kings 10:13). So Athaliah actually murdered her own grandsons in order to become queen! She was the only woman among the rulers of Judah and Israel.

One would assume that Jehosheba, mentioned in verse 2, was also Athaliah's daughter, although she is identified here only as the daughter of Jehoram and the sister of Ahaziah. But Chronicles reports that Jehosheba was the wife of Jehoiada, the high priest. And since Athaliah was a Baal worshiper and would not therefore have allowed her own daughter to marry a priest of Yahweh, Jehosheba must not have been her daughter after all. She may have been the child of Jehoram and one of his concubines.[2] Her name, "Jehosheba," is a variant of the name "Jehoshabath" in Chronicles, which in turn is a variant of the name "Elizabeth."[3]

Seeing what Athaliah was plotting, Jehosheba acted quickly to save one of the royal heirs, her infant nephew, Jehoash. She and her husband, the priest, hid him and his nurse in their living quarters in the temple compound. This was one place in Jerusalem where Queen Athaliah would not be likely to go. We are not told whether Athaliah suspected that Jehoash had escaped her purge nor why she did not search for him if she thought he was still alive. So apparently she assumed that he had been killed with the others. Neither did the temple guards and escorts in verse 4 seem aware of any rumors that one of the royal heirs had survived. Jehosheba and Jehoiada had guarded their secret well for six years.

Jehoash must have been almost eight years old when the events in verse 4 took place. It was the seventh year of Queen Athaliah's reign, and Jehoash was probably a one-year-old child when he was rescued by his aunt. The author of Kings does not explain how Jehoiada convinced the temple officials and the military personnel that the seven-year-old boy he presented to them was indeed Prince Jehoash. Maybe he bore an unmistakable family resemblance to his father the king, whose features they knew very well. Perhaps they simply trusted the integrity of the high priest and believed him when he told them who Jehoash was.

Traditionally, the temple guard, as well as the priests and Levites, served in shifts on a rotating basis. The military contingent who guarded the temple also had the responsibility for protecting the royal palace in Jerusalem. Since the shifts changed on the Sabbath, Jehoiada chose the next Sabbath day as the time for his carefully planned coup. That was when the company of soldiers guarding the palace marched to the temple to relieve the guards there. Consequently, all the contingents of soldiers would be at the temple at the same time, giving Jehoiada full military strength to carry out his plan. It also meant that neither the concentrated gathering of soldiers nor the noisy crowd of people in the temple on that day would attract the queen's attention and arouse her suspicions.

Each man knew his instructions. The guards were to surround the young prince and protect him *"as he goes out,"* that is, to be publicly presented to the people, and *"as he comes in,"* that is, to be crowned (v. 8). In addition to the regular weapons they routinely carried, Jehoiada also issued them the ceremonial spears and shields that were kept in the treasure house of the temple (v. 10). When he was king, David had confiscated the beautiful golden shields from the Ammonites whom he had defeated in battle. For years, they had been displayed in the temple until they were pillaged by Shishak (1 Kings 14:26). Later, less expensive bronze copies were made to replace the priceless gold shields, and it was these bronze ceremonial weapons that Jehoiada distributed to the guards. Even though they were not made of gold, they were still quite expensive and beautiful and were used only when Judah's royalty visited the temple. Hence Jehoiada acted properly in using them for the coronation ceremony being planned for Jehoash.[4]

Standing by the appropriate pillar near the altar in the temple court, the boy prince received the royal crown on his head. In verse 12 the word for "crown" is *nēzer,* from the same root as the word "nazirite," conveying the general idea of consecration. Not much is said in Scripture about the coronation jewels of Judah nor the fashion of the particular crown used here. This one may have been kept in the temple treasury; or, conceivably, the palace guards, acting on Jehoiada's instructions, may have secretly confiscated the queen's own crown from the palace to the temple.

Jehoash also received in his hands *"the Testimony,"* that is, a copy of the law. The word in verse 12 is *ʿēdûth,* meaning a scroll of the

Torah. It is from this passage that the custom of handing a Bible to the British Monarch as a part of the coronation ceremony comes.[5]

Young Jehoash was now officially the king of Judah. Like Samuel before him, his childhood home had been the temple, and his first impressions growing up were the singing of the Levites, the sounds and aromas of daily sacrifices, the white-robed priests, the jubilant worshipers, and the reading of the sacred Scriptures. His early environment was vastly superior to what it might have been had he grown up in the palace next door with all its pagan influences and godless lifestyle.

For years, cynics have perpetuated the myth that "preacher's kids" are typically mischievous delinquents who, because of their strict religious upbringing, usually rebel and turn out to be failures. But that tired, overworked caricature is simply not true. Recent studies show that on the contrary, children of ministers are actually more likely to succeed than the children of any other professionals. Their home environments more often produce the qualities—healthy faith and strong character—that result in successful and meaningful lives.

This was true in Jehoash's case as Jehoiada, the high priest, and Jehosheba, his courageous wife, shaped the faith and moral character of the new king. They brought him up "in the training and admonition of the Lord" (Eph. 6:4). And, as a result, Chronicles says, "[Jehoash] did what was right in the sight of the Lord all the days of Jehoiada the priest" (2 Chron. 24:2).

Athaliah Is Killed and Jehoash Is Enthroned

11:13 Now when Athaliah heard the noise of the escorts *and* the people, she came to the people *in* the temple of the LORD.

14 When she looked, there was the king standing by a pillar according to custom; and the leaders and the trumpeters were by the king. All the people of the land were rejoicing and blowing trumpets. So Athaliah tore her clothes and cried out, "Treason! Treason!"

15 And Jehoiada the priest commanded the captains of the hundreds, the officers of the army, and said to them, "Take her outside under guard, and slay

with the sword whoever follows her." For the priest
had said, "Do not let her be killed in the house of the
LORD."

16 So they seized her; and she went by way of the
horses' entrance *into* the king's house, and there she
was killed.

17 Then Jehoiada made a covenant between the
LORD, the king, and the people, that they should be
the LORD's people, and *also* between the king and the
people.

18 And all the people of the land went to the temple of Baal, and tore it down. They thoroughly broke
in pieces its altars and images, and killed Mattan the
priest of Baal before the altars. And the priest appointed officers over the house of the LORD.

19 Then he took the captains of hundreds, the
bodyguards, the escorts, and all the people of the
land; and they brought the king down from the house
of the LORD, and went by way of the gate of the escorts to the king's house. Then he sat on the throne of
the kings.

20 So all the people of the land rejoiced; and the
city was quiet, for they had slain Athaliah with
the sword *in* the king's house.

21 Jehoash *was* seven years old when he became
king.

2 Kings 11:13–21

Sounds of the tumultuous celebration in the temple could be heard all the way to the royal palace. Although it isn't mentioned until verse 14, it can be assumed that in addition to the loud clapping and the shouts of "Long live the king!" there was also the jubilant blowing of the shophar, the ceremonial trumpet. Her curiosity aroused, Queen Athaliah came running to the temple courtyard to see what was causing the commotion. This scene is reminiscent of the events in 1 Kings 1:38ff. when Adonijah, the unsuccessful pretender to the throne, wondered what was happening when he heard the sounds of celebration at the coronation of King Solomon.

When she arrived, no one had to tell the queen what was happening. She understood all too clearly the joyous acclamation of the crowd, "Long live the king!" Furthermore, she saw the young prince standing in the official place where royalty customarily stood when they came to the temple. She recognized her own crown on his head. The queen's small retinue of personal guards, who had not participated in the regular change of shifts at the temple and who were therefore not informed about the coup, were totally outnumbered. To deal with the possibility that some of them might be foolhardy enough to try to defend her, Jehoiada publicly commanded his captains to *"slay with the sword whoever follows her"* (v. 15). She was alone and defenseless.

Although he had not specifically ordered her execution, Jehoiada knew what the people had in mind, so his concern then turned to protecting the sanctity of the temple. *"Do not let her be killed in the house of the Lord"* (v. 15). Respecting his concern, the guards led her out of the temple compound by way of the back gate, the one used for horses being led to the royal stables. Choosing such an ignoble spot for her execution was an intentional insult to the wicked woman who was the only queen ever to reign in Jerusalem.

Ceremonial renewal of the covenant, a frequently repeated ritual in the history of God's people, often led to national revival and spiritual rebirth. In this case, the renewal of the covenant (v. 17) resulted in an immediate campaign to rid Jerusalem of the blight of Baal worship. Aroused by the emotion of the impressive ceremony, the populace stormed the temple of Baal and killed its priest, Mattan (v. 18). Unlike Jehu's similar purge in Samaria, in which all the gathered Baal worshipers were massacred, here only the queen and the priest of Baal were put to death.

Since this is the only scriptural reference to a Baalist temple in Jerusalem, and since no specific location is given, we have no way of knowing precisely where it stood.[6] It may have been merely an open-air enclosure with an altar or a small covered shrine dedicated to Baal. While not shedding any light on its exact location, Josephus reports that it was built by Queen Athaliah. If so, the pagan shrine may have been adjacent to the royal palace, or perhaps even within the temple compound itself.[7] It does appear from this passage that wherever it was located, it could not have been very far from the temple, because the people were able to destroy it and then return to escort their new king from the temple to the palace all within a brief time span.

Notice the contrast between verse 19 and verse 16. The condemned queen was taken out by the lowly horse's gate, while the newly crowned monarch was led out through the prestigious royal gate used by the kings and their escorts.

This same contrast between the wicked Athaliah and the innocent Jehoash is dramatically portrayed throughout this chapter. Athaliah was a true daughter of Jezebel, a tigress of a woman with an unscrupulous character. Her disregard for human life was demonstrated by the incredible, cold-blooded murder of her own grandsons. When this evil woman angrily stormed into the temple, she came face to face with innocence and purity, personified in the boy prince standing beside the altar. What a contrast! The childlike Jehoash makes Athaliah look ugly and perverse.

Lift up the true king, and all other tyrannies will look bleak and intolerable by contrast. When Jesus said, "And I, if I am lifted up from the earth, will draw all peoples to Myself" (John 12:32), He was primarily referring to His death on the cross. But it is also true that when we lift up the true King of kings by our witness, our preaching, our Christian examples, His perfect personality will draw searching humanity to Himself. Beside Him, all other alternative religions and world views appear anemic, colorless, and trivial.

> Turn your eyes upon Jesus,
>   Look full in His wonderful face,
> And the things of earth,
>   Will grow strangely dim,
> In the light of His glory and grace.[8]

Jehoash Restores the Temple

> 12:1 In the seventh year of Jehu, Jehoash became king, and he reigned forty years in Jerusalem. His mother's name *was* Zibiah of Beersheba.
>
> 2 Jehoash did *what was* right in the sight of the LORD all the days in which Jehoiada the priest instructed him.
>
> 3 But the high places were not taken away; the people still sacrificed and burned incense on the high places.
>
> 4 And Jehoash said to the priests, "All the money of the dedicated gifts that are brought into the house

of the LORD—each man's census money, each man's
assessment money—*and* all the money that a man purposes in his heart to bring into the house of the LORD,
5 "let the priests take *it* themselves, each from his
constituency; and let them repair the damages of the temple, wherever any dilapidation is found."
6 Now it was so, by the twenty-third year of King
Jehoash, *that* the priests had not repaired the damages to the temple.
7 So King Jehoash called Jehoiada the priest and
the *other* priests, and said to them, "Why have you not repaired the damages of the temple? Now therefore, do not take *more* money from your constituency, but deliver it for repairing the damages of the temple."
8 And the priests agreed that they would neither
receive *more* money from the people, nor repair the damages of the temple.
9 Then Jehoiada the priest took a chest, bored a
hole in its lid, and set it beside the altar, on the right side as one comes into the house of the LORD; and the priests who kept the door put there all the money brought into the house of the LORD.
10 So it was, whenever they saw that *there was*
much money in the chest, that the king's scribe and the high priest came up and put it in bags, and counted the money that was found in the house of the LORD.
11 Then they gave the money, which had been ap-
portioned, into the hands of those who did the work, who had the oversight of the house of the LORD; and they paid it out to the carpenters and builders who worked on the house of the LORD,
12 and to masons and stonecutters, and for buying
timber and hewn stone, to repair the damage of the house of the LORD, and for all that was paid out to repair the temple.
13 However there were not made for the house of
the LORD basins of silver, trimmers, sprinkling-bowls, trumpets, any articles of gold or articles of silver, from the money brought into the house of the LORD.
14 But they gave that to the workmen, and they
repaired the house of the LORD with it.

15 Moreover they did not require an account from
the men into whose hand they delivered the money
to be paid to workmen, for they dealt faithfully.
16 The money from the trespass offerings and the
money from the sin offerings was not brought into
the house of the LORD. It belonged to the priests.

2 Kings 12:1–16

Jehu was in his seventh year on the throne in Samaria, the capital of the Northern Kingdom, when the boy king, Jehoash, was crowned in Jerusalem, the capital of the Southern Kingdom. For the next twenty years these two neighboring rulers held the line against Baalism in their respective nations. We know nothing about Jehoash's mother except that her hometown was Beersheba, and that her name was Zibiah, which means "gazelle" (v. 1). "Zibiah" is the equivalent of the New Testament name "Tabitha" (Acts 9:36).[9] It seems strange that she is not mentioned during the crisis when her son narrowly escaped death through the courageous intervention of her sister-in-law Jehosheba, nor during the six years he lived in the temple quarters. Possibly Zibiah died in childbirth or a few months later, before these events took place. On the other hand, it may be that she was a concubine of King Ahaziah and was given no legitimate involvement in the rearing of their son.

There is an unusual recurrence in these verses of references to the number seven, *šebaʿ* in Hebrew. It appears in the proper names Beer*sheba,* the home of Zibiah, and Jeho*sheba,* who rescued Jehoash. The number turns up also in time references. The coronation takes place in the seventh year of Jehu's reign, which is also the seventh year of Athaliah's reign. Jehoash is seven years old. Seven is a very important number in Jewish numerology, but its repetition here seems to have no particular significance and is probably coincidental.

The author of Kings gives Jehoash high marks for his leadership, but not straight A's. His early report card reads, *"Jehoash did what was right in the sight of the Lord."* However, his good grades continued only as long as he remained under the godly influence of his adoptive father, the priest (v. 2). Jehoiada's instruction had been meticulous, even to the point of picking out the king's wives for him! (2 Chron. 24:3). But as soon as Jehoiada died and his oversight of the young king ended, Jehoash began to drift away from the ways of the Lord (2 Chron. 24:2, 17ff.).

His primary failure was that he allowed the people to continue the practice of offering sacrifices to Yahweh on the *"high places,"* former sites of pagan shrines. Even though at times God had seemed to overlook this practice, it was still forbidden. Like the use of the images in the worship of Yahweh at Dan and Bethel in the North, these compromising sacrifices at the high places in the South inclined the people toward idolatry and weakened their commitment to Yahweh, the only true God. Jehoash was guilty of looking the other way and permitting his people to continue this popular practice without punishment.

Otherwise, Jehoash was a good king. His greatest accomplishment, in fact his only recorded accomplishment during his forty-year reign, was his restoration of the temple in Jerusalem, which was in need of repair. Solomon's majestic temple, one of the architectural marvels of the ancient world, was now about 140 years old. Its shabby and dilapidated condition was not altogether the result of its age and long years of benign neglect. Chronicles adds another reason why the repairs were needed. Athaliah and her wicked sons had "broken into the house of God, and had also presented all the dedicated things of the house of the Lord to the Baals" (2 Chron. 24:7). So some of the deterioration was due to their malicious vandalism. To make matters worse, when Queen Athaliah controlled the treasury and the nation's resources, she probably diverted any money for temple maintenance into the support of Baalism, leaving the temple to deteriorate.[10]

Three categories of revenue were assigned by Jehoash to be used in the restoration project: (1) *"Census money,"* that is, the half shekel per year paid by each Israelite past the age of twenty (Exod. 30:13). (2) *"Assessment money,"* that is, literally, "each man the money of the souls of his estimating." This was a kind of property tax based on the personal assessment of each individual (Lev. 27:2). (3) *"The money that a man purposes in his heart to bring,"* that is, freewill offerings over and above the required donations.[11]

New Testament patterns of stewardship which present-day churches try to follow include a similar balance between *"assessments"* (the tithe) and *"the money a man purposes in his heart to bring"* (freewill offerings). The first category belongs primarily to the Old Testament economy of law, and the second category belongs primarily to the New Testament economy of love. Ideal Christian stewardship should begin then with the tithe. We certainly would hold up as a minimum standard nothing less than that which was required of a faithful Jewish steward in Old Testament days. But motivated not only by obedience but by love, the Christian steward should go beyond the law and bring "offerings" to the Lord, over and above the tithe, remembering the New Testament teaching, "God loves a cheerful giver" (2 Cor. 9:7).

Verses 4 and 5 report Jehoash's first attempt at a building fund drive. It should have succeeded, but it didn't. Why not? Jones proposes that the failure was caused by a lack of response on the part of the priests, which in turn may have been due to the fact that Jehoiada was quite aged now and therefore unable to control the temple officials. He could no longer command their loyalty and obedience.[12]

Twenty-three years later, when the king was thirty years old, the repairs had still not been made, so he took matters into his own hand and instituted a new plan (vv. 7–12). He took the responsibility for collecting the money away from the priests and assigned it to his own secretary (the king's scribe, v. 10). Then he placed a collection chest in a strategic location on the right side of the altar, giving the repair project a high priority and a corresponding high visibility.

Since the earliest indication of coins in the Bible is found in Ezra 2:69, the *"money"* in these verses was probably not in the form of currency or coins, but precious metals and valuable jewels. Careful accountability seems to be the added factor that ensured the success of Jehoash's second program. The king set up precise, businesslike procedures. For example, two people, the scribe and the high priest, were assigned the responsibility for counting the offerings. (This is a precursor to present-day church practices of using a tellers committee to count the offerings and co-signers to endorse the church's checking account.)

Understandably, the public gets suspicious when they hear about instances of embezzlement or improper handling of church contributions. This problem seems to occur more frequently with independent, personality-centered media ministries where there is little supervision or accountability. Write a letter to one of these independent operations requesting a financial report or an audit, and even if you're a regular contributor to their work, you're not likely to receive substantial information. But make that same request of one of our legitimate denominational ministries and you will receive a report of the expenditure of every penny. The difference is accountability.

In 1986, six of the leading television evangelists had a combined income equivalent to the mission giving of the 14.6 million Southern Baptists through their churches. *U.S. News & World Report* indicated that in 1986 these television ministries took in $684 million. That same year, Southern Baptists gave about $635 million to mission causes through their denomination. Between them, the six TV evangelists, in addition to their television programs, supported four schools, a hospital, three churches, two ministries to needy children, a home for unwed mothers, and a ministry to the needy, *U.S. News* said. Meanwhile, with about the same money, Southern Baptists supported 67 denominational colleges and universities with more than 200,000 students, dozens of children's homes, hospitals, and homes for the aged. They paid for 3,756 foreign missionaries in more than 100 nations and 3,637 home missionaries in the United States. They provided for ministries to students on 1,100 public campuses in the U.S. and for the work of the Southern Baptist Radio and Television Commission which has established a national Christian network. Southern Baptists also supported six accredited theological seminaries. One of every five seminary students in the United States is enrolled in one of these six schools.[13]

Unlike some of the television ministries, most denominational mission programs are undergirded by a financial system of openness and accountability. From the local church to the missionary on the foreign field, every penny given is accounted for. And the pennies buy considerably more service and ministry than most independent enterprises put together.

Jehoash's approach in verse 3 was to transfer the responsibility for the money from the priests to the secular scribes who were more skilled in finance. When he did, the problems were solved, and the restoration was completed. Sometimes, churches and other religious organizations make the mistake of putting financial matters in the hands of well-meaning ministers who have had no training or experience in fiscal management. This is done in spite of the fact that most of these organizations have lay persons with enormous capabilities in this area. Perhaps we need to take a lesson in ministerial delegation and lay involvement from Judah's ancient king.

Only two other times in the Bible was such a team of craftsmen assembled: when Solomon built the temple in 1 Kings 5, and later when Josiah repaired it in 2 Kings 22. At first there appears to be an inconsistency between verse 13, which says that the money was not spent for vessels and implements of worship, and 2 Chron. 24:14, which says that these vessels and implements *were* paid for by the offerings. The answer seems to be that no money was spent for this purpose until all the structural repairs were made. Then the surplus funds were spent to supply new vessels and implements. The only reason given for exempting the trespass and sin offerings is the statement in verse 16 that these monies belonged to the priests.

It is interesting to notice that it was the king who grew up in the temple who led the campaign to repair it. Jehoash must have loved the beautiful old sanctuary filled with memories from his childhood, and he grieved to see it neglected. Now, as an adult, reinforced by the spiritual principles instilled in him by early childhood impressions and experiences in the temple, he steadfastly set out to repair it. Today, when a child grows up in a positive church environment, those early impressions will have an immense effect on good character and conduct in later years. Parents who are fearful of forcing religious values on impressionable young lives, and who for that reason do not make their children go to church, forget that deep impressions are being stamped on the child's personality by *not* going to church too. To neglect early religious training is to rob the child of rich spiritual resources.

There is a lesson too in Jehoash's concern for maintaining the facilities that had been built by the sacrifices of previous generations and handed to him and his contemporaries as a gift. A significant feature of responsible stewardship is to maintain the church buildings and institutional facilities that have been placed in our hands today. At Southwestern Seminary, the cost of our aggressive program of planned maintenance is sometimes questioned. But that program is based on the philosophy that the facilities built by generous "construction" gifts from the past must be passed on to future students by generous "maintenance" gifts from the present. The president of one of our leading state colleges said, "University landscaping is academically relevant." I agree. And it is also true that seminary maintenance is spiritually relevant.

JEHOASH PAYS TRIBUTE TO SYRIA AND DIES

12:17 Hazael king of Syria went up and fought against
Gath, and took it; then Hazael set his face to go up to
Jerusalem.
18 And Jehoash king of Judah took all the sacred
things that his fathers, Jehoshaphat and Jehoram and
Ahaziah, kings of Judah, had dedicated, and his own
sacred things, and all the gold found in the treasuries of the house of the LORD and in the king's
house, and sent *them* to Hazael king of Syria. Then
he went away from Jerusalem.
19 Now the rest of the acts of Joash, and all that he
did, *are* they not written in the book of the chronicles
of the kings of Judah?
20 And his servants arose and formed a conspiracy, and killed Joash in the house of the Millo, which
goes down to Silla.
21 For Jozachar the son of Shimeath and Jehozabad the son of Shomer, his servants, struck him. So
he died, and they buried him with his fathers in the
City of David. Then Amaziah his son reigned in his
place.

2 Kings 12:17–21

The historical setting of the events in this passage was given in 2 Kings 10:32–33. During the last days of Jehu's reign in Israel, King Hazael of Syria conquered parts of that nation. Later he pushed south along the Mediterranean coast toward Judah. The Syrians made their way into neighboring Philistia, conquering the border town of Gath, just twenty-five miles from Jerusalem (v. 17). According to Chronicles, Hazael actually attacked Jerusalem and, even though he was outnumbered, defeated Jehoash's large army and took away the treasures of the city, leaving Judah's king severely wounded (2 Chron. 24:23). Leaving out this information, 2 Kings 12:18 implies that Jehoash volunteered the treasures of the temple and the palace as a tribute to Hazael, following the precedent of King Asa in 1 Kings 15:18. Both accounts are true, and the Syrian king was content to leave Jerusalem with his booty. All the effort and expense of supplying the newly renovated temple with new vessels and implements went to waste as these valuable treasures were carted away to Damascus.

We must turn again to the parallel account in Chronicles to read the details of Jehoash's death. The sparse sketch here simply speaks of a conspiracy of servants who murdered the king. The more detailed report in Chronicles tells about the king's order to kill the son of Jehoiada the priest. According to 2 Chron. 24:25, the motive for Jehoash's murder was revenge, "because of the blood of the sons of Jehoiada the priest." But there is also likelihood that the killing could have been motivated by the tensions arising out of Jehoash's decision during the restoration project to take over some of the fiscal responsibilities that belonged to the priests. The place names "Millo" and "Silla" are unknown, as are the names of the murderous servants, which are given slightly different spellings in Chronicles. The parallel passage also adds that Jehoash was not buried in the official tombs of the kings.

NOTES

1. M. Pierce Matheney and Roy Honeycutt, "1–2 Kings," in *The Broadman Bible Commentary,* ed. Clifton J. Allen, vol. 3 (Nashville: Broadman, 1970), 255.

2. C. F. Keil, *The Books of the Kings,* Biblical Commentary on the Old Testament, ed. C. F. Keil and F. Delitzsch, vol. 4 (Grand Rapids: Eerdmans, 1950), 355.

3. John Gray, *I and II Kings,* Old Testament Library (Philadelphia: Westminster, 1963), 514.

4. Gwilym H. Jones, *1 and 2 Kings,* New Century Bible Commentary, ed. Ronald E. Clements (Grand Rapids: Eerdmans, 1984), 478.

5. I. W. Slotki, *Kings* (London: Soncino Press, 1950), 230.

6. T. R. Hobbs, *2 Kings,* Word Biblical Commentary, ed. John D. W. Watts, vol. 13 (Waco, TX: Word Books, 1985), 143.

7. Gray, 524.

8. Helen H. Lemmel, "Turn Your Eyes upon Jesus," in *Baptist Hymnal* (Nashville: Convention Press, 1975), no. 198.

9. Jones, 489.

10. Keil, 365.

11. Slotki, 234.

12. Jones, 489.

13. Orville Scott, "Televangelist Ministries Scant Compared to Cooperative Program," *Baptist Press,* 11 May 1987; cf. "An Unholy War in the TV Pulpit," *U.S. News & World Report,* 6 April 1987, 58–66, esp. 63.

CHAPTER SIXTEEN

The Reigns of Jehoahaz, Jehoash, and Jeroboam II of Israel; Amaziah and Azariah of Judah; the Last Days of Elisha

2 Kings 13:1–15:7

JEHOAHAZ REIGNS IN ISRAEL

13:1 In the twenty-third year of Joash the son of
Ahaziah, king of Judah, Jehoahaz the son of Jehu became king over Israel in Samaria, *and reigned* seventeen years.
2 And he did evil in the sight of the LORD, and
followed the sins of Jeroboam the son of Nebat, who
had made Israel sin. He did not depart from them.
3 Then the anger of the LORD was aroused against
Israel, and He delivered them into the hand of Hazael
king of Syria, and into the hand of Ben-Hadad the son
of Hazael, all *their* days.
4 So Jehoahaz pleaded with the LORD, and the
LORD listened to him; for He saw the oppression of
Israel, because the king of Syria oppressed them.
5 Then the LORD gave Israel a deliverer, so that
they escaped from under the hand of the Syrians; and
the children of Israel dwelt in their tents as before.
6 Nevertheless they did not depart from the sins
of the house of Jeroboam, who had made Israel sin,
but walked in them; and the wooden image also remained in Samaria.
7 For He left of the army of Jehoahaz only fifty
horsemen, ten chariots, and ten thousand foot

soldiers; for the king of Syria had destroyed them
and made them like the dust at threshing.
8 Now the rest of the acts of Jehoahaz, all that he
did, and his might, *are* they not written in the book
of the chronicles of the kings of Israel?
9 So Jehoahaz rested with his fathers, and they
buried him in Samaria. Then Joash his son reigned in
his place.

2 Kings 13:1–9

About halfway through the forty-year reign of Jehoash in Judah, the very year he grew weary of the delay in repairing the temple, Jehu's son Jehoahaz became king in neighboring Israel. His father, the military hero who had purged Israel of Baalism, did what was right in the sight of the Lord, so the Lord promised that his sons would sit on the throne of Israel to the fourth generation. Jehoahaz, whose name means "Yahweh has grasped," was the first of these promised generations. Since his father died a natural death, he must have had ample time to prepare his son for the responsibilities of the kingdom. Furthermore, Jehu named his son after Yahweh, dramatizing his hope that his son would continue to "do right in the sight of the Lord," just as he had done. Unfortunately, that was not to be; verse 2 says Jehoahaz *"did evil in the sight of the Lord."*

The writer of Kings will not let any of the monarchs, especially those who ruled in Israel, pass through the pages of his history without being critically assessed, and verse 2 follows the writer's customary formula for describing a king's failures. Jehoahaz was guilty of perpetuating the *"sins of Jeroboam,"* that is, preserving the calf images at Dan and Bethel. He did not prohibit the people from using these forbidden icons when they worshiped Yahweh at these two great cultic centers. Originally, Jeroboam set up these molten bulls, symbolizing the strength and virility of Yahweh, hoping thereby to entice the people to give up their custom of going to Jerusalem's temple and worship in Israel instead. But God had commanded, "You shall not make for yourself a carved image—any likeness of anything that is in heaven above, or that is in the earth beneath, or that is in the water under the earth" (Exod. 20:4). So no matter how obedient a king might otherwise be, if he did not lead the people to obey this command and turn away from the use of the molten bulls, that king was condemned.

Already, during the last years of Jehu, Hazael of Syria had encroached on the territory of Israel (2 Kings 10:32–33). And now, His anger aroused against Israel, God allowed the Syrian king and his son Ben-Hadad, who succeeded him, to conquer Israel.

The oppression of Syria, mentioned in verse 4, is more specifically described in verse 7, after a parenthetical insertion in verses 5 and 6. Syria had reduced Jehoahaz's large army to a small force of ten chariots, with fifty charioteers, and ten thousand ordinary infantrymen. The rest of the army, primarily his chariot forces, had been crushed like dust trampled underfoot on a threshing floor. This Syrian domination is spoken of in Amos 1:3–5. God's plan was successful. It brought Jehoahaz and his people to their knees in repentance, so that the king began to pray. The term *"pleaded with the Lord"* comes from a word meaning "to be sick," implying weakness and dependency.[1] Jehoahaz was at the end of his rope.

Some people turn to the Lord only when they are desperate. Like the troubled sailors in David's psalm, "They reel to and fro, and stagger like a drunken man, and are at their wits' end. Then they cry out to the Lord in their trouble" (Ps. 107:27–28). As a pastor, I have dealt with a number of people who came to the Lord with this kind of "foxhole" faith. I remember "Ben," who had a problem with alcohol. His wife and children were active in the life of the church, but Ben, although a member, seldom attended. His business was doing well, and his weekends were spent at the country club, more often in the men's locker room around the card table with a drink than on the golf course. With the usual trite excuses, he rebuffed every attempt to draw him back into the fellowship of the congregation: "I'm so busy now. My weekends are the only time I have to relax. These contacts at the club are important to my work, and Sunday is the only time I can meet them." Almost smug in his financial success, Ben made it clear he didn't need "a crutch." He was quite sufficient in himself without those "hypocrites" down at the church.

But there came that terrible day when his teenaged daughter was seriously injured—ironically, in an automobile accident caused by a drinking driver. She was in a coma for weeks. During regular visits to the hospital it became clear that Ben's proud self-sufficiency was eroding. He began to realize how helpless he was. The doctors were doing all they could, and told him so. There was nothing his money and success could do to help. He, like Jehoahaz in Israel, was at the end of his human resources. Like the sailors in the psalm, he was reeling, staggering, at his wits' end.

It was then that Ben began to pray and to respond to pastoral counsel. He even began to accompany his wife and their other children to worship and Bible study. When his daughter finally recovered, he came forward one Sunday morning at the end of the service to thank the congregation for their support, to praise God for His help, and to rededicate his life to the Lord. His commitment was genuine. He remains an active church member to this day.

Remember that in David's psalm, when the desperate men "cried out to the Lord in their trouble," He heard them and calmed the storm. Sometimes, desperation can drive a person to the Lord, and a genuine, healthy faith emerges. Ben had that experience. But unfortunately, "desperation faith" is more likely to be weak and short-lived. I have known others who came to the Lord out of a crisis, only to turn away again as soon as the danger was over. Religion at wits' end is religion all right, but it is usually poor religion. True faith is walking with God all the time, not just in the emergencies of life.

When Jehoahaz was desperate, he turned to the Lord, and *"the Lord listened to him."* However, the answer to his prayer for deliverance from the Syrians did not come immediately, but during the reign of his son King Jehoash (v. 25). The *"deliverer"* in verse 5 may refer to an Assyrian king (some say Adad-Nirari III) whose military approach to Syria drew the attention of Hazael and Ben-Hadad away from Israel to defend their own borders.[2] Keil and Delitzsch believe the deliverer was not another army, nor an angel, nor Elisha, nor some Israelite general who rallied their outnumbered troops to victory, as some other commentators guess, but one or both of the next two kings of Israel: Jehoash and Jeroboam.[3]

"Dwelt in their tents as before" is an idiomatic expression meaning "they had peace"; that is, the soldiers were able to return to their homes and pursue civilian life again. The phrase also refers to the fact that during war times, the people who lived in the open countryside had to move into the fortified villages clustered on the hilltops. When the conflict was over, they could once again pitch their tents and live in their plowed lands and grazing fields.[4]

Israel's repentance was not complete and was obviously short-lived. Not only did they resume their forbidden worship at the shrines of the molten bulls (the sin of Jeroboam), but they also allowed wooden images to remain in Samaria. *"The wooden image"* is literally *'ăšērâ,* the name of a goddess (Asherah) associated with the Phoenician worship of Baal. It may have been a carved pole or the decorated stump of a tree.[5] Jezebel set up such an idol in Samaria with the approval of King Ahab (1 Kings 16:33). If these images were removed during the purge of Baalism under Jehu, they had apparently been replaced. *"Walked"* in verse 6 is singular, indicating that each one of the people sinned. Relationship with God always has an individual as well as a national dimension.

JEHOASH REIGNS IN ISRAEL

> 13:10 In the thirty-seventh year of Joash king of Judah, Jehoash the son of Jehoahaz became king over Israel in Samaria, *and reigned* sixteen years.
>
> 11 And he did evil in the sight of the LORD. He did not depart from all the sins of Jeroboam the son of Nebat, who made Israel sin, *but* walked in them.
>
> 12 Now the rest of the acts of Joash, all that he did, and his might with which he fought against Amaziah king of Judah, *are* they not written in the book of the chronicles of the kings of Israel?
>
> 13 So Joash rested with his fathers. Then Jeroboam sat on his throne. And Joash was buried in Samaria with the kings of Israel.
>
> *2 Kings 13:10–13*

For a time, both Israel and Judah simultaneously had kings named Jehoash. Judah's Jehoash was the young prince who had been rescued from his grandmother's murderous purge and hidden in the temple by Jehoiada the priest and his wife Jehosheba. He was a young man on the throne in Jerusalem when the son of Jehoahaz, also named Jehoash, began to rule in Samaria in the Northern Kingdom. The difference in spelling here and there in the narrative seems to reflect an attempt on the part of translators to distinguish between the two kings.

These four verses give only a brief summary of Jehoash's sixteen-year reign; however, the rest of this chapter and the first sixteen verses of the next chapter give detailed information on it, dwelling particularly on Jehoash's relationship with the prophet Elisha, who died during his reign. Some believe that the writer intentionally separated the death of Elisha from the rest of his report on King Jehoash because he did not want the prophet to be linked with the wicked king's idolatry.[6] Support for this view is found in the fact that the customary conclusion to the reign of Jehoash is given in verses 12–13 and repeated in 2 Kings 14:15–16, as though the writer isolated the story of Elisha from the rest of the account of Jehoash with the stylistic equivalent of parentheses.

Briefly, in this passage, the writer condemns Jehoash for committing *"the sins of Jeroboam"* and then mentions his successful war against Amaziah of Judah, which he neither condemns nor praises. This warfare is described in greater detail in 2 Kings 14:8–15. *"Sat on his throne"* in verse 13 is unusual. Customarily the writer uses the phrase "reigned in his place." Some translators omit the phrase altogether, believing it was not in the original.[7] Jehoash's son Jeroboam II represents the third generation of Jehu's dynasty.

ELISHA PROPHESIES AND DIES

13:14 Elisha had become sick with the illness of which he would die. Then Joash the king of Israel came down to him, and wept over his face, and said, "O my father, my father, the chariots of Israel and their horsemen!"

15 And Elisha said to him, "Take a bow and some arrows." So he took himself a bow and some arrows.

16 Then he said to the king of Israel, "Put your hand on the bow." So he put his hand *on it,* and Elisha put his hands on the king's hands.

17 And he said, "Open the east window"; and he opened *it.* Then Elisha said, "Shoot"; and he shot. And he said, "The arrow of the LORD's deliverance and the arrow of deliverance from Syria; for you must strike the Syrians at Aphek till you have destroyed *them.*"

18 Then he said, "Take the arrows"; so he took *them.* And he said to the king of Israel, "Strike the ground"; so he struck three times, and stopped.

19 And the man of God was angry with him, and
said, "You should have struck five or six times; then
you would have struck Syria till you had destroyed
it! But now you will strike Syria *only* three times."
20 Then Elisha died, and they buried him. And
the *raiding* bands from Moab invaded the land in the
spring of the year.
21 So it was, as they were burying a man, that
suddenly they spied a band *of raiders;* and they put
the man in the tomb of Elisha; and when the man
was let down and touched the bones of Elisha, he
revived and stood on his feet.

2 Kings 13:14–21

Elisha has not been mentioned in the narrative of Kings for fifty years, since his anointing of Jehu in 2 Kings 9:1–10. (The sons of the prophets also fade from the picture about the same time.) Here Elisha is an old man, sick and at the point of death. Unlike the flamboyant Elijah, whose life ended in a dramatic whirlwind exit in a fiery chariot, Elisha died from a wasting illness. But God was just as near to him as he passed through the shadows of the valley of death as He had been to Elijah as he passed through the skies on his fiery chariot.

Jehoash *"came down to him."* This suggests that the king came to Samaria, where Elisha had a home, although it could refer to Elisha's ancestral home in Abel Meholah or to Gilgal, where he also lived at times. Actually, Gilgal better fits the situation in verse 20, since it was closer to the source of the Moabite raids mentioned there. Elisha was apparently buried near the location of these raids, so a good guess is that he spent his last days of illness at his home in Gilgal and then was buried there instead of in the ancestral tombs.[8]

Jehoash's weeping lament over the *"chariots of Israel and their horsemen!"* has been variously interpreted. Some suggest that he was describing a situation similar to that in 2 Kings 2:12 when the chariot of fire transported Elijah to heaven. According to this view, chariots like those of the army of Israel had come to take Elisha home.[9] Others believe that this was merely the king's sad lament over the loss of Israel's chariotry to the forces of the Syrians (2 Kings 13:7).[10] Still others believe that Jehoash considered Elisha himself to be a miraculous substitute for their lost military forces. They didn't need horses and chariots; they had Elisha on their side.[11] This seems to be the interpretation of Josephus, who says Elisha had been their chariotry and cavalry and now that he was dying, they were being left unarmed and defenseless before the Syrians.[12]

It was characteristic of Elisha to use symbolic actions to reinforce his prophecies. He was a "show-and-tell" prophet with a flair for using visual aids effectively. So the last act of the prophet was a visual symbol using a bow and some arrows, dramatizing the future victory of Israel. Elisha put his hand on the bow also, either in order to free the king's hand to open the window or else to endow the act with prophetic spirit and power. The window was opened eastward toward Syria and specifically toward Aphek (v. 17), the most strategic site between Damascus and Samaria. Aphek was the city where Ahab had defeated the Syrians years earlier (1 Kings 20:26).

Most commentaries understand verse 18 to mean that the king held the arrows in his hand and struck them against the floor of Elisha's room. Keil and Delitzsch, however, point out that the word in verse 18 is *"ground,"* not "floor." They submit that when the word *"strike"* is used of an arrow, it means "shoot." Therefore, what Elisha was asking Jehoash to do was to continue to shoot arrows into the ground through the east window. He shot only three arrows and stopped.[13]

Either way, the point of the passage is that the king stopped too soon. He lacked perseverance and determination. He was content with half measures and incomplete achievement, and therefore the future victory over Syria would be a limited victory. If he had continued to "strike" with the arrows, Israel's victory would have been absolute (v. 19). Angry over the king's lack of grit and enthusiasm, the fierce prophet must have died with some misgivings as to the future of his country. The fulfillment of the prophet's prediction is reported in 2 Kings 13:22–25.

Verses 20–21 tell the curious account of Elisha's burial and the crowning miracle of his career. As indicated above, we can only guess at the location of the tomb, a hewn-out sepulcher with a stone rolled across the entrance. Gray makes a strong case for Gilgal, near the Moabite invasions.[14] The verb tense in verse 20 indicates that the Moabites, from east of the Dead Sea, "used to invade"; that is, the raids happened regularly year by year, probably in the spring and summer when the crops would provide food for soldiers and horses.[15] So the event described in these verses could have happened some time after Elisha had been buried. In fact, according to verse 21, his body had already deteriorated so that nothing but bones remained.

Who the dead man was is not disclosed. But as he was being carried to the burial site, suddenly a Moabite raiding-party appeared, and the pallbearers were forced to implement a contingency plan. Instead of preparing the man's own tomb, as they no doubt had planned, they stopped at the first sepulcher they could find, rolled away the stone, and quickly deposited the linen-wrapped body. But before they could reposition the stone and flee from the approaching invaders, a strange thing happened. When the dead man touched the decaying bones of the body already in the tomb, *"he revived and stood on his feet"* (v. 21). It was then they discovered that the tomb they had chosen belonged to Elisha, and the occurrence was listed as his last miracle.

Some commentators suggest that since the term *"revived"* is used here, the man was not actually dead but merely unconscious. Either the trauma of being thrown violently into the tomb or else the cool interior of the burial place resuscitated him and he stood up.[16] I suppose that if the man were not dead, being suddenly dropped on top of a decaying corpse would be trauma enough to revive him! Most interpreters, however, see the account as a resurrection miracle attributed to Elisha.

Elisha remained faithful to his task till his last breath, his own determination and perseverance in sharp contrast to the weakness of the sluggish King Jehoash. If Elisha had held those arrows in his hand, there is little doubt that he would have struck the ground repeatedly, with typical enthusiasm and grit. As a matter of fact, the reason he used that dramatic symbol instead of delivering a routine sermon was that he hoped that by vivid action and direct involvement, the young king might catch some of Elisha's own contagious spirit. Sometimes spiritual lessons are more easily caught than taught.

Learning to ski on the man-made snow of the north Georgia mountains was one of the greatest challenges of my life. My rented boots didn't fit very well, and the worn-out skis had no edges at all. Add to that the fact that the artificial snow had frozen over, making the slopes solid ice. They were one long skating rink! But we were determined to learn.

We discovered that reading ski magazines and how-to-do-it books was not enough. Neither was it enough to listen to the instructor's theoretical explanation of a "snowplow" position. If we were going to learn, we had to plunge in and try it. So the ski instructor said, "Watch me, and do what I do." He pointed his ski tips together in the shape of a plow and began to make slow graceful turns down the beginner's slope. "Now you try it," he said; and we did. And after a while, not so much by talking as by demonstrating, the teacher had us ready to ride the lift for our first run down the slope.

I'll never forget it. Pointing my ski tips together, just as I had seen the expert do, I pushed off down the icy mountain, gaining speed every foot of the way. The rented skis with dull edges glided over the glazed ice with no bite whatsoever. No matter how hard I tried to force the edges into the snow and slow down, I kept getting faster, my skis making a sickening clattering sound as they bounced over the ice.

One thing a skier has to do, of course, is look cool. So even though I was petrified with fear on the inside, on the outside I tried to appear as though I knew exactly what I was doing as I flew out of control past astonished fellow skiers. Now, on the ski slopes of north Georgia, unless you happen to be there following an infrequent snowstorm, the man-made snow ends abruptly at the bottom of the slope. And I was rapidly approaching the place where the snow ended and where a gravel road and a plowed field began. Remembering that above all things, a skier has to look cool, I faithfully held my skis in a perfect snowplow, clattered off the end of the icy snow, across the gravel road, and twenty yards out into the plowed field before coming to an embarrassing halt. Casually, I snapped off my muddy skis, put them over my shoulder and walked back to the lift looking cool, as though I did that sort of thing regularly and intentionally. At least I didn't fall!

Later, on the beautiful packed powder of the Colorado Rockies, with better equipment and a talented instructor, I finally managed to get the feel of it. Now skiing has become our favorite family sport—one that can only be learned by following the example of a good teacher and doing it yourself.

Giving lectures on faith is not enough. If we want to help others learn what the Christian life is all about, we have to demonstrate it, not just once, but consistently, and in a way that will encourage them to trust Christ for themselves. A convincing witness, lived out as well as taught, will make unbelievers want to experience such a life for themselves, and will draw them to Christ.

ISRAEL RECAPTURES CITIES FROM SYRIA

> 13:22 And Hazael king of Syria oppressed Israel all
> the days of Jehoahaz.
> 23 But the LORD was gracious to them, had compassion on them, and regarded them, because of His covenant with Abraham, Isaac, and Jacob, and would not yet destroy them or cast them from His presence.
> 24 Now Hazael king of Syria died. Then Ben-Hadad his son reigned in his place.
> 25 And Jehoash the son of Jehoahaz recaptured from the hand of Ben-Hadad, the son of Hazael, the cities which he had taken out of the hand of Jehoahaz his father by war. Three times Joash defeated him and recaptured the cities of Israel.
>
> *2 Kings 13:22–25*

Picking up again the story of Jehoash, which he began in 2 Kings 13:10, the writer now adds more detail to his brief reference to Syria's oppression of Israel and explains how Yahweh, in spite of Syria's opposition, kept His promise to deliver Israel. Here we see only the turning of the tide in favor of Israel; but their complete domination of Syria, in fulfillment of God's promise, would come during the next reign, that of Jeroboam II. *"Oppressed"* in verse 22 is in the pluperfect tense, signifying "had oppressed" (cf. 2 Kings 13:4, 7). From his own perspective at the time he wrote this, the writer indicates that so far, because of His grace, compassion, and faithfulness to His covenant, God had not allowed Israel to be destroyed. *"Yet"* in verse 23 means "until now." Of course, in a few years, because of her sin, Israel would be defeated and led into captivity.

Ben-Hadad the son Hazael came to power in Syria during the reign of King Jehoash of Israel. This is the third Syrian king of that name referred to in Kings. Israel's victories over Ben-Hadad probably came when Adad-Nirari III, king of Assyria, attacked Syria, giving Israel the opportunity, while Ben-Hadad was distracted, to seize again the cities Hazael had taken from them.[17] The cities were those east of the Jordan, in the territory known as Transjordan. Notice that Israel overcame the Syrian army on three different occasions, equivalent to the number of times Jehoash had struck the ground with the arrows (2 Kings 13:19).

AMAZIAH REIGNS IN JUDAH

14:1 In the second year of Joash the son of Jehoahaz, king of Israel, Amaziah the son of Joash, king of Judah, became king.

2 He was twenty-five years old when he became king, and he reigned twenty-nine years in Jerusalem. His mother's name was Jehoaddan of Jerusalem.

3 And he did *what was* right in the sight of the LORD, yet not like his father David; he did everything as his father Joash had done.

4 However the high places were not taken away, and the people still sacrificed and burned incense on the high places.

5 Now it happened, as soon as the kingdom was established in his hand, that he executed his servants who had murdered his father the king.

6 But the children of the murderers he did not execute, according to what is written in the Book of the Law of Moses, in which the LORD commanded, saying, "Fathers shall not be put to death for their children, nor shall their children be put to death for their fathers; but a person shall be put to death for his own sin."

7 He killed ten thousand Edomites in the Valley of Salt, and took Sela by war, and called its name Joktheel to this day.

8 Then Amaziah sent messengers to Jehoash the son of Jehoahaz, the son of Jehu, king of Israel, saying, "Come, let us face one another *in battle.*"

9 And Jehoash king of Israel sent to Amaziah king of Judah, saying, "The thistle that *was* in Lebanon sent to the cedar that *was* in Lebanon, saying, 'Give your

daughter to my son as wife'; and a wild beast that *was*
in Lebanon passed by and trampled the thistle.
10 "You have indeed defeated Edom, and your heart
has lifted you up. Glory *in that,* and stay at home; for
why should you meddle with trouble so that you fall-
you and Judah with you?"
11 But Amaziah would not heed. Therefore Jehoash king of Israel went out; so he and Amaziah
king of Judah faced one another at Beth Shemesh,
which *belongs* to Judah.
12 And Judah was defeated by Israel, and every
man fled to his tent.
13 Then Jehoash king of Israel captured Amaziah
king of Judah, the son of Jehoash, the son of Ahaziah,
at Beth Shemesh; and he went to Jerusalem, and broke
down the wall of Jerusalem from the Gate of Ephraim
to the Corner Gate—four hundred cubits.
14 And he took all the gold and silver, all the articles that were found in the house of the LORD and in
the treasuries of the king's house, and hostages, and
returned to Samaria.
15 Now the rest of the acts of Jehoash which he
did—his might, and how he fought with Amaziah
king of Judah—*are* they not written in the book of the
chronicles of the kings of Israel?
16 So Jehoash rested with his fathers, and was
buried in Samaria with the kings of Israel. Then Jeroboam his son reigned in his place.
17 Amaziah the son of Joash, king of Judah, lived
fifteen years after the death of Jehoash the son of
Jehoahaz, king of Israel.
18 Now the rest of the acts of Amaziah, *are* they
not written in the book of the chronicles of the kings
of Judah?
19 And they formed a conspiracy against him in
Jerusalem, and he fled to Lachish; but they sent after
him to Lachish and killed him there.
20 Then they brought him on horses; and he was
buried at Jerusalem with his fathers in the City of
David.
21 And all the people of Judah took Azariah, who

was sixteen years old, and made him king instead of his father Amaziah.

22 He built Elath and restored it to Judah, after the king rested with his fathers.

2 Kings 14:1–22

Following his rotation pattern, the historian now switches from Israel back to Judah and begins his account of King Amaziah. Jehoash, the young prince who grew up in Jerusalem's temple, was assassinated by his servants, Jozachar and Jehozabad, after a commendable reign of forty years. His son Amaziah followed him, assuming the throne of Judah two years after Jehoash the son of Jehoahaz became king in Israel. Amaziah's mother was from Jerusalem, and her name, "Jehoaddan," means, "May God give sexual pleasure."[18]

Amaziah followed his father's good example but still did not receive the unqualified approbation of the writer. Compared to David, he fell short (v. 3). Like his father, he was guilty of permitting the people to worship Yahweh on the *"high places,"* the former pagan cultic sites that the people of Judah had transformed into centers of Yahweh worship (v. 4). It was not until Josiah's reformation years later that this sinful practice was finally corrected. Despite his shortcomings, Amaziah was commended for his long reign (v. 2), his revenge on his father's murderers (v. 5), his restraint in sparing the children of the murderers (v. 6), and his victory over Edom (v. 7).

Ironically, his clemency in sparing the children of his father's killers may have led to his own death. Some commentators believe the assassins who put Amaziah to death in verse 19 may have been the very children whom Amaziah had spared. They, in turn, were exacting vengeance for Amaziah's executions.

The quotation in verse 6 is from Deut. 24:16 and is the second reference in Kings to *"the Book of the Law of Moses."* The first is in 1 Kings 2:3. It was probably this scroll that Josiah found when he restored the temple.[19]

Most of the enemies of Judah came and went like the waves of the sea: the Moabites, Syrians, Assyrians, Egyptians. But the Edomites were always there. The Edomites were the descendants of Esau, the twin brother of Jacob. These twins were competitors all their lives.

Even before they were born, their mother, Rebekah, complained that the twins "struggled together within her" (Gen. 25:22). At birth, Esau was first, but Jacob had a grip on his brother's ankle, so they named him "Supplanter," meaning, "one who trips or supplants another." Jacob and Esau constantly competed with each other, and the nations descended from them, Israel and Edom, continued the feud. These two nations hated and scorned each other with a relentlessness unmatched in the history of kindred and neighboring nations. From Gen. 25:30 to Mal. 1:5 there are biblical records of hostility between them. It was one of these frequent feuds that occasioned the Book of Obadiah, which is a prophetic condemnation of the Edomites.

The land of Edom was located in the great red mountains of the Arabian wilderness south of the Dead Sea. Their capital, Petra, was literally carved out of those mountains and was inaccessible except through a narrow canyon called the Siq. Therefore, Petra was an easy city to defend, and because of their perceived invincibility, the Edomites were inclined to become proud and boastful.

The battle in verse 7 took place in the *"Valley of Salt,"* south of the Dead Sea. *"Sela"* means "rock" and probably stands for Petra, the Edomite capital carved from the sandstone mountains. There is no trace of the name *"Joktheel"* anywhere else in Scripture except in Josh. 15:38, and because of the location implied in that passage, it could not be referring to the same city. In 2 Chronicles 25, more details of this battle are given. Amaziah hired a hundred thousand mercenaries from Israel, but when an unnamed prophet warned him against using them in the battle, he discharged them and, disregarding their angry protests, sent them back home. In addition to the ten thousand Edomites killed in battle (v. 7), Chronicles says Amaziah executed another ten thousand Edomite captives by casting them from the top of Mount Petra.

Overconfident because of his stunning success in the Edomite campaign, Amaziah declared war on Israel (v. 8). After all, his army had killed twenty thousand Edomites, and since Jehoash had only ten chariots and ten thousand infantrymen, he assumed he could easily defeat them too (cf. 2 Kings 13:7). The war may have erupted over a border dispute between the two nations.[20] Or, according to Keil and Delitzsch, it may have been precipitated when the discharged Israelite mercenaries returned in anger from the Edomite campaign.

They went back home, plundering Judean villages on the way.[21] This caused Amaziah to challenge Jehoash to meet him in battle.

Jehoash's parable teaches the folly of overestimating one's importance. In essence the parable says, "The thistle, imagining himself to be equal with the cedar, presumptuously suggested a marriage alliance between them. The difference between them was made obvious when a wild beast passed through and crushed the thistle underfoot. Of course the beast was powerless to injure the cedar." A similar parable is found in Judg. 9:8ff. The Arabs also have a comparable parable, "The mule says the horse is his father."[22]

Beth Shemesh, on the border of Judah and Dan, was an unlikely place to fight a battle. The fact that they fought there adds credence to the idea that the war was precipitated by a border dispute, perhaps in the vicinity of Beth Shemesh.[23] Jehoash's army won the battle, as he had boasted it would. Chronicles adds that Amaziah's defeat was a punishment from God because Judah had begun to worship Edomite gods.

Not only did the army of Israel win the battle of Beth Shemesh, they also captured King Amaziah, who was deserted by his retreating army. Then they pillaged the city of Jerusalem. The *"Gate of Ephraim"* in verse 13, now known as the Damascus Gate, was on the north side of the city, facing Ephraim—that is, the kingdom of Israel. A section of the wall about two hundred feet long was destroyed, leaving the city unprotected to the north. After confiscating treasures from the temple and the palace and taking a number of hostages as well, Jehoash left Amaziah in Jerusalem to continue as a vassal king over a ruined capital. The *"hostages,"* literally, "sons of pledges" were apparently taken to ensure Amaziah's continued capitulation. Verses 15 and 16 are identical with 13:12ff. and are repeated here to mark the end of the interlude intentionally inserted after the summary of Jehoash's reign.

No reason is given for the conspiracy against Amaziah in verse 19, but it may have been fostered by the families of the servants who were executed by the king when he was enthroned. Others suggest that Amaziah was killed by citizens who were angry that he had allowed Jerusalem to be plundered and the temple violated.[24] Another theory advanced is that Azariah, his son and successor, plotted the coup.[25] Lachish was a Judean stronghold about thirty-five miles southwest of Jerusalem. The use of the plural *"horses"* in verse 20 suggests that the king's body was brought back on a wagon.

Azariah is called Uzziah in 2 Chronicles and in Isaiah. There is a difference of only one letter between the two names in Hebrew and some commentators believe a scribe may have accidentally dropped a letter in copying the text.[26] As they are spelled, the two names are related in meaning: "Azariah" means "Yahweh is a help"; "Uzziah" means "Whose strength is Yahweh." The names are used interchangeably for this king throughout the Old Testament. When the writer says in verse 21 that *"all the people of Judah"* chose Azariah as king, he implies that the choice was unanimous or at least very popular. His statement could also point to widespread national hostility against Amaziah.

Elath was a seaport town on the Gulf of Aqaba. Archaeological excavations there have uncovered a seal bearing the inscription "belonging to Jotham." This is evidence of the presence of Azariah and his son Jotham in the area.[27] Later the harbor was lost again to Syria (2 Kings 16:6).

The lesson of this sad chapter in the continuing conflict between the Southern and the Northern Kingdoms is "Pride goes before destruction, and a haughty spirit before a fall" (Prov. 16:18).

Jeroboam II Reigns in Israel

14:23 In the fifteenth year of Amaziah the son of Joash, king of Judah, Jeroboam the son of Joash, king of Israel, became king in Samaria, *and reigned* forty-one years.

24 And he did evil in the sight of the LORD; he did not depart from all the sins of Jeroboam the son of Nebat, who had made Israel sin.

25 He restored the territory of Israel from the entrance of Hamath to the Sea of the Arabah, according to the word of the LORD God of Israel, which He had spoken through His servant Jonah the son of Amittai, the prophet who *was* from Gath Hepher.

26 For the LORD saw *that* the affliction of Israel *was* very bitter; and whether bond or free, there was no helper for Israel.

27 And the LORD did not say that He would blot
out the name of Israel from under heaven; but He
saved them by the hand of Jeroboam the son of
Joash.
28 Now the rest of the acts of Jeroboam, and all that
he did—his might, how he made war, and how he re-
captured for Israel, from Damascus and Hamath, *what
had belonged* to Judah—*are* they not written in the
book of the chronicles of the kings of Israel?
29 So Jeroboam rested with his fathers, the kings
of Israel. Then Zechariah his son reigned in his place.

2 Kings 14:23–29

Now we return to Israel and the story of the monarchical succession there. After sixteen years on the throne, characterized by spectacular military victories over Syria and Judah, Jehoash died a natural death and was buried in Samaria with the other kings of Israel. His son Jeroboam, the second of that name to rule in Israel, ascended to the throne.

It is obvious from the abbreviated treatment given to Jeroboam II by the writer of Kings that his purpose is not to give a classical historical account. Secular historians would have spent significant time on Jeroboam because his rule was one of the longest in the history of Israel, forty-one years. Not since the days of Solomon had the people of Israel known such prosperity, power, and grandeur as was achieved during the reign of Jeroboam II. But our historian casually mentions him, almost in passing. He has another goal, namely, to give a spiritual and theological account of God's dealings with His people: how His people sinned, how they were judged and punished, how God continued to work with them to fulfill His eternal purpose. With this in mind, the author skips lightly over events that technical historians would dwell on, and conversely, spends much time on incidents that secular writers would hardly consider worthy of mention.

While secular recorders would appraise Jeroboam II's reign as great, our writer perfunctorily calls it sinful because the king continued to disobey Yahweh by following the sins of the first Jeroboam, the son of Nebat (v. 24). This is consistent with Amos's depiction of Israel under Jeroboam as an overripe summer fruit doomed to speedy decay (Amos 8:1–2). The author refuses to give Jeroboam II credit for his successes and nonchalantly explains the achievements as God's blessing on the kingdom because of His promise (v. 27).

In verse 25 the writer refers to another of the canonical prophets, Jonah, the son of Amittai, from Gath Hepher. The incident referred to is not mentioned in Jonah's book. Tradition says he was the one chosen from among the sons of the prophets to anoint Jehu (2 Kings 9:1).[28]

At the end of Jeroboam II's long reign, Zechariah his son became king of Israel in his place (v. 29). Zechariah was the fourth generation of the Jehu dynasty. God had promised Jehu that his sons would rule in his place to the fourth generation (2 Kings 10:30). After Zechariah, the dynasty of Jehu came to an end, and the kingdom passed into other hands.

Azariah Reigns in Judah

15:1 In the twenty-seventh year of Jeroboam king of Israel, Azariah the son of Amaziah, king of Judah, became king.

2 He was sixteen years old when he became king, and he reigned fifty-two years in Jerusalem. His mother's name *was* Jecholiah of Jerusalem.

3 And he did *what was* right in the sight of the LORD, according to all that his father Amaziah had done,

4 except that the high places were not removed; the people still sacrificed and burned incense on the high places.

5 Then the LORD struck the king, so that he was a leper until the day of his death; so he dwelt in an isolated house. And Jotham the king's son *was* over the *royal* house, judging the people of the land.

6 Now the rest of the acts of Azariah, and all that he did, *are* they not written in the book of the chronicles of the kings of Judah?

7 So Azariah rested with his fathers, and they buried him with his fathers in the City of David. Then Jotham his son reigned in his place.

2 Kings 15:1–7

Now we go back to Judah once again to pick up the drama there. Following the tragic events that brought King Amaziah's reign to an end, Jerusalem was in disarray, a major section of its protective wall destroyed, its temple and palace emptied of their treasures, and some of its inhabitants taken away to Israel as hostages. Azariah, or Uzziah as he is also known, had his work cut out for him. His long reign of fifty-two years may have included a coregency with his father, Amaziah, at the beginning and, because of his illness, a coregency with his son Jotham toward its conclusion.[29]

He was a good king, but the writer does not mention a single accomplishment. In the parallel account, Chronicles tells how he elevated Judah to great earthly power and prosperity, waging successful wars against the Philistines and the Arabs, rebuilding the wall of Jerusalem and adding strong towers, constructing watchtowers in the desert, constructing cisterns, and developing vineyards and other agricultural interests (2 Chron. 26:5ff.). Chronicles also adds that his leprosy, mentioned in verse 5, was a punishment from God because he had presumed to burn incense in the temple (2 Chron. 26:16).

Verse 5 implies that his son took over administrative tasks in a kind of coregency when he was about fifteen years old. Since Jotham was only twenty-five years old when Azariah died (2 Kings 15:33), Azariah's illness probably began during the last ten years of his reign.[30] *"Isolated house"* in verse 5 comes from the word meaning "free" and may imply several things. It may mean he lived free from his duties as king, his son taking over the responsibility for him.[31] Or it could mean he lived on "unmolested" (Moffat's translation). Or it could mean he was quarantined in a separate dwelling.[32]

Since the word for "leprosy" is a generic term denoting a variety of skin diseases, his case may not have been a serious one. However, Chronicles indicates it was serious enough that because of the disease he was not buried with the other kings of Judah. An Aramaic inscription uncovered near Jerusalem in 1931 reads, "Hither we brought the bones of Uzziah, do not open." This supports the passage in 2 Chron. 26:23, which suggests that his remains were easily identifiable because he had been buried apart from the regular royal tombs.[33]

His death is significant for another reason. It was in that year that Isaiah was called to be a prophet. "In the year that King Uzziah died, I saw the Lord" (Isa. 6:1). Chronicles refers to a record of Ahaziah's work written by Isaiah, but the record has not been found.[34]

NOTES

1. T. R. Hobbs, *2 Kings,* Word Biblical Commentary, ed. John D. W. Watts, vol. 13 (Waco, TX: Word Books, 1985), 165.
2. M. Pierce Matheney and Roy Honeycutt, "1-2 Kings," in *The Broadman Bible Commentary,* ed. Clifton J. Allen, vol. 3 (Nashville: Broadman, 1970), 258.
3. C. F. Keil, *The Books of the Kings,* Biblical Commentary on the Old Testament, ed. C. F. Keil and F. Delitzsch, vol. 4 (Grand Rapids: Eerdmans, 1950), 373.
4. John Gray, *I and II Kings,* Old Testament Library (Philadelphia: Westminster, 1963), 539.
5. Matheney and Honeycutt, 258.
6. I. W. Slotki, *Kings* (London: Soncino Press, 1950), 241.
7. Gwilym H. Jones, *1 and 2 Kings,* New Century Bible Commentary, ed. Ronald E. Clements (Grand Rapids: Eerdmans, 1984), 501.
8. Gray, 541.
9. Slotki, 242.
10. Hobbs, 169.
11. Gray, 541.
12. Hobbs, 169.
13. Keil, 376.
14. Gray, 541.
15. Slotki, 242.
16. Keil, 376.
17. Jones, 505.
18. Gray, 547.
19. Ibid.
20. Matheney and Honeycutt, 260.
21. Keil, 379.
22. Gray, 547.
23. Hobbs, 178.
24. Matheney and Honeycutt, 260.

25. Jones, 512.
26. Norman H. Snaith, Ralph W. Sockman, and Raymond Calkins, "The First and Second Books of Kings," in *The Interpreter's Bible,* vol. 3 (Nashville: Abingdon, 1954), 260.
27. Jones, 512.
28. Slotki, 249.
29. Ibid., 250.
30. Keil, 386.
31. Gray, 558.
32. Matheney and Honeycutt, 263.
33. Jones, 520.
34. Snaith, Sockman, and Calkins, 266.

CHAPTER SEVENTEEN

The Last Six Kings of Israel, Jotham and Ahaz of Judah, and the Captivity of Israel

2 Kings 15:8–17:41

ZECHARIAH, SHALLUM, AND MENAHEM REIGN IN ISRAEL

15:8 In the thirty-eighth year of Azariah king of Judah, Zechariah the son of Jeroboam reigned over Israel in Samaria six months.

9 And he did evil in the sight of the LORD, as his fathers had done; he did not depart from the sins of Jeroboam the son of Nebat, who had made Israel sin.

10 Then Shallum the son of Jabesh conspired against him, and struck and killed him in front of the people; and he reigned in his place.

11 Now the rest of the acts of Zechariah, indeed they *are* written in the book of the chronicles of the kings of Israel.

12 This *was* the word of the LORD which He spoke to Jehu, saying, "Your sons shall sit on the throne of Israel to the fourth *generation.*" And so it was.

13 Shallum the son of Jabesh became king in the thirty-ninth year of Uzziah king of Judah; and he reigned a full month in Samaria.

14 For Menahem the son of Gadi went up from Tirzah, came to Samaria, and struck Shallum the son of Jabesh in Samaria and killed him; and he reigned in his place.

15 Now the rest of the acts of Shallum, and the conspiracy which he led, indeed they *are* written in the book of the chronicles of the kings of Israel.

16 Then from Tirzah, Menahem attacked Tiphsah,
all who *were* there, and its territory. Because they did
not surrender, therefore he attacked *it.* All the women
there who were with child he ripped open.
17 In the thirty-ninth year of Azariah king of Judah, Menahem the son of Gadi became king over Israel, *and reigned* ten years in Samaria.
18 And he did evil in the sight of the LORD; he did
not depart all his days from the sins of Jeroboam the
son of Nebat, who had made Israel sin.
19 Pul king of Assyria came against the land; and
Menahem gave Pul a thousand talents of silver, that
his hand might be with him to strengthen the kingdom under his control.
20 And Menahem exacted the money from Israel,
from all the very wealthy, from each man fifty shekels
of silver, to give to the king of Assyria. So the king of
Assyria turned back, and did not stay there in the land.
21 Now the rest of the acts of Menahem, and all
that he did, *are* they not written in the book of the
chronicles of the kings of Israel?
22 So Menahem rested with his fathers. Then
Pekahiah his son reigned in his place.

2 Kings 15:8–22

Having stepped on the slippery slope of apostasy and disobedience, Israel was careening with accelerating speed toward an inevitable destiny of destruction and captivity. Within the next forty-three years half a dozen "pseudo-kings" would reign in rapid succession, one murderer replacing another on the throne, as the nation tottered on the brink of anarchy. Only one king, Menahem, died a natural death and was succeeded by his son on the throne of Samaria. The other five were violently dethroned by rebels. Most of the rulers were not so much kings as robbers and tyrants, unworthy of the august name of "king."

It did not require special insight for Hosea to conclude that such political bedlam signified the approaching doom of Israel. Sadly he declared to his countrymen the word of the Lord: "I will avenge the bloodshed of Jezreel on the house of Jehu, and bring an end to the kingdom of the house of Israel" (Hos. 1:4). In a few short years, the Northern Kingdom would be no more.

Jeroboam II had brought Israel to a level of stability, power, and grandeur beyond any other period of prosperity since Solomon, but those good days came to a swift end when his son Zechariah assumed the throne. Zechariah hardly ruled Israel long enough to be appraised—only six months—but his character was well enough established that the writer of Kings could label him another of those who *"did evil in the sight of the Lord, as his fathers had done"* (v. 9). His name, meaning "Yahweh remembers," should have encouraged him to remember the commandments of the Lord and the warnings of the prophets, but his memory was faulty, and like Jeroboam I, he *"made Israel sin."*

Nothing is known about Shallum, the usurper who conspired against Zechariah to take the throne by force. The designation *"son of Jabesh"* may mean "man from Jabesh." According to verse 10 Shallum killed Zechariah *"in front of the people,"* a phrase that translates one word in the Hebrew text, *gābāl-ʿam.* If that is the correct translation, it emphasizes that Shallum must have had a strong popular following to be able to carry out his plan in public.[1] Notice, however, that both the Targum and the Vulgate read here the Hebrew word *yiblĕʿām,* interpreting it as "Ibleam," the name of the well-known city. (This reading actually only differs by a single consonant.)

Accepting that explanation, some modern translations construe the verse to mean that Zechariah was murdered at Ibleam, the same location where Jehu massacred the princes of the royal house of Judah when he usurped the throne of Israel (2 Kings 10:14).[2] Ironically, this would mean that the dynasty of Jehu began and ended at the same place, Ibleam.

Zechariah was the fourth generation of the sons of Jehu to reign in Israel (v. 12). God had promised Jehu that because of his obedience, even though it was imperfect, four generations of his sons would succeed him on the throne of Samaria (2 Kings 10:30). So, even though Zechariah was unworthy to rule the nation, he was still allowed six months on the throne to fulfill God's promise. The story of his brief reign ends at verse 11 with the usual concluding formula for the kings of Israel, except that no mention is made of his burial. In the case of each of these last kings of Israel, with the exception of Menahem, the usual notice of burial is missing.

Now it was Shallum's turn to be king. If Zechariah's term was scandalously brief, Shallum's term was a joke—so short the author of Kings seems to struggle to find an appropriate term to describe it. Literally, he says Shallum reigned "a month of days," that is, a full month. Of all the kings of Israel, only Zimri reigned for a shorter period—seven days!

The name "Shallum" means "he for whom compensation has been made." It may refer to the fact that at his birth his parents discharged some vow they had made.[3] The same name is incorporated into the names of two of David's sons, Absalom and Solomon.[4] If Jabesh is a place name rather than the personal name of his father, then Shallum came from Jabesh-Gilead on the other side of the Jordan (v. 13). He may have been assisted in his conspiracy against Zechariah by the Syrians.[5]

Within a matter of thirty days Shallum lost his throne to still another usurper. Menahem (probably a general in Zechariah's army) launched a military coup d'état, killed Shallum, and assumed the throne himself. Apparently, the people of Tiphsah had supported Shallum, so Menahem destroyed the city with the uncommon cruelty described in verse 16. Such atrocities were characteristic of pagan invaders, but, with this one exception, were never committed by the soldiers of Israel.[6]

Not much more could be said about Shallum's accomplishments than the terse conclusion in verse 15 that mentions only his conspiracy against Zechariah. Assyrian records identify Israel's King Shallum as "the son of nobody."[7]

Compared to the short-term reigns of the kings before and after him, Menahem's ten-year reign appears quite lengthy. When he became king, it meant that four different kings had ruled Israel in less than a year. Their tenures were so brief that the historical account often says more about their usurpers than about the kings themselves. Meanwhile in the south, Judah was enjoying the relative calm of King Azariah's long and stable fifty-two-year reign (v. 17). The contrast between the two nations at this point is dramatic.

If, as Josephus declares, Menahem was Israel's commander in chief before he became king, than it was probably from Tirzah that he launched his coup. It appears that Menahem and the army had been stationed at Tirzah preparing for an assault on the nearby city of Tiphsah, where an uprising had recently broken out. So, leaving the main body of troops at Tirzah, Menahem took a small battalion of soldiers with him to Samaria, three hours away, where he killed

Shallum and declared himself king. Then it was back to Tirzah to solidify his hold on the military by leading the entire army to destroy the disloyal city of Tiphsah.

Menahem was unlike the other kings of Israel during this turbulent period in that his reign lasted a full ten years. But he was very much like the other kings in that he too *"did evil in the sight of the Lord"* (v. 18). Because of a problem with chronology, some commentators believe Menahem did not immediately become king following the death of Shallum but continued to struggle for the throne in a civil war that lasted several months.

Because he needed Assyria's help to strengthen his hold on the throne, Menahem willingly paid tribute to Tiglath-Pileser III, even though this meant that Israel became a vassal state. Here in verse 19, the nation of Assyria makes its first contact with Israel, which it eventually destroyed. Pul is another name for Tiglath-Pileser III, a throne name that he assumed when he usurped royal power in 729 B.C. The amount of the tribute (v. 19) was enormous. *"A thousand talents"* is equal to 844,800 ounces of silver. At a price of $5 an ounce, the tribute would be equivalent to $4,224,000. At an assessment of fifty shekels per man, about $100, it would require 42,000 men to meet such an obligation. Supposedly, then, there were many families in Israel at this time who could fit the category *"wealthy"* as defined in verse 20.[8]

This tribute payment is briefly mentioned in the annals of Tiglath-Pileser III:

> As for Menahem, I overwhelmed him like a snowstorm, and he . . . fled like a bird, along, and bowed to my feet. I returned him to his place and imposed tribute upon him, to wit: gold, silver, linen garments with multicolored trimmings, . . . great . . . I received from him.[9]

Ironically, the name "Menahem" means "comforting."

PEKAHIAH AND PEKAH REIGN IN ISRAEL

> 15:23 In the fiftieth year of Azariah king of Judah, Pekahiah the son of Menahem became king over Israel in Samaria, *and reigned* two years.

24 And he did evil in the sight of the LORD; he did
not depart from the sins of Jeroboam the son of
Nebat, who had made Israel sin.
25 Then Pekah the son of Remaliah, an officer of
his, conspired against him and killed him in Samaria,
in the citadel of the king's house, along with Argob
and Arieh; and with him were fifty men of Gilead.
He killed him and reigned in his place.
26 Now the rest of the acts of Pekahiah, and all
that he did, indeed they *are* written in the book of
the chronicles of the kings of Israel.
27 In the fifty-second year of Azariah king of
Judah, Pekah the son of Remaliah became king over
Israel in Samaria, *and reigned* twenty years.
28 And he did evil in the sight of the LORD; he did
not depart from the sins of Jeroboam the son of
Nebat, who had made Israel sin.
29 In the days of Pekah king of Israel, Tiglath-
Pileser king of Assyria came and took Ijon, Abel Beth
Maachah, Janoah, Kedesh, Hazor, Gilead, and Galilee,
all the land of Naphtali; and he carried them captive to
Assyria.
30 Then Hoshea the son of Elah led a conspiracy
against Pekah the son of Remaliah, and struck and
killed him; so he reigned in his place in the twentieth
year of Jotham the son of Uzziah.
31 Now the rest of the acts of Pekah, and all that
he did, indeed they *are* written in the book of the
chronicles of the kings of Israel.

2 Kings 15:23–31

Azariah had been on the throne of neighboring Judah for half a century when Pekahiah, the son of Menahem, became king in the troubled nation of Israel. His name means "Yahweh opens or illumines."[10] Isn't it amazing that the kings continued to take religious names, indicating their devotion to the Lord God of Israel, when their hearts were so far from Him? The writer has nothing to say about Pekahiah's two years as king except the usual words of condemnation, *"he did evil in the sight of the Lord"* (v. 24).

There is another problem here for those who try to harmonize the chronology of the kings. Some suggest that there was a two-year interim without a king before Pekahiah took over after the death of his father Menahem. If so, it may be that the Assyrians intentionally imposed this waiting period so they could officially test Pekahiah's loyalty as their vassal.[11] Whatever the timing, once the king was crowned, it didn't take long for the political instability of Israel to breed another coup.

Once again the rebellion started in the military, and this time it was led by an army officer with the same name as the king he deposed! Pekah is a shortened form of Pekahiah and was apparently a common name. A jar found in the archaeological dig at Hazor has an inscription reading, "belonging to Pekah Samdar."[12] Pekah is called an *"officer"* in verse 25. This translates the Hebrew word *šālîš*, which specifically means "captain."

With the help of fifty Gileadites, Pekah boldly assaulted the fortified wing of the royal palace in Samaria and put the king to death. Josephus adds that the attack took place during an official banquet in the palace.[13] *"Argob,"* the name of a district in Bashan, probably identifies a man who was the governor there. He, along with Arieh, remained loyal to King Pekahiah to the last and suffered death with him. *"Arieh"* means "lion," but nothing more is known about him.[14]

According to verse 27, Pekah's reign lasted *"twenty years,"* which presents yet another sticky chronological challenge to those who try to harmonize royal successions. Some say the verse should read "five years," some say "two years."[15] Others draw the conclusion that Pekahiah was a fictitious king, that he never existed. But this conclusion is more a gesture of despair on the part of frustrated harmonizers than the fruit of careful historical analysis.[16]

Later, in 2 Kings 15:37, we are told about an alliance between Pekah and King Rezin of Syria. The two of them tried to enlist Ahaz of Judah to join an alliance with them, and when he refused, they attacked the Southern Kingdom in what is known as the Syrian-Ephraimite invasion.[17] It may have been this alliance with Rezin that caused Tiglath-Pileser III of Assyria to launch the attack against Israel (v. 29), fearing that they might try to rebel with the help of their new friend.

Assyria's invasion of Israel is also referred to in several other inscriptions, including one in Tiglath-Pileser's royal annals. According to this account, he created three districts from the conquered territory: (1) Meggido, covering Galilee and the Northern Plains; (2) Dor, including the Plain of Sharon and extending to the Philistine border; and (3) Gilead, in the Transjordan area.[18] The inscription also says, "They overthrew their king Peqaha and I placed Ausi [Hoshea] as king over them." This indicates that Tiglath-Pileser III may have actually participated in Hoshea's conspiracy to kill King Pekah (v. 30).[19] Archaeological evidence of the invasion has also been unearthed in the excavations at Hazor.[20] Together, all the cities mentioned in verse 29 make up *"the land of Naphtali"* (synonymous with Galilee). Igon is the most northerly of the cities listed and was therefore the first to fall before the Assyrian invaders, who came from that direction.

This oppression in 733 B.C., a precursor of the major captivity in 722 B.C., seems to be the first test of Assyria's strategy of reducing a conquered nation into an Assyrian province by deporting the upper classes to another part of the empire and replacing them with foreign immigrants.[21] For another graphic picture of this grim period in Israel's history read Hosea 13:11, 7:11, 4:17, 4:1–2, and 8:2.

These were dark days for Israel, her territory now reduced to a tiny kingdom only thirty miles wide by forty miles long. The Northern Kingdom was down to its last ruler. Hoshea would be the final king of this dying nation. No wonder these tragic events became the occasion for the "Immanuel" passages in Isaiah 7:1ff.

Nowhere in the Word of God is there a clearer illustration of the consequences of sin. Israel was helpless to save herself. Even the powerful preaching of the prophets could not stem the tide. Destruction was inevitable. And it's still that way today. Sin still brings consequences so overpowering that even the strongest human efforts cannot withstand them.

The Bible makes it clear that in spite of our impressive technological sophistication, without Christ, our own generation, like Israel, is dead in trespasses and sins. Even our unprecedented scientific power cannot save us. Nothing short of a divine miracle can defeat Satan and redeem the sinner. That's why this passage in Kings points us so plaintively to the cross of Calvary, God's ultimate solution to humankind's lostness. Over seven hundred years after Israel's captivity, on a cross just outside the walls of Jerusalem, another monarch, this time a perfect descendant of David—Jesus Christ, the King of kings—gave His life for the sins of the world, so that those who believe in Him might not perish, but have eternal life. No wonder the Bible calls that atoning event "the good news!"

Before completing the story of Israel's tragic finale, the historian switches his attention back to Judah for a brief look at two of the kings there.

JOTHAM AND AHAZ REIGN IN JUDAH

15:32 In the second year of Pekah the son of Remaliah, king of Israel, Jotham the son of Uzziah, king of Judah, began to reign.

33 He was twenty-five years old when he became king, and he reigned sixteen years in Jerusalem. His mother's name *was* Jerusha the daughter of Zadok.

34 And he did *what was* right in the sight of the LORD; he did according to all that his father Uzziah had done.

35 However the high places were not removed; the people still sacrificed and burned incense on the high places. He built the Upper Gate of the house of the LORD.

36 Now the rest of the acts of Jotham, and all that he did, *are* they not written in the book of the chronicles of the kings of Judah?

37 In those days the LORD began to send Rezin king of Syria and Pekah the son of Remaliah against Judah.

38 So Jotham rested with his fathers, and was buried with his fathers in the City of David his father. Then Ahaz his son reigned in his place.

16:1 In the seventeenth year of Pekah the son of Remaliah, Ahaz the son of Jotham, king of Judah, began to reign.

2 Ahaz *was* twenty years old when he became king, and he reigned sixteen years in Jerusalem; and he did not do *what was* right in the sight of the LORD his God, as his father David *had done.*

3 But he walked in the way of the kings of Israel; indeed he made his son pass through the fire, according to the abominations of the nations whom the LORD had cast out from before the children of Israel.

4 And he sacrificed and burned incense on the high places, on the hills, and under every green tree.

5 Then Rezin king of Syria and Pekah the son of

Remaliah, king of Israel, came up to Jerusalem to *make* war; and they besieged Ahaz but could not overcome *him.*

6 At that time Rezin king of Syria captured Elath for Syria, and drove the men of Judah from Elath. Then the Edomites went to Elath, and dwell there to this day.

7 So Ahaz sent messengers to Tiglath-Pileser king of Assyria, saying, "I *am* your servant and your son. Come up and save me from the hand of the king of Syria and from the hand of the king of Israel, who rise up against me."

8 And Ahaz took the silver and gold that was found in the house of the LORD, and in the treasuries of the king's house, and sent *it as* a present to the king of Assyria.

9 So the king of Assyria heeded him; for the king of Assyria went up against Damascus and took it, carried *its people* captive to Kir, and killed Rezin.

10 Now King Ahaz went to Damascus to meet Tiglath-Pileser king of Assyria, and saw an altar that *was* at Damascus; and King Ahaz sent to Urijah the priest the design of the altar and its pattern, according to all its workmanship.

11 Then Urijah the priest built an altar according to all that King Ahaz had sent from Damascus. So Urijah the priest made *it* before King Ahaz came back from Damascus.

12 And when the king came back from Damascus, the king saw the altar; and the king approached the altar and made offerings on it.

13 So he burned his burnt offering and his grain offering; and he poured his drink offering and sprinkled the blood of his peace offerings on the altar.

14 He also brought the bronze altar which *was* before the LORD, from the front of the temple—from between the *new* altar and the house of the LORD—and put it on the north side of the *new* altar.

15 Then King Ahaz commanded Urijah the priest, saying, "On the great *new* altar burn the morning burnt offering, the evening grain offering, the king's burnt sacrifice, and his grain offering, with the burnt

offering of all the people of the land, their grain offering, and their drink offerings; and sprinkle on it
all the blood of the burnt offering and all the blood
of the sacrifice. And the bronze altar shall be for me
to inquire *by.*"
16 Thus did Urijah the priest, according to all that
King Ahaz commanded.
17 And King Ahaz cut off the panels of the carts,
and removed the lavers from them; and he took
down the Sea from the bronze oxen that *were* under
it, and put it on a pavement of stones.
18 Also he removed the Sabbath pavilion which
they had built in the temple, and he removed the
king's outer entrance from the house of the LORD, on
account of the king of Assyria.
19 Now the rest of the acts of Ahaz which he did,
are they not written in the book of the chronicles of
the kings of Judah?
20 So Ahaz rested with his fathers, and was buried
with his fathers in the City of David. Then Hezekiah
his son reigned in his place.

2 Kings 15:32–16:20

Following an internship of about ten years during which he carried the responsibilities of state for his ailing father, King Azariah, young Prince Jotham was crowned king of Judah. Repulsed by the sorry state of affairs he had witnessed in the Northern Kingdom, Jotham determined that it would be different in Judah. He set his course to continue the worthy tradition of his father's commendable reign. According to the historian's report card, he *"did what was right in the sight of the Lord"* (v. 34).

"Jotham" means "Yahweh is complete, or perfect." As explained above, "Uzziah," the name of his father, is another spelling for the name "Azariah." His mother, Jerusha, was the daughter of a priestly family and therefore was probably a well-known personality. This may explain why, in the case of Jerusha, the writer did not follow his usual practice of telling where the queen mother was from.[22]

Among the accomplishments of Jotham, the historian mentions the building of the *"Upper Gate"* of the temple. This was the famous gate near the palace, which was used primarily by the royal family. Actually, since the gate was already in existence, the verse means that Jotham rebuilt or repaired it.[23] Chronicles adds that he also built several cities in the mountains of Judah, castles and watchtowers in the forests, and additions to the Ophel (2 Chron. 27:3–4). He was also commended for his success in subduing the Ammonites. But, like every other Judean king until Josiah, he did not forbid the people to worship Yahweh on the high places. For this he was rebuked by the author (v. 35).

During Jotham's reign, the combined forces of King Rezin of Syria and King Pekah of Israel began their invasion of Judah, but the full impact of these military assaults was not felt until Jotham's son became king (v. 37).

At the age of forty-one King Jotham died, leaving the kingdom to his twenty-year-old heir, Ahaz. Ahaz was immature and did not possess the godly spirit of his father and grandfather. His weak and unprincipled reign was a devastating step backward after a long period of progress in Judah.

The list of Ahaz's failures is staggering:

1. He introduced the worship of the Canaanite god Molech and actually sacrificed his own children in the ceremonial fire (v. 3).

2. He not only permitted worship at the "high places" but burned sacrifices there himself.

3. According to 2 Chronicles 28, he lost 120,000 Judean soldiers, 200,000 civilian hostages, and his own son in the battle with Rezin and Pekah.

4. He surrendered the Judean port city of Elath to the Syrians and later to the Edomites (v. 6).

5. According to Isa. 7:1–11, he spurned the prophet's advice and decided to look to Assyria for help.

6. He closed down the temple, refusing to let the people worship there (2 Chron. 28:24).

7. He removed the pavilion (a sheltered colonnade used by the priests in the temple) and bricked up the Upper Gate of the temple, which his father had built (v. 18).

8. He confiscated the gold and silver treasures of the house of God and the royal palace to finance a bribe (the literal meaning of the word "present") to Tiglath-Pileser III (v. 8).

9. He placed a pagan altar in the central position in the temple, having copied the design from an altar he saw on a visit to a pagan temple in Damascus (vv. 10–11, 15).

10. He usurped the function of the priests and offered sacrifices in the temple himself (vv. 12–13).

11. He relocated the bronze altar built by Solomon and on that sacred altar he examined the entrails of dead animals for a sign, introducing pagan witchcraft into the temple itself. The phrase *"for me to inquire by"* (v. 15) refers to the practice of fortune-telling or divining by reading the livers and other organs of animals.[24]

Ahaz was the consummate syncretist. He tried anything from anybody's religion that might give him any kind of advantage. Bored by what he considered to be the humdrum routine of the faith of his forefathers, Ahaz wildly experimented, trying to inject the religion of Judah with new life. He seemed to be drawn to the most lurid elements in the pagan religions around him. Like the Athenians in Acts 17 who "spent their time in nothing else but either to tell or to hear some new thing," Ahaz was addicted to the lure of the sensational.

A few years ago the newspapers carried the spectacular story of a strange occurrence in Port Neches, Texas. One afternoon, while enjoying a picnic in the backyard of a modest home there, neighbors noticed a strange image on the screen door of the house, caused by the reflection of the sun on the uneven surface of the wire. The image was a perfect representation of what they considered to be the bearded face of Jesus Christ. For several hours at a certain time each afternoon the image was visible.

The neighbors told others about it, and they in turn told others, and soon crowds were coming from everywhere to view the miraculous manifestation. News wire pictures in the papers were very convincing. The screen-door image did resemble those traditional paintings of the face of Jesus with which we are all familiar. Reporters and television cameramen trampled into the backyard for a look at the phenomenon and for interviews with the people gathered there. Some of the spectators knelt in worship, others took candid snapshots, and still others made plans to buy the house and construct a permanent shrine on the site.

Pretty soon, the street became a traffic hazard and the neighbors, who at first enjoyed the national publicity, began to complain that it was a public nuisance. Eventually, the homeowner had to call in the police to restrict access to the backyard. The excitement soon wore off, and I haven't heard anything about the miraculous image since then.

It was another example of that ancient human lust for something new, something spectacular, especially in religion. That's what drove so many in Jesus' day to ask for a sign, a miracle, a sensational evidence of the validity of the faith. And that same urge led Ahaz to import so many sensational elements from the pagan religions of his neighbors.

When all the uproar over the incident in south Texas died down, I couldn't help but be amused. I wanted to tell everybody that I didn't need a reflection on a dented screen door to convince me that Jesus was real in Port Neches. For it was in that very town, in the First Baptist Church of Port Neches, Texas, in 1939, that I met Jesus Christ as my Savior and Lord. I walked down the aisle of the church at the age of nine and publicly committed my life to Christ in repentance and faith, and He saved me. His presence has been vividly real to me ever since. My experience may not be as sensational as the reflection of a mysterious face on somebody's screen door, but in the words of the gospel song:

> You ask me how I know He lives?
> He lives within my heart.[25]

It would be difficult to draw a more drastic contrast than the one between the godly reigns of Azariah and Jotham over the previous seventy-five years and the disastrous record of King Ahaz. No wonder Chronicles adds that when Ahaz was buried, he was not allowed to rest in the tombs of the kings of Judah (2 Chron. 28:27).

Since Ahaz offered his own children in the fire to Molech, Judah was fortunate to have a royal heir left. In the Talmud there is a tradition that his son Hezekiah, who followed him on the throne, had survived because his mother smeared his body with the blood of a salamander before the wicked king sacrificed him in the flames. According to the legend, the blood somehow prevented the fire from consuming young Hezekiah and he was spared to reign in his father's place.[26]

HOSHEA REIGNS IN ISRAEL

> 17:1 In the twelfth year of Ahaz king of Judah, Hoshea the son of Elah became king of Israel in Samaria, *and he reigned* nine years.

> 2 And he did evil in the sight of the LORD, but not as the kings of Israel who were before him.
>
> 3 Shalmaneser king of Assyria came up against him; and Hoshea became his vassal, and paid him tribute money.
>
> 4 And the king of Assyria uncovered a conspiracy by Hoshea; for he had sent messengers to So, king of Egypt, and brought no tribute to the king of Assyria, as *he had done* year by year. Therefore the king of Assyria shut him up, and bound him in prison.
>
> *2 Kings 17:1–4*

Here we finally come to Hoshea, the last king in the long list of those who ruled over the Northern Kingdom from the time of its separation from Judah after the death of Solomon. Hoshea took over the crown by force, killing his predecessor Pekah in a coup that apparently was sponsored by Tiglath-Pileser III, who claims credit for putting Hoshea on the throne of Israel. "Hoshea" means "Yahweh saves." It is similar to the names Hosea, Joshua, and even Jesus.

Ironically, while he was not without failures, this final king of Israel was a significant improvement over the pitiful list of "pseudo-kings" who immediately preceded him. Verse 2 says, *"he did evil in the sight of the Lord, but not as the kings of Israel who were before him."* We are not told in what ways he was better than the others. Some have suggested that he may have allowed the people of Israel to go to Jerusalem to worship.[27] But in spite of his commendable qualities, it was during his reign that the full judgment of destruction burst upon the sinful nation.

Shalmaneser, the son of Tiglath-Pileser III, was now the king of Assyria, ruling from 725 B.C. to 722 B.C. He continued the assault on Israel that his father had begun (2 Kings 15:19), and when he learned that Hoshea had conspired against him by attempting to form an alliance with Egypt, Shalmaneser stepped up the intensity of the assault (v. 4). *"So, king of Egypt"* is sometimes identified with Shabaka (whose name means "wild cat"), the Ethiopian ruler who founded the twenty-fifth Egyptian dynasty. Others consider him to be the king named Sibi whom Sargon defeated at Raphia in 720 B.C.[28] Jones makes a third guess. He points out that there was no Egyptian ruler with that exact name, but there was an Egyptian city named So. It was the capital of the delta region. Therefore, Jones interprets the text to say that Hoshea appealed to an Egyptian king, whom he does not name, who was in the city of So. The ruler in So at that time, according to Jones, was Tefnakhte, who reigned 726–716 B.C.[29]

Shalmaneser attacked Samaria, captured King Hoshea, and put him in chains as prisoner (v. 4). The details of this three-year siege of Samaria are given in the next section. Sometime during the battle for Samaria, King Shalmaneser died, and his brother Sargon II completed the assault and conquered the capital in the ninth year of Hoshea's reign (2 Kings 17:6).

ASSYRIA CARRIES ISRAEL INTO CAPTIVITY

17:5 Now the king of Assyria went throughout all the land, and went up to Samaria and besieged it for three years.

6 In the ninth year of Hoshea, the king of Assyria took Samaria and carried Israel away to Assyria, and placed them in Halah and by the Habor, the River of Gozan, and in the cities of the Medes.

7 For so it was that the children of Israel had sinned against the LORD their God, who had brought them up out of the land of Egypt, from under the hand of Pharaoh king of Egypt; and they had feared other gods,

8 and had walked in the statutes of the nations whom the LORD had cast out from before the children of Israel, and of the kings of Israel, which they had made.

9 Also the children of Israel secretly did against the LORD their God things that *were* not right, and they built for themselves high places in all their cities, from watchtower to fortified city.

10 They set up for themselves *sacred* pillars and wooden images on every high hill and under every green tree.

11 There they burned incense on all the high places, like the nations whom the LORD had carried away before them; and they did wicked things to provoke the LORD to anger,

12 for they served idols, of which the LORD had
said to them, "You shall not do this thing."
13 Yet the LORD testified against Israel and against
Judah, by all of His prophets, every seer, saying,
"Turn from your evil ways, and keep My commandments *and* My statutes, according to all the law which
I commanded your fathers, and which I sent to you by
My servants the prophets."
14 Nevertheless they would not hear, but stiffened
their necks, like the necks of their fathers, who did
not believe in the LORD their God.
15 And they rejected His statutes and His
covenant that He had made with their fathers, and
His testimonies which He had testified against
them; they followed idols, became idolaters, and
went after the nations who *were* all around them,
concerning whom the LORD had charged them that
they should not do like them.
16 So they left all the commandments of the LORD
their God, made for themselves a molded image *and*
two calves, made a wooden image and worshiped all
the host of heaven, and served Baal.
17 And they caused their sons and daughters to
pass through the fire, practiced witchcraft and soothsaying, and sold themselves to do evil in the sight of
the LORD, to provoke Him to anger.
18 Therefore the LORD was very angry with Israel,
and removed them from His sight; there was none
left but the tribe of Judah alone.
19 Also Judah did not keep the commandments
of the LORD their God, but walked in the statutes of
Israel which they made.
20 And the LORD rejected all the descendants of Israel, afflicted them, and delivered them into the hand
of plunderers, until He had cast them from His sight.
21 For He tore Israel from the house of David, and
they made Jeroboam the son of Nebat king. Then Jeroboam drove Israel from following the LORD, and
made them commit a great sin.
22 For the children of Israel walked in all the sins
of Jeroboam which he did; they did not depart from
them,

> 23 until the LORD removed Israel out of His sight, as He had said by all His servants the prophets. So Israel was carried away from their own land to Assyria, *as it is* to this day.
>
> *2 Kings 17:5–23*

You might say that, up to this point in the book, the history of the Northern Kingdom has been similar to the "whereases" that appear before the "therefores" in a legal document. Everything the inspired writer has written so far has been leading up to these next verses, which tell the climactic conclusion of God's judgment. The ultimate purpose of 1 and 2 Kings is to show that disobeying God's law inevitably brings punishment. "Whereas" the people sinned, "therefore" they have become slaves to Assyria. That's the theme of the entire story.

The actual captivity is described in two brief verses (vv. 5–6). We know from other sources that the three-year siege ended in 722 B.C. The fact that it took Assyria that long to break Samaria's resistance is a testimony to the good wall Omri and Ahab had built around the capital city. Samaria also had an inner wall laid on rock-hewn foundation trenches around the palace and citadel itself.[30]

Shalmaneser died in 722 B.C., just before Samaria fell, so his brother and successor, Sargon II, completed the captivity of the people. Sargon claims in his annals that he confiscated fifty chariots, carried away 27,290 captives, and allowed the rest of the people to keep their property in Samaria. Then he imported foreigners to live there with the remnant of Israel, ruled by a governor whom he appointed.[31] Not much is known about the Assyrian cities to which the captives were taken (v. 6).

Verse 7 marks the beginning of a theological explanation of why Israel fell. It sounds like an obituary of the Northern Kingdom—not a eulogy, but a dirge. What a sad list of failures! Their sin can be traced all the way back to the Exodus, to the gracious and miraculous act of God in delivering them from Egyptian bondage (v. 7). They should have remembered His goodness and served the Lord faithfully, but they didn't. So Israel's first failure on the historian's list is: 1. spiritual forgetfulness and ingratitude. The remainder of this embarrassing catalog of sins is as follows:

2. They feared other gods (v. 7).
3. They adopted the customs of the pagan Canaanites (v. 8).

4. They tried to keep their wrongdoings secret (v. 9).

5. They covered the land with *"high places"* (v. 9). *"From watch-tower to fortified city"* was a familiar figure of speech used to denote "everywhere"—that is, "hamlet to metroplex."

6. They set up idolatrous pillars and wooden images everywhere (v. 10). *"On every high hill and under every green tree"* is another idiomatic expression meaning "everywhere."

7. They burned incense on the *"high places"* (v. 11).

8. They served idols (v. 12).

9. They would not listen to the warnings of the prophets whom the Lord sent to them (vv. 13–14).

10. They became stiff-necked and rebellious (v. 14).

11. They rejected God's statutes, His covenant, and His testimonies (v. 15).

12. They followed idols, and thereby became idolatrous, adopting the empty customs of pagan nations (v. 15).

13. They disobeyed all the commandments of the Lord their God (v. 16).

14. They made molded images of two calves (v. 16).

15. They made a wooden image (Asherah) and worshiped *"the host of heaven"*—that is, the sun, moon, and stars (v. 16).

16. They served Baal (v. 16).

17. They burned their children in the fire as sacrifices to Molech (v. 17).

18. They practiced witchcraft and soothsaying (v. 17).

19. They sold themselves to do evil (v. 17).

20. They provoked God to anger (v. 17).

What a list! Now for the *"therefore."* Since Israel had sinned so grievously, *therefore* they will be destroyed (v. 18). The ten tribes of the North disappeared after this, never to be heard from again. These ten lost tribes of Israel have been a mystery through the years. People have tried to find them in the Jewish communities of southern Arabia, in various tribes in India, in China, in Turkey, in Cashmir, in Afghanistan, in the American Indians; but not a trace remains. Verse 23 says, *"the Lord removed Israel out of His sight."*

Only Judah remained, and in verse 19 the writer inserts a parenthetical reminder that within 160 years, Judah also would follow in the same tragic pattern.

Unlike technical secular historians, the purpose of the Old Testament historians was not to catalogue various events in chronological order, nor to analyze the various movements in history, but to declare God's righteous dealings with His people. Therefore, great events like the fall of a kingdom were of little significance to them unless they revealed the righteous purpose of God. The main thing about this passage then is not the details of the siege, nor the names of the Assyrian kings, nor the military strategies, nor the political maneuvering—items which secular historians would have emphasized. The main thing for the biblical historian is the long list of the reasons for God's judgment on Israel.

Here, the important message is the postmortem inquiry into the spiritual diseases that killed the kingdom, because that message becomes a warning for nations of all ages. In this passage are warnings against the danger of ingratitude, the danger of stiff-necked resistance to the word of God, the danger of yielding to the unhealthy influences of godless people around us, the folly of secret transgressions, the impotence of cheap, convenient religion, the danger of pride, the peril of provoking God to anger, the hazards of idolatry (which is still practiced in many diverse forms today), the warning of inevitable judgment.

But one of the most vivid lessons in this passage is in verse 15. The New King James Version translates the phrase, *"They followed idols, became idolaters."* The original is more accurate at this point: "They worshiped emptiness and became empty." The word here is *hebel* meaning "air," "delusion," or "vanity."[32] The idea is that they became like the gods they worshiped. They bowed down to nothingness and became nothing.

In my opinion, some of the worst of the abominations of modern technology are those ubiquitous electric hand dryers you find in public washrooms. Most people really despise them. I sympathize with the message some disgruntled user had scratched on one I saw recently. The frustrated customer had added another step to that list of useless instructions you always find on the front of the dryer: (1) Shake excess water from hands. (2) Push button. (3) Briskly rub wet hands together under the flow of air. He had scratched in (4) "Then wipe your hands on your shirt." I agree!

On a visit to Auburn University in Alabama a few years ago, I stepped into a rest room in the administration building that had a wall full of those electric dryers and discovered that someone had added another appropriate message to one of the machines: "Push this button and hear a message from our beloved president." Nothing but hot air!

The writer of Kings describes the religion of idolatry with the same vivid phrase. It is *hebel*—nothing but hot air. And the tragedy was that the followers of that empty religion had become empty themselves: their lives lacked substance, their personalities became trivial, their characters lacked depth. As one man described his friend, "Down deep, he's shallow!"

"Trivial Pursuit" is not just the name of a popular American game, it is the sad but accurate description of the lives of many people today. Their lives are trivial. They go through the motions of routine daily schedules without anything to excite them, to challenge their best, to ennoble their existence. They have put first in their lives those things that have no eternal value, and as a result, they have become as empty as their "gods." Someday, they will conclude, as the author of Ecclesiastes did, "Vanity of vanities . . . All is vanity" (Eccl. 12:8).

ASSYRIA RESETTLES SAMARIA

17:24 Then the king of Assyria brought *people* from
Babylon, Cuthah, Ava, Hamath, and from Sepharvaim, and placed *them* in the cities of Samaria instead
of the children of Israel; and they took possession of
Samaria and dwelt in its cities.
25 And it was so, at the beginning of their dwelling
there, *that* they did not fear the LORD; therefore the
LORD sent lions among them, which killed *some* of
them.
26 So they spoke to the king of Assyria, saying,
"The nations whom you have removed and placed in
the cities of Samaria do not know the rituals of the
God of the land; therefore He has sent lions among
them, and indeed, they are killing them because they
do not know the rituals of the God of the land."
27 Then the king of Assyria commanded, saying,

"Send there one of the priests whom you brought from there; let him go and dwell there, and let him teach them the rituals of the God of the land."

28 Then one of the priests whom they had carried away from Samaria came and dwelt in Bethel, and taught them how they should fear the LORD.

29 However every nation continued to make gods of its own, and put *them* in the shrines on the high places which the Samaritans had made, *every* nation in the cities where they dwelt.

30 The men of Babylon made Succoth Benoth, the men of Cuth made Nergal, the men of Hamath made Ashima,

31 and the Avites made Nibhaz and Tartak; and the Sepharvites burned their children in fire to Adrammelech and Anammelech, the gods of Sepharvaim.

32 So they feared the LORD, and from every class they appointed for themselves priests of the high places, who sacrificed for them in the shrines of the high places.

33 They feared the LORD, yet served their own gods—according to the rituals of the nations from among whom they were carried away.

34 To this day they continue practicing the former rituals; they do not fear the LORD, nor do they follow their statutes or their ordinances, or the law and commandment which the LORD had commanded the children of Jacob, whom He named Israel,

35 with whom the LORD had made a covenant and charged them, saying: "You shall not fear other gods, nor bow down to them nor serve them nor sacrifice to them;

36 "but the LORD, who brought you up from the land of Egypt with great power and an outstretched arm, Him you shall fear, Him you shall worship, and to Him you shall offer sacrifice.

37 "And the statutes, the ordinances, the law, and the commandment which He wrote for you, you shall be careful to observe forever; you shall not fear other gods.

38 "And the covenant that I have made with you, you shall not forget, nor shall you fear other gods.

39 "But the LORD your God you shall fear; and He will deliver you from the hand of all your enemies."
40 However they did not obey, but they followed their former rituals.
41 So these nations feared the LORD, yet served their carved images; also their children and their children's children have continued doing as their fathers did, even to this day.

2 Kings 17:24–41

With these verses, the second section of the Book of Kings comes to a close. (Section I, From David to the Divided Kingdom, 970–932 B.C.; Section II, From the Divided Kingdom to the Fall of Israel, 932–722 B.C.; Section III, From the Fall of Israel to the Fall of Judah, 722–587 B.C.) *"The king of Assyria"* in verse 24 is probably Sargon II, unless the events described here occurred somewhat later, in which case the king would be Ashurbanipal.

"Cuthah" refers to the Babylonian city of Kutu, northeast of the capital. In the Talmud, all Samaritans are referred to as "Cutheans."[33] Very little is known about the other cities mentioned here. It is interesting to note that here for the first time the entire area of the Northern Kingdom is referred to as Samaria. These verses, then, give us the origin of the group of people who came to be known, especially in New Testament times, as Samaritans. After foreign colonists had been transplanted in Samaria to live with the Israelites who were left in the land, and after the two groups had become fused so that there arose a mixed Samaritan people of predominantly pagan character, it was impossible to speak any longer of the people of Ephraim in the land of Israel. The phrase *"to this day"* in verses 34 and 41 indicates that already antagonism was developing between the Jews and the Samaritans.

Lions were somewhat common in Old Testament times. They may have been attracted to Samaria at this time because of the unburied carcasses following the war and because of the depopulation of areas that had formerly been inhabited. Their proliferation was seen as a further punishment from God because the people *"did not fear the Lord"* (v. 25).

What a pantheon of weird deities is found in verses 30 and 31! Succoth-Benoth was a Babylonian god that, according to the Talmud, was shaped like a hen and her chickens. The first word, "Succoth," means "hen" and the second one, "Benoth," means "daughters" or "chicks." Nergal was a deity of the Babylonian netherworld and was similar to the Roman war god, Mars. It looked like a wild cock. The god Ashima is of unknown origin, but the Talmud says it looked like a "hairless he-goat." Nibhaz was an unknown dog-shaped deity, while Tartak looked like a donkey. Finally, Adrammelech and Anammelech were, as their compound names suggest, Molech-like gods. Talmudic tradition says that they took the forms of a mule and a horse. Sennacherib named one of his sons Adrammelech.[34]

This passage shows the futility of false religion. False religion is

1. *A religion of fear.* The Samaritans would have never turned to God if it had not been for the plague of lions that threatened their lives. So today there are those who pray only when they are ill or in trouble.

2. *A religion of form.* The Samaritans believed that acceptable religion depended on practicing the appropriate rituals and customs. If the formalities were performed correctly, then the god would be pleased. So today there are those who go through the motions of formal ecclesiastical practices believing that in so doing they are pleasing God.

3. *A religion of facilitation. "They feared the Lord, yet served their own gods"* (v. 33). This is a religion that compromises, makes allowances for all viewpoints, and seeks the lowest common denominator. Its followers find it easy to accommodate their religion to the surrounding culture, for such religion takes its color from the environment in which its followers live. But God is a jealous God who will not share His dominion with any rivals. *"The Lord, who brought you up from the land of Egypt with great power and an outstretched arm, Him you shall fear . . . you shall not fear other gods"* (vv. 36–37).

NOTES

1. I. W. Slotki, *Kings* (London: Soncino Press, 1950), 252.
2. John Gray, *I and II Kings,* Old Testament Library (Philadelphia: Westminster, 1963), 562.
3. Ibid., 563.

4. T. R. Hobbs, *2 Kings,* Word Biblical Commentary, ed. John D. W. Watts, vol. 13 (Waco, TX: Word Books, 1985), 195.

5. Gray, 563.

6. M. Pierce Matheney and Roy Honeycutt, "1-2 Kings," in *The Broadman Bible Commentary,* ed. Clifton J. Allen, vol. 3 (Nashville: Broadman, 1970), 265.

7. Norman H. Snaith, Ralph W. Sockman, and Raymond Calkins, "The First and Second Books of Kings," in *The Interpreter's Bible,* vol. 3 (Nashville: Abingdon, 1954), 267.

8. Robert C. Dentan, *Kings and Chronicles,* Layman's Bible Commentary, vol. 7 (Richmond: John Knox Press, 1964), 79.

9. *Ancient Near Eastern Texts,* ed. J. B. Pritchard, 3d ed. (Princeton: Princeton University Press, 1969) 281ff., cited by Matheney and Honeycutt, 264.

10. Ibid.

11. Ibid.

12. Hobbs, 200.

13. Ibid.

14. Slotki, 254.

15. Matheney and Honeycutt, 264.

16. Hobbs, 200.

17. Dentan, 81.

18. Gwilym H. Jones, *1 and 2 Kings,* New Century Bible Commentary, ed. Ronald E. Clements (Grand Rapids: Eerdmans, 1984), 529.

19. Gray, 569.

20. Ibid., 568.

21. Jones, 529.

22. Gray, 570.

23. Slotki, 257.

24. Ibid.

25. Alfred H. Ackley, "He Lives," in *Baptist Hymnal* (Nashville: Convention Press, 1975), no. 438.

26. Slotki, 257.

27. C. F. Keil, *The Books of the Kings,* Biblical Commentary on the Old Testament, ed. C. F. Keil and F. Delitzsch, vol. 4 (Grand Rapids: Eerdmans, 1950), 409.

28. Slotki, 262.

29. Jones, 546.

30. Gray, 585.

31. Slotki, 264.

32. Jones, 549.

33. Slotki, 266.

34. Ibid.

SECTION THREE

The Kingdom of Judah from the Fall of Samaria to the Fall of Jerusalem 722–587 B.C.

2 Kings 18:1–25:30

CHAPTER EIGHTEEN

The Reign of Hezekiah in Judah

2 Kings 18:1–20:21

HEZEKIAH'S INITIAL REFORMS

18:1 Now it came to pass in the third year of Hoshea
the son of Elah, king of Israel, *that* Hezekiah the son
of Ahaz, king of Judah, began to reign.
2 He was twenty-five years old when he became
king, and he reigned twenty-nine years in Jerusalem.
His mother's name *was* Abi the daughter of Zechariah.
3 And he did *what was* right in the sight of the
LORD, according to all that his father David had done.
4 He removed the high places and broke the *sacred* pillars, cut down the wooden image and broke
in pieces the bronze serpent that Moses had made;
for until those days the children of Israel burned incense to it, and called it Nehushtan.
5 He trusted in the LORD God of Israel, so that
after him was none like him among all the kings of
Judah, nor who were before him.
6 For he held fast to the LORD; he did not depart
from following Him, but kept His commandments,
which the LORD had commanded Moses.
7 The LORD was with him; he prospered wherever
he went. And he rebelled against the king of Assyria
and did not serve him.
8 He subdued the Philistines, as far as Gaza and
its territory, from watchtower to fortified city.
9 Now it came to pass in the fourth year of King
Hezekiah, which *was* the seventh year of Hoshea the
son of Elah, king of Israel, *that* Shalmaneser king of
Assyria came up against Samaria and besieged it.

10 And at the end of three years they took it. In
the sixth year of Hezekiah, that *is,* the ninth year of
Hoshea king of Israel, Samaria was taken.
11 Then the king of Assyria carried Israel away
captive to Assyria, and put them in Halah and by
the Habor, the River of Gozan, and in the cities
of the Medes,
12 because they did not obey the voice of the LORD
their God, but transgressed His covenant *and* all that
Moses the servant of the LORD had commanded; and
they would neither hear nor do *them.*
13 And in the fourteenth year of King Hezekiah,
Sennacherib king of Assyria came up against all the
fortified cities of Judah and took them.
14 Then Hezekiah king of Judah sent to the king of
Assyria at Lachish, saying, "I have done wrong; turn
away from me; whatever you impose on me I will
pay." And the king of Assyria assessed Hezekiah king
of Judah three hundred talents of silver and thirty talents of gold.
15 So Hezekiah gave *him* all the silver that was
found in the house of the LORD and in the treasuries
of the king's house.
16 At that time Hezekiah stripped *the gold from* the
doors of the temple of the LORD, and *from* the pillars
which Hezekiah king of Judah had overlaid, and
gave it to the king of Assyria.

2 Kings 18:1–16

Most outlines of 1 and 2 Kings divide the story into three sections, and most agree where the divisions ought to fall:

Section I, From the Last Days of David to the Divided Kingdom, 1 Kings 1:1–11:43.

Section II, From the Divided Kingdom to the Fall of Israel, 1 Kings 12:1–2 Kings 17:41.

Section III, From the Fall of Samaria to the Fall of Jerusalem, 2 Kings 18:1–25:30.

Although he was crowned half a dozen years before the actual fall of Samaria, Hezekiah's reign in Judah is an appropriate place to begin this third and final section of the two books of the Kings.

One way of determining how important the author considered

each king in his story to be is to calculate how much space he allocated to each one. According to such a computation, Solomon was the most important, because the author of Kings gave 395 verses to his reign. In the same way, the least important king was Shallum of Israel, on whose story he spent only 2 verses. One might say, therefore, that Hezekiah was considered very important to the story, because the author gave 70 verses to the telling of his account. If the sections during Hezekiah's reign that deal primarily with Isaiah the prophet are included, the number goes up to 95. With the exception of Solomon, whose story occupies 13 percent of the total of both books, only King Ahab was given more space than Hezekiah. Hezekiah's reign is also described in two other places in the Old Testament, Isaiah 36–39 and 2 Chronicles 29–32.

Hezekiah came to power during the Northern Kingdom's final gasps of survival. His royal counterpart in the North, Hoshea, would soon be the prisoner of Sargon II, and the entire nation would be transported as captives of Assyria. The nation that had been known as Israel since it broke away from the other tribes would no longer exist. From this time on, the Southern Kingdom would be known not only by the name "Judah" but also by the ancient name "Israel." Because of its importance to the future of Judah, the author inserts at verse 9 a repetition of his earlier account of the fall of Samaria.

Realizing that his father, King Ahaz, had taken Judah down the same path of disobedience that led Israel to her doom, Hezekiah moved quickly to reverse national policy and bring Judah back to the Lord. In this respect, he was more like his grandfather, Jotham, than his father. Hezekiah's name means, "Yahweh strengthens," which may have reinforced his determination to do *"what was right in the sight of the Lord"* (v. 3).

The parallel account in Chronicles refers to a number of godly achievements that are omitted here, but verses 4–6 mention a select few. Going much further than other good kings of Judah, Hezekiah removed the *"high places,"* that is, the former sites of pagan worship that the people had transformed into altars for the worship of Yahweh. God was never happy about this practice, but none of the other good kings ever found the courage to forbid it. Hezekiah did. Not only that, but he boldly broke down the sacred pillars and the wooden images (v. 4). (The Hebrew word translated *"wooden image"* is *ʾăšērâ,* which may also be the proper name of a Canaanite goddess, Asherah.)

One of Hezekiah's reforms in verse 4 is not found anywhere else in Scripture. He broke in pieces the bronze serpent that Moses had made in the wilderness. It had apparently been preserved in Jerusalem and had become something of an idol before which some of the people were offering incense. When God instructed Moses to fashion the bronze serpent, He intended it to be used as a symbol reminding them that they were to put their trust in Him (Num. 21:6–9). But now, centuries later, the people were treating it as a divine relic and worshiping it as a god. The means had become the end.

So widespread had this idolatrous practice become that the people gave the serpent a popular name, *"Nehushtan,"* meaning "Bronze Thing" (v. 4). It was a clever play on words, since the word for "serpent" is *nāḥāš* and the word for "bronze" is *nĕḥōšet.* Another theory proposes that the name was given to the serpent after it was broken in pieces, as though the people were saying, "The mighty Nachash (serpent) has become nothing more than Nehushtan (a bronze thing, just a pile of scrap metal)."[1]

Hezekiah earned one of the highest scores on the author's royal report card. The language the author used to praise him is almost effusive, ranking him even above Solomon and David. *"After him was none like him among all the kings of Judah, nor who were before him"* (v. 5). Some have pointed out that the author was inconsistent in his praise, since later he said essentially the same thing about Josiah: "Now before him there was no king like him . . . nor after him did any arise like him" (2 Kings 23:25). One explanation of this apparent inconsistency is that Hezekiah was praised for his confidence in God, while Josiah was praised for his obedience to the Mosaic law.[2]

What else did Hezekiah do to deserve such unprecedented applause? In addition to the destruction of idols in verse 4, the king is also lauded because *"he trusted in the Lord God of Israel"* (v. 5), *"he held fast to the Lord"* (v. 6), *"he did not depart from following Him"* (v. 6), and he *"kept His commandments"* (v. 6). In the long parallel passage in 2 Chronicles 29–30, other reforms are listed:

1. He opened the doors of the temple, which his father, Ahaz, had closed.
2. He led the Levites to sanctify themselves and begin their ministry again in the house of God.
3. He restored the traditional worship of Yahweh in the temple.
4. He reinstituted the Passover feast of unleavened bread.

5. He invited the remnant of the Northern tribes to worship with the people of Judah in Jerusalem.
6. He returned the nation to the Lord, so that He heard their prayers.

As a result of this enviable record of righteousness and faith, the Lord was with Hezekiah, so that he prospered wherever he went, he was enabled to resist the Assyrian oppression, and he totally subdued the Philistines (vv. 7–8). The author's high regard for Hezekiah shows that he was measuring history from a religious and theological perspective rather than from a political and secular one. Viewed through the eyes of a technical, classical historian, Hezekiah's reign had serious political and international problems. He paid quite a price for his rebellion against Assyria, for example. But our author's purpose is to relate these events exclusively in the light of God's control over the destiny of nations.[3]

Things went well in Judah for fourteen years, but then trouble appeared in the form of Sennacherib, king of Assyria, who invaded from the north and captured *"all the fortified cities"* of Judah (v. 13). Sennacherib was the son of Sargon II, who had enslaved Israel before he died in battle in 705 B.C. Taking up where his father had left off, Sennacherib occupied the Assyrian throne until 681 B.C., and the details of his eight military expeditions, including this one against Judah, are preserved in his royal annals. There he claims to have captured forty-six major cities and an unspecified number of villages in Judah and hemmed up Hezekiah in Jerusalem "like a bird within its cage."[4] The attack on Judah was apparently provoked by Hezekiah's refusal to continue paying tribute to Assyria as his father Ahaz had done. Surprised at Sennacherib's quick retaliation, Hezekiah tried to head off a worse fate by volunteering to pay tribute to Assyria after all (v. 14).

The foreign army captured Lachish, an important Judean city on the road to Egypt, and encamped there. An interesting wall relief taken from the excavation of Sennacherib's royal palace in Nineveh is preserved in the British Museum. It portrays the Assyrian king on a portable throne in his military camp outside Lachish. Prisoners of war are marching by on foot, and all the booty from the city is being displayed on ox-wagons. The inscription reads, "Sennacherib, king of all, king of Assyria, sitting on his 'nimedu-throne' while the spoil of the city of Lachish passes before him."[5]

In order to pay Sennacherib's assessment, Hezekiah surrendered all the silver in the temple and in the royal treasury (v. 15) and stripped the gold overlay from the temple doors and pillars. According to verse 14, that amounted to three hundred talents of silver and thirty talents of gold. Sennacherib's annals say the amount was eight hundred talents of silver and thirty talents of gold, the difference being explained by the fact that the biblical account probably measured only the amount that was taken from the Temple.[6] In present-day currency the tribute would amount to $1,267,200 in silver and $3,379,000 in gold, for a total of $4,646,200.

The Assyrian annals add that Hezekiah was forced to include in the tribute "precious stones, antimony, large cuts of red stone, couches inlaid with ivory, nimedu-chairs inlaid with ivory, elephant hides, ebony wood, boxwood, and all kinds of valuable treasures."[7] This initial encounter with Assyria's army was only the beginning of a long military engagement between Hezekiah and Sennacherib that becomes the primary subject of the next two chapters of 2 Kings.

Hezekiah is a noble example of a leader who achieved godliness in a difficult situation. He was able to please God in a day of limited revelation, whereas we today are the fortunate recipients of the full revelation of Jesus Christ. He remained faithful even though surrounded by the temptations of monarchy and power, whereas most of us live in humbler, less distracting circumstances. By this contrast, it is evident that our record of godliness ought to be significantly greater than it is.

Hezekiah's good report in spite of unfavorable circumstances judges us and encourages us to imitate certain characteristics of his religious faith. This passage describes four marks of Hezekiah's godly life.

First, Hezekiah wholeheartedly *"trusted"* in the Lord (v. 5). A pro-Assyrian party in Jerusalem wanted Hezekiah to put his trust in Assyria. A pro-Egyptian party, on the other hand, encouraged him to put his trust in that country; but Hezekiah did neither. He put his trust in the Lord. Simple trust in God is foundational to every other element in a godly life. The word translated "trust" here is *bāṭaḥ,* the common word for reliance upon God. It literally means, "he leaned all his weight on the Lord." Hezekiah knew so little about God and yet leaned so much on Him. We know so much and sometimes lean so little on Him. Because of our abundant spiritual advantages, it ought to be easier for us to lean all our weight on the Lord.

Second, Hezekiah tenaciously *"held fast"* to the Lord (v. 6). Here the word is *dābaq,* which means "cleave" like ivy on a tree trunk. If simple trust is the foundation of the house of faith, then this tenacious cleaving to the Lord is the first floor. This phrase conveys the picture of a believer who hangs on for dear life to the God he has trusted, in the face of obstacles, distractions, and temptations. Like Jacob, who wrestled with God, the believer will not let go. It is the same word used to describe the union of husband and wife in marriage, calling to mind the admonition of the book of Acts that we "should continue with the Lord" (Acts 11:23).

Third, Hezekiah steadfastly followed the Lord (v. 6). This idea of actively *"following"* after God seems incongruent with the idea of clinging to Him. Can faith be expressed in both union and pursuit? Yes. No matter how closely we cling to the Lord, there is always the possibility of clinging closer, of trusting him more profoundly, of following Him more obediently. A healthy, growing faith discovers that there is always a challenging distance yet out ahead. We never achieve that perfect union with God because the closer we get to Him, the more we become aware of how far short we fall. Spiritual goals seem to be always receding so that we can never claim to have finally arrived. Even at the end of his life, Paul testified that he was still pressing on toward the mark of the prize of the upward call of God.

Fourth, Hezekiah consistently obeyed the Lord (v. 6). This is the upper story on the house of godly living. Built on the foundation of faith, the believer must next construct a life of union and discipleship which should then naturally issue in practical obedience. You might say that trusting in the Lord, clinging to the Lord, and following the Lord are not worth much if they do not issue in obedience to the Lord. On the other hand, human attempts to obey God's will are futile if they don't begin with faith and spring from a spiritual walk with God. Peter wrote, "Add to your faith virtue, to virtue knowledge, to knowledge self-control, to self-control perseverance, to perseverance godliness, to godliness brotherly kindness, and to brotherly kindness love" (2 Pet. 1:5–7). The modern songwriter expressed it:

Trust and obey, for there's no other way
To be happy in Jesus,
But to trust and obey.

SENNACHERIB'S BOAST AGAINST THE LORD

18:17 Then the king of Assyria sent *the* Tartan, *the*
Rabsaris, and *the* Rabshakeh from Lachish, with a
great army against Jerusalem, to King Hezekiah. And
they went up and came to Jerusalem. When they had
come up, they went and stood by the aqueduct from
the upper pool, which *was* on the highway to the
Fuller's Field.
18 And when they had called to the king, Eliakim
the son of Hilkiah, who *was* over the household,
Shebna the scribe, and Joah the son of Asaph, the
recorder, came out to them.
19 Then *the* Rabshakeh said to them, "Say now to
Hezekiah, 'Thus says the great king, the king of
Assyria: "What confidence *is* this in which you
trust?
20 "You speak of *having* plans and power for war;
but *they are* mere words. And in whom do you trust,
that you rebel against me?
21 "Now look! You are trusting in the staff of this
broken reed, Egypt, on which if a man leans, it will
go into his hand and pierce it. So *is* Pharaoh king of
Egypt to all who trust in him.
22 "But if you say to me, 'We trust in the LORD our
God,' *is* it not He whose high places and whose altars Hezekiah has taken away, and said to Judah
and Jerusalem, 'You shall worship before this altar
in Jerusalem'?"'
23 "Now therefore, I urge you, give a pledge to my
master the king of Assyria, and I will give you two
thousand horses—if you are able on your part to put
riders on them!
24 "How then will you repel one captain of the least
of my master's servants, and put your trust in Egypt
for chariots and horsemen?
25 "Have I now come up without the LORD against

this place to destroy it? The LORD said to me, 'Go up against this land, and destroy it.'"

26 Then Eliakim the son of Hilkiah, Shebna, and Joah said to *the* Rabshakeh, "Please speak to your servants in Aramaic, for we understand *it;* and do not speak to us in Hebrew in the hearing of the people who *are* on the wall."

27 But *the* Rabshakeh said to them, "Has my master sent me to your master and to you to speak these words, and not to the men who sit on the wall, who will eat and drink their own waste with you?"

28 Then *the* Rabshakeh stood and called out with a loud voice in Hebrew, and spoke, saying, "Hear the word of the great king, the king of Assyria!

29 "Thus says the king: 'Do not let Hezekiah deceive you, for he shall not be able to deliver you from his hand;

30 'nor let Hezekiah make you trust in the LORD, saying, "The LORD will surely deliver us; this city shall not be given into the hand of the king of Assyria."'

31 "Do not listen to Hezekiah; for thus says the king of Assyria: 'Make *peace* with me by a present and come out to me; and every one of you eat from his own vine and every one from his own fig tree, and every one of you drink the waters of his own cistern;

32 'until I come and take you away to a land like your own land, a land of grain and new wine, a land of bread and vineyards, a land of olive groves and honey, that you may live and not die. But do not listen to Hezekiah, lest he persuade you, saying, "The LORD will deliver us."

33 Has any of the gods of the nations at all delivered its land from the hand of the king of Assyria?

34 'Where *are* the gods of Hamath and Arpad? Where *are* the gods of Sepharvaim and Hena and Ivah? Indeed, have they delivered Samaria from my hand?

35 'Who among all the gods of the lands have delivered their countries from my hand, that the LORD should deliver Jerusalem from my hand?'"

36 But the people held their peace and answered

> him not a word; for the king's commandment was, "Do not answer him."
>
> 37 Then Eliakim the son of Hilkiah, who *was* over the household, Shebna the scribe, and Joah the son of Asaph, the recorder, came to Hezekiah with *their* clothes torn, and told him the words of *the* Rabshakeh.
>
> *2 Kings 18:17–37*

Hezekiah's last-minute attempt to placate Sennacherib by paying tribute was not successful. Even though the Assyrian king got his gold and silver, he did not leave Jerusalem alone. In fact, it appears Hezekiah's capitulation simply emboldened Sennacherib, and he sent a three-man delegation with a detachment of soldiers from Lachish to Jerusalem to call for Judah's surrender.

The King James Version regards the terms *"Tartan," "Rabsaris,"* and *"Rabshakeh"* in verse 17 to be proper names, but most recent translations consider them to be official titles. In footnotes, the New King James Version suggests that the titles could be translated "Commander in Chief," "Chief Officer," and "Chief of Staff" or "Governor." The New International Version translates the words "Supreme Commander," "Chief Officer," and "Field Commander." It is difficult to find exact equivalent ranks in present-day military terminology, but obviously the three officers were in high places of responsibility in Sennacherib's military command.

Intending to intimidate Hezekiah with a sizable show of force, they came with *"a great army."* Exactly where the parley between the servants of Hezekiah and the servants of Sennacherib took place has been much disputed by biblical scholars. The description in verse 17 is detailed and precise, and must have been familiar to the first readers of Kings: *"by the aqueduct from the upper pool, which was on the highway to the Fuller's Field."*

Modern scholarship, however, is divided in its opinion of the location. Some say the *"upper pool"* referred to here is Siloam, and the lower pool into which the aqueduct or canal carried the water they identify as Birket al-Hamra, which is now an orchard at the lower end of the Tyropoean Valley. Others believe the "upper pool" is the Birket al-Hamra and the lower one was an unknown pool above Ain Rogel (the name "Rogel" means "fuller"). Gray, offering a totally different solution, suggests that the location was northwest of Jerusalem where flood waters from the natural basin called Ard al-birkeh probably flowed by a canal along the "great north road" into the upper city to the Pool of Siloam. The *"Fuller's Field"* (or "Washerman's Field") in verse 17 was obviously a well-known location somewhere beside the canal.[8]

Since Sennacherib had not come himself but sent an envoy, Hezekiah decided to respond in a similar fashion. Although the Assyrian delegation demanded that Hezekiah talk to them, he sent his court officials Eliakim, Shebna, and Joah to represent him. A face-to-face summit meeting between the two heads of state themselves might have been better, but it was left to the negotiators to channel the messages back and forth between the two kings.

The arrogance of Sennacherib's boastful taunt is detected in the opening address of the Rabshakeh where he uses the term *"the great king,"* which was probably Sennacherib's self-designated title. He proudly disdained the national power of Egypt, calling that nation a *"broken reed,"* literally "a crushed or broken stalk." Since this is the same terminology Isaiah used to symbolize Egypt (Isa. 42:3) some have suggested that Sennacherib was familiar with Isaiah's prophecies and quoted the prophet here to imply he was carrying out Yahweh's will.[9] Further support for this idea is found in verse 25 where Sennacherib seemed to be aware of Isaiah's statement that Assyria was a rod which Yahweh would use to punish Judah (Isa. 10:5).

According to Sennacherib's pagan theology, Judah could no longer call on Yahweh because under Hezekiah they had destroyed the high places, which he assumed were the primary sites of Yahweh worship (v. 22). He also expressed arrogant contempt for Judah's army, making a wager with Hezekiah that even if he were given two thousand horses he couldn't find enough soldiers to ride them (v. 23). The word translated *"pledge"* literally means "a wager," or "a bet."

When Hezekiah's ambassadors requested that the parley be continued in the Aramaic language, the international language of commerce and diplomatic discourse in western Asia, they were trying to avoid a panic on the part of the population of Jerusalem who were listening from the city wall. The Assyrian delegation refused this request because they wanted to lure the people of Jerusalem to rebel as they listened to the attractive offers the Assyrians were making to

Hezekiah. If they would *"come out,"* that is, surrender, they would be allowed to eat their own fruit and drink from their own wells rather than being forced to eat their own dung and drink their own urine during a siege (v. 27). Surrender would mean that they would eventually be transplanted safely to a prosperous and comfortable location in Assyria. The Rabshakeh hoped this offer would sound like a better alternative to the beleaguered people on the wall (vv. 31–32).

To the credit of the people of the city, they obeyed their king's command to hold their peace and they refused to answer Sennacherib's taunt. Hezekiah had asked them not to speak, lest they betray any sign of uneasiness or fear (v. 36). But uneasiness and fear there was aplenty. Eliakim, Shebna, and Joah returned to the king's palace *"with their clothes torn,"* indicating their heavy hearts and grievous concern for the situation.

Once again it was like David confronting Goliath. The helpless little community of Jerusalem was facing the overwhelming odds of Assyria's mighty army. From every reasonable and pragmatic perspective Jerusalem was in no position to resist. Surrender seemed to be the only choice. It was either that or be totally destroyed by the cruel Assyrians. No wonder the people on the wall held their peace. What was there to say?

Well, the answer lay deeper than reason or pragmatic common sense. Jerusalem's hope and strength were not to be found in the visible measurements of military manpower or defensive strategies, but in moral and spiritual resources that were invisible. Judah's secret weapon was her trust in the Lord, her confidence in the invisible presence of God whose power is unlimited.

Centuries later, Paul reminded the Corinthian believers that the power to see it through is not to be found in accommodating circumstances, nor in physical strength, human abilities, or military might. It is to be found by trusting in "the God who commanded light to shine out of darkness, who has shone in our hearts to give the light of the knowledge of the glory of God in the face of Jesus Christ" (2 Cor. 4:6). He went on to say, "But we have this treasure in earthen vessels, that the excellence of the power may be of God and not of us." That is why we can be "hard pressed on every side, yet not crushed . . . struck down, but not destroyed." Paul declares that the Christian's spiritual secret is that "we do not look at the things which are seen, but at the things which are not seen. For the things which are seen are temporary, but the things which are not seen are eternal" (2 Cor. 4:18).

So Judah looked to "the things which are not seen"; they placed their hope and confidence in God. The next section describes how their faith led them to seek God's word from Isaiah and to seek God's face in prayer. He would surely deliver them.

ISAIAH'S PROPHECY OF DELIVERANCE

> 19:1 And so it was, when King Hezekiah heard *it*, that he tore his clothes, covered himself with sackcloth, and went into the house of the LORD.
>
> 2 Then he sent Eliakim, who *was* over the household, Shebna the scribe, and the elders of the priests, covered with sackcloth, to Isaiah the prophet, the son of Amoz.
>
> 3 And they said to him, "Thus says Hezekiah: 'This day *is* a day of trouble, and rebuke, and blasphemy; for the children have come to birth, but *there is* no strength to bring them forth.
>
> 4 'It may be that the LORD your God will hear all the words of *the* Rabshakeh, whom his master the king of Assyria has sent to reproach the living God, and will rebuke the words which the LORD your God has heard. Therefore lift up *your* prayer for the remnant that is left.'"
>
> 5 So the servants of King Hezekiah came to Isaiah.
>
> 6 And Isaiah said to them, "Thus you shall say to your master, 'Thus says the LORD: "Do not be afraid of the words which you have heard, with which the servants of the king of Assyria have blasphemed Me.
>
> 7 "Surely I will send a spirit upon him, and he shall hear a rumor and return to his own land; and I will cause him to fall by the sword in his own land."'"
>
> *2 Kings 19:1–7*

Hezekiah's reaction upon hearing the boastful and blasphemous words of Sennacherib through his spokesman the Rabshakeh was commendable. He humbled himself, tearing his royal robes and replacing them with sackcloth as a gesture of repentance and remorse. Then he *"went into the house of the Lord"* (v. 1). Here is a pungent example of a person with power and position who has come to that painful place where he must admit that he is not sufficient in himself.

I remember visiting with a family in New England who had been members of a church I pastored in the South. When I unexpectedly knocked at their door, they told me the shocking news. Just twenty-four hours earlier, their little eight-year-old daughter had been kidnapped from a playground across the street from their house. A doll and one little tennis shoe were found near the swing set as the only clue to her disappearance. Of course, the parents were frantic—trying to keep the phone clear in case the kidnapper tried to deliver a ransom message—jumping with fright whenever it rang—returning disappointed when there was no news. It was a heartbreaking scene to witness. They did everything they could, even appearing on television and radio to appeal for her release or for information that might help, but nothing worked. Weeks later police found the body of their daughter discarded in a field. The search was over, but not the grief.

Indelibly stamped on my memory is the testimony of that angry and grief-stricken father. He was a brilliant executive with a leading computer firm. As they waited anxiously for some word, he said:

> All my life I've been trained to solve problems, and I'm good at it. Just give me the data, and with the help of the computer I can analyze those data and come up with solutions to the problem. But this problem just doesn't compute! All of my training and professional experience are useless. It's like I was back in kindergarten again, trying to learn my ABC's. I'm as helpless as if I'd never learned anything.

He acknowledged that the only thing he had left when he sifted through all his assets—professional, intellectual, and material—was his faith in God. Grateful for that faith, he wondered, as I often do, how people face such crises when they do not know God.

Hezekiah was smart enough to acknowledge that all his royal power and political position were insufficient in the face of Sennacherib's attack. Wisely, he did not try to meet the blasphemies of

Sennacherib with weapons, but with tears and sackcloth, and prayer. He went into the house of the Lord to arrange for a delegation to go to Isaiah the prophet. Hezekiah didn't need politicians, or princes, or secular advisors. He didn't need war councils, or military strategists, or fortune tellers. He needed a word of authority from one who was in fellowship with God.

Seeing Hezekiah's reliance on the prophet should encourage ministers of the gospel today who feel their work is somehow inferior to that of the physician or attorney or business leader. Here is another reminder that the person who is called to speak for God has a vital and irreplaceable role in guiding others to find their help in the Almighty.

This is the first time Isaiah is mentioned in 1 and 2 Kings, even though he had been active since the reign of Hezekiah's grandfather, Ahaziah (Uzziah) (v. 2). In fact, this is the first canonical prophet to appear in the historical books of the Old Testament, which are remarkably silent on the ministries and roles of the prophets whose writings are included in the canon of Scripture. (Some believe 2 Kings 14:25 refers to another canonical prophet, Jonah.)

Since Eliakim, Shebna, and the elders also put on sackcloth before going to see Isaiah, it may be that Hezekiah had commanded a public fast. Perhaps he led all the people of Jerusalem to join him as he withdrew from public life and retreated to the temple to pray.

The king may have used a popular proverb in verse 3 when he compared Jerusalem to a mother who was about to have a child but was too weak to deliver the baby.[10] In verse 4 he seems to be saying that although the people of Jerusalem do not deserve God's intervention, maybe He will interfere because of the blasphemy of the Assyrians. *"Remnant"* here is used in the sense that Jerusalem was the only Judean city left uncaptured. All the other fortress cities had fallen to Sennacherib's army (2 Kings 18:13). The word for "prayer" here is *tĕpillâ,* which means primarily intercessory prayer.

Verse 6 gives the impression that Isaiah didn't wait for the king's plea to be delivered by the royal delegation. He knew they were coming and already had an answer for the king before they asked the question. Hezekiah and the people of Jerusalem were not the only ones who listened to Sennacherib's reproach. God had listened to the blasphemous words too, and He had already set in motion His judgment upon the Assyrian king.

It is interesting to note that the word used for the servants of the king of Assyria in this verse is a different word from the one used for the servants of Hezekiah in verse 5. Here the word is one that literally means "the boys" of the king of Assyria. God dismissed the boastful threats of the Rabshakeh and his comrades as the bluster of little children, not the serious threats of officers of a great army.[11]

The *"spirit"* referred to in verse 7 was probably a spirit of fear or uncertainty sent to undermine the determination and confidence of Sennacherib. The rumor that God predicted Sennacherib would hear was that the king of Ethiopia, Tirhakah, was approaching to make war against Assyria (v. 9). In the light of such a rumor, what else could Sennacherib do but give up his siege of Jerusalem and return to Assyria to defend his own country? Later the Assyrians returned to attack Jerusalem, only to be routed by the miracle described in 2 Kings 19:35. After this defeat, Sennacherib was assassinated in his homeland, fulfilling the word of the Lord in verse 7.

HEZEKIAH'S PRAYER FOR HELP

19:8 Then *the* Rabshakeh returned and found the king of Assyria warring against Libnah, for he heard that he had departed from Lachish.

9 And the king heard concerning Tirhakah king of Ethiopia, "Look, he has come out to make war with you." So he again sent messengers to Hezekiah, saying,

10 "Thus you shall speak to Hezekiah king of Judah, saying: 'Do not let your God in whom you trust deceive you, saying, "Jerusalem shall not be given into the hand of the king of Assyria."

11 'Look! You have heard what the kings of Assyria have done to all lands by utterly destroying them; and shall you be delivered?

12 'Have the gods of the nations delivered those whom my fathers have destroyed, Gozan and Haran and Rezeph, and the people of Eden who *were* in Telassar?

13 'Where *is* the king of Hamath, the king of Arpad, and the king of the city of Sepharvaim, Hena, and Ivah?'"

14 And Hezekiah received the letter from the hand
of the messengers, and read it; and Hezekiah went
up to the house of the LORD, and spread it before the
LORD.
15 Then Hezekiah prayed before the LORD, and
said: "O LORD God of Israel, *the One* who dwells *between* the cherubim, You are God, You alone, of all the
kingdoms of the earth. You have made heaven and
earth.
16 "Incline Your ear, O LORD, and hear; open Your
eyes, O LORD, and see; and hear the words of Sennacherib, which he has sent to reproach the living
God.
17 "Truly, LORD, the kings of Assyria have laid
waste the nations and their lands,
18 "and have cast their gods into the fire; for they
were not gods, but the work of men's hands—wood
and stone. Therefore they destroyed them.
19 "Now therefore, O LORD our God, I pray, save
us from his hand, that all the kingdoms of the earth
may know that You *are* the LORD God, You alone."

2 Kings 19:8–19

Sennacherib's envoys returned with their report of Hezekiah's response to discover that the Assyrian army had left Lachish to attack the nearby city of Libnah (v. 8). Libnah was a strong military fortress in the lowland between the Mediterranean and the mountains of Judah. However, before he could complete the Libnah assault, Sennacherib heard the rumor about the threatened attack of Ethiopia's king, Tirhakah. Tirhakah was also known as Tarakos, the third and last of the twenty-fifth dynasty of Egypt. Now he was king of Ethiopia only, but later he became the ruler of all the Nile nations.[12] So before Sennacherib rushed back to defend his own capital against a new enemy, he fired one last verbal missile at Hezekiah (vv. 10–13).

This time the swaggering threat was issued in the form of a letter. Its message was similar to the earlier threat, repeating most of the same arguments Sennacherib had used the first time to try to convince Hezekiah that his position was futile (2 Kings 18:35). One subtle difference, however, is that the first threat accused Hezekiah of deceiving himself, while this second threat claimed that it was

God who was doing the deceiving (v. 10). Another difference is that Sennacherib added the names of additional nations that Assyria had conquered (vv. 12–13).

In verse 14, Hezekiah reacted to the second letter in a different manner. He didn't go to Isaiah. He went to the temple and prayed alone, taking his plea directly to the Lord. Both kinds of prayer are appropriate for the believer who is facing a crisis. We should follow the biblical admonition to share our concerns with fellow believers so they may intercede on our behalf. We should bear one another's burdens, according to the Scriptures. But we can't stop there. We must also petition the Lord ourselves, claiming the promise that "whatever things you ask when you pray, believe that you receive them, and you will have them" (Mark 11:24).

The word for *"letter"* in verse 14 is plural, indicating that the letter was lengthy, probably written in Aramaic on several leather or papyrus scrolls. We are given only a summary of its message in this chapter.[13] Hezekiah carried the letter into the temple and *"spread it before the Lord"* in a symbolic act, displaying the blasphemy in God's presence, and calling for His help in response to it. Gray suggests that the reference to the cherubim in verse 15 might mean that Hezekiah was in the Holy of Holies itself. Since as king he possessed some sacral status, he might well have been standing before the ark between the two cherubs that symbolized the presence of Yahweh.[14]

Hezekiah's prayer is a commendable model. It contains an invocation addressed to God as *"Lord God of Israel,"* who is enthroned above the cherubim, who is alone the God of all the nations, and who made heaven and earth (v. 15). It contains a plea for God to hear and attend to the matter at hand (v. 16). It contains the complaint about Sennacherib's assault (vv. 17–18). It contains a final plea for God's intervention, to *"save us from his hand"* (v. 19). Finally, it contains a motivation or reason for the request, *"that all the kingdoms of the earth may know that You are the Lord God, You alone"* (v. 19). God heard the prayer, and He was already preparing an answer.

ISAIAH'S WORD CONCERNING SENNACHERIB

19:20 Then Isaiah the son of Amoz sent to Hezekiah,
saying, "Thus says the LORD God of Israel: 'Because

you have prayed to Me against Sennacherib king of
Assyria, I have heard.'

21 "This *is* the word which the LORD has spoken
concerning him:
'The virgin, the daughter of Zion,
Has despised you, laughed you to scorn;
The daughter of Jerusalem
Has shaken *her* head behind your back!
22 'Whom have you reproached and blasphemed?
Against whom have you raised *your* voice,
And lifted up your eyes on high?
Against the Holy *One* of Israel.
23 By your messengers you have reproached the
LORD,
And said: "By the multitude of my chariots
I have come up to the height of the mountains,
To the limits of Lebanon;
I will cut down its tall cedars
And its choice cypress trees;
I will enter the extremity of its borders,
To its fruitful forest.
24 I have dug and drunk strange water,
And with the soles of my feet I have dried up
All the brooks of defense."
25 'Did you not hear long ago
How I made it,
From ancient times that I formed it?
Now I have brought it to pass,
That you should be
For crushing fortified cities *into* heaps of ruins.
26 Therefore their inhabitants had little power;
They were dismayed and confounded;
They were *as* the grass of the field
And the green herb,
As the grass on the housetops
And *grain* blighted before it is grown.
27 'But I know your dwelling place,
Your going out and your coming in,
And your rage against Me.
28 Because your rage against Me and your tumult
Have come up to My ears,
Therefore I will put My hook in your nose

And My bridle in your lips,
And I will turn you back
By the way which you came.
29 'This *shall be* a sign to you:
You shall eat this year such as grows of itself,
And in the second year what springs from the same;
Also in the third year sow and reap,
Plant vineyards and eat the fruit of them.
30 And the remnant who have escaped of the house of Judah
Shall again take root downward,
And bear fruit upward.
31 For out of Jerusalem shall go a remnant,
And those who escape from Mount Zion.
The zeal of the LORD of hosts will do this.'
32 "Therefore thus says the LORD concerning the
king of Assyria:
'He shall not come into this city,
Nor shoot an arrow there,
Nor come before it with shield,
Nor build a siege mound against it.
33 By the way that he came,
By the same shall he return;
And he shall not come into this city,'
Says the LORD.
34 'For I will defend this city, to save it
For My own sake and for My servant David's sake.'"
35 And it came to pass on a certain night that the
angel of the LORD went out, and killed in the camp of
the Assyrians one hundred and eighty-five thousand;
and when *people* arose early in the morning, there
were the corpses—all dead.
36 So Sennacherib king of Assyria departed and
went away, returned *home,* and remained at Nineveh.
37 Now it came to pass, as he was worshiping in the
temple of Nisroch his god, that his sons Adrammelech
and Sharezer struck him down with the sword; and
they escaped into the land of Ararat. Then Esarhaddon
his son reigned in his place.

2 Kings 19:20–37

Even though Isaiah was not directly consulted, he responded to Hezekiah's prayer. It appears that God decided to answer the king through the words of the prophet: *"Because you have prayed to Me . . . I have heard. This is the word which the Lord has spoken concerning him [Sennacherib]"* (vv. 20–21). While Hezekiah was praying the prophet Isaiah was receiving a divine revelation, which he then forwarded to the king.

There follows next a fourteen-verse poem, or song, from the pen of Isaiah. Biblical scholars liken it to other similar poetic writings that use the Hebraic "gina measure." Such poetic writings fall into the literary genre called "taunt songs."[15] For example, this one is similar to another gina-measure "taunt song" in Isa. 10:5–29.

The *"virgin"* and the *"daughter"* in verse 21 both refer to Jerusalem, which had not been "violated" since the days of David. In other words, no enemy had succeeded in capturing the city. It was uncontaminated by heathens. So Jerusalem could shake her head in derision and scorn at Sennacherib's threat.

God asked Sennacherib in verse 22, *"Whom have you reproached and blasphemed?"* Obviously, the answer is not just "Jerusalem" or "Judah," for Sennacherib had also reproached *"the Holy One of Israel"* Himself. This is Isaiah's favorite term for God, describing Him as the God of both kingdoms, Judah and Israel. God then quotes Sennacherib's own boast in verses 23–24. Since Assyria had few trees, Sennacherib was obviously impressed by the plentiful forests of Lebanon. He considered the cypress and cedar wood a prime spoil of conquest (v. 23). In the British Museum is a letter found at Nineveh written by Sennacherib's successor on the Assyrian throne, King Esarhaddon, which bears out this fact:

> I sent all of these to drag with pain and difficulty to Nineveh, the city of my dominion, as supplies needed for my palace, big beams, long posts, and trimmed planks of cedar and cypress wood, products of the Sirara and Lebanon mountains, where for long they had grown tall and thick. . . .[16]

It is not easy to interpret verse 24. *"I have dug and drunk strange water"* is a metaphor for successful achievement. *"Strange water"* may refer to water in foreign lands, indicating that he had conquered many nations. *"With the soles of my feet"* was Sennacherib's boast that he commanded so many soldiers that when they marched across riverbeds, they literally dried up the rivers.[17] It is not clear in the Hebrew whether the phrase translated *"brooks of defense"* means "rivers of the delta," referring to Egypt, or "rivers of the fortress," meaning a defensive barrier. The same Hebrew word can easily be read either way.[18] Whichever interpretation is preferred, the phrase represents an empty boast, especially since as far as we know, Sennacherib had never been to Egypt.

In verse 25, God speaks again through the prophet's song. Sennacherib's success has been possible only because God allowed it. His boasting has no foundation because it was God who brought all his accomplishments to pass. Verse 26 adds that even the lack of defense on the part of the cities that the king had conquered was God-ordained. *"Little power"* in verse 26 is literally "short of hands." Adding to this idea in Isa. 10:5, the prophet declares that God considered Sennacherib His instrument, using him like a rod or a staff in His divine hand.

Verse 27 means that every step Sennacherib took, every word he said, was seen and heard by God, and his continued existence was possible only because God allowed it. The *"rage against Me"* refers to the boasts and threats in Sennacherib's letter and the earlier message delivered by the Rabshakeh.

In verse 28 God promises to turn back the Assyrian king. While the phrases *"hook in your nose"* and *"bridle in your lips"* sound like a description of cruel treatment of animals, there is evidence that Assyrian conquerors actually humiliated their enemies by leading them away captive in this cruel manner.[19]

In verse 29 God addresses Hezekiah through the medium of Isaiah's song. How encouraging it must have been to hear the Lord promise that Sennacherib's siege of Jerusalem would not last long and that prosperity would flourish again in Jerusalem. During the first year of the Assyrian invasion, the war would prevent the people of Jerusalem from planting. They would have to eat what *"grows of itself"* without cultivation. The next year they would have to live on *"what springs from the same,"* that is, what comes up naturally from the uncultivated crops of the past year. But in the third year, the residents would be able to *"sow and reap"* because the siege would be lifted. One should not attempt to use this verse to calculate an exact chronology for the Assyrian assault. It seems to say that residents of

Jerusalem would not cultivate the land for two consecutive autumns, but this could refer to two years or a little over one year.

Continuing the horticulture metaphor, verse 30 suggests that those who survive the crisis will dwell securely and will flourish. But verse 31 warns them that this miraculous deliverance will take place, not because Judah is deserving of such salvation, but because of *"the zeal of the Lord of hosts."*

"Therefore" in verse 32 seems to refer to verse 28. Because Sennacherib has blasphemed God, he will be prevented from conquering Jerusalem.

He shall not come into this city.
Nor shoot an arrow there,
Nor come before it with shield,
Nor build a siege mound against it.

This encouraging promise of the inviolability of Jerusalem was later cheapened by the people in Jeremiah's day. They began to presume on this word and changed it from a doctrine of hope to a false claim that God would save them no matter what they did. Using these verses of the song, they presumed upon God and boasted in their own safety, and soon the city fell.

The fulfillment of God's promise in verse 33 that Sennacherib would turn away is described in verse 35. The beautiful song of Isaiah ends with the promise of God in verse 34, *"For I will defend this city, to save it for My own sake and for My servant David's sake."*

With little detail, almost matter-of-factly, the author of Kings declares that the angel of Lord wiped out the army of Sennacherib in one night. The king and whoever else survived awakened to find 185,000 soldiers dead. It is interesting to note that Herodotus records a similar Egyptian tradition telling of another calamity that befell Sennacherib. A plague of field mice broke out in his military camp at Pelusium in Egypt. In one night, according to the record, the mice gnawed through the leather thongs of the soldier's shields and their leather bowstrings, and, by depriving them of their weapons, exposed them helpless to their enemies.[20]

Notice how the author stacks up the series of verbs in verse 36: Sennacherib *"departed . . . went away . . . returned home . . . remained."* This unusual linguistic construction suggests the speed of the defeated king's frantic retreat.

The end of Sennacherib's story is given in verse 37. Obviously, some period of time elapsed between his siege of Jerusalem and his death. The god Nisroch is found only here and in the parallel passages of the Old Testament. Some scholars identify him with Nusku, an Assyrian sun god. Ararat, of course, is the famous mountain in Armenia.

HEZEKIAH'S ILLNESS AND GOD'S CURE

20:1 In those days Hezekiah was sick and near death. And Isaiah the prophet, the son of Amoz, went to him and said to him, "Thus says the LORD: 'Set your house in order, for you shall die, and not live.'"

2 Then he turned his face toward the wall, and prayed to the LORD, saying,

3 "Remember now, O LORD, I pray, how I have walked before You in truth and with a loyal heart, and have done *what was* good in Your sight." And Hezekiah wept bitterly.

4 And it happened, before Isaiah had gone out into the middle court, that the word of the LORD came to him, saying,

5 "Return and tell Hezekiah the leader of My people, 'Thus says the LORD, the God of David your father: "I have heard your prayer, I have seen your tears; surely I will heal you. On the third day you shall go up to the house of the LORD.

6 "And I will add to your days fifteen years. I will deliver you and this city from the hand of the king of Assyria; and I will defend this city for My own sake, and for the sake of My servant David."'"

7 Then Isaiah said, "Take a lump of figs." So they took and laid *it* on the boil, and he recovered.

8 And Hezekiah said to Isaiah, "What *is* the sign that the LORD will heal me, and that I shall go up to the house of the LORD the third day?"

9 Then Isaiah said, "This is the sign to you from the LORD, that the LORD will do the thing which He has spoken: *shall* the shadow go forward ten degrees or go backward ten degrees?"

10 And Hezekiah answered, "It is an easy thing for
the shadow to go down ten degrees; no, but let the
shadow go backward ten degrees."
11 So Isaiah the prophet cried out to the LORD and
He brought the shadow ten degrees backward, by
which it had gone down on the sundial of Ahaz.

2 Kings 20:1–11

These next eleven verses tell about a miraculous event that took place sometime before the Assyrian army was annihilated by the angel of the Lord. Since the miraculous healing extended the life and reign of Hezekiah *"fifteen years"* (v. 6), it must have taken place in about the middle of Hezekiah's twenty-nine-year reign. When the king heard Isaiah's diagnosis that his illness was terminal, he turned his face away from the people gathered around his sick bed, prayed, and literally "wept a great weeping" (v. 3).

His prayerful request for divine healing was grounded in four personal characteristics that he felt deserved the Lord's attention: (1) He had walked before God. This was the same trait with which the Bible describes men like Enoch, Noah, Abraham, Isaac, David, and others. (2) He had been faithful, or true. His relationship with God had been one of genuine sincerity and reliability. (3) He had served God *"with a loyal heart,"* literally "with a whole heart." There was no duplicity or deceit in his faith. (4) He had done what was good.

God heard the king's prayer, and once again used Isaiah as the channel through whom He communicated His promised healing to Hezekiah (vv. 4–6). Applying the poultice of figs to the infection was a remedy used in that day for both humans and animals to draw the poison from a boil or wound. "Recovered" here refers to the local infection, leaving the king still in a weakened and sickly condition so that he continued to ask Isaiah for some sign that God would complete the healing process.

As a sign, Isaiah allowed Hezekiah to choose whether to have the shadow on a sundial go miraculously ten degrees backward or ten degrees forward. *"The sundial of Ahaz"* in verse 11 is literally "the steps of Ahaz." The phrase could be the proper name of a sundial built by Ahaz for use in astral worship. That is credible since we are told that he was guilty of worshiping the "host of heaven." The Septuagint, on the other hand, supposes that the phrase "the steps of

Ahaz" refers not to a sundial but literally to a flight of steps in the palace arranged so that the shadow on them could tell the time.[21] Either way, the miracle does not necessarily require some reverse movement of the earth. It may be that God miraculously moved the shadow on the dial itself in some supernatural way.

BABYLON'S ENVOYS AND HEZEKIAH'S DEATH

20:12 At that time Berodach-Baladan the son of Baladan, king of Babylon, sent letters and a present to Hezekiah, for he heard that Hezekiah had been sick.
13 And Hezekiah was attentive to them, and showed them all the house of his treasures—the silver and gold, the spices and precious ointment, and all his armory—all that was found among his treasures. There was nothing in his house or in all his dominion that Hezekiah did not show them.
14 Then Isaiah the prophet went to King Hezekiah, and said to him, "What did these men say, and from where did they come to you?" So Hezekiah said, "They came from a far country, from Babylon."
15 And he said, "What have they seen in your house?" So Hezekiah answered, "They have seen all that *is* in my house; there is nothing among my treasures that I have not shown them."
16 Then Isaiah said to Hezekiah, "Hear the word of the LORD:
17 'Behold, the days are coming when all that *is* in your house, and what your fathers have accumulated until this day, shall be carried to Babylon; nothing shall be left,' says the LORD.
18 'And they shall take away some of your sons who will descend from you, whom you will beget; and they shall be eunuchs in the palace of the king of Babylon.'"
19 So Hezekiah said to Isaiah, "The word of the LORD which you have spoken *is* good!" For he said, "Will there not be peace and truth at least in my days?"
20 Now the rest of the acts of Hezekiah—all his

> might, and how he made a pool and a tunnel and brought water into the city—*are* they not written in the book of the chronicles of the kings of Judah?
> 21 So Hezekiah rested with his fathers. Then Manasseh his son reigned in his place.
>
> *2 Kings 20:12–21*

Having given extensive coverage to the long reign of Hezekiah of Judah, the author now brings the account of one of Judah's greatest kings to a close. Ironically, this last incident in Hezekiah's commendable reign was not a very complimentary one. It depicted an uncharacteristic naïveté on the part of the king, which was rebuked by Isaiah. One never knows the full impact of a person's life, not even a noble one like Hezekiah's, until the very end.

Berodach-Baladan, the king of Babylon, is also mentioned in Isa. 39:1, where his name is spelled Merodach-Baladan. He is identified with Mardukhabaliddina who seized the Babylonian throne in 721 B.C., was deposed by Sargon of Assyria, and then came back to rule again for a short time about 704 B.C.[22] He sent letters and a present to Hezekiah because he had heard about his illness. In his parallel account, Isaiah adds that Hezekiah had by now recovered, and Chronicles adds that the Babylonian king wanted to know more about the miraculous recovery and the miracle of the sundial. Josephus adds still more, declaring that the visit of Berodach-Baladan was to secure the friendship of Judah as an ally in his fight against the Assyrians.

At any rate, the visit of the envoys was not an altogether innocent or friendly one, since Isaiah predicted that it would eventually lead to the destruction of Jerusalem.

A rabbinic tradition infers that Isaiah's question in verse 14 was intended to test Hezekiah, just as God had tested Cain and Balaam. He should have answered, "You are a prophet of God to whom secrets are known, why then do you ask me?" Instead, he made a show of his own greatness by boasting how two great leaders came such a distance to see him and his prosperous court and to solicit his friendship. So on account of his arrogance and lack of faith in God, Hezekiah was punished by the ominous prophecy of Isaiah in verses 16–18.[23]

Whether or not this rabbinic tradition is true, it is clear that instead of showing off his wealth, Hezekiah should have shown his foreign visitors the temple and the evidence of God's power and holiness. He should have used the opportunity to introduce them to Yahweh and to demonstrate how they worshiped Him as the one true God. But instead he showed them nothing but what they could have expected to see in any pagan country.

Hezekiah's famous water tunnel is referred to briefly in verse 20. This remarkable engineering project was discovered in 1880, still intact, with an inscription carved in the wall describing the cutting of the tunnel. (For a complete translation of the inscription, see M. Pierce Matheney and Roy Honeycutt, "1-2 Kings," *The Broadman Bible Commentary,* ed. Clifton J. Allen, vol. 3 [Nashville: Broadman, 1970], 282.) It is quite an impressive experience to walk through the tunnel today and marvel at the achievement of Hezekiah's skilled workmen who started at each end and met in the middle of the rock with very little variation.

So Hezekiah died, and although the author of Kings doesn't mention it, Chronicles indicates that he was buried in "the upper tombs of the sons of David; and all Judah and the inhabitants of Jerusalem honored him at his death." Jewish tradition says he was buried next to David and Solomon.

A group of tombs discovered by archaeologists in the city of David may be those of the kings, but they were so badly damaged that identification of individual tombs was impossible.[24]

NOTES

1. I. W. Slotki, *Kings* (London: Soncino Press, 1950), 270.
2. C. F. Keil, *The Books of the Kings,* Biblical Commentary on the Old Testament, ed. C. F. Keil and F. Delitzsch, vol. 4 (Grand Rapids: Eerdmans, 1950), 430.
3. John Gray, *I and II Kings,* Old Testament Library (Philadelphia: Westminster, 1963), 607.
4. Ibid.
5. M. Pierce Matheney and Roy Honeycutt, "1–2 Kings," in *The Broadman Bible Commentary,* ed. Clifton J. Allen, vol. 3 (Nashville: Broadman, 1970), 273.

6. Gray, 607.
7. Gwilym H. Jones, *1 and 2 Kings,* New Century Bible Commentary, ed. Ronald E. Clements (Grand Rapids: Eerdmans, 1984), 561.
8. Gray, 618.
9. Keil, 434.
10. Gray, 621.
11. Jones, 574.
12. Slotki, 281.
13. Ibid.
14. Gray, 624.
15. Ibid., 625.
16. British Museum Tablet K. 1295, cited by Matheney and Honeycutt, 277.
17. Slotki, 283.
18. Gray, 625.
19. Ibid.
20. Slotki, 283.
21. Keil, 460.
22. Slotki, 290.
23. Ibid.
24. T. R. Hobbs, *2 Kings,* Word Biblical Commentary, ed. John D. W. Watts, vol. 13 (Waco, TX: Word Books, 1985), 294.

CHAPTER NINETEEN

The Reigns of Manasseh and Amon

2 Kings 21:1–26

MANASSEH REIGNS IN JUDAH

21:1 Manasseh *was* twelve years old when he became king, and he reigned fifty-five years in Jerusalem. His mother's name *was* Hephzibah.

2 And he did evil in the sight of the LORD, according to the abominations of the nations whom the LORD had cast out before the children of Israel.

3 For he rebuilt the high places which Hezekiah his father had destroyed; he raised up altars for Baal, and made a wooden image, as Ahab king of Israel had done; and he worshiped all the host of heaven and served them.

4 He also built altars in the house of the LORD, of which the LORD had said, "In Jerusalem I will put My name."

5 And he built altars for all the host of heaven in the two courts of the house of the LORD.

6 Also he made his son pass through the fire, practiced soothsaying, used witchcraft, and consulted spiritists and mediums. He did much evil in the sight of the LORD, to provoke *Him* to anger.

7 He even set a carved image of Asherah that he had made, in the house of which the LORD had said to David and to Solomon his son, "In this house and in Jerusalem, which I have chosen out of all the tribes of Israel, I will put My name forever;

8 "and I will not make the feet of Israel wander anymore from the land which I gave their fathers—only if they are careful to do according to all that I

> have commanded them, and according to all the law
> that My servant Moses commanded them."
> 9 But they paid no attention, and Manasseh se-
> duced them to do more evil than the nations whom
> the LORD had destroyed before the children of Israel.
>
> *2 Kings 21:1–9*

It would be difficult to imagine a more dramatic reversal in character and practice than that which took place when Manasseh assumed the throne of Judah in the place of his father. If Hezekiah was the best king Judah had, then his son Manasseh must have been the worst. Hezekiah received the high distinction of being compared to David, but Manasseh was the only king of Judah who was likened to wicked king Ahab of Israel (v. 3). Under Manasseh the greatest infidelity and apostasy against Yahweh in the history of Judah emerged. Of Hezekiah, the author of Kings writes: "He did what was right in the sight of the Lord . . . so that after him was none like him among all the kings of Judah, nor who were before him" (18:3, 5). But of Manasseh, the author writes, *"He did much evil in the sight of the Lord, to provoke Him to anger"* (v. 6). The prophets declare that "he has acted more wickedly than all the Amorites who were before him" (2 Kings 21:11).

How could the son of such a noble father turn out so bad? A more important question is, "How does the same thing happen today?" Obviously the old adage "Like father, like son" is not always true.

One pastor I know, whose daughter went astray, tried to blame her failures on the university she attended. But universities, even denominational schools, are not designed to be remedial institutions. They can't correct in four years what parents have failed to accomplish in eighteen or twenty years. Another well-known religious leader said recently, "Inevitably, the children of famous personalities who are popular and constantly in the public arena always turn out to be problem children." As you might guess, his own children were sad disappointments to him and his wife.

It seems illogical to us that children of godly parents should turn out bad, so we naturally look for something or someone to blame. Who or what can be blamed for the unprecedented spiritual collapse of Hezekiah's son Manasseh?

One clue to the puzzle may be the statement in verse 1 that

Manasseh was only twelve years old when his father died and he began to reign. He must have been born in the third of the extra fifteen years of life God gave Hezekiah after his serious illness (2 Kings 20:6). Unlike King Joash, who also assumed the throne as a young boy after his father's death but who was surrounded by godly advisers like Jehosheba and Jehoiada (2 Kings 11:1–12), young Manasseh must have fallen under the influence of godless counselors. Some idolatrous faction in the court of Hezekiah must have gained control of the young and inexperienced monarch early in his reign in order to get their way in Judah and return the country to pagan worship. His fifty-five-year reign was not only the worst but also the longest of any king in Judah or in Israel.

Manasseh's name means "he causes to forget." It may have been given to him because he brought consolation to Hezekiah his father after the loss of an earlier child or because his coming caused his mother Hephzibah to forget the pain of childbirth.[1] Her name, incidently, means "my delight is in her." Isaiah used that name poetically to suggest that Zion would be blessed by God. He said that Zion's name would be Hephzibah ("my delight is in her") rather than Azubah ("forsaken") or Shemamah ("desolate") (Isa. 62:4).

"Abominations" in verse 2 can be literally translated "disgusting actions," and the *"abominations of the nations"* is a generic, inclusive term for all the sins listed in the next verses.[2] Here is the catalogue of Manasseh's transgressions:

1. He rebuilt the high places his father had torn down (v. 31; cf. 2 Kings 16:4; 18:4).

2. He built altars to Baal and images to Asherah, the consort of Baal, just as Ahab had done in Israel (v. 3; cf. 1 Kings 16:33).

3. He went beyond the sins of Ahab, however, by introducing into Judah the Assyrian practice of worshiping the sun, moon, and stars—that is, the *"host of heaven"* (v. 3). Archaeologists have discovered a seal from the time of Manasseh's reign that bears the inscription, "[belonging] to Manasseh, son [or steward] of the king." On the seal are a six-pointed star and a crescent, suggesting that the owner worshiped the *"host of heaven."* It has been dated close to the beginning of Manasseh's reign, and if it did indeed belong to him, it indicates that he became a practicing idolater as a young man.

4. He actually erected altars to the sun, moon, and stars in the temple itself (vv. 4–5). Since the temple as described in 1 Kings 6

had only one court, the second court mentioned in this verse must refer to the palace court next door. This was called "the middle court" and was considered almost a part of the temple.[3]

5. He sacrificed his son on the fiery altar of the god Molech and apparently encouraged the people of Jerusalem to do the same thing (v. 6).

6. He practiced soothsaying or augury (v. 6). The word is *ʿônēn.* Because of the similarity of this word to *ʿānān,* which means "cloud," some believe the word points to the practice of telling fortunes by looking at the changing patterns of the clouds.[4] Others assert that *ʿônēn* is an onomatopoeic word based on the crooning sound made by the soothsayer himself in imitation of the cooing of a dove as he drifted into a trance before telling fortunes.[5]

7. He practiced witchcraft or divination (v. 6). This might refer to snake charming or hydromancy, that is, the telling of fortunes by looking at water.[6]

8. He consulted spiritists and mediums (v. 6). Some translators say the two words here should be translated "mediums" and "wizards." Either way, they both refer to foretelling the future by making contact with the dead or calling up departed spirits (necromancy).

9. He set up a newly carved image of Asherah in the holy temple of Yahweh (v. 7). This last sin was serious because of God's promise to David and Solomon that His presence would dwell in that temple in a special way (2 Sam. 7:13; 1 Kings 8:27). He also promised that He would bless and protect His people as long as they obeyed *"the law that My servant Moses commanded them"* (v. 8).

What a dreadful list of deplorable sins! Paying no attention to the warnings of God, the people let Manasseh "seduce them" into following his example so that they became more pagan than the pagans, doing *"more evil than the nations whom the Lord had destroyed before the children of Israel"* (v. 9).

The prophets make much of this theme that God's people should have behaved better than their neighbors who worshiped idols (cf. Amos 9:7; Jer. 2:9–13). That theme even finds its way into the teaching of Jesus: "It will be more tolerable for Tyre and Sidon in the day of judgment than for you" (Matt. 11:22).

The contrast between the wicked reign of Manasseh and the commendable reign of his father Hezekiah is so dramatic that it leads one to suspect that Manasseh deliberately repudiated his father's reforms.

Some scholars have pointed out that the terrible idolatry during this period might have been due to Judah's domination by Assyria, but Manasseh's radical reversal of national religious practice in the very opposite direction of godliness seems too intense to have been circumstantial. Manasseh was plainly on an intentional anti-Yahweh crusade.

It may be that the young king yielded to pressures from a group in Jerusalem who did not agree with his father's reforms and influenced him toward apostasy and infidelity, but it is difficult to place the blame anywhere but on Manasseh himself.

Isaiah was dead, and there was no prophet in Judah strong enough to oppose the royal campaign for idolatry. Furthermore, some of the people were restless and unhappy because Hezekiah had taken away the pleasures of their pagan worship practices. To worship only Yahweh, with His insistence on justice and morality, seemed to them too narrow, too strict. Even the priests probably favored a return to worshiping Yahweh in the pagan high places because such decentralization of worship, scattering worship sites throughout the land rather than only in Jerusalem, brought in more money.

In spite of extenuating circumstances, even though conditions were somewhat stacked against him, Manasseh was responsible for what has been called the era of the greatest infidelity and apostasy in the history of Judah. Years later, when Jerusalem fell to the Babylonians, the writer would blame Judah's punishment on the sins of Manasseh (2 Kings 24:3–4).

The Prophets Judge Manasseh and He Dies

> 21:10 And the LORD spoke by His servants the prophets, saying,
>
> 11 "Because Manasseh king of Judah has done these abominations (he has acted more wickedly than all the Amorites who *were* before him, and has also made Judah sin with his idols),
>
> 12 "therefore thus says the LORD God of Israel: 'Behold, *I* am bringing *such* calamity upon Jerusalem and Judah, that whoever hears of it, both his ears will tingle.
>
> 13 'And I will stretch over Jerusalem the measuring line of Samaria and the plummet of the house of

Ahab; I will wipe Jerusalem as *one* wipes a dish,
wiping *it* and turning *it* upside down.
14 'So I will forsake the remnant of My inheritance and deliver them into the hand of their enemies; and they shall become victims of plunder to all
their enemies,
15 'because they have done evil in My sight, and
have provoked Me to anger since the day their fathers came out of Egypt, even to this day.'"
16 Moreover Manasseh shed very much innocent
blood, till he had filled Jerusalem from one end to
another, besides his sin by which he made Judah sin,
in doing evil in the sight of the LORD.
17 Now the rest of the acts of Manasseh—all that
he did, and the sin that he committed—*are* they not
written in the book of the chronicles of the kings of
Judah?
18 So Manasseh rested with his fathers, and was
buried in the garden of his own house, in the garden
of Uzza. Then his son Amon reigned in his place.

2 Kings 21:10–18

Fifty-five years is a long time for wickedness in high places to continue without challenge, but eventually the long-suffering of God reached its limits, and He judged Manasseh through *"His servants the prophets."* Literally the verse says He spoke "by the hand of" His servants the prophets.

Who were these nameless spokesmen for God? Not Jeremiah. He had not yet begun his ministry. It was neither Micah nor Isaiah, since they were no longer on the scene. In fact, one tradition says that Manasseh was the one who put Isaiah to death. In a pseudepigraphal book called *The Martyrdom of Isaiah,* there is a story of a false prophet named Belchira of Bethlehem who accused Isaiah of disloyalty before the court of Manasseh. The passage from the book says:

> And he [Belchira] brought many accusations against Isaiah and the prophets before Manasseh. But Beliar [angel of lawlessness and ruler of this world] dwelt in the heart of Manasseh . . . and he sent and seized Isaiah. And he sawed him asunder with a wood-saw. . . . But Isaiah was [absorbed] in a vision of the Lord, and though his eyes were open, he saw them [not].[7]

It was not Jeremiah, Micah, nor Isaiah, but perhaps one of the prophets referred to in verse 10 was Habakkuk, since he so vividly predicted the Babylonian judgment in his book (Hab. 1:5).

The authoritative message from Yahweh through these anonymous prophetic voices is recorded in verses 11 through 15. The Amorites in verse 11 were one of the original peoples who occupied Canaan when the children of Israel entered the promised land. Here the name stands for all the idolatrous inhabitants of Canaan. Because of Judah's disobedience, God's calamitous judgment would soon fall on Judah and its capital city of Jerusalem. The punishment would be of such magnitude that hearing the news of it would cause the ears of the hearer to tingle (v. 12). In other words, such calamity had never been heard of before. This metaphor of tingling ears is also used in 1 Sam. 3:11 and Jer. 19:3.

Another metaphor for the judgment soon to fall upon Judah is taken from the vocabulary of the builder. The *"measuring line"* would be used to calculate the extent of her destruction. The *"plummet"* may refer either to the instrument used in demolition or to the plumb line by which a builder determines whether or not a wall is perpendicular. Amos used this same symbol when he pictured God as a judge with a plumb line in His hand, using it to determine if Israel was leaning away from the standard of His law (Amos 7:7–8).

When the bricklayers were building the walls of the new library on our seminary campus a few years ago, I was surprised to see that after all these years of advancing technology these skilled craftsmen were still using the ancient plumb line to keep the walls perfectly straight. Suspended from the scaffold on which the bricklayers worked was a piece of heavy string. Tied to the end of the string was a pointed piece of lead. (The Latin word *plumbum* means "lead.") When the weighted string, hanging just an inch from the new wall, stopped swinging and stood still, it told the bricklayers whether or not the wall was perfectly vertical. Later, when the architect came by to inspect their work in order to approve it so we could pay them, he also carried a plumb line to measure the perpendicular quality of the wall.

The Bible says that God judges us in the same way. He has a plumb line in His hand to measure whether our lives are straight according to His standard, or whether they lean away from the vertical ideal of the Ten Commandments.

Another prophetic symbol is found in verse 13; this time it comes from the kitchen. Before the modern convenience of electric dishwashers, the familiar scene in family kitchens for centuries was the busy cook with a dish towel in hand, drying the freshly washed dishes. In rural areas, after a sumptuous feast, I can remember seeing the cook put the dried plates back on the clean tablecloth upside down, ready for the next meal. Supposedly, this was designed to keep the plates free from dust until they were used again. When the host said "amen" after the blessing at the next meal, all of us would ceremoniously turn our plates right side up in readiness to pass the fried chicken and mashed potatoes.

In verse 13, God says, *"I will wipe Jerusalem as one wipes a dish, wiping it and turning it upside down."* This could indicate that, once cleansed by His judgment, Jerusalem would be ready for His use again. Or the symbol may mean that God was turning the dish upside down to show that not a drop remained in it, indicating that Jerusalem would be completely depopulated. This seems to be the meaning in Jer. 51:34, "Nebuchadnezzar the king of Babylon . . . has made me an empty vessel."

The *"remnant"* in verse 14 refers to the people in the Southern Kingdom. They were the only ones remaining since the ten tribes of the North had already been deported. *"Forsake"* is a strong, forceful word used to describe the skinning of an animal. It is sometimes translated "cast off."[8]

Several explanations have been proposed for the shedding of innocent blood mentioned in verse 16. One suggestion is that it refers to Manasseh's sacrificing of children to the god Molech.[9] Another is that, like Ahab, the king was guilty of executing innocent victims in order to confiscate their property.[10] Still another explanation is that the shedding of innocent blood refers to Manasseh's killing of God's prophets, particularly Isaiah, according to the Jewish legend described above. Josephus (*Antiquities* 10.3.1) indicates that Manasseh killed a few prophets every day during his reign! Whoever was being killed, their blood filled Jerusalem from *"one end to another."* This is an interesting phrase meaning literally, "from mouth to mouth"—that is, from one entrance of the city to another.

Manasseh died a natural death at the age of sixty-seven and was buried *"in the garden of his own house, in the garden of Uzza"* (v. 18). Apparently the regular burial place for Judean kings in the southern extremity of the old city of David was already full, or maybe Manasseh's apostasy precluded his being buried with the others. Notice, however, that his father Hezekiah, the good king, was not buried with the other kings either, so the explanation that there was no more space in the traditional tombs is more likely (2 Chron. 32:33).

Scholars are not sure where the grave site named *"the garden of Uzza"* was located. The name "Uzza" may be a shortened form of "Uzziah," leading some to suggest that the garden had been built by Uzziah as an addition either to the royal palace in Jerusalem or perhaps to one of his summer or winter palaces. Gray believes that "Uzza" is the name of a Canaanitish desert deity, maybe of Arabian origin, and that a shrine to this god was built in the king's garden. Therefore, the garden took its name from this pagan deity.[11] Wherever it was located, Manasseh's son Amon was also buried there (2 Kings 21:26).

According to the parallel passage in 2 Chronicles 33, Manasseh was put in chains and carried to Babylon by the king of Assyria. There he repented and prayed to God, who accepted his supplication and restored him to his throne in Jerusalem. He then abolished the pagan idols, rebuilt the altar of the Lord, and called upon the people of Judah to serve Him alone. But the repentance was too little too late. The clock of divine judgment had already begun its countdown.

AMON REIGNS IN JUDAH

> 21:19 Amon *was* twenty-two years old when he became king, and he reigned two years in Jerusalem. His mother's name *was* Meshullemeth the daughter of Haruz of Jotbah.
>
> 20 And he did evil in the sight of the LORD, as his father Manasseh had done.
>
> 21 So he walked in all the ways that his father had walked; and he served the idols that his father had served, and worshiped them.
>
> 22 He forsook the LORD God of his fathers, and did not walk in the way of the LORD.
>
> 23 Then the servants of Amon conspired against him, and killed the king in his own house.

24 But the people of the land executed all those who had conspired against King Amon. Then the people of the land made his son Josiah king in his place.

25 Now the rest of the acts of Amon which he did, *are* they not written in the book of the chronicles of the kings of Judah?

26 And he was buried in his tomb in the garden of Uzza. Then Josiah his son reigned in his place.

2 Kings 21:19–26

Because of his long and wicked reign, Manasseh looms large on the pages of Judah's history. His son Amon, on the other hand, is dismissed as not much more than a worthless cipher, a wretched footnote at the bottom of the historical page. Since he was twenty-two years old when he began to reign and had therefore been under the influence of Judah's wickedest king for nearly a quarter of a century, it is no surprise that he too *"did evil in the sight of the Lord"* (v. 20). In fact, his father dramatized Amon's pagan upbringing by naming him for an Egyptian deity. Amon's mother, who bore the Arabian name "Meshullemeth," is mentioned only here.[12] Her father's name, "Haruz," is also thought to be Arabian, which might give credence to the idea that "the garden of Uzza" mentioned above was indeed the location of a shrine to an Arabian desert god. Manasseh might well have included such a deity among his many idols if indeed his father-in-law was Arabian. Num. 33:33 mentions Haruz's hometown of Jotbah. It has been identified with a location in Edom about twenty miles north of Aqaba. This also supports the Arabian connection.[13]

Amon's assassins, called his *"servants"* in verse 23, may have been representatives of a priestly party in the royal household who objected to the idolatry and apostasy of Manasseh and his son and took advantage of the young king before he could consolidate his royal power. But another party, perhaps pro-Assyrian in their loyalty, quickly executed the assassins and established Amon's eight-year-old son, Josiah, on the throne of Jerusalem. These *"people of the land"* no doubt assumed that they could manipulate the boy-king to carry out their policies. Amon was buried beside his father Manasseh in the garden of Uzza.

If it is difficult to understand how such an outstanding leader as

Hezekiah could have had a son as wicked as Manasseh, it is even more incredible that such a weak and wicked character as Amon could have had such an illustrious son as Josiah. The only positive contribution Amon made to the history of Judah was to produce one of the best kings to reign on the throne of Jerusalem. The story of Josiah, a noble king like his grandfather, Hezekiah, is told in the next chapter.

NOTES

1. Robert C. Dentan, *Kings and Chronicles,* Layman's Bible Commentary, vol. 7 (Richmond: John Knox Press, 1964), 94.
2. T. R. Hobbs, *2 Kings,* Word Biblical Commentary, ed. John D. W. Watts, vol. 13 (Waco, TX: Word Books, 1985), 304.
3. Gwilym H. Jones, *1 and 2 Kings,* New Century Bible Commentary, ed. Ronald E. Clements (Grand Rapids: Eerdmans, 1984), 595.
4. Ibid.
5. Norman H. Snaith, Ralph W. Sockman, and Raymond Calkins, "The First and Second Books of Kings," in *The Interpreter's Bible,* vol. 3 (Nashville: Abingdon, 1954), 310.
6. Jones, 595.
7. M. Pierce Matheney and Roy Honeycutt, "1–2 Kings," in *The Broadman Bible Commentary,* ed. Clifton J. Allen, vol. 3 (Nashville: Broadman, 1970), 283.
8. John Gray, *I and II Kings,* Old Testament Library (Philadelphia: Westminster, 1963), 645.
9. Ibid.
10. I. W. Slotki, *Kings* (London: Soncino Press, 1950), 295.
11. Gray, 645.
12. Jones, 601.
13. Gray, 648.

CHAPTER TWENTY

The Reign and Reforms of Josiah

2 Kings 22:1–23:30

THE DISCOVERY OF THE BOOK OF THE LAW

22:1 Josiah *was* eight years old when he became king, and he reigned thirty-one years in Jerusalem. His mother's name *was* Jedidah the daughter of Adaiah of Bozkath.

2 And he did *what was* right in the sight of the LORD, and walked in all the ways of his father David; he did not turn aside to the right hand or to the left.

3 Now it came to pass, in the eighteenth year of King Josiah, *that* the king sent Shaphan the scribe, the son of Azaliah, the son of Meshullam, to the house of the LORD, saying:

4 "Go up to Hilkiah the high priest, that he may count the money which has been brought into the house of the LORD, which the doorkeepers have gathered from the people.

5 "And let them deliver it into the hand of those doing the work, who are the overseers in the house of the LORD; let them give it to those who *are* in the house of the LORD doing the work, to repair the damages of the house—

6 "to carpenters and builders and masons—and to buy timber and hewn stone to repair the house.

7 "However there need be no accounting made with them of the money delivered into their hand, because they deal faithfully."

8 Then Hilkiah the high priest said to Shaphan the scribe, "I have found the Book of the Law in the

house of the LORD." And Hilkiah gave the book to
Shaphan, and he read it.
9 So Shaphan the scribe went to the king, bringing the king word, saying, "Your servants have gathered the money that was found in the house, and have
delivered it into the hand of those who do the work,
who oversee the house of the LORD."
10 Then Shaphan the scribe showed the king, saying, "Hilkiah the priest has given me a book." And
Shaphan read it before the king.
11 Now it happened, when the king heard the
words of the Book of the Law, that he tore his clothes.
12 Then the king commanded Hilkiah the priest,
Ahikam the son of Shaphan, Achbor the son of
Michaiah, Shaphan the scribe, and Asaiah a servant
of the king, saying,
13 "Go, inquire of the LORD for me, for the people
and for all Judah, concerning the words of this book
that has been found; for great *is* the wrath of the
LORD that is aroused against us, because our fathers
have not obeyed the words of this book, to do according to all that is written concerning us."

2 Kings 22:1–13

Along with his great-grandfather, Hezekiah, Josiah ranks as one of the most important of all the kings of Judah. Most commentators would grade him slightly above Hezekiah in importance because he avoided even the minor failures of his great-grandfather's later years and because his reign came during the climactic final chapter of Judah's history. Momentous events were erupting around the biblical world in 638 B.C. when Josiah came to the throne in Jerusalem in 638 B.C. As the powerful influence of Assyria was waning, the savage invasion of the Scythians emerged on the horizon and lasted until 624 B.C. Finally, in 612 B.C. the capital of Assyria fell before a combined army of Scythians, Medes, and Babylonians. That paved the way for the ominous rise to world power of Babylon, whose "innocent" envoys had visited the court of Josiah's great-grandfather (2 Kings 20:12). In 627 B.C. the articulate voice of Jeremiah, reinforced by the preaching of Zephaniah and Nahum, began to be heard in Judah. While not one of these events is mentioned in this historical account of Josiah's reign, they must have had an enormous impact on the king, both during his formative years and during the active years of his national reforms.

Since he was only eight years old when the people of the land crowned him, Josiah spent his first eighteen years as king under the tutelage and guardianship of the priests and elders. His first recorded independent act as king is recorded in this chapter when, at the age of twenty-six, he ordered the restoration of the temple. Chronicles, however, says that after seeking the God of his father David at the age of sixteen, Josiah, at twenty, began his crusade to purge Judah of idolatry.

Not much is known about his mother, Jedidah, except her mother's name and hometown. "Jedidah" means "beloved," and she must have been a godly woman who, along with pious leaders of the temple and the court, helped her son overcome the influence of his wicked father. Since at the most impressionable time in the young king's life he encountered the violence, bloodshed, and revolution of his father Amon's brief reign, it would have been natural for him to repeat that paternal pattern. So there must have been some wise heads and strong arms and loyal hearts around him. With the exception of Jedidah, however, their names have perished. Under the influence of these nameless heroes, Josiah grew up to do *"what was right in the sight of the Lord, and he walked in all the ways of his father David"* (v. 2). Like his great-grandfather Hezekiah, Josiah received the rare unqualified commendation of the author of Kings. The final grade on his royal report card was an A+.

Recalling, perhaps, an early history lesson during his years of training, Josiah remembered that one of his predecessors, King Jehoash, had developed an ingenious plan for rebuilding the temple (2 Kings 12). He decided to employ that same plan to restore the sadly neglected temple in his day. Shaphan, a trusted scribe (some say he was the secretary of state) with a well-known and commendable family pedigree, was assigned the responsibility for the project (v. 3). He and his sons, one of whom is mentioned in verse 12, were described as helpers of Jeremiah (Jer. 26:24; 29:3). With the assistance of Hilkiah the high priest, Shaphan's first task was to allocate the contributions of temple worshipers so that the trusted craftsmen could begin the restoration. But, as often happens, the construction project was halted because of an archaeological discovery.

In the news recently was a fascinating story with similar implications. Jim Siler, a Santa Fe woodworker, was digging the foundation for his new house near Glorieta, New Mexico when his backhoe operator yelled at him. He ran over to where the digging was taking place and saw a human skull in the ditch. Wisely, Jim Siler stopped any further digging and contacted the museum of New Mexico. A few days later, a team of archaeologists had uncovered a double row of thirty-two skeletons, arms crossed over their chests, neatly stacked side by side and two deep in the corner of Siler's foundation. Researchers are convinced they had found the mass grave of Texas Volunteers who died in the battle of Glorieta Pass, March 26, 1862. For six hours on that cold spring day over 125 years ago, two thousand Confederate soldiers from Texas and Colorado had clashed with Union troops in a battle that dashed the Confederacy's hopes of seizing New Mexico in the War Between the States. The next day the Confederates hastily buried their dead in the hard ground—most of them in a mass grave. Then they withdrew, leaving New Mexico, and leaving their fallen comrades' graves lost to history.

Shirt buttons, shoe leather, hats, rings, bullets, coins, pocketknives, combs, and other artifacts were retrieved from the grave. Three of the victims wore Union Army belt buckles bearing the initials "U.S." But they were worn upside down, the way Confederate soldiers wore confiscated Union buckles. Comparing the artifacts with the official roster of the missing casualties may shed light on the identities of the bodies. The discovery will also help scholars learn more about the general history of the event as well.

New Mexico archaeologists said, "It's a startling find. If it's not a once-in-a-lifetime find, it's pretty close to it!" But Jim Siler, the home builder, said he had had about all the excitement he could handle. "Later, when we were out there digging for the septic tank," he said, "I sure was praying we wouldn't find anything else."[1]

As the ancient workers began the repair of the long-neglected temple, they made a "once-in-a-lifetime" discovery. Hilkiah the priest said to Shaphan the scribe, *"I have found the Book of the Law in the house of the Lord"* (v. 8). The Hebrew sentence is more dramatic. It literally says, "The Book of the Law I have found." Apparently the Scripture scroll had lain lost and forgotten for seventy-five years—the fifty-five years of Manasseh's reign, the two years of Amon's reign, and the eighteen years between Josiah's coronation as an eight-year-old and the discovery when he was twenty-six. The people of Jerusalem had become steeped in idolatry, temple worship had been neglected, and most copies of the Book of the Law had been destroyed. The scroll discovered in the temple must have been hidden in some secret chamber years earlier by faithful priests. A few scholars surmise that Hilkiah knew where to look for the book because he had hidden and protected it for many years.[2] Josephus, enlarging on the Chronicles account, advanced the theory that the scroll was discovered in the bottom of one of the temple treasure chests when the money was taken out.[3]

Exactly what was this mysterious scroll or book? Hilkiah obviously recognized it because he called it *"the"* Book of the Law (v. 8). Later when Shaphan presented it to the king, he called it *"a"* book, because the king was not aware of its identity. It was probably a scroll written on animal skin similar to the scrolls discovered at Qumran, although as indicated by the clay seals uncovered at Lachish, papyrus was also in use during this period as a writing material.[4]

Usually, the term *"Book of the Law"* refers to the entire Pentateuch, the first five books of the Old Testament. Because Chronicles adds the words "given by Moses" in 2 Chron. 34:14, Grotius and others have inferred that this was the original copy of the Pentateuch written in Moses' own hand.[5] But since the days of Jerome most biblical scholars have believed that it was an ancient scroll of the Book of Deuteronomy, which was also popularly known as *"the Book of the Law."*[6]

Shaphan, who had first taken time to read the book for himself (v. 8), now brought it before King Josiah and read the book aloud. Chronicles explains that he read certain passages from the book, and one wonders what sections he selected. Surely Shaphan included the blessings and cursings in chapter 28. Whatever the text, the reading of the word of God, as it always does, spoke to the heart of the young king and stirred his spirit to conviction and repentance.

Such genuine spiritual conviction always leads to action, and Josiah did indeed begin to act. He *"tore his clothes"* as a symbol of repentance, and then he appointed a delegation to prayerfully study the book. *"Inquire of the Lord for me,"* he commanded. This was a technical word that meant they were to find a godly interpreter who could explain the book's meaning (v. 12).

The deputation was made up of Hilkiah the priest, whose name means "Yahweh is my spirit" and whose grandson Seraiah would be the last high priest before the exile; Ahikam the son of Shaphan the scribe, a faithful supporter of Jeremiah; Achbor the son of Michaiah; Asaiah the servant of the king, who held a post of great importance in the court; and of course, Shaphan the scribe.

It is interesting to note the popularity of animal names for persons in this period. "Shaphan" means "rock badger" and "Achbor" means "mouse." "Huldah," the name of the prophetess introduced in the next section, means "mole." They were obviously not disrespectful names, but they may have been affectionate nicknames. Shaphan may have played on the rocks as a little boy and thereby picked up the nickname "rock badger." Huldah may have acquired her name when she emerged from the Siloam tunnel carrying a jar of water one day. Most biblical characters were given names with spiritual significance or that described some personal characteristic, but these names seem to have had a more lighthearted meaning.

This passage is laden with lessons and truths with relevance for today. Notice that Josiah found the Book of the Law only after he had started the repairs on the temple and other national religious reforms. It's still true that we learn more about God's will when we are engaged in doing it. When we apply whatever limited knowledge of His will we already have, He reveals more of that will in the midst of our obedience. God's will is seldom laid out before us like the selections on a cafeteria line so that we can pick and choose those elements in His will we would like to obey. Instead, He reveals His will to those who are already committed to it and who are presently engaged in obeying the part of His will that they already know. "If any man will do His will, he will know of the doctrine" (John 7:17).

All across the U.S. the FAA maintains a complex system of air navigation aids that guide pilots through a network of invisible "highways" in the sky. The primary system is made up of routes called VOR airways. Every few miles along these airways there is a VOR radio transmitter, which sends out its signal in all directions of the compass. A pilot can tune the navigation radio in his plane to one of the stations and adjust an indicator on the instrument panel. When this has been done, the needle will tell him which direction he must take to fly to that station. Along the pilot's route, the needle will drift to the right or to the left if he is off course, so he must keep the needle centered in order to fly directly to the VOR station.

When flying from Houston to Dallas, for example, the pilot of a small private plane cannot receive the VOR radio signal at his destination, because Dallas is too far away. The "line of sight" broadcast of a VOR radio transmitter usually has a range of no more than forty or fifty miles at low altitudes. So he must tune in the nearest VOR station on his route and keep the needle centered as he flies to that first point. Then as he crosses that VOR, a flag on the instrument panel flips to tell him he has just passed the station. He can then tune his radio to the next VOR on his route, keep the needle centered as he flies to this point, and continue the process until he is in range of his destination, the Dallas VOR. In other words, every time he reaches one VOR on the airway he will then have sufficient guidance to enable him to fly toward another, and so on until he reaches his destination.

That's the way it is with the will of God. Every believer knows some things that are God's will for him or her right now. If we take those steps we know to be His will, He is always faithful to show us another step, and so on, until we find His complete will for our lives. God may reveal His ultimate will to some people, but He leads most of us a step at a time. When people with a lantern walk in darkness, the lantern illuminates only a few steps ahead at a time. But when they begin to walk into the slim circle of light they have, the circle pushes ahead of them and reveals a few more safe steps they can take. So, if they keep walking slowly, letting the light push forward in the darkness, they can eventually reach their destination.

Josiah obeyed what little light he had about the will of God, but when he took those first steps, God revealed more of His will to him. It was in the midst of obeying God's will that the king discovered the Book of the Law.

How could the written word of God have been lost for seventy-five years? The simple answer is neglect. Whenever we disregard spiritual values, they gradually slip out of sight. One Christmas a few years ago, the pastor of a Cuban congregation in Atlanta complained about a problem he had encountered in preparing for the church's annual pageant. His church was made up primarily of refugees from Cuba who did not speak English, so their worship services and Bible studies were all in Spanish. Unlike their parents, however, the little children in the church quickly learned English, and, since they seldom spoke Spanish, even at home, they began to forget their native tongue. And therein lay the problem the Cuban pastor faced when preparing the Christmas pageant. He said, "I not only have to encourage the children in the pageant to memorize the Scripture passages they are to recite, but I have to teach them how to say the passages in Spanish!" Because of neglect and lack of use, they were losing the ability to speak the language they had learned as infants.

The Bible had been neglected for seventy-five years in Judah, so it is no wonder it had been lost and forgotten. I'm afraid that if the preservation of the Scriptures for future generations depended on the value that some people in our day place on it, the Bible would have been lost long ago.

This remarkable passage reminds us that the providential transmission of the Bible through the centuries is just as miraculous as its inspiration. In the seventh century B.C. it was this one copy alone, as far as we know, that kept the chain of transmission alive in order to pass it on to the future. Like a trickle of water that finds its way through the rock and sand to become at last a great river in the valley below, so God has preserved and transmitted His word from generation to generation, sometimes through a channel that seems precariously thin. There are millions of copies now, but this one dusty forgotten scroll lay buried in the rubble of the temple for seventy-five years as the only link to the Bible's future. We can be thankful for God's providential watch-care over the long process of transmission that brought the Bible to us today.

This passage also teaches the important truth that the inspired word of God carries its own credentials and its own power. When presenting it to King Josiah, Shaphan the scribe called it simply *"a book."* He gave it no name, but left it to authenticate its own message in the king's heart. Doesn't this tell us that the Bible needs no man-made defense? It stands by its own power, without the need for human apologists or protectors. Dwight Moody is supposed to have said, "Defend the Bible? You might as well try to defend a lion. All you have to do is open his cage. The lion will defend himself." So, the word of God does not need to be defended; it needs to be obeyed, studied, preached, and taught. It can take care of itself.

Notice, however, that it was necessary for Josiah to have a trained, dedicated, God-called interpreter to explain the meaning of the Book. That's why the skill of interpretation, called hermeneutics, is such a vital subject in the seminary curriculum today. It is true, of course, that as Luther said, the most uneducated person who loves the Lord and prays for understanding can, with the illumination of the Holy Spirit, interpret the Bible better than an unbelieving scholar. But it is also true that reverent scholarship can open up insights in God's Word that less skilled interpreters might miss. The treasures of the Bible are so innumerable that its students must constantly sharpen their skills of exposition while at the same time praying for the Holy Spirit's guidance in order to dig out the treasures for themselves and those whom they teach. It is the Bible—properly interpreted—that is our authority for living. Josiah was wise when he called for the biblical scholars of his day and said, *"Inquire of the Lord for me, for the people and for all Judah, concerning the words of this book"* (v. 13).

THE PROPHECY OF HULDAH

> 22:14 So Hilkiah the priest, Ahikam, Achbor, Shaphan, and Asaiah went to Huldah the prophetess, the wife of Shallum the son of Tikvah, the son of Harhas, keeper of the wardrobe. (She dwelt in Jerusalem in the Second Quarter.) And they spoke with her.
>
> 15 Then she said to them, "Thus says the LORD God of Israel, 'Tell the man who sent you to Me,
>
> 16 "Thus says the LORD: 'Behold, I will bring calamity on this place and on its inhabitants—all the words of the book which the king of Judah has read—
>
> 17 'because they have forsaken Me and burned incense to other gods, that they might provoke Me to anger with all the works of their hands. Therefore My wrath shall be aroused against this place and shall not be quenched.'"'
>
> 18 "But as for the king of Judah, who sent you to inquire of the LORD, in this manner you shall speak to him, 'Thus says the LORD God of Israel: *"Concerning* the words which you have heard—

19 "because your heart was tender, and you humbled yourself before the LORD when you heard what I spoke against this place and against its inhabitants, that they would become a desolation and a curse, and you tore your clothes and wept before Me, I also have heard *you,*" says the LORD.
20 "Surely, therefore, I will gather you to your fathers, and you shall be gathered to your grave in peace; and your eyes shall not see all the calamity which I will bring on this place."'" So they brought back word to the king.

2 Kings 22:14–20

In the light of so much discussion about women in ministry today, one cannot avoid asking the question at this point in the book, "Why did the king's delegation go to Huldah the prophetess, a relatively unknown woman, when there were several famous prophets in Judah who were men?"

We don't know much about Huldah or her family. Her husband's father was a *"keeper of the wardrobe,"* that is, of the priestly vestments in the temple or the royal garments of the court. She lived in the *"Second Quarter"* of Jerusalem. According to Neh. 3:9–12 and Zeph. 1:10, ancient Jerusalem was divided into two neighborhoods or sectors. Which one of these is intended by the term in verse 14 is uncertain. The word for "quarter" here can also be translated "college."

Jeremiah and (probably) Zephaniah and Nahum were already at work at this time, and were certainly better known. As men, they were probably considered more traditional candidates for the role of royal interpreter. Prophetesses are mentioned in the Old Testament only a few times: Miriam, Deborah, Noadiah, and Huldah. Isaiah's wife is called a prophetess, but probably in the sense of a prophet's wife and not one who held the office. Anna is mentioned as a prophetess in the New Testament.

So, why Huldah? The ancient rabbis answered the question in several ways. Some said the delegation went to a woman because they believed that she would be more tenderhearted and, rather than rebuking the people for their transgressions, would be inclined to pray for them, realizing they had sinned in ignorance. Others taught that Jeremiah had only begun his prophetic ministry and had not yet attained widespread recognition. Huldah, on the other hand, already had a good reputation for her work in Jerusalem. Still others explain that Huldah was the wife of one of the priests and therefore well known to them for her gifts.[7]

If they thought Huldah, being a woman, would somehow soften the message of the word of God, they were mistaken. Using the traditional *"thus says the Lord God of Israel,"* the prophetess delivered a forthright, clear, powerful, intense proclamation of the meaning of the book (vv. 15–20).

"The man who sent you to Me" might be a general reference to the king, or, more likely, may have referred to someone else who recommended Huldah to the king's delegation. The first part of Huldah's interpretation applied to the people of Judah in general (vv. 16–17), but the last part was directed to the king himself (vv. 18–20). Josiah was to be spared the calamities written in the book because he had responded to its message receptively, with tenderhearted humility.

Some have interpreted the phrase *"gathered to your grave in peace"* to indicate that Josiah was to die a natural death, when in fact he was killed in battle against Pharaoh Necho at Megiddo (2 Kings 23:29). But the meaning is that at his death Judah would still be intact as a nation, and he would die without experiencing the terrible tragedies to come. The word translated *"grave"* here is plural and may refer to a royal mausoleum that contained several sepulchers.

THE REFORMS OF JOSIAH

> 23:1 Now the king sent them to gather all the elders of Judah and Jerusalem to him.
>
> 2 The king went up to the house of the LORD with all the men of Judah, and with him all the inhabitants of Jerusalem—the priests and the prophets and all the people, both small and great. And he read in their hearing all the words of the Book of the Covenant which had been found in the house of the LORD.
>
> 3 Then the king stood by a pillar and made a covenant before the LORD, to follow the LORD and to keep His commandments and His testimonies and His statutes, with all *his* heart and all *his* soul, to perform the words of this covenant that were written

in this book. And all the people took a stand for the covenant.

4 And the king commanded Hilkiah the high priest, the priests of the second order, and the doorkeepers, to bring out of the temple of the LORD all the articles that were made for Baal, for Asherah, and for all the host of heaven; and he burned them outside Jerusalem in the fields of Kidron, and carried their ashes to Bethel.

5 Then he removed the idolatrous priests whom the kings of Judah had ordained to burn incense on the high places in the cities of Judah and in the places all around Jerusalem, and those who burned incense to Baal, to the sun, to the moon, to the constellations, and to all the host of heaven.

6 And he brought out the wooden image from the house of the LORD, to the Brook Kidron outside Jerusalem, burned it at the Brook Kidron and ground *it* to ashes, and threw its ashes on the graves of the common people.

7 Then he tore down the *ritual* booths of the perverted persons that *were* in the house of the LORD, where the women wove hangings for the wooden image.

8 And he brought all the priests from the cities of Judah, and defiled the high places where the priests had burned incense, from Geba to Beersheba; also he broke down the high places at the gates which *were* at the entrance of the Gate of Joshua the governor of the city, which *were* to the left of the city gate.

9 Nevertheless the priests of the high places did not come up to the altar of the LORD in Jerusalem, but they ate unleavened bread among their brethren.

10 And he defiled Topheth, which *is* in the Valley of the Son of Hinnom, that no man might make his son or his daughter pass through the fire to Molech.

11 Then he removed the horses that the kings of Judah had dedicated to the sun, at the entrance to the house of the LORD, by the chamber of Nathan-Melech, the officer who *was* in the court; and he burned the chariots of the sun with fire.

12 The altars that *were* on the roof, the upper

chamber of Ahaz, which the kings of Judah had
made, and the altars which Manasseh had made in
the two courts of the house of the LORD, the king
broke down and pulverized there, and threw their
dust into the Brook Kidron.
13 Then the king defiled the high places that *were*
east of Jerusalem, which *were* on the south of
the Mount of Corruption, which Solomon king
of Israel had built for Ashtoreth the abomination of
the Sidonians, for Chemosh the abomination of the
Moabites, and for Milcom the abomination of
the people of Ammon.
14 And he broke in pieces the *sacred* pillars and cut
down the wooden images, and filled their places
with the bones of men.
15 Moreover the altar that *was* at Bethel, *and* the
high place which Jeroboam the son of Nebat, who
made Israel sin, had made, both that altar and the
high place he broke down; and he burned the high
place *and* crushed *it* to powder, and burned the
wooden image.
16 As Josiah turned, he saw the tombs that *were*
there on the mountain. And he sent and took the bones
out of the tombs and burned *them* on the altar, and
defiled it according to the word of the LORD which the
man of God proclaimed, who proclaimed these words.
17 Then he said, "What gravestone *is* this that I
see?" So the men of the city told him, "*It is* the tomb
of the man of God who came from Judah and proclaimed these things which you have done against
the altar of Bethel."
18 And he said, "Let him alone; let no one move
his bones." So they let his bones alone, with the
bones of the prophet who came from Samaria.
19 Now Josiah also took away all the shrines of the
high places that *were* in the cities of Samaria, which
the kings of Israel had made to provoke the LORD to
anger; and he did to them according to all the deeds
he had done in Bethel.
20 He executed all the priests of the high places
who *were* there, on the altars, and burned men's bones
on them; and he returned to Jerusalem.

21 Then the king commanded all the people, saying, "Keep the Passover to the LORD your God, as *it is*
written in this Book of the Covenant."
22 Such a Passover surely had never been held
since the days of the judges who judged Israel, nor in
all the days of the kings of Israel and the kings of
Judah.
23 But in the eighteenth year of King Josiah this
Passover was held before the LORD in Jerusalem.
24 Moreover Josiah put away those who consulted
mediums and spiritists, the household gods and
idols, all the abominations that were seen in the
land of Judah and in Jerusalem, that he might perform the words of the law which were written in the
book that Hilkiah the priest found in the house of
the LORD.
25 Now before him there was no king like him,
who turned to the LORD with all his heart, with all
his soul, and with all his might, according to all the
Law of Moses; nor after him did *any* arise like him.
26 Nevertheless the LORD did not turn from the
fierceness of His great wrath, with which His anger
was aroused against Judah, because of all the
provocations with which Manasseh had provoked
Him.
27 And the LORD said, "I will also remove Judah
from My sight, as I have removed Israel, and will
cast off this city Jerusalem which I have chosen, and
the house of which I said, 'My name shall be there.'"
28 Now the rest of the acts of Josiah, and all that
he did, *are* they not written in the book of the chronicles of the kings of Judah?
29 In his days Pharaoh Necho king of Egypt went to
the aid of the king of Assyria, to the River Euphrates;
and King Josiah went against him. And *Pharaoh Necho*
killed him at Megiddo when he confronted him.
30 Then his servants moved his body in a chariot
from Megiddo, brought him to Jerusalem, and buried
him in his own tomb. And the people of the land took
Jehoahaz the son of Josiah, anointed him, and made
him king in his father's place.

2 Kings 23:1–30

Now Josiah takes center stage and personally directs the entire population in national reforms. He had delegated the temple repair and the interpretation of the Book of the Law to others, but the vast reforms would be led by the king himself. The best way to grasp the remarkable extent of Josiah's reformation is to list his accomplishments by categories and then examine them more closely.

I. The Renewal of the Covenant (vv. 1–3)
   A. He read the Book of the Law to the people.
   B. He made a personal recommitment to the covenant.
   C. He led the people to renew the covenant.
II. The Removal of Idols from Judah (vv. 4–14)
   A. He removed the idols from the temple and burned them.
   B. He removed the idolatrous priests.
   C. He destroyed the wooden image of Asherah.
   D. He destroyed the booths of the perverted persons.
   E. He closed down the high places and brought the wayward priests back to Jerusalem.
   F. He destroyed the fiery altar of Molech in Hinnom.
   G. He wiped out the pagan worship of the sun, moon, and stars.
   H. He destroyed the altars of Ashtoreth, Chemosh, and Milcom.
   I. He destroyed the sacred pillars.
III. The Removal of Idols from Bethel (vv. 15–20)
   A. He destroyed Jeroboam's molten bulls in Bethel.
   B. He burned human bones on the altars to defile them.
   C. He honored the grave of the prophet from Judah.
   D. He destroyed the high places in Samaria.
   E. He executed the idolatrous priests in Samaria.
IV. The Reinstitution of the Passover Feast (vv. 21–23)
V. The Removal of Superstitions from Judah (vv. 24–25)
   A. He put away those who consulted mediums.
   B. He prohibited the use of household gods.
   C. He destroyed all the abominations in Judah.

I. The Renewal of the Covenant (vv. 1–3)

The entire population of Jerusalem was invited to join leaders from all across Judah to enter the temple for a ceremonial renewal of the covenant. *"Small and great"* in verse 2 means "young and old." Chronicles has the word "Levites" in the place of the word *"prophets"* here. In leading the ceremony, the king stood by the pillar just as the boy-king Jehoash had done when Jehoiada the chief priest seized the throne for him and proclaimed him king (2 Kings 11:14). It was evidently the proper and traditional place for the king to stand when he worshiped in the temple.

"[He] made a covenant" is literally "[he] cut a covenant," which goes back to the practice of cutting the carcass of an animal and separating the parts so the contracting parties could seal their agreement by walking between them[8] (cf. Gen. 15:17; Jer. 34:18). In this case, the promise that the king and the people made was to keep the words of the book. The phrase *"took a stand for the covenant"* in verse 3 is literally "stood in the covenant."

II. The Removal of Idols from Judah (vv. 4–14)

Josiah's grandfather (Manasseh) had installed all sorts of pagan idols in the temple and his father (Amon) had reinforced idol worship; but now Josiah ordered the idols all removed, burned outside the city, and the ashes taken away to Bethel. Bethel was a defiled place from which idolatry had spread throughout the Northern Kingdom and, supposedly, into Judah as well. It was at Bethel that Jeroboam had set up the infamous molten bulls to lure the people of Israel to worship there instead of Jerusalem.

In verse 5, the word for priests is *kĕmārîm,* which is used rarely in the Old Testament and only for idolatrous priests. In Aramaic it is the regular word for all priests. It was formerly thought that it came from a Hebrew root meaning "to be black," on the grounds that the priests were supposedly always dressed in black. But we now know that following an ancient custom, the Jerusalem priests wore white; therefore, it is unlikely that the word carries this meaning. A better explanation is that the word comes from a root word meaning "to lay prostrate," the priest thus being the man who prostrates himself before God.[9] The priests referred to in this verse were the ones who led the rituals on the *"high places"* throughout Judah. Even though they were supposedly worshiping Yahweh, they were doing it on the sites of pagan altars and were probably intermingling idolatrous practices with the worship of Yahweh. The Lord had consistently forbidden such syncretism.

Other priests who were removed by Josiah were those who presided over the worship of the *"host of heaven,"* that is, the sun, moon, and stars. The word translated "constellations" in verse 5 is the word *mazzālôt,* which literally means "a place of standing." Most linguists believe it refers to the Assyrian zodiac.[10]

The word translated "wooden image" in verse 6 is *ʾăšērâ.* Asherah was a Canaanite goddess who was considered the consort of Baal. Throwing the ashes of the idol on the graves of the common people outside the city was not intended to defile their graves, but the very opposite. Any contact with death was believed to be an act of defilement, so scattering the dust on the graves served to defile the idols. Also the act symbolized the fact that the idol appropriately belonged in the cemetery because it was not a living god. The word for *"graves"* here is singular, probably indicating a mass grave. Customarily, the wealthy people were buried in caves hollowed out of hillsides. This burial place, on the contrary, was probably a large death pit where the poor were laid to rest (cf. Jer. 26:23).

"Perverted persons" in verse 7 refers to male and female prostitutes who participated in pagan religious rituals. Even though this native Palestinian practice was regularly abolished by reforming kings, it found its way back again as soon as the time of the reforms was past. Such practice was strictly forbidden in the Mosaic law (Deut. 23:17). The word translated *"hangings"* likely refers to a fabric woven by idol worshipers for curtains behind which the ritual obscenities were practiced.[11] Others explain that the hangings were garments to be worn by the pagan priests or to be draped on the images they worshiped.[12]

Next, Josiah called in the country priests who led worship at the rural high places across Judah. A popular proverbial phrase, *"from Geba [in the north] to Beersheba [in the south],"* is used to describe the fact that these shrines were scattered throughout the entire nation. He brought these erring priests back to Jerusalem, but he reduced their status and responsibility (v. 9). Nowhere else in Scripture is the *"Gate of Joshua"* mentioned, and its precise location is not known, although obviously to the first readers of Kings it was a familiar feature of the city of Jerusalem. It might have been a current nickname for a gate known to us by a different, more formal name.[13]

In the Valley of Hinnom, a gruesome place throughout the history of Judah, King Manasseh had built an altar to the pagan god, Molech. There the children of worshipers were burned on a fiery altar as sacrifices to the pagan god. *"Topheth"* means "fireplace" or "furnace" and was probably the name of the pit dug in the ground for this abominable ritual. The unknown original spelling of this name was changed by the Masoretic scholars to include the vowels from the word *bōšet,* which means "shameful thing."[14]

Apparently, the references in verses 11 and 12 are to various ceremonies involved in the worship of the sun, moon, and stars. Chariots and horses played a big part in the worship of the sun, probably because of the idea that the sun god drives across the sky in his chariot. In the literature of other nations, the sun god is pictured riding in a winged chariot.[15] Here, the horses and chariots mentioned were probably large statues, though they may have been miniature figurines used in astral worship. Rooftop shrines like those described in verse 12 were also related to this same pagan cult, which was introduced by King Ahaz.

Scholars differ widely on the meaning of the term *"Mount of Corruption"* in verse 13. Its literal translation is "Mount of the Destroyer." Some see it as an allusion to the location where the angel of destruction stood and stretched out his hand to bring a plague on Jerusalem (2 Sam. 24:16). It is taken, therefore, to be the southern extremity of the Mount of Olives, which is still called "the Mount of Offence."[16] Here Solomon built his infamous altars to the pagan deities of his wives.

III. The Removal of Idols from Bethel (vv. 15–20)

In his zeal, Josiah even extended his iconoclastic purge beyond the borders of Judah, into what was left of the Northern Kingdom. Bethel was the place where Jeroboam had built the altar to the molten bulls (or golden calves) in an effort to keep his people from going south to Jerusalem to worship Yahweh. Even though Yahweh was the god worshiped at Bethel, the altar had become the symbol of the idolatry and apostasy that eventually brought down the Northern Kingdom.

After he had destroyed the images on the mountain in Bethel, Josiah looked around the moutainside and saw the cemetery mentioned in verse 16. He knew that spreading the ashes of the dead on the altar of Bethel would be an appropriate way to defile the site, so he dug up some of the anonymous graves, removed and burned the bones on Bethel's famous altar, and thereby desecrated the shrine. The author points out that this was in fulfillment of the prophecy of the man of God in 1 Kings 13:1–3. Evidently, two of the graves were marked to identify the persons buried there. One was the grave of *"the man of God who came from Judah,"* and the other was the grave of *"the prophet who came from Samaria."* Respecting these two men, neither of whom is named, Josiah commanded that their burial places remain undisturbed. After executing the idolatrous priests who were in charge of the shrine at Bethel, Josiah returned to Jerusalem.

IV. The Reinstitution of the Passover Feast (vv. 21–23)

For seventy-five years there had been no Passover feast held in Jerusalem, and even before that the ceremony had been diluted and revised to fit the whims of previous rulers. For example, Hezekiah observed the feast in the second month instead of the prescribed first month, and he did it without the proper purification of some of the people (2 Chron. 30:2–3, 17–20). Josiah was determined to do it right, according to the Book of the Law (Deut. 16:1–8).

The word for *"Passover"* is *pesaḥ,* which may come from the root word "to jump." If so, it suggests the death angel "jumping" the houses of the Israelites on the night of the Exodus. Another explanation is that the word comes from a root meaning "a blow, or stroke." This would suggest that Yahweh struck the Egyptians on the night of the plague.[17] Since the observance of the Passover feast involved both a home ceremony and a public feast, most of those who observed it on this occasion must have lived in or very near Jerusalem.

V. The Removal of Superstitions from Judah (vv. 24–25)

Consulting the dead through mediums and spiritists in order to foretell the future is an ancient practice that still prevails today, even in the scientific twentieth century. It was always forbidden by God. The term *"household gods"* is the translation of the Hebrew word *tĕrāpîm.* They were images of various sizes, big enough to be mistaken for a man in a bad light (1 Sam. 19:13–16), or small enough to be packed in the saddle bags of camels (Gen. 31:32, 34). Sometimes prophets like Hosea seemed to have accepted them as legitimate (Hos. 3:4).

Both Josiah and his great-grandfather Hezekiah are praised as the best kings of Judah—Hezekiah for his absolute confidence in God even under duress, Josiah for his absolute adherence to the Mosaic law. However, in spite of Josiah's moral and religious greatness, God's judgment against Judah would not be turned back. His reforms were noble, but they could not save the nation from inevitable destruction (vv. 26–27). Once again, the terrible fate of Judah is predicted, and the blame is laid at the feet of sinful King Manasseh, Josiah's grandfather.

Josiah's untimely death at the age of thirty-nine is described briefly in verses 28–30. Pharaoh Necho II was the son of Psamtik I and therefore the second Pharaoh of the twenty-sixth dynasty.[18] Just before he assumed the throne of Egypt, Nineveh, the capital of Assyria, was destroyed by the Babylonians, Scythians, and Medes (612 B.C.). Since Egypt and Assyria were allies, Necho II was probably marching northward to try to reinforce what was left of the retreating Assyrian army, and simultaneously to claim expanded territories for his empire (v. 29).

Why Josiah had gone to Megiddo is not known, but he may have been trying to do the same thing Necho II was doing—that is, extending his kingdom and authority in the wake of Assyria's downfall. After killing Josiah, Necho's combined army of Egyptians and Assyrians marched to Carchemish, where in 605 B.C. they engaged the Babylonians and were annihilated, bringing an end to the Egyptian bid for world power.

The death of Josiah was a disaster of the highest magnitude for Judah. The nation mourned him greatly (2 Chron. 35:25), and the apocryphal book of Ecclesiasticus tells how the king's memory was greatly treasured in Israel for centuries (Ecclus. 49:1–3). All this happened at Megiddo, which in Greek is called Armageddon. This battlefield came to be the traditional site for the last great fight against the enemies of God (Rev. 16:16).

NOTES

1. *Dallas Morning News,* 4 July 1987.

2. Norman H. Snaith, Ralph W. Sockman, and Raymond Calkins, "The First and Second Books of Kings," in *The Interpreter's Bible,* vol. 3 (Nashville: Abingdon, 1954), 317.

3. C. F. Keil, *The Books of the Kings,* Biblical Commentary on the Old Testament, ed. C. F. Keil and F. Delitzsch, vol. 4 (Grand Rapids: Eerdmans, 1950), 476.

4. John Gray, *I and II Kings,* Old Testament Library (Philadelphia: Westminster, 1963), 656.

5. Keil, 478n.

6. M. Pierce Matheney and Roy Honeycutt, "1–2 Kings," in *The Broadman Bible Commentary,* ed. Clifton J. Allen, vol. 3 (Nashville: Broadman, 1970), 285.

7. I. W. Slotki, *Kings* (London: Soncino Press, 1950), 301.

8. Ibid., 302.

9. Snaith, Sockman, and Calkins, 321.

10. T. R. Hobbs, *2 Kings,* Word Biblical Commentary, ed. John D. W. Watts, vol. 13 (Waco, TX: Word Books, 1985), 332.

11. Slotki, 302.

12. Gray, 662.

13. Hobbs, 332.

14. Snaith, Sockman, and Calkins, 323.

15. Ibid.

16. Slotki, 302.

17. Gray, 673.

18. Snaith, Sockman, and Calkins, 326.

CHAPTER TWENTY-ONE

The Last Days of Judah and the Fall of Jerusalem

2 Kings 23:31–25:30

Jehoahaz's Reign and Captivity

23:31 Jehoahaz *was* twenty-three years old when he
became king, and he reigned three months in Jerusalem. His mother's name *was* Hamutal the daughter
of Jeremiah of Libnah.
32 And he did evil in the sight of the LORD, according to all that his fathers had done.
33 Now Pharaoh Necho put him in prison at
Riblah in the land of Hamath, that he might not reign
in Jerusalem; and he imposed on the land a tribute of
one hundred talents of silver and a talent of gold.
34 Then Pharaoh Necho made Eliakim the son of
Josiah king in place of his father Josiah, and changed
his name to Jehoiakim. And *Pharaoh* took Jehoahaz
and went to Egypt, and he died there.

2 Kings 23:31–34

As a noble ruler, Josiah gave thirty-one years of his life to an intensive national crusade for righteousness, but he obviously did not spend enough time with his sons. They both succeeded him on the throne, and both of them *"did evil in the sight of the Lord."* Even though it has a contagious quality, faith is not automatically transmitted from parent to child. Surrender to the will and power of God is an individual decision. It cannot be passed on to others like an inheritance or a royal title. Josiah's sons could accede automatically to the throne of Judah, but their relationship with the King of kings must be settled deliberately and singularly. Everyone must choose whether he or she will surrender to the Higher Power or foolishly try to go it alone.

Recently I walked through the grounds of the Alamo in San Antonio, Texas. Overshadowed by the giant glass skyscrapers surrounding it, the weathered little sandstone mission with its familiar rounded facade and columned portico seems inappropriately small considering the significant events that occurred there in March, 1836. Originally called San Antonio de Valero, the little church, established in 1718, was later named "the Alamo" from the Spanish word for the cottonwood trees surrounding it. In times of danger, the mission doubled as a fort for the early Texas settlers who lived nearby.

During the war for Texas independence, about 150 Texas soldiers under the command of Colonel William Barret Travis held the fort against 5,000 Mexican troops led by General Antonio Lopez de Santa Anna. Refusing to surrender, even when their ammunition was exhausted, the Texas patriots fought the enemy in hand-to-hand combat, using their empty muskets as clubs. Finally, all of them were killed, including the famous border heroes James Bowie and Davy Crockett. This heroic battle has been likened to the battle of Thermopylae, where a small band of Greek soldiers held off a superior Persian army.

Out of the drama of that historical battle has come the legend of a last-hour conference within the Alamo before the final Mexican assault. Travis told his men they had no ammunition and no chance of surviving Santa Anna's next attack. Drawing his sword, the colonel drew a line in the dirt floor of the mission. He said, "I have promised we will never surrender, so if you wish to remain and fight to the death, step across this line. Those who do not may escape under cover of darkness tonight." One by one, each courageous soldier stepped across the line with Travis. There was even one fighter who was wounded and asked that his cot be carried across the line to be on the side of those heroic martyrs. Even the Mexican soldiers were awed by the courage and determination of the little band. No wonder the motto for the War of Independence became "Remember the Alamo!"

We have always been stirred by heroism, and we honor those who refuse to retreat or give in. The very idea of surrender to a stronger force is abhorrent to us. Maybe that's why some people rebel at the idea of surrendering to God. They wince at the thought of becoming a "slave of God."

It must be especially difficult for a king, surrounded by constant reminders of his autonomous authority, to yield his will to a Higher Power. But the Bible says this kind of surrender is not only appropriate; it is essential. And the good news is that when we surrender to Him, we do not become less; we become more! When we yield our wills to His sovereign will, we can tap into His unlimited power, and it enables us to be our best. So many have testified that it works that way.

Faith in God allows poets to become more eloquent in their poetry, runners to run at full speed, musicians to sing more beautifully, preachers to preach with more persuasion, doctors to operate with greater skill. If more contemporary men and women discovered this truth, teenagers wouldn't choose suicide, actors wouldn't resort to cocaine, athletes would no longer feel the need for steroids to push themselves to full potential, and television evangelists wouldn't need all that secular hype to get their message across. Instead, they would discover that the Power to which they have surrendered is sufficient to fulfill every potentiality.

If it is difficult for ordinary persons to admit their limitations and surrender to God's omnipotence, how much more difficult it must be for a potentate, a ruler, a king. Even with the evidence before them of how faith enabled their father to accomplish so much, Jehoahaz and Eliakim, the sons of King Josiah, decided to go their own way without God.

Jehoahaz was two years younger than his brother Eliakim. Under the normal rules of royal accession, Eliakim should have been king in place of his father. But "the people of the land" deliberately short-circuited the normal process and anointed the younger son, Jehoahaz, as king. Maybe they chose him because he favored the popular anti-Egyptian position of his father.[1] Or maybe they hoped his youthful vigor and energy would enable the nation to throw off the threat of Necho II of Egypt. Another factor which supports this idea of an anti-Egyptian faction is the identity of his mother. The supposition is that his mother, Hamutal, who came from the rebellious city of Libnah, was a strong supporter of the anti-Egyptian party in Jerusalem. Later, another of her sons, Zedekiah, was chosen by the king of Babylon to be the vassal king of Judah, obviously because of his anti-Egyptian sentiment (2 Kings 24:17–18). The supporters of Jehoahaz quickly anointed him, even before he was crowned, in order to confirm his appointment and head off any opposition from his older brother.

Jehoahaz's name, which is the same as that borne by a king of Israel during Elisha's time, means "Yahweh has grasped." However, Jeremiah calls him Shallum in Jer. 22:11. Since Shallum was a weak king who also reigned only a few days, Jeremiah may have called Jehoahaz by that name as a term of derision and scorn. Others are convinced that his throne name was Jehoahaz and his private name was Shallum.[2] Ezekiel compares Jehoahaz to a young lion who learned to catch his prey and devour men, but as soon as the nations heard of him he was trapped in their pit and led by nose-rings to Egypt (Ezek. 19:3).

In only three months on the throne, the young king's wickedness was sufficiently demonstrated to justify the author's condemnation *"he did evil in the sight of the Lord, according to all that his fathers had done"* (v. 32).

How did Necho II, who was still engaged in consolidating his army with the remnants of the defeated Assyrians, manage to imprison Jehoahaz and place Judah under tribute? Some believe he simply summoned the young king to come to Riblah, where the Egyptians were headquartered in the Orontes Valley on the road from Jerusalem to Babylon.[3] It would have been foolish, however, for the king voluntarily to leave the safety of Jerusalem and risk the exposure such a trip would entail.

Other commentators suggest the following scenario. After his victory over Josiah at Megiddo, Necho II intended to continue his march to the Euphrates, but on hearing that Jehoahaz had ascended to the throne, and perhaps encouraged by complaints from Eliakim that he had been passed over as king, he ordered a division of his army to march against Jerusalem. While the main army was moving slowly to Riblah to establish headquarters there, the smaller Egyptian force captured Jerusalem, dethroned Jehoahaz, laid the land under tribute, and appointed Eliakim as a vassal king. Then, the Egyptians brought the deposed Jehoahaz in chains to Riblah and eventually to Egypt, where he died, evidently of natural causes.[4]

Compared with the heavy tribute Sennacherib extracted from Judah in 2 Kings 18:14, the one hundred talents of silver and one talent of gold in verse 33 seem insignificant. The total came to only $760,320, and it may indicate a conciliatory spirit on the part of Necho II. Since his conflict with Babylon was not yet settled, the Pharaoh did not need another rebellious nation at his heels. So the reasonable tribute was a wise strategy to keep Judah relatively pacified.

Eliakim, the older brother of Jehoahaz, was put in place as a puppet of Necho, and his name was changed to Jehoiakim as a symbol of his subservience. Later, Nebuchadnezzar did the same thing in changing King Mattaniah's name to Zedekiah (2 Kings 24:17). In Eliakim's case, the change was only in the first part of his name, from "El" to "Jehoi," from "God establishes" to "Yahweh establishes." This minor change may indicate another conciliation on the part of Necho II. Conceivably, he even allowed Eliakim to pick his own new name.

Notice verse 34 says the Egyptian king caused him to reign *"in place of his father Josiah"* rather than "in place of his brother Jehoahaz." Necho never did officially recognize the brief reign of Jehoahaz as legitimate. Eliakim must have been more loyal to the pro-Egyptian party in Jerusalem.[5]

Jehoiakim's Reign

23:35 So Jehoiakim gave the silver and gold to Pharaoh; but he taxed the land to give money according to the command of Pharaoh; he exacted the silver and gold from the people of the land, from every one according to his assessment, to give *it* to Pharaoh Necho.

36 Jehoiakim *was* twenty-five years old when he became king, and he reigned eleven years in Jerusalem. His mother's name *was* Zebudah the daughter of Pedaiah of Rumah.

37 And he did evil in the sight of the LORD, according to all that his fathers had done.

24:1 In his days Nebuchadnezzar king of Babylon came up, and Jehoiakim became his vassal *for* three years. Then he turned and rebelled against him.

2 And the LORD sent against him *raiding* bands of

Chaldeans, bands of Syrians, bands of Moabites, and
bands of the people of Ammon; He sent them against
Judah to destroy it, according to the word of the LORD
which He had spoken by His servants the prophets.
3 Surely at the commandment of the LORD *this*
came upon Judah, to remove *them* from His sight because of the sins of Manasseh, according to all that
he had done,
4 and also because of the innocent blood that he
had shed; for he had filled Jerusalem with innocent
blood, which the LORD would not pardon.
5 Now the rest of the acts of Jehoiakim, and all
that he did, *are* they not written in the book of the
chronicles of the kings of Judah?
6 So Jehoiakim rested with his fathers. Then
Jehoiachin his son reigned in his place.
7 And the king of Egypt did not come out of his
land anymore, for the king of Babylon had taken all
that belonged to the king of Egypt from the Brook of
Egypt to the River Euphrates.

2 Kings 23:35–24:7

How quickly world dominance shifted between the powerful nations in these days. Like some gigantic game of "king of the mountain," Moab, Edom, Syria, Egypt, Assyria, and Babylon scrambled to the peak in turn, only to be toppled and replaced by another. No sooner had Jehoiakim paid his tribute to Egypt than another power shift removed that enemy from the scene altogether. Only three years after Jehoiakim became king, Necho II was defeated at Carchemish in 605 B.C., and Jehoiakim was unexpectedly freed from his dominance (cf. Jer. 25:1; 46:2). But he soon encountered a worse enemy in the person of Nebuchadnezzar of Babylon.

Jehoiakim was twenty-five years old when he became king, two years older than his deposed brother Jehoahaz. Notice that while Josiah was the father of both men, Jehoiakim had a different mother (v. 36). His mother was not Hamutal but Jebudah. We know nothing about her or about Rumah from which her parents came.

It fell to Jehoiakim's lot to scrape together the Egyptian tribute imposed during the short reign of his brother, but he could not draw the gold and silver from the treasuries of the temple or the palace since these had been depleted. His only recourse was to extract the money from the people of Judah in the form of an assessment (v. 35). Apparently he had to pay the tribute to Egypt for only three years, after which Nebuchadnezzar subdued Jerusalem and abruptly transferred Jehoiakim's loyalty to Babylon.

In typical terminology, verse 37 accused the new king of doing evil in the sight of the Lord as his ancestors, especially Manasseh and Amon, had done. The prophet Jeremiah added his unflattering judgment: "Your eyes and your heart are for nothing but your covetousness, for shedding innocent blood, and practicing oppression and violence" (Jer. 22:17). The prophet also accused him of cutting up and burning the word of God (Jer. 36:22–26). Unlike his noble father, Jehoiakim never really fulfilled the role of leader of his people. He merely played the part, went through the motions, and used the office for his own covetous purposes.

That same kind of "play-acting" has infected the Christian ministry today. There is a familiar television commercial that features a man clad in a physician's white jacket who says, "I'm not a real doctor, but I play one on TV." Most people recognize the actor immediately as a regular on an afternoon soap opera. After that classic "opener," the actor goes on to describe the medical products he is selling. Advertising researchers believe the average consumer is gullible enough to accept the word of an actor, even when he deals with matters relating to our health.

With the embarrassing antics of so many television preachers being exposed today, perhaps another version of that TV commercial is in order: "I'm not a real preacher, but I play one on TV." The public has often been duped into believing that these glamorous stars of television evangelism are typical of the church's ministers. One preacher friend of mine said, "To tell the truth, I'm still partial to the hometown physician who knows me and helps me when I need him. And I'm still partial to the preacher who calls his people by name when they leave the service and is available to minister to their spiritual and physical needs. I don't play a pastor on TV, but I do try to be one in real life."

Jehoiakim began his ineffective eleven-year reign in 608 B.C. and ruled until 598 B.C., just three months before the fall of Jerusalem. The most significant event in this entire period is recorded in 24:1, the appearance of Nebuchadnezzar of Babylon. Like his father

Nabopolasser, he was named for the Babylonian god Nebo. His name probably means "May Nebo protect my boundary stone."[6] He is also known in scripture as "Nebuchadrezzar," primarily in the books of Jeremiah and Ezekiel. Although "Nebuchadrezzar" is closer to the Akkadian spelling, "Nabu-kudurri-usur," it is used only thirty-three times in the Bible compared to fifty-eight times for "Nebuchadnezzar."[7]

Having assumed the Babylonian throne in the place of his father in 605 B.C., he defeated Pharaoh Necho II at Carchemish and marched against Jerusalem. Although not much is said in Kings about this subjection of Jerusalem, the details are included in the books of Chronicles and Daniel. There we are told that Nebuchadnezzar defeated the city, put Jehoiakim in bronze fetters, and threatened to carry him off to Babylon. But apparently, when he bowed to Babylonian authority, he was allowed to stay as Nebuchadnezzar's puppet ruler in Jerusalem (2 Chron. 36:4, 6; Dan. 1:1–4). Nebuchadnezzar did, however, take back to Babylon on this occasion some of the sacred vessels from the temple and a number of choice Hebrew young men, including a young prophet named Daniel.

About three years later, in 601 B.C., Egypt tried one more time to return to power by attacking Babylon's army. Catching Nebuchadnezzar's troops by surprise, they won the battle but were unable to pursue the enemy any further and returned to Egypt (v. 7). It was after this brief Egyptian victory that Jehoiakim, hoping to renew his alliance with the Pharaoh against Babylon, rebelled against Nebuchadnezzar (v. 3), an action Jeremiah sharply condemned.

Limping a little from his defeat at the hand of Egypt, Nebuchadnezzar was unable to put down Jehoiakim's rebellion. For the next two or three years he had to remain in Babylon to rebuild his army. However, he did the next best thing to keep Jehoiakim off balance and to contain his revolt. He hired mercenaries from among the Syrians, Moabites, and Ammonites to join the few soldiers he had left in Judah, and he kept them fighting against Jerusalem until he could muster his main army for a major assault. The term *"Chaldeans"* in verse 2 is another word for "Babylonians." According to the author, the attack of these marauding bands was not coincidental, but was ordained of God as a punishment for their sins (v. 3). Probably the prophets who are mentioned in verse 2 were Isaiah, Micah, Habakkuk, and Jeremiah.

In Jeremiah 26, some of the *"rest of the acts of Jehoiakim"* (v. 5) are described in detail. Incidentally, this is the last reference in the Book of Kings to *"the book of the chronicles of the kings of Judah."* Jehoiakim's burial is not mentioned, but Jeremiah wrote:

> "They shall not lament for him,
> Saying, 'Alas, my brother!' or 'Alas, my sister!'
> They shall not lament for him,
> Saying, 'Alas, master!' or 'Alas, his glory!'
> He shall be buried with the burial of a donkey,
> Dragged and cast out beyond the gates of
> Jerusalem."
>
> *Jer. 22:18–19*

Jehoiakim's death can be dated precisely from the Babylonian Chronicle as 7 December 598 B.C., just three months and ten days before the fall of Jerusalem. Jeremiah predicted, "none of his descendants shall prosper, sitting on the throne of David . . . ," but his son Jehoiachin did ascend to the throne for three months. There is a sense in which such a short reign could not legitimately be construed as "sitting on the throne of David."

The fall of Jerusalem didn't come about in one cataclysmic battle; it occurred in stages. First came Nebuchadnezzar's initial subjection of the city about 605 B.C. Next was the cumulative destruction caused by Nebuchadnezzar's marauding bands from about 601 to 598 B.C. Then, during Jehoiachin's reign, Nebuchadnezzar's main army besieged Jerusalem and it fell on 16 March 597 B.C. Most of the leading citizens were transported to Babylon. Finally, when the puppet king Zedekiah again rebelled against Babylon, Nebuchadnezzar returned to completely destroy and depopulate the city in the summer of 586 B.C.

Nothing could now avert the inevitable judgment that had been building up against Judah through all the history of the kings. The final denouement was about to begin.

Jehoiachin's Reign and the First Deportation

> 24:8 Jehoiachin *was* eighteen years old when he became king, and he reigned in Jerusalem three months.

His mother's name *was* Nehushta the daughter of
Elnathan of Jerusalem.

9 And he did evil in the sight of the LORD, according to all that his father had done.

10 At that time the servants of Nebuchadnezzar king of Babylon came up against Jerusalem, and the city was besieged.

11 And Nebuchadnezzar king of Babylon came against the city, as his servants were besieging it.

12 Then Jehoiachin king of Judah, his mother, his servants, his princes, and his officers went out to the king of Babylon; and the king of Babylon, in the eighth year of his reign, took him prisoner.

13 And he carried out from there all the treasures of the house of the LORD and the treasures of the king's house, and he cut in pieces all the articles of gold which Solomon king of Israel had made in the temple of the LORD, as the LORD had said.

14 Also he carried into captivity all Jerusalem: all the captains and all the mighty men of valor, ten thousand captives, and all the craftsmen and smiths. None remained except the poorest people of the land.

15 And he carried Jehoiachin captive to Babylon. The king's mother, the king's wives, his officers, and the mighty of the land he carried into captivity from Jerusalem to Babylon.

16 All the valiant men, seven thousand, and craftsmen and smiths, one thousand, all *who were* strong *and* fit for war, these the king of Babylon brought captive to Babylon.

2 Kings 24:8–16

With a name very similar to his father's, Jehoiachin, a teenaged prince, was crowned as king in the palace of Jerusalem. Chronicles says he was eight years old, but that was probably his age at the time his father Jehoiakim designated him to be the next king (cf. 2 Chron. 36:9). He was also known by the name Jeconiah in Chronicles and by the name Coniah in Jeremiah. His reign lasted only three months, and no deeds are recorded here except his surrender to Nebuchadnezzar. Briefly he appeared on the scene as a pitiful pawn of fate, but after only ninety days the author knew enough about his potential for apostasy and his evil character to judge him. *"He did evil in the sight of the Lord"* (v. 9).

According to the Babylonian Chronicle, on 29 November 598 B.C., Nebuchadnezzar mustered his army for the assault on Judah. The description of what happened follows:

> . . . and having marched to the land of Hatti [northern Syria], besieged the city of Judah, and on the second day of the month of Adar took the city and captured the king. He appointed therein a king of his own choice, received its heavy tribute and sent [them] to Babylon.[8]

An advance assault division of Babylonian troops was sent ahead to commence the siege before King Nebuchadnezzar arrived. *"Servants of Nebuchadnezzar"* in verse 10 refers to his officers and men. Realizing that the situation was hopeless, young Jehoiachin, his mother Nehushta, his servants, his princes, and his officers (verse 15 adds *"the king's wives"*) *"went out to the king,"* that is, to surrender. They were apparently well treated, held under some kind of limited imprisonment in Babylon. Later, Jehoiachin was released from imprisonment and allowed to live in dignity in Babylon, supported by a stipend from the king himself (2 Kings 25:27).

Since Nebuchadnezzar had already plundered the temple a few years earlier (cf. Dan. 1:1–4), there were few easily accessible treasures left. This time, with considerable effort, he removed the gold plating from the larger vessels such as the altar of burnt offerings, the table of shew bread, and the ark of the covenant.[9] So there was not much of value left when the temple was finally destroyed in 586 B.C.

Babylon's initial deportation of Jerusalem's population occurred in 597 B.C., during the eighth year of Nebuchadnezzar's reign. This is the first time in Kings that an event in the history of Israel is dated by a foreign era.[10] Those who were deported were those who might be able to threaten Babylon by organizing military resistance or building weapons. Anyone with rank, wealth, power, or skill was carried away (v. 14). There were ten thousand in all: eight thousand from among the groups listed in verse 16 and two thousand from among the common people.

Zedekiah's Reign as a Vassal

> 24:17 Then the king of Babylon made Mattaniah, *Jehoiachin's* uncle, king in his place, and changed his name to Zedekiah.
>
> 18 Zedekiah *was* twenty-one years old when he became king, and he reigned eleven years in Jerusalem. His mother's name *was* Hamutal the daughter of Jeremiah of Libnah.
>
> 19 He also did evil in the sight of the LORD, according to all that Jehoiakim had done.
>
> 20 For because of the anger of the LORD *this* happened in Jerusalem and Judah, that He finally cast them out from His presence. Then Zedekiah rebelled against the king of Babylon.
>
> *2 Kings 24:17–20*

To fill the empty throne with a friendly king, Nebuchadnezzar reached back a generation and chose another son of Hamutal, the wife of Josiah. She was a loyal follower of the anti-Egyptian philosophy in Jerusalem, and Nebuchadnezzar assumed that her son would share her political views. His name was Mattaniah, but to dramatize his subjection, Nebuchadnezzar named him Zedekiah, which means "the righteousness of Yahweh." Verse 19 indicates that he chose as his working political model the wicked rule of his brother Jehoiakim.

Apparently he imitated his model perfectly, for, according to Jeremiah, he was weak and vacillating in character and, even though most of the talented people had been taken to Babylon, he was completely dominated by stronger men in the kingdom. He had no courage nor power to offer resistance and be his own man. It appears that those who manipulated the young king represented the pro-Egyptian party. They encouraged him to rebel against Babylon and to appeal to Egypt for a military alliance. Jeremiah warned him of the folly of this tactic, but Zedekiah did not obey the words of the Lord that came through Jeremiah (Jer. 38).

There is nothing more pitiful than a weak character who cannot resist the temptation to "go with the flow," follow the lines of least resistance, and cater to the majority.

I have watched people like this in important business meetings.

They wait to vote on an issue until they see some signal of how the "ruling party" is voting. I have smiled at their awkward confusion when the chairman unexpectedly calls for a show of hands on some decision before the party "floor manager" has had time to signal what the vote should be. Rather than weighing the issues prayerfully and making an independent decision, these weaklings, like the puppet kings of Judah, waver while they test the wind. Then they play it safe and go with the winning side.

In so many places, the Bible calls us to individual responsibility. Ps. 49:7 says, "None of them can by any means redeem his brother, nor give to God a ransom for him." Jesus asked His disciples in Matt. 16:13ff. not only, "Who do men say that I, the Son of Man, am?" but, "Who do *you* say that I am?" On another occasion, Jesus underscored the importance of individual responsibility when He confronted Pilate with the question "Are you speaking for yourself about this, or did others tell you this concerning Me?" (John 18:34).

Zedekiah's vacillating capitulation to the influential crowd and his unwillingness to stand courageously for the word of the Lord led to his foolish decision to rebel. And that rebellion was the last straw that brought on the final destruction of Jerusalem.

The Siege and Fall of Jerusalem

25:1 Now it came to pass in the ninth year of his reign, in the tenth month, on the tenth *day* of the month, *that* Nebuchadnezzar king of Babylon and all his army came against Jerusalem and encamped against it; and they built a siege wall against it all around.

2 So the city was besieged until the eleventh year of King Zedekiah.

3 By the ninth *day* of the *fourth* month the famine had become so severe in the city that there was no food for the people of the land.

4 Then the city wall *was* broken through, and all the men of war *fled* at night by way of the gate between two walls, which was by the king's garden, even though the Chaldeans *were* still encamped all around against the city. And *the king* went by way of the plain.

5 But the army of the Chaldeans pursued the
king, and they overtook him in the plains of Jericho.
All his army was scattered from him.
6 So they took the king and brought him up to
the king of Babylon at Riblah, and they pronounced
judgment on him.
7 Then they killed the sons of Zedekiah before
his eyes, put out the eyes of Zedekiah, bound him
with bronze fetters, and took him to Babylon.
8 And in the fifth month, on the seventh *day* of
the month (which *was* the nineteenth year of King
Nebuchadnezzar king of Babylon), Nebuzaradan the
captain of the guard, a servant of the king of Babylon, came to Jerusalem.
9 He burned the house of the LORD and the king's
house; all the houses of Jerusalem, that is, all the
houses of the great, he burned with fire.
10 And all the army of the Chaldeans who *were
with* the captain of the guard broke down the walls
of Jerusalem all around.
11 Then Nebuzaradan the captain of the guard carried away captive the rest of the people *who* remained
in the city and the defectors who had deserted to the
king of Babylon, with the rest of the multitude.
12 But the captain of the guard left *some* of the
poor of the land as vinedressers and farmers.
13 The bronze pillars that *were* in the house of the
LORD, and the carts and the bronze Sea that *were* in
the house of the LORD, the Chaldeans broke in pieces,
and carried their bronze to Babylon.
14 They also took away the pots, the shovels, the
trimmers, the spoons, and all the bronze utensils
with which the priests ministered.
15 The firepans and the basins, the things of solid
gold and solid silver, the captain of the guard took
away.
16 The two pillars, one Sea, and the carts, which
Solomon had made for the house of the LORD, the
bronze of all these articles was beyond measure.
17 The height of one pillar *was* eighteen cubits,
and the capital on it *was* of bronze. The height of
the capital was three cubits, and the network and

> pomegranates all around the capital were all of bronze. The second pillar was the same, with a network.
>
> 18 And the captain of the guard took Seraiah the chief priest, Zephaniah the second priest, and the three doorkeepers.
>
> 19 He also took out of the city an officer who had charge of the men of war, five men of the king's close associates who were found in the city, the chief recruiting officer of the army, who mustered the people of the land, and sixty men of the people of the land *who were* found in the city.
>
> 20 So Nebuzaradan, captain of the guard, took these and brought them to the king of Babylon at Riblah.
>
> 21 Then the king of Babylon struck them and put them to death at Riblah in the land of Hamath. Thus Judah was carried away captive from its own land.
>
> *2 Kings 25:1–21*

Siege warfare was a cruel but effective military strategy of the ancient East. Rather than making a concentrated assault to break down fortifications and overwhelm the defenders of a city, siege warriors simply surrounded the city and cut off all access to food and in some cases water. Then they patiently waited until the inhabitants ran out of supplies, began to starve, and were ready to surrender. This tactic took longer, but it cost fewer lives on the part of the invaders. The *"siege wall"* in verse 1 was a mound of earth piled up by slave labor to a level somewhat higher than the city wall itself. From the siege wall, the attackers could shoot at the defenders on the walls of the city. If the siege wall was close enough, as it was in some cases, battering rams could be used to break down the defenses.

A few years ago, standing on the hilltop fortress of Masada near the Dead Sea, I looked down on a siege wall that the Romans had built nearly two thousand years before in order to overwhelm that stubborn garrison. From the hilltop you can see ruins of the series of Roman garrisons that were set up in a ring around Masada to cut off its supplies. But the ingenious fortress built by Herod the Great held enough food and water to last for years. Furthermore, its elevated location and high wall made it practically unapproachable by enemy troops.

The only way the superior Roman army could conquer Eleazor, the commander of Masada, and the heroic Jewish defenders was to build a dirt assault ramp that would allow the imperial troops to storm Masada's walls. Furthermore, that task would have been impossible if the Roman general, Silva, had not used thousands of Jewish slaves to build the ramp. For from their superior position on the fortifications high above the plain, Eleazor and his soldiers could have easily killed any workers who attempted to construct such a ramp. But when they discovered that the ramp builders were Jewish slaves, they could not bring themselves to kill their own countrymen.

So the defenders of Masada watched helplessly as the ramp grew longer and higher each day. Finally, one evening in the spring of A.D. 73, it became obvious that the next morning the Roman siege-machines and battering rams would be pushed up the ramp, and the fortress would be conquered. That night Eleazor and his brave zealots decided to take their own lives rather than let Rome kill them or enslave them. Each soldier killed his own family, and then ten were selected to kill the rest. One of the ten was picked to kill the nine others, and then, after setting fire to the fortress, to take his own life. When the invaders broke through the next morning they discovered 960 bodies of courageous people who chose death over slavery.

The dirt ramp is still there, 200 feet high and 645 feet long. Nebuchadnezzar's siege wall at Jerusalem must have looked a lot like it (v. 1).

Inasmuch as Jerusalem was practically void of weapons and skilled soldiers, why did it take the powerful Babylonian army under the leadership of king Nebuchadnezzar nearly two years to break through the walls and conquer the city? Some say it was because the city itself was strategically located for natural defense, and its fortifications were unusually well built and difficult to penetrate. Others point out that during the siege, Egypt once again made what turned out to be a feeble and unsuccessful attempt to attack Babylon. Therefore, Nebuchadnezzar's attention was temporarily diverted from Jerusalem while he dealt with Egypt, thus extending the siege.[11]

Eventually, since the siege interrupted two harvest seasons and halted the cultivation of the land, and since the circle of troops prevented any produce from coming into the city, the ensuing famine brought the people in the city to the point of starvation. Their will to fight waned; the defense broke down; and encountering little resistance, Nebuchadnezzar's troops were able to break through the wall. The breach was probably made in the most vulnerable part of the wall on the north side. The cowardly King Zedekiah and his troops tried to escape through a narrow corridor in the southeast wall that gave access to the Kidron Valley (v. 4). Verse 5 says the Babylonians *"overtook him in the plains of Jericho."*

A Jewish legend tells of a mysterious subterranean passage extending from the palace to the plains of Jericho. Zedekiah attempted to escape through this secret passage, but God decreed that a deer should run along the surface just above the roof of the underground passage, revealing to the Babylonians its location. All they had to do was to chase the animal until they reached the plains of Jericho. Their arrival coincided with the emergence of the hapless king into the open.[12]

It seems ironic that here, at the very spot where Israel first set foot on the Promised Land, the last of the Davidic kings was captured and his monarchy shattered. Here, where Israel experienced her first victory as the walls of Jericho fell before unarmed men who trusted God, was the scene of her last defeat. At the location where the covenant was renewed and the reproach of Israel was taken away, the broken covenant was now finally avenged and abrogated. The end came back to the beginning.

Babylonian justice meted out its cruel punishment on Zedekiah. Before binding him, they forced him to watch the murder of all his sons. We are not told how many there were, but the Babylonians certainly intended to cut off all claimants to the throne. Zedekiah, the last king in David's line, was now led in bronze fetters to Babylon; like Samson, he was weak and blind in enemy hands. The last thing his eyes saw was the death of his sons. As a young man of thirty-two, he had little to look forward to but the dark misery of blind imprisonment. Zedekiah's death is not mentioned here, but Ezekiel has a brief reference indicating that he died in Babylon (Ezek. 12:13).

About a month after the capture of the city, Nebuchadnezzar brought in a Babylonian specialist in urban demolition. His name was Nebuzaradan and he is called *"the captain of the guard"* (v. 8).

That title in Hebrew is literally "the chief executioner" or "the slaughterer." Methodically, he set about to demolish the beautiful city, burning the palace and chief buildings, breaking down the walls, and wrecking the temple. The Talmud declares that when the Babylonians entered the temple, they held a two-day feast there to desecrate it; then, on the third day, they set fire to the building. The Talmud adds that the fire burned throughout that day and the next.[13] Verses 13–17 give details about the temple destruction, including the tearing down of the two famous bronze columns, which in 1 Kings 7:21 were named Jachin and Boaz (v. 17).

Then "the Slaughterer" rounded up the inhabitants, both those inside the walls and those who had surrendered to the troops outside, and started them on their long journey into exile (v. 11). Leaving a few peasants to keep the land cultivated for the benefit of Babylon, he marched about seventy religious, political, and military leaders in chains to Nebuchadnezzar's headquarters in Riblah, where they were executed. "The Slaughterer's" job was now done. The Holy City lay empty and in rubble.

Some believe the original book of 2 Kings ended here at verse 21 and that the next two sections were added later as an appendix.[14]

The reader cannot help but be struck by the passionless tone of the narrative in this chapter. Not once does the author show his feelings, even though he is describing the tragic downfall of his country. We have to turn to the Book of Lamentations for weeping and groaning. That book describes the emotion of devout hearts who mourned over the desolation of the beautiful City of David, but here in Kings we have the calm historical record of God's judgment.

In Hebrew, the first twelve verses of the chapter are one long sentence, each verse beginning with "and." Clause is heaped upon clause in a kind of cadence, as if each one were another tick of the clock counting down Jerusalem's final hours.

Nor can the reader help but be impressed with the revelation throughout these chapters of God's patience and His reluctance to punish. More than four hundred years had passed since Solomon first disobeyed God and introduced the children of Israel to pagan idolatry. Faithfully, through all those years, a steady stream of prophets clearly proclaimed the warnings of punishment. Varying disasters confirmed their messages, vividly previewing what was to come if the people did not repent and turn to God. With steadfast love, God tried again and again to seek and save His people, but they mocked His warnings, killed His prophets, and would not listen to His reproof. So finally the hour struck and the impending crash came. The harshness of the judgment is somehow softened by the recognition that the Lord is indeed long-suffering toward His people. But His patience and steadfast love are balanced with justice. The destruction is a reminder that we must not presume on His grace and mercy.

I have to admit that having studied 1 and 2 Kings for this writing project, having been caught up in the story from the exciting days of the building of Jerusalem, chapter by chapter through the vivid action of each monarchy, coming to this final chapter was a profound emotional experience. On many occasions previously, I have studied and preached from these passages in a fragmentary fashion, but never have I tried to master the books in one concentrated and intense period of time. Over these past months, I have become very much a part of the drama. So, to read this final chapter, after all that involvement, is to be gripped in an unusual way by the emotion of the tragedy.

The Appointment of Gedaliah and the Release of Jehoiachin

25:22 Then he made Gedaliah the son of Ahikam, the son of Shaphan, governor over the people who remained in the land of Judah, whom Nebuchadnezzar king of Babylon had left.

23 Now when all the captains of the armies, they and *their* men, heard that the king of Babylon had made Gedaliah governor, they came to Gedaliah at Mizpah—Ishmael the son of Nethaniah, Johanan the son of Careah, Seraiah the son of Tanhumeth the Netophathite, and Jaazaniah the son of a Maachathite, they and their men.

24 And Gedaliah took an oath before them and their men, and said to them, "Do not be afraid of the servants of the Chaldeans. Dwell in the land and serve the king of Babylon, and it shall be well with you."

25 But it happened in the seventh month that Ishmael the son of Nethaniah, the son of Elishama, of

the royal family, came with ten men and struck and
killed Gedaliah, the Jews, as well as the Chaldeans
who were with him at Mizpah.
26 And all the people, small and great, and the
captains of the armies, arose and went to Egypt; for
they were afraid of the Chaldeans.
27 Now it came to pass in the thirty-seventh year
of the captivity of Jehoiachin king of Judah, in
the twelfth month, on the twenty-seventh *day* of the
month, *that* Evil-Merodach king of Babylon, in
the year that he began to reign, released Jehoiachin
king of Judah from prison.
28 He spoke kindly to him, and gave him a more
prominent seat than those of the kings who *were*
with him in Babylon.
29 So Jehoiachin changed from his prison garments, and he ate bread regularly before the king all
the days of his life.
30 And as for his provisions, *there was* a regular
ration given him by the king, a portion for each day,
all the days of his life.

2 Kings 25:22–30

In some ways these last two sections of the book seem anticlimactic. It's not hard to see why some scholars suggest that they were added to the book later. But, even though they appear to be an addendum, they are very important to the history because they conclude the story on a positive and upbeat note. After the horrible account of the destruction of Jerusalem, these last verses offer a glimmer of hope for the future.

We don't know much about Gedaliah except that his father was one of Jeremiah's friends whom King Josiah appointed to the delegation that went to the prophetess Huldah to get her interpretation of the Book of the Law (2 Kings 22:12). Since Nebuchadnezzar was fond of Jeremiah, Gedaliah's relationship with the prophet could have influenced Nebuchadnezzar's choice of him as the governor of Judah.

The *"captains of the armies"* in verse 23 were Judean soldiers who had escaped from the city with King Zedekiah during the Babylonian siege along with other soldiers who had been assigned to various fortresses across Judah and therefore were not exiled with the defenders of Jerusalem. The governor's residence must have been at Mizpah. Gedaliah's plea for the men to give up their resistance and *"serve the king of Babylon"* fell on deaf ears as far as one of the officers was concerned. Ishmael and ten of his men returned later to assassinate Gedaliah, whom they considered a traitor. Then they fled to Egypt for asylum.

Twenty-six years after the fall of Jerusalem, about 560 B.C., Nebuchadnezzar died. Jewish commentators explain that the Babylonian king died on the twenty-fifth day of the twelfth month and was buried on the twenty-sixth. Then, the next day, on the order of his successor, Evil-Merodach, his body was exhumed and dragged through the streets of the capital.[15] It was on this same day that Evil-Merodach issued the decree that released Jehoiachin, king of Judah, from prison (v. 27). We are not told why the Babylonian monarch extended this generous gesture to his Jewish prisoner, but perhaps he did it to dramatize his own noble character in contrast to that of the cruel Nebuchadnezzar.

The Book of Kings, in its last four verses, ends on a bright note. The last surviving sovereign of Judah is set free from the rigors and humiliation of Babylonian prison. He is shown honor and good will. Here is a hopeful sign that a better future is in store for God's people. Someday the exile will end, and ultimately the Davidic monarchy will be restored.

NOTES

1. I. W. Slotki, *Kings* (London: Soncino Press, 1950), 302.
2. John Gray, *I and II Kings,* Old Testament Library (Philadelphia: Westminster, 1963), 681.
3. Gwilym H. Jones, *1 and 2 Kings,* New Century Bible Commentary, ed. Ronald E. Clements (Grand Rapids: Eerdmans, 1984), 630.
4. C. F. Keil, *The Books of the Kings,* Biblical Commentary on the Old Testament, ed. C. F. Keil and F. Delitzsch, vol. 4 (Grand Rapids: Eerdmans, 1950), 496.
5. M. Pierce Matheney and Roy Honeycutt, "1–2 Kings," in *The Broadman Bible Commentary,* ed. Clifton J. Allen, vol. 3 (Nashville: Broadman, 1970), 290.

6. T. R. Hobbs, *2 Kings,* Word Biblical Commentary, ed. John D. W. Watts, vol. 13 (Waco, TX: Word Books, 1985), 349.

7. Matheney and Honeycutt, 290.

8. British Museum No. 1–21946 rev. 11–13, plate 5, cited by Matheney and Honeycutt, 291.

9. Keil, 507.

10. Gray, 691.

11. Ibid., 695.

12. Slotki, 317.

13. Ibid.

14. Jones, 642.

15. Slotki, 322.

Bibliography

Albright, W. F. "The Chronology of the Divided Monarchy of Israel." *Bulletin of the American Schools of Oriental Research* 100 (1945): 16.

———."Ivory and Apes of Ophir." *The American Journal of Semitic Languages* 37 (1920–21): 144.

Alexander, Pat. "I and II Kings." In *Eerdmans' Handbook to the Bible,* edited by David Alexander and Pat Alexander, 250–85. New York: Guideposts, 1973.

Anderson, Bernhard W. *Understanding the Old Testament.* Englewood Cliffs: Prentice-Hall, 1957.

Bähr, Karl Chr. W. F. *The Books of the Kings.* Commentary on the Holy Scriptures, edited by John Peter Lange. Grand Rapids: Zondervan, 1960.

Box, G. H. *The Second Book of Kings.* 2nd ed. Cambridge: Cambridge University Press, 1928.

Burney, Charles F. *Notes on the Hebrew Text of the Books of Kings.* Oxford: Clarendon Press, 1903.

Childs, Brevard S. *Introduction to the Old Testament as Scripture.* Philadelphia: Fortress Press, 1979.

Clark, Walter Eugene. "The Sandalwood and Peacocks of Ophir." *The American Journal of Semitic Languages* 36 (1920): 103.

Cook, Stanley A. *The Religion of Ancient Palestine in Light of Archaeology.* London: Oxford University Press, 1930.

Crockett, William Day. *A Harmony of the Books of Samuel, Kings, and Chronicles.* Grand Rapids: Baker Book House, 1959.

Dentan, Robert C. *Kings and Chronicles.* Layman's Bible Commentary, vol. 7. Richmond: John Knox Press, 1964.

DeVries, Simon J. *1 Kings.* Word Biblical Commentary, edited by John D. W. Watts, vol. 12, Waco, TX: Word Books, 1985.

Engnell, Ivan. *Studies in Divine Kingship in the Ancient Near East.* Uppsala: Almqvist and Wiksells, 1943.

Francisco, Clyde T. "Chronological Chart of the Kingdom of Israel." In *Introducing the Old Testament,* 243–71. Nashville: Broadman Press, 1953.

———. "First and Second Kings." In *Introducing the Old Testament,* 67–68. Nashville: Broadman Press, 1953.

Glueck, Nelson. "Ezion-Geber." *The Biblical Archaeologist* 28 (1965): 70.

Gottwald, Norman K. *All the Kingdoms of the Earth: Israelite Prophecy and International Relations in the Ancient Near East.* New York: Harper & Row, 1964.

Gray, John. *I and II Kings.* Old Testament Library. Philadelphia: Westminster Press, 1963.

Harrison, Roland K. *Introduction to the Old Testament.* Grand Rapids: Eerdmans, 1973.

Heaton, E. W. *The Hebrew Kingdoms.* The New Clarendon Bible, vol. 3. London: Oxford University Press, 1968.

Hobbs, T. R. *2 Kings.* Word Biblical Commentary, edited by John D. W. Watts, vol. 13. Waco, TX: Word Books, 1985.

Hulse, E. V. "The Nature of Biblical 'Leprosy' and the Use of Alternative Medical Terms in Modern Translations of the Bible." *Palestine Exploration Quarterly* 107 (1975): 87.

Johnson, Aubrey R. *Sacral Kingship in Ancient Israel.* Cardiff: Wales University Press, 1967.

Jones, Gwilym H. *1 and 2 Kings.* New Century Bible Commentary, edited by Ronald E. Clements. Grand Rapids: Eerdmans, 1984.

Josephus, Flavius. *The Life and Works of Flavius Josephus.* Translated by William Whiston. Philadelphia: J. C. Winston, 1957.

Keil, C. F. *The Books of the Kings.* Biblical Commentary on the Old Testament, edited by C. F. Keil and F. Delitzsch. Vol. 4. Grand Rapids: Eerdmans, 1950.

Klein, Ralph W. "Jeroboam's Rise to Power." *Journal of Biblical Literature* 89 (1970): 217.

La Sor, William Sanford. "1 and 2 Kings." In *The New Bible Commentary: Revised,* edited by D. Guthrie and J. A. Motyer, 320–68. Grand Rapids: Eerdmans, 1970.

Lumby, J. Rawson. *I and II Kings.* The Cambridge Bible, edited by J. J. S. Perowne. Cambridge: Cambridge University Press, 1889.

Maclaren, Alexander. *Second Samuel and the Books of Kings.* Expositions of Holy Scripture, vol. 2. Grand Rapids: Eerdmans, 1952.

Malamat, A. "The Last Kings of Judah and the Fall of Jerusalem." *Israel Exploration Journal* 18 (1968): 137.

Marty, Martin E. "The Hope that Outlived Hitler." *Context* 18, no. 10 (15 May 1986): 5.

Matheney, M. Pierce, and Roy Honeycutt. "1-2 Kings." In *The Broadman Bible Commentary,* edited by Clifton J. Allen, vol. 3, pp. 146–296. Nashville: Broadman Press, 1970.

Mauchline, John. "I and II Kings." In *Peake's Commentary on the Bible,* edited by Matthew Black and H. H. Rowley. London: Thomas Nelson and Sons, 1962.

Miller, J. Max. "So Tibni Died (1 Kings xvi 22)." *Vetus Testamentum* 18 (1968): 392.

Montgomery, James A. *A Critical and Exegetical Commentary on the Books of Kings.* International Critical Commentary, edited by Henry Snyder Gehman, vol. 10. New York: Scribner, 1951.

Myres, J. L. "King Solomon's Temple and Other Buildings and Works of Art." *Palestine Exploration Quarterly* 80 (1948): 14.

Pfeiffer, Charles F. *Baker's Bible Atlas.* Grand Rapids: Baker Book House, 1961.

Robinson, J. *The First Book of Kings.* Cambridge Bible Commentary. Cambridge: Cambridge University Press, 1972.

Skinner, John. *Kings.* The Century Bible, edited by Henry Frowde, vol. 4. London: Caxton, 1900.

Slotki, I. W. *Kings: Hebrew Text and English Translation with an Introduction and Commentary.* London: Soncino Press, 1950.

Snaith, Norman H., Ralph W. Sockman, and Raymond Calkins. "The First and Second Books of Kings." In *The Interpreter's Bible,* vol. 3. Nashville: Abingdon Press, 1954.

Tatum, Scott L. "I and II Kings." In *The Teacher's Bible Commentary,* 194–219. Nashville: Broadman Press, 1972.

Thiele, Edwin R. *The Mysterious Numbers of the Hebrew Kings.* Grand Rapids: Academie Books, 1978.

Traylor, John H., Jr. *1 & 2 Kings, 2 Chronicles.* Layman's Bible Book Commentary, vol. 6. Nashville: Broadman Press, 1981.

Watts, J. Wash. *Old Testament Teaching.* Nashville: Broadman Press, 1967.

Wiener, Aharon. *The Prophet Elijah in the Development of Judaism.* London: Routledge and Kegan Paul, 1978.

Wylie, C. C. "On King Solomon's Molten Sea." *The Biblical Archaeologist* 12 (1949): 86.

Young, Robert. *Analytical Concordance to the Bible.* New York: Funk and Wagnalls, 1936.